As Near to Heaven
by Sea

As Near to Heaven by Sea

A History of
Newfoundland
and Labrador

Kevin Major

PENGUIN

VIKING

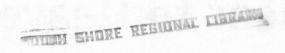

VIKING
Published by the Penguin Group
Penguin Books Canada Ltd, 10 Alcorn Avenue, Toronto, Ontario, Canada M4V 3B2
Penguin Books Ltd, 27 Wrights Lane, London W8 5TZ, England
Penguin Putnam Inc., 375 Hudson Street, New York, New York 10014, U.S.A.
Penguin Books Australia Ltd, Ringwood, Victoria, Australia
Penguin Books (NZ) Ltd, cnr Rosedale and Airborne Roads, Albany, Auckland 1310,
New Zealand

Penguin Books Ltd, Registered Offices: Harmondsworth, Middlesex, England

First published 2001

1 3 5 7 9 10 8 6 4 2

Printed and bound in Canada on acid-free paper ∞
Text design and typesetting by Laura Brady

CANADIAN CATALOGUING IN PUBLICATION DATA

Major, Kevin, 1949–
As near to heaven by sea : a history of Newfoundland & Labrador

Includes bibliographical references and index.
ISBN 0-670-88290-9

1. Newfoundland—History. I. Title

FC2161.M34 2001   971.8   2001-900574-1
F1123.M34 2001

Visit Penguin Canada's website at www.penguin.ca

For Anne

Contents

They change their clime, not their frame of mind, who rush across the sea.

—Horace

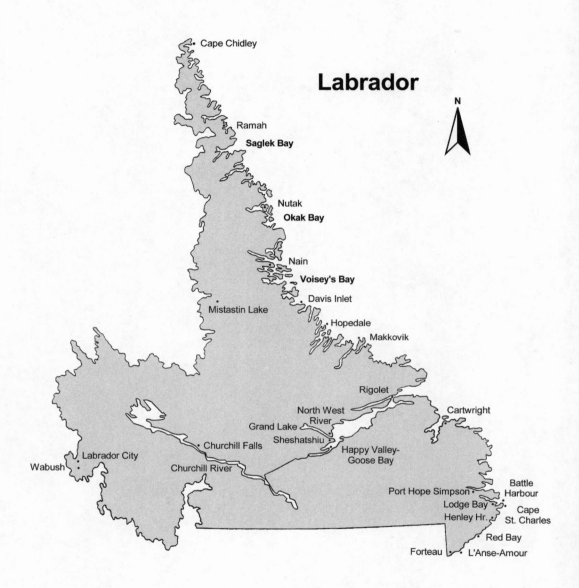

Labrador

N

- Cape Chidley
- Ramah
- **Saglek Bay**
- Nutak
- **Okak Bay**
- Nain
- **Voisey's Bay**
- Davis Inlet
- Mistastin Lake
- Hopedale
- Makkovik
- Rigolet
- Cartwright
- North West River
- Grand Lake
- Sheshatshiu
- Churchill Falls
- Happy Valley-Goose Bay
- Labrador City
- Wabush
- Churchill River
- Port Hope Simpson
- Battle Harbour
- Lodge Bay
- Cape St. Charles
- Henley Hr.
- Red Bay
- Forteau
- L'Anse-Amour

L'Anse aux Meadows

Strait of Belle Isle

St. Anthony

Newfoundland

Port au Choix
Point Riche

GREAT
NORTHERN
PENINSULA

Englee

N

White Bay

Fleur de Lys

Cape St. John

Tilt Cove

Twillingate

Fogo

Bonne Bay

**Notre Dame
Bay**

Bay of Islands

Botwood

Gander

Greenspond

Bonavista Bay

Corner Brook

Grand Falls -
Windsor

Gambo

Salvage

Cape Bonavista

Stephenville

Red Indian Lake

Port Union

Trinity

Bay St. George

Trinity Bay

Cape
Anguille

Channel - Port
aux Basques

Conne River

Come By Chance

Conception Bay

St. John's

Cape Ray

Cupids

Cape Spear

Isle aux Morts

Burgeo

AVALON
PENINSULA

Fortune Bay

Placentia

Ferryland

Grand Bank

Placentia Bay

Burin

St. Lawrence

St Mary's Bay

Cape Race

Trepassey

It's About Time

The people of Newfoundland and Labrador made our Canadian family complete in the twentieth century. And tonight they are showing us the way into the twenty-first century.

—Jean Chrétien, 1 January 2000 in Newfoundland

(31 December 1999 in the rest of Canada)

The dawn of the second millennium strikes North America.

Dawn

In the early hours of 1 January 2000, hundreds of us gathered at Cape Spear, the most easterly point in North America, to witness the dawn. We were all hoping for a spectacular crown of sunrays to rise up from the Atlantic. Instead, the light ascended unobtrusively behind a ridge of cloud, diffuse and subdued.

Ah, well. As Newfoundlanders and Labradorians we have learned to temper our optimism. We were relieved it wasn't blowing a gale, or we weren't ourselves shrouded in cloud. We cheered on the dawn, and basked in the spectacular allure of our place in history.

That first light followed a midnight when we revelled in the thousand years since the Norse sailed our way. By virtue of our half-hour time zone, we were the first in North America to roar into 2000. And rant and roar we did, before a billion TV viewers, the quirk of our clock handing us double our fifteen minutes of fame. We were spotlit before the world. The foreign networks were even pronouncing the name of our province correctly. It all boded well for our future.

High Noon

There's a new confidence at work in this province. We are thankfully past the era of looking over our shoulders for direction. We assert our own perspective, lashing back at national media who see us as quaint money-grabbers in Confederation. We seemed to have turned a corner when Clyde Wells faced down the federal government over Meech Lake. Then Brian Tobin hung foreign fishing practices out to dry. Mary Walsh taking the sword to pompous politicians week after week on national television is clearly a boost. As is Rex Murphy's vocabulary.

We're in a fighting mood. Tobin sported a sealskin parka one day, then went head-to-head with INCO and Diane Francis the next. Great Big Sea flatly refused to don sou'westers and be towed onto the Canada Day stage in Ottawa in a dory. A vehement backlash erupted against the word 'Newfie.' The gloves are off. There's fire in our bellies.

Our stage is set for better things. At the turn of the new century we lead the country in economic growth. The exodus of families out of the province has finally showed signs of coming to an end. Tourism is up, unemployment is down. Government is investing $50 million in a smashing new museum-archives-art gallery complex.

It won't ever be smooth sailing, of course. And we know better than to get cocky, being bred of a history snarled by setbacks. Some initiatives will flounder, others waste too much money. It is unlikely there will ever be a full recovery of the codfishery. And, to add to that tragedy, some rural communities won't see out this new century.

But there's an attitude afloat that we've been able to cast off the harnesses of geography and climate and lack of conviction about our own expertise. We'll be damned if we'll let these opportunities slip away.

Night Watch

It's all reason to plunge into our past. No sense trying to forge ahead, if we don't understand what we've left behind. I knew too little about that past when I started this book, and my sons seemed destined to know even less. It became a personal exploration, and a means to understanding our collective character.

The history of Newfoundland and Labrador has drawn a great deal of published analysis in recent decades. This book owes its existence to the work of many scholars and amateur historians. Ultimately, the narrative merely adds to the voices that emerge from Newfoundland and Labrador. For none of us who live in this place are without strong opinions of it.

At Cape Spear we stood with the Atlantic and Europe before us, the rest of North America at our backs.

From here, where the gulf between continents is narrowest, the look at our past begins.

1 | Taking Shape

There is a giant spirit who lives in the north—the great Torngak. When he blows his breath, violent snowstorms occur. Other spirits . . . breathe soft winds and summer weather. Female spirits dwell to the south. They send the flowers and summer rain.

—Native mythology of Labrador

The Torngat Mountains of northern Labrador, as photographed by Holloway.

Joey and the Colliding Continents

In my younger days I usually spent a week each summer teaching canoeing at Mint Brook in central Newfoundland. The camp was the only human activity then found on the site, but scattered through the woods were rusted remnants of a sawmill. By the turn of the twentieth century Mint Brook had become a thriving little community, said by some to be the first in Newfoundland to be built out of sight of saltwater. Among its inhabitants was the infant Joseph Roberts Smallwood, who, born in nearby Gambo, had come with his parents to Mint Brook where his father worked as a forest surveyor. In fifty years 'Joey' (the only word needed in Newfoundland and Labrador to identify him) would emerge from the political woods to become the single most important figure in our history. But at that time he was a mere babe in his mother's arms.

I recall Mint Brook for the clarity of its night sky, and I sometimes wondered if the young Joey ever looked up into that sky. When I was there the whole camp would sometimes gather after dark in an open field and survey the constellations, feeling such minute pinpricks of life in the vast universe. If the infant Joseph did gaze skyward for a time he couldn't help being impressed, especially having been born as he was on December twenty-fourth. Given his later political self-image, some might contend he would have blinked, thinking a star in the east had glinted in his eye.

In any case, the inestimable vastness of the cosmos and its billions of years of history impress most all of us, young and old, leader and follower. And leave us to wonder . . . where does Newfoundland and Labrador fit into this bigger picture, this far greater one than our own? How long after the 'big bang' did we take on the shape we have today, give or take a little coastal erosion or alluvial deposit?

Let's start with a figure that would impress even Joey, who during his political heyday grew so fond of ventures on a grand scale. 'Not one million, not ten million, not fifty million, but *six hundred million* years ago . . .'

The theory of plate tectonics tells us the earth's crust is a shell of rigid, yet movable plates. Not unlike gigantic ice pans (of which we know more than our fair share), these plates, imbedded with continents and oceans, shift about on the surface of the earth. Six hundred million years ago much of what is now western Newfoundland was at the eastern rim of a continent we call Laurentia.

The ever-distant Avalon Peninsula, from Cape Spear to a sizable chunk beyond the isthmus, was part of a second continent, Gondwana. Between them stretched a thousand kilometres of the Iapetus Ocean.

As geological time moved on, so did the ocean. Through subduction its floor was reabsorbed into the earth's mantle. Some of the rock melted as it sank toward the hot liquid depths of the interior, but then, destined for greater things, it burst to the surface as volcanic islands. These islands gave rise to what is now central Newfoundland.

The last of the ocean shrank away as Laurentia and Gondwana rammed into each other. The crushing impact threw up a chain of mountains as high and jagged as the Rockies. Now weather-weary ghosts of their former selves, in North America they are the Appalachians, extending from Alabama all the way up to the west coast of Newfoundland. To our portion we give the name Long Range Mountains.

The continents bonded for 200 million years, only to part company in Early Jurassic times. The Appalachians left behind their northernmost links, in present-day Britain and Scandinavia. But, to make up for it, chunks of Gondwana (including Nova Scotia, and parts of New Brunswick and New England) detached from what is now southern Europe and northwestern Africa and were dragged along with the rest of Laurentia. So, too, was the Avalon Peninsula, but less willingly, to judge by how thin its isthmus neck was stretched.

Today, if you turn off the Trans-Canada Highway onto Route 320, go past the statue of Joey at Gambo, and on to Dover (stopping not far from the Salvation Army cemetery), you'll get a good view of that point of contact, where a piece of Gondwana was welded to the rest of North America. Where the otherworldly eastern reaches of the island were forced to share living space with central and western Newfoundland. Joey had picked a momentous place to be born.

It is called the Dover–Hermitage Fault. However, there's no need to panic. No need to widen the boundaries of the cemetery. The two continents are still moving away from each other (at a rate of three centimetres a year), and it's the other edge of our continent, the San Andreas one, that sees most all the action. Still, scientists speculate that eventually the movement of the continents will reverse, and North American and Euro-Asia will again start heading toward each other. Watch for a literal drop in the real-estate market in eastern Newfoundland in 100 million years.

Life Begins in Newfoundland

Offshore lies a part of Newfoundland and Labrador as important as the land mass itself, and three times its size. It is an extension of its bedrock overlain with sedimentary deposits—the continental margin.

As the continents separated, seas washed over this extension, and in its relatively shallow depths there thrived rudimentary life forms. In some cases their organic remains became trapped through the natural processes of slumping and faulting that accompanied the drifting of the continents. It is in these sandstone reservoirs, capped by shale, where lie the oilfields that have recently been the cause of so much excitement.

Another discovery, of something originally laid down in fine volcanic ash, gets some of us even more excited. At Mistaken Point, near Cape Race, in what was once a piece Gondwana, are to be found the oldest deepwater fossils in the world. These 620-million-year-old traces of soft-bodied marine creatures are almost three times older than the oldest dinosaurs. Paleontologists have termed it the most spectacular assemblage of Precambrian animals anywhere on earth. Most 'defy identification with any known living organism.' This fossil bed and its matching site along the coast of North Africa offer up some of the most potent evidence for the theory of continental drift.

In the eyes of many scientists Mistaken Point is central to the whole debate about the origins of life on this planet. They tell us that in these fossils lie the beginnings of animal life as we know it today. Others would have us think of them as the remains of a life form that eventually became extinct. In their view, the key to human origins lies somewhere other than a remote, windswept headland in Newfoundland. Such little faith.

Labrador Rocks

Joey Smallwood was known to refer to his beloved province as 'this poor bald rock.' Today, the hippest FM station in the capital city refers to itself as 'The Rock of the Rock.' Mainlanders, and Newfoundlanders turned mainlanders, are fond of referring to the Island as 'The Rock.' It is an Alcatraz-like reference that doesn't escape easily the vocal cords of most people who actually inhabit this place.

The rock, in all its striations and exposed cross-sections and mineral concentrations, has served us well. With the extraordinary orange-hued Tablelands of our west

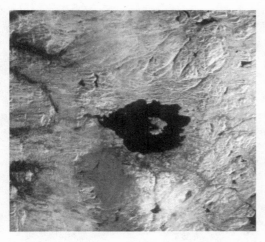

A space shuttle flight captures Labrador's Mistastin Lake in winter.

coast we can boast that 'nowhere else in North America are the rocks of the earth's interior displayed so well.' These vast toxic mounds that spewed to the surface from the mantle 500 million years ago draw the curious from across the world.

Amateur rockhounds love what they find in Newfoundland and Labrador. As do geologists and paleontologists. And mining companies rave on about it when their stock prices are high. It has offered up incredible scenery, as well as slate for the roofs of Europe, and gold, copper, gypsum, fluorspar, iron ore and more . . . much of it for smelters and processors in the rest of North America.

And in the fish lured to the waters of the continental margin is to be found the very reason for the populating of this place, the reason generations build their houses upon the surface rock of its shores.

But this is only half the geological story. Or a third of the story, if you compare the land mass of the Island of Newfoundland with that of its partner, Labrador.

For Labrador has some of the oldest dated rock on earth. ('The Rock of All Rock' if FM radio in Labrador were ever inclined to do Newfoundland one better.) In the Saglek Fiord along the far northern coast of Labrador are found rocks dating back 3.8 *billion* years. That's just a billion or so shy of the estimated formation of the earth. Joey would have loved it if he had only known.

Unlike Newfoundland, Labrador is part of the Canadian Shield. And proud of it. No endless coastline twisted into every conceivable shape of peninsula known to humankind. Basically a solid, if somewhat frigid, mass of rock, a buttress between the North Atlantic and the rest of North America. To drive home the point it has a meteoritic full stop near its border with Quebec. Thirty-eight million years ago the heavens sent down a chunk of rock that dug a crater three kilometres deep and twenty kilometres in diameter, now Mistastin Lake.

It was a sharp and decisive bit of cosmic punctuation. All land to the east of

Spawning capelin pile ashore.

this mark shall be reserved for a hardy breed willing to face the treacheries of ocean wind and weather and whatever Gondwanians/Europeans sail its way. The indentation and all the lands surrounding it were encased in several ice ages to seal their fate.

It was only when the last one retreated, when the ice melted and the waters parted, some filling the indentations, the rest cascading into the seas, only then did humankind venture here, having trekked all the way across the continent. They could go no farther. The seas washing the edge of the continent were brimming with the animal species that millions of years of marine evolution had produced. Sustenance, they must have thought . . . enough for evermore.

2 | Treks through Prehistory

osweet (caribou) . . . *ozrook* (ice) . . . *beothuk* (people)

Caribou escape the flies on a summer snowbed in the Long Range Mountains.

The Legacy of Ice

The last ice age in North America ended a mere eight to twelve thousand years ago. At its height it covered most of the northern half of the continent, with ice mounded in places to a thickness of three kilometres. In Labrador, only the highest peaks of the Torngat and Mealy Mountains were visible; and on the Island, perhaps a few of the Long Range poked through.

The formidable mass of ice pressed the land deeper into the underlying mantle. And in its slow crawl over the land, it reshaped much of the surface. Evidence of glacial action is everywhere—the rounded Signal Hill of St. John's, the huge boulders that dot our many barrens, the deep inlets of the Labrador coast.

As the ice cap melted, land that was once beneath the ocean rose again. In one case it turned beachfront property into prime alpine-skiing terrain. Marble Mountain near Corner Brook (what Nancy Greene Raine calls 'the best skiing east of the Rockies') has ledges of rock encrusted with fossilized shells. And in another case, the rising land created the scenic centrepiece of Gros Morne National Park. Western Brook Pond was once open to the ocean, gouged out by the forward end of a glacier. As the ice melted, the land rose. The sea drained away and the crater filled with fresh water to become the spectacular sixteen-kilometre-long inland fiord it is today.

Ancient Burial Plot

This freshly thawed landscape, much of it rock-bare or left with only a glazing of soil, gradually gave rise to lichens and mosses and wind-skewed conifers, rangy birch and alder. Tough flora it had to be. It was plenty, though, to sustain the migration of land mammals, the caribou prime among them. In pursuit of caribou the first humans to come our way ventured along the north shore of the St. Lawrence and into southern Labrador.

Ours was the last corner of the continent to be reached by these wandering bands of hunters, descendants of the Paleoindian peoples who had crossed the land bridge from Asia, over what is now the Bering Strait. (Or so scientists have traditionally believed. Recent evidence points to a much earlier arrival on the west coast of North America by boat. Some even contend there was a prehistoric crossing of the Pacific.) However they came, they made it here about nine thousand

The Maritime Archaic burial site at L'Anse-Amour.

years ago. It appears to have been worth the effort, to judge by the chipped-stone blades discovered in a scattering of shoreline campsites.

It took the investigation in southern Labrador of a curious pile of small boulders to confirm the sustained presence of such a people. In 1973, near the community of L'Anse-Amour, a low, wide mound of rock was discovered by road construction workers. Who had expended the time and effort to bring the rocks from the mouth of a river to this sandy terrace, and for what reason?

The following year archaeologists from Memorial University arrived at the site. With the bush and grasses cleared, the mound was found to measure nearly ten metres in diameter. The covering layers of rock were carefully removed. At a metre below the surface more rocks were found, these on edge and aligned in two rows, delineating what appeared to be a chamber. Its excavation proved disappointing, with nothing removed but sand.

Then, at a depth of close to two metres, the crew came upon an incredible component of our prehistorical record—a human skeleton, that of a twelve-year-old child, face down in the sand. The skeleton was completely extended, the head to the west, the feet to the east. A large flat rock rested on the child's back.

Near the head were several chipped-stone knives and spear points, and beneath the skeleton parts of a toggling harpoon, clear indication of the sophisticated hunting techniques of this people. And, among several other artifacts, the archaeologists uncovered a musical instrument. The child had been buried with a two-holed flute made from the hollow bone of a bird.

The child's flute.

The excavation revealed the remains of two fires, one to the north, the other to the south of the remains. Radiocarbon dating of charcoal from one of the fires set the burial at 7,500 years ago, some 3,000 years before the building of the Egyptian pyramids. The elaborate effort undertaken to bury this child made it an extraordinary site for the study of any hunter-gatherer tradition. For its age and the complexity of the culture it revealed, it had no counterpart anywhere in the world.

Questions about the site at L'Anse-Amour remain. Why would there be such a burial for this child? What is the significance of the position of the skeleton, and the fact that it was weighed down by a large rock? Did those who buried the child feel a need to be rid of some negative spirit the child was thought to possess? It is unlikely these questions will ever be fully answered.

The First of Our Peoples

Those who dug this large pit and stood near its fires, gazing intently at the remains of the child, were part of a band of people who gradually spread along the whole coast of Labrador, reaching their most northerly hamlet at Ramah Bay about five thousand years ago. They also moved southward, venturing across the strait of open sea to the Island of Newfoundland, and a thousand years later had come to occupy much of its coast. In recognition of their strong ties to the marine environment, archaeologists have named these people the Maritime Archaic.

Excavations at another site, in the present-day community of Port au Choix, have been our greatest source of information about the Maritime Archaic. Here, on the western side of the Great Northern Peninsula, some 3,500 years ago, there existed a community as thriving as any to have ever occupied the area.

The Maritime Archaic were a vigorous people, in stature and health the equal of any inhabitants of the continent at the time. In facial features they resembled other ancient Indian peoples, with relatively broad heads, pronounced cheekbones, and narrow noses. The physical prowess necessary to their work—felling trees and digging out boats with stone tools, erecting hide-clad shelters, spearing seals and caribou, hauling home carcasses—made them tough and muscular, particularly strong in their upper bodies. Bearing in mind that they likely had a diet rich in protein and a relative absence of disease, it is not surprising that many of them survived well into their fifth decade.

And perhaps that kind of longevity was in part due to the richness of their spiritual lives. Among the many artifacts uncovered at Port au Choix is a stone carving of a killer whale. This species of marine mammal was legendary for its ability to hunt seals. The bearer of the whale-piece probably drew his faith in the seal

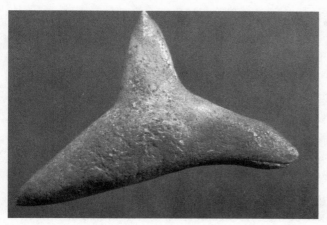

A killer whale, carved in stone.

hunt from this carving, as others linked their success at other hunts to the wearing of a string of fox teeth, or the bill of a loon. Certainly, the placement of these objects in the graves, and the use of red ochre to cover the remains, speak of powerful and strongly imbedded spiritual beliefs. The precision of these burials seem to have been as much for the living as for the dead.

Our first people, the Maritime Archaic, inhabited Labrador and Newfoundland for five thousand years, far longer than any group that would come after. They were the sole occupants of this place; no group would ever again roam over both land masses alone. They spread to many of its bays, but were never separated by language or traditions. Important discoveries of one band, such as Ramah chert, the prized flint-like stone from Labrador, found its way to all bands. (And was coveted for spearheads by American cousins, as revealed by excavations in Maine.)

Body and soul were well tended. If plenty to eat, an amiable distance from neighbours, and time to give voice to innermost emotion through stone carving are any measure of contentment, then the Maritime Archaic knew good times, even during the coldest months of winter.

Face to Unknown Face

This peaceful, familial existence was not to continue undisturbed. One day, some four thousand years ago, the northernmost band of Maritime Archaic stood at their encampment in utter incredulity at the sight before them. Over the frozen landscape were walking a people other than their own kind, humans such as they never knew existed—short and stocky, with broad facial features and straight black hair. The upper part of their skin coverings was shaped into a high collar, the spears they held in their hands were barbed but simple, without a toggling end, and when they spoke, there was no sense to be made of a single word.

The Maritime Archaic had come face to face with the group we have since named Paleoeskimos. These newcomers had crossed into Labrador from Greenland, their ancestors having traversed the top of the world from Alaska five centuries earlier. They were hunters in pursuit of land and sea mammals, just like the people they encountered.

What transpired between the two groups is not entirely clear. Some contend the Maritime Archaic who had occupied the northern and central coasts of Labrador gave way to the new arrivals and retreated south, to join their own people. Others speculate that physical conflict led to their extinction.

The Paleoeskimos took over the empty campsites, as well as establishing new ones. They held firm and before long expanded south and onto the Island of Newfoundland. They seem to have displaced the Maritime Archaic people everywhere they went. Yet some have theorized that remnants of the Maritime Archaic tradition lived on to the time of the European discovery of Newfoundland.

The Paleoeskimos made a surprisingly rapid adaption to their new world. As with any peoples who have come to these shores, the abundant population of sea mammals became a focus of their hunting. To their arsenal of weapons they added the harpoon technology of the people they replaced. The toggling harpoon, with its end that detaches from the harpoon shaft and twists in the wounded animal, prevented the animal's escape, and so was a much more efficient means of killing. (In turn, their use of the bow and arrow may have passed on to the Maritime Archaic.)

But the early Paleoeskimos did not turn completely to the sea for subsistence. They would move from site to site in a somewhat organized pattern of hunting and gathering—to the caribou, the sea birds and their eggs, the salmon and trout of the freshwater streams. It was many centuries later, when these early Paleo-eskimos dwindled in number and were replaced by another group, that a definite shift in the way of life took place. The second wave of this culture, now referred to as Dorset Eskimos, became less migratory. The Dorsets often spent the winter and spring in semi-permanent encampments along the coast, in pursuit of the herds of harp seals that arrived with the northern ice floes.

Seal oil was used as fuel for cooking and, in soapstone lamps, as fuel for heat and light. The prime area for soapstone were the cliffs at Fleur de Lys on the Baie Verte Peninsula. There, blocks of the stone were removed and shaped into vessels. Perhaps it was an early practical venture into carving that led to a distinct feature of many Dorsets—their figurative work in soapstone, ivory, antler, and bone. Residents of one site in Labrador—Shuldham Island in Saglek Bay—were particularly gifted carvers. Their miniature, stylistic depictions are treasures of fine art, testament to the deep-seated creative inclinations of Arctic peoples.

Some of the carvings would seem central to the belief system of the Dorsets. They no doubt drew inspiration from the depiction of polar bears, a confirmation of their own hunting abilities. Perhaps the carving of a bird head and neck functioned as a stopper for a special vessel. A seashell might have been used to placate nature's spirits or carved purely for the joy of its form. Certainly the images of an adult polar bear and her cub, the latter sitting with its forepaws extending to touch its hind toes, go beyond the ceremonial into art, with the stone transformed into the curious, pensive, and wonderfully playful.

The Dorset Eskimos disappeared from the Island of Newfoundland about 1,300 years ago, and from Labrador 700 years later. The exact cause of their demise remains a mystery. Perhaps the marine food resources had declined to the point they could no longer sustain the population. Perhaps the Dorsets, who in Newfoundland had settled farther south than their counterparts in any other region of the continent, could not adapt to the climatic warming that was taking place. Or they may have retreated from other groups who were moving into the region at that same time, including the ancestors of the present-day Inuit of Labrador. In any event, Labrador and Newfoundland had seen a second distinct culture come and go. Survival in the northeastern region of the continent was clearly unpredictable. A prehistoric warning, as clear as the ocean waves, was sounding.

More Cultures Find a Home

In recent years it has become clear that the Dorset Eskimos were not alone at the time of their occupation of Newfoundland and Labrador. Perhaps unbeknownst to many of them, they were sharing the land with another group, a second Indian population that has come to be referred to as Recent Indians. The artifacts of these people differ markedly from those of the Maritime Archaic, yet an archaeological linkage may someday be found, and a line of continuous Indian occupation established. Some of these Recent Indians are thought to have left the coast each year to establish campsites for the hunting of caribou, becoming the first inhabitants of the interior of Labrador. It is these people who are believed to be the ancestors of the present-day Innu Nation.

What can be said with certainty is that one group of these Recent Indians were the native people of Newfoundland encountered by the first Europeans to sail across the Atlantic and land on our shores. Like the ancient Maritime Archaic, they used red ochre to cover themselves and their dead.

The Greenland Europeans who came our way were quick to name them 'skrael-ings.' In later times, they were labelled 'Red Indians.' The fate of these people, the Beothuk, resonates through the history of this Island like no other.

3 | Seafarers from the East

They went ashore and looked about them. The weather was fine. There was dew on the grass, and the first thing they did was to get some of it on their hands and put it to their lips, and to them it seemed the sweetest thing they had ever tasted.

—Saga of the Greenlanders

The Greenland Norse sight new land.

Who Was the First?

It would appear that Labrador, and then Newfoundland, were first inhabited by peoples who had either trekked over the land bridge from Asia or traversed the Pacific by boat, and who then made their way across the northern reaches of North America. It would only be a matter of time before migration to this eastern rim of the continent would take place from the opposite direction, from Europe, across the North Atlantic.

Just how many centuries had passed before a second arrival took place no one knows for sure. What stood in its way, of course, was the unpredictability of the northern seas. Crossing them was much riskier than traversing terra firma. It would have had to await the evolution of ocean-going vessels sufficiently seaworthy or a breed of people sufficiently adventuresome (or foolhardy, or divinely driven) to go beyond that broad and vacant horizon. Luckily, there was a string of islands from the north of Scotland to Greenland to serve as stepping stones for the brave of heart.

Who out of the fogs of time first sailed our way? What breed of European first set foot on these eastern shores of North America? The island of Greenland is but eight hundred kilometres from the coast of Labrador. It would seem logical, given that Greenland was inhabited by about A.D. 985, that some daring souls would want to know what lay beyond its western coast.

One lithe academic mind (of which there have been more than a few drawn to the question of our provenance) has dispensed with even this notion, and has gone so far as to suggest that Odysseus's fabled journey landed him in our part of the world. That the Greek hero could have given up cruising the Mediterranean for a voyage among the ice floes off Bonavista is a bit of a stretch, even for those most desperate to put John Cabot in his rightful place.

Some would have it that it was St. Brendan the Navigator, with a crew of fellow monks in an ox-hide boat in the sixth century, forsaking all worldly temptations, and seeking a place for prayer and solitude. It does seem certain that the goodly Irish saint voyaged to Scotland, and possibly to the Orkney and Shetland Islands, and maybe even as far west as the Faroes. But the legend of *Navigatio Sancti Brendani Abbatis*, as recorded several centuries later, has led some to nudge his ox-hide a little farther, to Iceland, propelled by evidence of Irish monks living in Iceland before the Norse arrived there about A.D. 860. Some are even willing to

An imperturbable St. Brendan en route to the promised land.

inflate his sail all the way to North America, conveniently ignoring the nature of the legend as a religious allegory, one in which St. Brendan passes en route to the promised land (among others) a fire-breathing giant and a highly harmonious trio of choirs, fully robed and perched upon an island. Of course, there are some who would point to Newfoundland's strong tradition of choral music as support for St. Brendan and his crew. And others who assert that the land of the legend is assuredly ours because upon approaching its shores 'a great fog enveloped them.' However, it's really not a great deal on which to build a case, even when you add the fact that Tim Severin and crew in 1977 proved that an ox-hide boat of the type St. Brendan would have used was able to make it all the way across the Atlantic.

(Still, for many of us, discovery of the new world, a promised land, by St. Brendan the Navigator, has a seductive ring to it. Some think of it as zealous foresight, in anticipation of the eventual spread of the Church of Rome. Others, myself included, wonder if St. Brendan might just have been the one, given that the shores he sought were dubbed 'The Land of Promise of the Saints.' Could it not have been in anticipation of the multitude of unfulfilled promises, saintly and otherwise, that have come our way in the many centuries that followed?)

Most recently, no less a literary adventurer than Farley Mowat has entered the fray with his notion that the first sailors to strike our shores were a group of

Indo-Europeans he calls 'The Albans,' arriving here in the tenth century, again by way of the islands of the North Atlantic. Never one to hold back when a good dose of speculation could stir archaeologists (or the book-buying public) to action, Mowat would have us believe that the descendants of these Albans are to be found today living in Bay St. George, on the west coast of Newfoundland. (Having grown up in this part of Newfoundland, I find myself only too thrilled at such a prospect.) However, the fate of that theory lies in other hands. Perhaps in a DNA testing lab. Scepticism is nothing new to Mowat, of course, clearly recalling as he does the response of many a certified historian when, a few short decades ago, it was suggested that proof would be found of Norse settlement in the New World.

Proof in a Spindle-whorl

That particular heap of disbelief was forever dispelled on a summer's day in 1964, at a site called L'Anse aux Meadows, on the tip of Newfoundland's Great Northern Peninsula. A team of archaeologists led by Anne Stine, wife of Helge Ingstad, the Norse discoverer of the site, uncovered a round piece of soapstone about four centimetres in diameter, with a hole through its centre. It was a spindle-whorl, a tool for spinning wool. Clearly identifiable as Norse, the object is completely unrelated to any artifacts of the indigenous cultures of the Island.

Here at last was indisputable proof that Norse women and men (for only women spun wool) had been in Newfoundland. Their high-gunwaled *knarr* had struck the New World a good five hundred years before the *Nina*, the *Pinta*, or the *Santa Maria*. Columbus and Cabot were abruptly jostled ahead in the history books.

It had been a lifelong dream of Ingstad to establish such proof as he found at L' Anse aux Meadows, although he was certainly not the first to suggest the area as the possible Vinland of the famous Icelandic sagas. A Newfoundland amateur historian, W. A. Munn, had done so in a booklet published in 1914. 'I believe when Leif started to come in towards the land, he was just south of Belle Isle . . . ' wrote Munn. 'They went ashore at Lancey Meadows [L'Anse aux Meadows].' In succeeding decades, expeditions to the area by a number of keen adherents to such a theory, well-respected foreign scientists among them, failed to advance the idea of Norse settlement.

The basis of all the interest was the *Saga of Eirik the Red* and the *Saga of the Greenlanders*, the latter generally considered to be the older and more reliable of these two accounts of the settling of Greenland and lands to the west of it. The *Saga of the Greenlanders*, like the other derived from oral tradition, appears to have made it to vellum in about A.D. 1200. The single remaining copy of the saga is today housed in Reykjavik.

The sagas are a condensation of events and impressions, formalized accounts put together without strict adherence to detail and timeline. As such, they can't be taken as word-for-word guides to the Norse time in North America. Yet they remain our starting point in deciphering the series of significant events that took place about the turn of the first millennium. The *Saga of the Greenlanders* tells first of the Norseman Bjarni Herjolfsson, blown off course while sailing from Iceland to a Greenland newly settled by Eirik the Red. After several stormy days, the seas calmed and its crew sighted land—one that was 'wooded, with low ridges.' It was definitely not Greenland. They decided not to go ashore, but sailed north, eventually reaching land that was 'high and mountainous,' and covered by ice. It still did not fit the description of the place settled by their people. Could they have been sailing along the coast of Labrador, with their final view of the place dominated by the Torngat Mountains? Bjarni and his crew turned the ship out to sea and four days later struck the land they had been looking for—a headland on Greenland's southwestern coast.

However, it is the next tale in the saga that has stirred the blood of many historians, as far back as the mid-nineteenth century when the sagas first became widely known. Here, Leif Eiriksson, son of the aging and crippled Eirik the Red, was said to have been so gripped by the story of new lands brought to Greenland by Bjarni that he gathered a crew of thirty-five and put to sea in search of them. He was especially keen on finding wood to bring back to the timber-hungry Greenlanders.

Their journey of a few days ended with the sighting of a land of glacier, with a vast expanse of flat rock from the edge of the ice to the shoreline. Leif and his crew went ashore and walked the rock, but only long enough to name it 'Helluland.' Not an uncommon reaction to a foreigner's first sight of Baffin Island or Labrador, but in this case a Norse word to describe a 'land of stone slabs.'

It was back out to sea then, and a journey farther south. They dropped anchor and rowed ashore a second time. 'We shall name this country after what it has to offer, and call it Markland.' They were walking on a stretch of white sandy beach (not unlike that near Cape Porcupine on the Labrador coast), though the name referred to the sight of the thick inland forests. They boarded their ship again.

A third jaunt southward landed them in 'a sound between the island and the headland that stuck out northwards from the mainland.' There, according to the saga, the Norse liked what they saw and built sod houses to spend the winter. Assuming at least one of the lands they struck on the first two stops was Labrador (and which they took to be another of the islands of the northern seas), then the headland would most likely be the tip of the Great Northern Peninsula. So con-cluded Munn and Ingstad and several others, who all pointed to a sixteenth-century map by Sigurdur Stefansson as addi-tional support for their case. The map clearly shows a long, narrow peninsula south of a coastline very similar to that of present-day Labrador.

Stefansson's 'Promontorium Winlandia' may well be our Great Northern Peninsula.

There were a few literary obstacles to be overcome, or at least to be put in perspective. The saga noted that 'there was no frost in winter, and the grass hardly withered at all.' But, further, there was an abun-dance of 'vines and grapes' to be found inland. Enough fruit, in fact, that in the spring the Norse filled their boats with it before heading back to Greenland. Leif, in a moment of blind optimism perhaps, settled on a name for this country. He called it 'Vinland the Good.'

Now the Great Northern Peninsula, particularly in winter, is no Vinland, if we were to take the saga at its word. Those in support of this area of Newfoundland as the place named in the saga contended that by 'grapes' the Norse were actually referring to berries, of which there certainly was an abundance. And indeed the winter climate was considerably milder than that of their native Greenland and Iceland. Perhaps the winters of the eleventh century were mild enough to be considered frost-free. Or perhaps Leif had named it Vinland as his father had named their frozen island home Greenland, with the hope that a little imaginative labelling might attract potential settlers.

But no matter, the Norse did establish a base settlement in Newfoundland for a time, and for an eventful time at that.

Helge Ingstad, who had spent years looking for possible Norse sites, first sailed into the small fishing village of L'Anse aux Meadows in the late summer of 1960. There he encountered a bristle-faced, pipe-smoking gentleman, the patriarch of the place, George Decker. When asked if he knew of any old sites of unknown origin, Decker led him to expanse of grassland near a river. Before them were several faintly elevated, overgrown mounds.

Over the following several summers the site was excavated, uncovering absolute proof of brief Norse settlement there about the year A.D. 1000. Whereas other regions of North America can only propose the possibility of a Norse sojourn to their shores, Newfoundland is home to the real thing. Minnesota, for example, has a very questionable rune-stone, said to have been found in a farmer's field in 1898, and bearing an inscription relating a visit by Norsemen in 1362. Despite the fact that it has been denounced as a fake countless times, the good folks of Alexandria, Minnesota, have used it to build a tourist industry and the state to name its NFL football franchise. We're content to hold up our doughnut-shaped spindle-whorl, or our cloak pin, and watch the others gnash their teeth in envy.

Most scholars now agree that L'Anse aux Meadows was but a home base for the Norse, that in summer many of them continued southward into the Gulf of St. Lawrence, returning in the fall from warmer climates, ones that did indeed bear grapes. From that perspective, the whole coastal area of the Gulf could rightly be termed 'Vinland.' Evidence for this is found in one particular group of artifacts unearthed from a bog at L'Anse aux Meadows—three butternuts and a burl of butternut wood. The butternut is a North American relative of the walnut, and

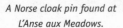

A Norse cloak pin found at L'Anse aux Meadows.

found only as far north as the indentations of the coast of New Brunswick at the head of the Gulf. Is it coincidence that this is also the northern limit of the wild grapes known to have flourished in the hardwood forests of eastern North America prior to European settlement? Is it coincidence that the oily, edible butternut ripens, as did the succulent grapes, in late summer? Could the Norse residents of L'Anse aux Meadows have gathered grapes and butternuts in New Brunswick and returned with them to their home at the tip of the Great Northern Peninsula, and perhaps manufactured wine during the winter before returning to Greenland the following spring?

Well, yes. And if so, then it is one of the earliest cases of mainland resources undergoing value-added processing in Newfoundland before being exported. Too bad the Norse didn't stick it out.

Unsettling Ways

As it happened, the Norse left Newfoundland permanently after a couple of decades. They seem to have initially planned to settle here, to judge by the size and solid construction of their buildings—multi-roomed halls framed with heavy timber and bearing steep roofs made from numerous layers of sod. Some of them could accommodate twenty-five or more people. One included a smithy for the forging of nails from bog iron. The *Saga of the Greenlanders* tells us that following Leif's journey, and the establishment of a settlement that came to be known as 'Leifsbudir,' his relatives made four more voyages.

The first of these was led by Leif's brother Thorvald, who set off for Vinland with a crew of thirty. There they spent the next two years, using the summer months to explore the coastline near Leifsbudir. All looked good ('well-wooded sandy shores'), until at one stop they discovered three mounds on a beach. The mounds proved to be skin-covered boats. Under each were three men.

In sod huts such as these, reconstructed at L'Anse aux Meadows, the Norse once lived.

By virtue of this contact, the human race had circled the globe.

This meeting closed the final gap, that between the Americas and Europe/Africa. Unfortunately, the welding of a last link in the human chain turned into a grievous event. Thorvald and his crew attacked the nine men, taking captive all but the one fortunate soul who managed to escape in his canoe. True to their image as callous warriors, the Norse killed all eight of them.

A counterattack by boatloads of natives ended with an arrow sunk in Thorvald's chest. His companions eventually laid him beneath the foreign soil and headed back the following year to Greenland. It was the beginning of the end for Norse settlement in the new world. A subsequent voyage by Thorstein Eiriksson, in hopes of bringing home his brother's body, ended when the crew lost its way and failed to reach Vinland. He was not long back in his home country when he died of the plague.

A few years later another attempt at settlement in Vinland was made, this time with sixty men and five women, and several head of cattle. It was led by Thorfinn Karlsefni, who had married Thorstein's widow, Gudrid. Together they were determined to make a life for themselves in Leifsbudir. Gudrid gave birth to a son, Snorri, believed to be the first European born in the new world. A thousand years later, in 1998, a replica of a *knarr*, named for the child, would complete a trip across the North Atlantic from Greenland. And from Iceland in July 2000 came the *Islendingur*, captained by a direct descendant of Leif Eiriksson. The sixty-two-foot replica of a Norse ship came ashore at L'Anse aux Meadows to a tumultuous welcome.

It was nothing like the contact the original settlers made with the natives of Newfoundland. Disputes over trading furs and leather for weapons ended in the death of still more of the skraelings. Constant fear of a revenge attack sent the Norse back home the following spring.

Be Not a Freydis

The final chapter in the story of Vinland belongs to Freydis, Leif's sister. It is a brutal tale, according to the sagas, a sad end to the hope the Norse had once pinned on their settlement in Vinland. Freydis tricked her husband into killing most of the crew after they landed in Vinland. She herself, in her best sword-wielding warrior pose, slaughtered all of the other women who had come along on the voyage.

She returned to Greenland in the spring, the sole owner of whatever treats

Vinland had to offer—grapes, no doubt among them. . . . Perhaps we could be persuaded to hand over this part of the sagas, the story of a fearsome Freydis, to New Brunswick. Or to Minnesota.

Then again, maybe we're missing the point. Some observers have been singling out these irrepressible women of the sagas as setting the stage for the strong role played by women in modern Nordic societies. Scandinavia has the highest proportion of female parliamentarians in the world, approaching 40 per cent in some countries. Iceland had the first female Western head of state. There are many who say we would do well to keep Freydis. Inspiration to stir up those male-infested political waters.

In fact, perhaps she's been reincarnated. What do you think, Mary Walsh—or should I say, Marg, Princess Warrior?

4 | Natives Alone

. . . before Europeans arrived . . . we had our own leaders, warriors, grand orators, musicians, religious experts and philosophers . . . we would have laughed and cried, tickled one another, played games, told jokes, sung lullabies to our kids, fallen in love, marvelled at glowing sunsets . . .

—Daniel Ashini of the Innu Nation

The Beothuk canoe was designed for rough coastal water.

What Tales They Would Tell

When the sad remnants of the last Norse expedition climbed aboard their *knarr* and the winds took charge of its great square sail, it was the last the Island would see of Europeans for nearly five hundred years. Their attempts at settlement had failed; the timber and fish and berries were not enough to draw back any of their descendants. The Greenlanders consigned the adventures westward to sagas, and let them serve as warnings that there was more to these new lands than the name Vinland the Good might indicate.

The aboriginal people were thankful to see the last of them. As they emerged from the forests and counted the cost of this brief encounter with these foreigners, they formed the tales of what had happened into an oral history of their own. Such stories never came to be written down or had the chance to develop the aura of the Norse sagas (nor the mountain of modern-day interpretations), but for the ancestors of the Innu and the Beothuk they would have served an equal purpose— a caution to the generations to come after them.

For the next five centuries these descendants had the Island to themselves. When European boats again struck the coasts of Newfoundland and the Beothuk again set eyes on such foreign men, they drew on the stories of their ancestors and kept their distance.

Changing Peoples of Labrador

In Labrador, the numbers of Dorset Eskimos declined. By the fifteenth century they were extinct and bands of Recent Indians had established themselves.

They, too, took to the sea for their food, augmenting it with caribou during the coldest months of the year. The preferred material for tool and weapon construction remained the translucent silicate, Ramah chert, and these ancestral Innu made regular treks north to secure it. They filled coastal sites as far as Nain, and spread deep in the bays, including to a dwelling place near present-day Sheshatshiu. In that site have been found the remains of structures thought to use long poles anchored in an oval base and covered with bark or hide, the centre of each outlined with flat rock to form a fire pit.

It was around such fire pits that the oral traditions of the Innu have their roots and the experience of the elders found its most powerful expression. Central to their beliefs had grown the concept of *kanauenitam*, the overseeing of the land in a manner that honoured its importance to their people. In the preservation of the land and its resources the ancestral Innu built their identity, reinforcing their spiritual affinity with the rest of nature.

In the early 1400s across open water from Baffin Island came people in large skin boats and slender kayaks. With the onset of winter, more arrived on sleds drawn by dogs. They have been given the name Thule Eskimo. They are the ancestors of today's Labrador Inuit.

These Inuit may have encountered the last of the Dorsets, for in their oral traditions are stories of a people they called 'Tunnit.' Whether such encounters led to the extinction of the Dorsets is not known. But what does seem certain is that Inuit contact with the Innu forced the Innu south and away from many of their coastal resources.

They took to the interior of Labrador, and to an increased dependence on hunting caribou, on trapping other land mammals, and on freshwater fishing. Relocation brought about a more nomadic, independent existence; they roamed at will much of the Labrador-Quebec Peninsula. This territory they shared with the other Innu peoples of eastern Quebec, a homeland called Nitassinan.

The Inuit Settle the Coast

The Inuit established themselves along Labrador's northern coast. With long-shafted harpoons tipped with bone or the prized chert, they hunted seals and whales. Specialized pronged spears secured salmon and char, after the fish had been channelled together with stone weirs. Like those before them, the Inuit built their lives around the resources of the sea, although a summer hunt of caribou (in open inland waters, using kayaks) proved a vital source of food and clothing.

For their winter hunting trips the Inuit constructed

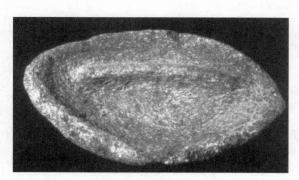

A prehistoric Inuit soapstone lamp.

snow houses, although their normal winter dwelling was an excavation walled with stone and covered with sod. In summer they slept inside skin-covered conical tents. The stone foundations of both dwellings still mark the landscape today.

In these houses, in the light of a soapstone lamp fuelled by seal oil, they told stories of the Tunnit, and of their first encounters with their new land. By day they ranged over more and more of its shoreline, eventually building a settlement as far south as Hamilton Sound. Firmly established along much of the coast, they undertook trips to the Strait of Belle Isle, and may even have made contact with the aboriginal people of Newfoundland.

The Beothuk Ways

It was the most settled period many of the native peoples would ever know. On the Island it led to the culture that today we call Beothuk. These people had chosen not to adopt the technology brought by the Norse, including the use of bog iron in forging tools and weapons. They preferred to refine the practices of their ancestors, which served them well, until the time they again encountered foreign men with firearms.

The Beothuk were never large in number, certainly nothing close to the exaggerated figures put forth by some writers in recent decades, overeager to demonstrate the magnitude of their decline. Estimates of the total population at the time of renewed European contact, based on written record and archaeological data, range from 500 to 1,600, with a figure closer to the lower estimate being the more likely.

In bands, each comprising fewer than fifty people, they spread into the major bays of the Island. They were coastline dwellers who took to the interior for the winter months. They practised no form of agriculture. Generally there was sufficient

This Beothuk wooden doll was found in a child's gravesite at Big Island, Pilley's Tickle.

food, although some bands must have experienced periods of starvation, as did most aboriginal people who lived off the land over long periods of time.

In as sheltered a site as they could find close to shore, they built their summer dwellings—'mamateeks'—often conical in shape, made of bark layered like shingles over a frame of poles. Inside each mamateek were dug sleeping hollows around a central fire pit. Nearby they erected storehouses for food and vapour baths.

They lived on an abundance of coastal fauna in their season—seals, porpoises, seabirds, salmon, even small whales. Larger mammals were hunted with spears and four-metre toggling harpoons. For smaller game, they preferred the bow and arrow, precisely fabricated from seasoned wood and caribou hide. One of the most prized sources of food was the flightless bird, the auk. Amazingly, the Beothuk of the northeast coast travelled regularly to their breeding grounds, the Funk Islands, some sixty kilometres offshore, paddling high-gunwaled birchbark canoes over the open ocean, often through dense fog.

In the fall the Beothuk moved inland by canoe, escaping the harshest months of the coastal winter, and turning their hunting skills to the annual migration of caribou. For the kill they sometimes built 'caribou fences,' lengthy stretches of felled trees that channelled the animals through narrow gaps where they would be slaughtered with relative ease.

The snows of winter would often find the Beothuk encamped near the shores of a lake. Well-nourished with venison and smaller game, they turned to making weapons, birchbark cooking vessels, and caribou-hide clothing. These garments they fringed with pendants of caribou bone, incised with precise patterns and rubbed with red ochre.

Though the Beothuk might have been descended from the Maritime Archaic people, and might even have been related to the Algonquin tribes of the northeastern part of the continent, at least linguistically, they had lived alone on the Island for so long they became a separate people in tradition and speech. Their solidarity they secured with an annual red-ochre ceremony. They mixed the ochre with grease, and covered their bodies with it. For the newly born the ceremony was an initiation, for the older a renewal of their identity as part of the land that sustained them. With this same red ochre they covered their dead.

What Breed of Foreigner?

In 1497 came the tracks of foreign men upon their shores.

These men arrived aboard a sailing ship, larger and far different from that of the foreigners five hundred years before. The Beothuk had seen them coming and took to the safety of the woods. They spied some of them climbing aboard a small boat and row toward land. Strange men in strange coverings, carrying long staffs the length of spears, with something loose at their ends flapping in the wind.

As the rowboat approached the shore, the foreigners jumped to dry land. They were overjoyed, much like their own Beothuk men when they returned in their canoes filled with auks from their journeys to the Funks.

The strangers came to a stop at the sight of the remnants of a fire. They looked up, searching the land around them, but the Beothuk remained unseen. On the ground not far from the fire they sighted animal dung. The inhabitants of this land must have farms, they said. And on the ground also a stick, pierced at both ends, and red in colour. They held it up for a closer look. We have reached the East, they said, the country of the Great Khan.

They ventured a little way from the fire and discovered a trail leading into the forest. They talked among themselves. No, they would not go farther. But what manner of people are they who live beyond this shore?

Straight of stature, firmly muscled from the rigours of the outdoors, they could never be confused with the wild animals of the forests.

Yet the foreigners who came after that first voyage, the ones to first lay eyes on the Beothuk, called them 'brute beasts.' For many of these foreigners the Beothuk, the Innu, and the Inuit became oddities, subhuman, something curious to be captured and displayed. And in their self-righteous benevolence the newcomers, who proclaimed ownership of the land in the name of the king and the pope, declared that for their own good these 'heathen savages' had to learn to cast aside their primitive ways. For those of Europeans were superior and, naturally, to be embraced.

5 | Cabot Sails the Vacant Sea

. . . to find, discover and investigate whatsoever islands, countries, regions or provinces of heathens and infidels, in whatsoever part of the world placed, which before this time were unknown to all Christians.

—Charter given to John Cabot by Henry VII, 1496

A colourful (if embellished) depiction of Cabot's departure from Bristol.

Adventurer from Venice

Of the first European to rediscover the Island of Newfoundland we know relatively little. The history books of our youth call him John Cabot. The tourist trade likes the flamboyant timbre of Giovanni Caboto. Documents of the day add Ioani, Johan, Zuan, and Zoanne to the list of possible first names.

Some contend he was born in Gaeta, Italy, others Genoa, the northern Mediterranean port where he spent his early childhood, and also home to the young Christopher Columbus. Their later rivalry may well have had roots in Genoa's streets and alleys.

As a young man, Caboto moved with his family to Venice. The city was the birthplace of Marco Polo, and there young Caboto soaked up exotic tales of voyages to the Orient. His father worked as a spice merchant, a lucrative trade abounding in such stories. Caboto joined the family enterprise, and began a life of travel, first to the ports of the Eastern Mediterranean and the Black Sea in search of new sources of spice. He claimed to have voyaged from Alexandria to the ancient Islamic holy city of Mecca (though it would have had to be in disguise, since he was a Christian.)

Caboto's reputation grew both as a cartographer and a master mariner, and with it his desire to find a new route to the East, one that circumvented the Arab rulers of Egypt who controlled the spice trade. In 1490, married and the father of three sons (and perhaps some daughters, given that female births were not recorded), Caboto moved to the Spanish seaport of Valencia. It was a promising place to generate interest in a voyage across the Atlantic.

It was through Valencia in 1493 that a jubilant Columbus passed on his way to tell his patrons, the Spanish monarchs Ferdinand and Isabella, that, indeed, he had found such a route, that he had been the first to sail west and reach the spice isles of Asia. His entourage of tanned 'Indians' captured on his voyage, together with a boisterous crew clutching pouches of gold dust and cages bearing brightly coloured parrots, was a vexing sight to the land-bound Caboto.

Caboto shook off Columbus's pronouncement that he had reached 'the land of the Great Khan.' Where were the tales of the fabled imperial cities of Cathay? Why were these 'Indians' so different in appearance from the Orientals Caboto had seen on his journeys east? It roused in the master mariner a craving to outdo his fellow Italian.

But Spanish backing for a voyage of his own was now out of the question, what with Columbus's triumphant entry to the royal court. And neither could he expect it from nearby Portugal. It had turned to sailing around the southern tip of Africa as a route to India.

So within a few years Caboto moved his family and his ambitions once more, this time to England. There, in the port of Bristol, a city of a mere ten thousand, he settled in and became known simply as John Cabot. And now his talk was of a shorter route across the open ocean, the northerly one. He sought out the city's wealthy merchants. This unclaimed route would provide not only new sources of spice but fish as well.

King Henry VII, still smarting from having rejected a proposal from the aspiring Columbus some years before, granted Cabot a charter. It was March 1496. Cabot's wanderlust would soon be quenched.

Just what new-found heathens awaited the royal blessing, neither the king nor Cabot had any way of knowing. The mariner quickly began preparations for the trip. Certainly such souls would welcome his arrival, or not violently resist it at least, or, better yet, choose not to cross paths with him.

Who Before Him?

Cabot was a master mariner whose explorations would lead to monumental changes on both sides of the North Atlantic. Yet, the ocean he was about to cross was not the vast expanse of unknown water that is sometimes depicted. Certainly not in the eyes of the Welsh who hold to the notion that one of their own, a Prince Madoc, landed in North America in 1170. Or in the eyes of the Scots, who champion an Earl of the Orkneys, Prince Henry Sinclair, as striking the New World in the late 1300s.

The Portuguese have their valiant prince as well, but hold a somewhat more plausible claim. In 1431, under the eager graces of Prince Henry the Navigator, they struck the Azores, that group of islands almost halfway between Portugal and Newfoundland. There is no proof they ever ventured beyond those shores and reached the mainland of North America, although some maps drawn late in the century throw open that possibility. The so-called Paris Map, circa 1490, depicts a group of three islands southwest of Iceland, and far to the west of Ireland, although roughly in the same latitude. These are labelled 'Islands of the Seven

Cities, now settled by the Portuguese.' Newfoundland, perhaps, together with some of its offshore isles?

'The Islands of the Seven Cities' and 'The Isle of Brasile' were legendary lands that held great fascination for sailors and map-makers of the Middle Ages. 'Brasile' seems to have come out of Gaelic folklore. The 'Seven Cities' were said to have been first discovered by seven bishops fleeing Portugal in the eighth century, a tale that . . . ummm . . . rather undermines its credibility. Yet, it was a substantial part of the picture of the Atlantic held by the sailors of the day. And any of these sailors who might have touched North America in their voyages would have thought they had landed in those very bishoprics.

Stronger evidence exists for voyages made by merchants of Bristol in the final decades of the century. They had long been engaged in trade with Iceland, where they exchanged woollen and linen goods for salted fish. They were always on the lookout for new markets. One document recounts a trip in search of the Isle of Brasile made in 1480 and lasting nine weeks before the Bristol crew returned home without success. 'For the last seven years the people of Bristol have equipped two, three, four caravels to go in search of the Island of Brasil and the Seven Cities.' In reference to Cabot, it claimed that the land where he came to shore 'was found and discovered in the past by the men of Bristol.' Yet, as tempting as it is to embrace such a notion, indisputable evidence to support it has not been found.

The *Matthew* Sets Sail

Ultimately we must pin our honours on John Cabot, Italian turned Englishman, backed by Bristol merchants and with a crew of Bristol men. Off he sailed in the summer of 1496. Initial preparations proved a little hasty, however, and a combination of bad weather, a shortage of food, and discontent among the crew forced him back to port.

Then, less than a year later, Cabot set sail again. With him was a crew of close to twenty, all local men but for two. Indispensable on the journey was Cabot's Genoese 'barber,' the profession at the time combining haircutting, surgery, and dentistry.

Their ship was the *Matthew*, likely named after Cabot's wife, Mathye. It was a three-masted caravel, built of oak, with a displacement of fifty tonnes, and a length of a mere twenty metres. In size, the ship was very close to the favoured smaller ship of Columbus, the *Nina*.

The *Matthew*'s mainmast held the large, square mainsail, the powerhouse of the ship, and at its top the crow's nest with its small topsail. The mast set aft carried a triangular lateen. And to the fore a smaller, square sail; and another, smaller still, on the bowsprit. In her sea trials in the Bristol Channel, the *Matthew*, properly trimmed and ballasted, proved a nifty, manoeuvrable craft. At the quay in Bristol in May 1497, she stood loaded with enough salted fish and meat, hardtack bread, and ale to last several months. Cabot's charm and foreign notions had been the talk of the place for months. His send-off was a fitting one (if a little less auspicious than that accorded Columbus), with the lord mayor proclaiming the good wishes of his citizenry and the clerics intoning their Latin benedictions for a safe return.

The *Matthew*'s voyage, though shorter, proved much colder and less predictable than that faced by Columbus in his trio of ships. Unlike that cruise to the Caribbean in the warmth of the prevailing winds, Cabot sailed *against* the prevailing winds and *against* the currents of the North Atlantic Drift. He confronted dense fog and towering icebergs. The North Atlantic was no Mediterranean, where Cabot had perfected his sailing skills. His five weeks at the helm proved that behind the clean-shaven face and embroidered doublet was a tough-minded, masterful navigator.

A reconstructed Matthew *faces the same perils of the North Atlantic as did Cabot's ship.*

Having ridden the swift outgoing tides of the Bristol Channel, Cabot steered for the west coast of Ireland, and from there (with compass, cross-staff, and astrolabe in hand), set a course into the open ocean. He likely heeded the advice of his Bristol crew and took a northwesterly route. The crew had made many trips to Iceland and knew the sense of avoiding the brunt of the ocean currents and atmospheric depressions faced by anyone sailing due west.

The ship's log has been lost and details of the thirty-five days at sea are gone with it. But on the twenty-fourth day of June 1497, the feast day of St. John the Baptist, Cabot and his crew saw an end to the ocean. New found land! Yet not some unknown world, for they were certain that the image forming in their spyglass was that of the eastern extremity of Asia, the rim of the great land of Khan.

Where Did Cabot's Foot Fall?

Given that Columbus's voyage of 1492 landed him in the Caribbean, and that he touched the mainland of the Americas in 1498 when he reached Venezuela, Cabot bears the honour of being the first European after the Norse to set foot in North America. But just where did his footprint settle?

It has been a point of disagreement for centuries. Over time the focus has been narrowed to Newfoundland and Cape Breton Island, with Newfoundland's claim in the lead by a significant margin in recent years. However, no one knows with certainty, and the best we can hope for is a balance of scholarly debate, outside the testy arena of provincial conceits and tourist gamesmanship.

(That said, we in Newfoundland know we have it hands down. We have the better statue of Cabot, and just where did the British monarch choose to visit in celebration of the quincentenary in 1997? She didn't freeze in near-zero weather in Bonavista for nothing.)

Actually, when you bring the experts in on the discussion, the currently favoured Bonavista appears to have no stronger a claim to it than do several other spots along Newfoundland's coast. Since we have no record of Cabot's journey in his own hand or that of any member of the crew, our sources have narrowed to descriptions written by others upon Cabot's return to England.

The best known of these is a relatively recent find (1955) in the Spanish National Archives. The title of the document had led previous researchers to think it concerned the discovery of the country of Brazil in South America, not the legendary Isle of Brasile. In the full light of Cabot scholarship it turned out to be a lengthy letter about the voyage written in the hand of one John Day, a Bristol merchant trading to Spain, and addressed to none other than Christopher Columbus. John Day, it appears, was a spy dutifully reporting on English voyages of discovery.

His letter of early 1498 had much to tell. One passage is particularly noteworthy. In reference to the 'cape' they first sighted, Day wrote: '. . .the cape nearest to Ireland is 1800 miles west of Dursey Head which is in Ireland, and the southern-most part of the Island of the Seven Cities is west of Bordeaux River, and . . . he landed at

Cabot's actual landfall was less frigid, but no more the land of Khan.

only one spot of the mainland, near the place where the land was first sighted.'

If Day's description is accurate (and we have no way of determining how reliable were his sources, or how reliable were Cabot's measuring devices), then 1,800 miles west of Dursey Head (latitude 51° 34' N) would put Cabot in sight of Cape Bauld, at the tip of the Great Northern Peninsula, and within a few kilometres of the location of the Norse settlement five centuries earlier! The southern extremity of his farther explorations (latitude 45° 35' N) would position him within sight of Cape Breton Island. (Of course, after making his one landing and exploring the coastline of Newfoundland, he'd had enough and headed back to England, leaving Cape Breton Island for another explorer on another day.)

In Day's description Cabot's first sighting was an island, one he sailed past to go ashore on the mainland. This description, too, would fit the Cape Bauld theory, the prominent Belle Isle being not far offshore. A sail along the western shore of Cape Bauld would have put Cabot and crew ashore at L'Anse aux Meadows. Did Cabot walk the very shores walked by the Norse? Is there any chance that in landing where he did Cabot was following a route he had heard of in Norse legend?

Certainly it's no less speculative than what has been generated by the various other claimants to the title of Cabot's first landfall. From Cape Bauld in Newfoundland to Cape North in Nova Scotia, the proclamations have been loud and long-standing, on more than one occasion tinged with the rhetoric of nationalism. A mayor of St. John's in the 1930s, in an attempt to settle the debate with a prominent Canadian historian, proclaimed without any regard to reason (as mayors of St. John's are oft prone to do): 'Cabot landed right out here in this bloody harbour!'

Cape Bonavista, despite its lack of a prominent island offshore, seems to have come out the winner of the battle of Cabot landfall sites, at least in the public mind. And, make no mistake, Bonavista had long been in the running, and over the years garnered some prominent supporters. And perhaps it's just as well. Someone needs to reap the benefits of the re-enactments, and the town does have a wonderful replica of the *Matthew*. Cabot would have felt proud that he is contributing to the economy, though he would never have thought it possible there would be an end to the codfish. The sea, Cabot was said to have recounted, was 'swarming with fish, which can be taken not only with the net, but in baskets let down with a stone.'

In the Name of the King, the Pope, and the Saints

Wherever John Cabot set foot, on 24 June 1497, he wasn't long coming to the realization that the land was not at all like the Asia of spices and gold. However, the piece of wood he picked up from the shore was red enough in colour to become 'brazil-wood,' so determined was he to draw a direct connection between it and the reddish wood native to India. He would never know that the wood had been rubbed with the red ochre of the Beothuk.

There was comfort to be had in that wealth of codfish crowding the waters where the *Matthew* lay at anchor. For the Bristol crewmen who had been employed in the uncertain fish trade with Iceland, it alone was worth the trip.

But then, when Cabot and his men looked up and saw a trail leading into the forest beyond, it sent a chill through them all. Who might be in that forest looking out? And (equally quick to mind), what weapons did they carry? The Europeans hastily planted the banners of King Henry VII, Pope Alexander VI, and St. Mark, erected a crucifix, and made a quick retreat back home to England.

6 | Uncertain Returns

. . . his majesty here has acquired a portion of Asia without a stroke of his sword.

—Raimondo de Soncino, ambassador
in the court of Henry VII, 1497

*This statue of Corte-Real stands assertively on the
shores of Newfoundland, a gift of the Portuguese.*

The Fortunes of the Admiral

With fair winds and weather, the *Matthew*'s return journey took but fifteen days, although a miscalculation landed them off the coast of Brittany rather than England. By early August 1497 Cabot and crew were back home in Bristol, and by the middle of the month the mariner had made his way to the court of Henry VII. With map in hand and a globe at the ready, he proclaimed the great success of his voyage. The king, though more than a little charmed and impressed, found it hard to hide his disappointment that the Italian hadn't appeared with an entourage bearing gold and spices and exotic beasts. It would only be a matter of time, Cabot reassured him, such time as a fleet of ships could be arranged to make another journey.

'He has brought here to the King certain snares which were spread to take game and a needle for making nets,' it was reported. The king pressed him further . . . exactly what riches, then, does this 'newe found launde' offer? The needle is of brazil-wood, red in colour and pierced at both ends, Cabot told him. The seas there swarm with fish . . . so many fish that his majesty's kingdom would have no further need of Iceland. And, declared Cabot, it is but the northern rim of the great lands of the East, where 'all the spices of the world have their origin, as well as the jewels.' And his plan—'to make London a more important mart for spices than Alexandria!'

Henry's teeth were said to be 'few, poor and blackish,' but Cabot's account of his voyage must surely have brought a self-congratulatory smile to the king's lips nonetheless. He had skirted the efforts of Spain and Portugal, to give himself a foothold in the new world. But Cabot's words also piqued the interest of the many foreign envoys whom Henry had so fondly welcomed to his court. Before long they were dashing off letters to their respective countries with details of Cabot's enterprise. At an appropriate moment the Spanish envoy suggested to the king that the lands to the south of Cabot's landfall were part of the territory granted to Spain by His Holiness Pope Alexander in the Treaty of Tordesillas, and indeed found by Columbus under the patronage of Ferdinand and Isabella. Henry, as the envoy noted in a letter to the Spanish monarchs, 'would not have it.'

In the days that followed, Cabot's stature in London and Bristol rose to new heights. The king conferred on the mariner a yearly pension of twenty pounds.

King Henry VII

'Vast honour is paid to him,' wrote Lorenzo Pasqualigo to his brothers in Venice, 'and he goes dressed in silk, and these English run after him like mad . . .' The admiral (as he now liked to be called) had little trouble convincing Henry to back him in a return voyage. The king promised ten armed ships and 'all the prisoners to be sent away.' Nor was there any problem in finding additional men to complete the crews, including 'some poor Italian friars' to whom Cabot promised bishoprics in the new world. And among those whose heads were bursting with the expectation of wealth was his Genoese barber/surgeon/dentist, for Cabot had granted him a whole island in the new-found lands for his part in the first voyage. (Leaving one to wonder just what island he was given. Belle Isle? One of the Funks? Fogo?) The gentleman now considered himself a count, and 'the Admiral esteems himself at least a prince.'

Cabot's head was awhirl with the possibilities of finding fortune and even greater fame with a second venture to the new world. Henry issued him a fresh charter, though he revised his promise of ships, providing him but one, though 'manned and victualled at the king's cost.' In May 1498 the ship, commanded by Cabot, together with three or four smaller vessels owned by London merchants, set sail. They had provisions to last at least a year and were well stocked with merchandise for bartering that included 'coarse cloth caps, laces, points, and other trifles.' Cabot was determined to make his way to land south of where his first voyage had taken him, to where his ships' store would trade for caravans of richly coloured spices, just like those he remembered from his long-ago travels as a young man.

Not far out on the high seas one of the ships was badly damaged in a storm. It turned back.

The remaining ships were never heard from again. Not a trace of Cabot and his vessels was ever found. Or if found, never reported. They had succumbed to the unpredictable North Atlantic. Or so it was assumed for centuries.

In recent years the parts of the puzzle of what happened to Cabot on his second voyage have been rearranged by some artful scholars. Could he have actually reached the new world a second time? And if so, did he sail south as he had planned, and into territory claimed by other adventurers? Could it have been a zealous competing nation out to stop his explorations, rather than stormy seas, that did him in?

At the centre of the puzzle is a remarkable map drawn in the year 1500 by the Spanish cartographer and adventurer Juan de la Costa. It is the very first world map to depict North America. Along its coastline were drawn five flags of England, with the inscription 'mar descubierto ingleses' (land discovered by the English). Where did Costa get his information? It may well have come from the Spanish envoy in the court of Henry VII, but Costa himself had travelled to the new world in May 1499, exactly one year after Cabot, in an expedition dispatched by Ferdinand and Isabella and led by one Alonso de Ojeda. Notorious for his ruthlessness, Ojeda was likely sent to assert Spain's claim on the territory where Columbus had landed. He terrorized the coast, killing many of the natives he encountered.

Did he (and Costa with him) also encounter Cabot wandering south as part of his voyage to the new world begun a year earlier? Did Costa gain his knowledge of North America directly from Cabot, and did Ojeda then put a brutal and decisive end to his English ambitions? Speculation certainly, but not without its tidbits of supporting evidence.

Ojeda returned to Spain, only to voyage again to the new world the following year, with a patent granted by the Spanish sovereigns that read in part: '. . . their Majesties make you a gift in the island of Hispaniola of six leagues of land . . . for the stopping of the English.' Centuries later, in 1829, an esteemed Spanish historian, writing of his country's early voyages to the Caribbean, concluded: 'It is certain that Ojeda in his first voyage encountered certain Englishmen . . .' There is no record of any other transatlantic journey at the time, only that of Cabot.

A further fact adds weight to the theory that Cabot reached North America in his voyage of 1498. A Portuguese expedition there in 1501 resulted in an encounter with natives bearing 'a broken piece of gilt sword which certainly seems to have been made in Italy,' and 'two silver (ear)rings which without doubt seem to have been made in Venice.' How did the natives obtain these curios? Certainly not from Cabot's first voyage in 1497, since there was no report of direct contact with native people on his one and only landfall. Could the Venetian Caboto have left them on his voyage of 1498? And then, moving farther south, come eye to eye with the vile Ojeda? The puzzle awaits a few more pieces.

The Portuguese Make Claim

The papal bull of 1493, and the resulting Treaty of Tordesillas, had given forceful notice to the countries of Europe about just who could undertake voyages of exploration, and in which direction they should sail. Only Spain and Portugal (for years the two dominant competitors in the race to find an oceanic route to Asia) received such rights; the less populous, more distant England was not included. Henry VII, as he noted to the letter-writing Spanish envoy dashing about the royal court, had other thoughts on the matter.

The treaty set a longitudinal line of demarcation in the Atlantic roughly 370 leagues (1,800 kilometres) to the west of the Cape Verde Islands off Africa, with Spain given the rights to the west of the line, and Portugal given rights to the east. Portugal had already undertaken extensive exploration in Africa, culminating in Diaz's rounding the Cape of Good Hope to the Indian Ocean in 1488, and Spain had followed with the initiatives of Columbus to the Caribbean in 1492. But Portugal was determined its rival would not have any influence in lands that had not yet been discovered to the east of the line, and so undertook expeditions to both the southern and northern extremities of the line.

This eventually led, in the south, to the exploration and colonization of Brazil (and its naming, because real brazil-wood had finally been found). In the north, it led to a landfall in Greenland, which the Norse had abandoned by the early 1400s. It would seem, however, that Greenland was not to the liking of the Portuguese and they chose instead to lay claim to the new-found lands southwest of Greenland, lands where the English had already set foot, and whose position relative to the line of demarcation was open to question.

Their first demonstrative step for a voyage north was the issuing of a patent by King Manuel I in 1499, granting João Fernandes rights of exploration in Portugal's 'sphere of influence.' Fernandes was a native of the Azores who appeared to have some connection with the merchants of Bristol, and must have been aware of Cabot's expeditions. He was a landowner, and as such bore the title 'lavrador.'

His success in heading northwest from the Azores and crossing the remainder of the Atlantic is evident from maps of the early sixteenth century. On one of these the land mass of Greenland where Fernandes landed bears the title *Terra Laurador*, on another *Terra Laboratoris*. Later in the century the name would come to refer to the bulk of land to the southwest of Greenland. And thus we have the naming of the 'Labrador' as it is today.

When Fernandes left Greenland he forsook his home country. He sailed to Bristol and there joined in a partnership with some of its merchants. The alliance found favour with Henry VII, who issued them a patent. They sailed off in 1501 and probably headed for the lands as reported by Cabot. But Fernandes was not heard from again. Another voyage was undertaken in 1502. Indeed, 'The Company of Adventurers to the New Found Lands,' as the alliance came to be called, continued its forays across the Atlantic until at least 1505. Its goal was to combine exploration with commercial interests. In 1502, with the return of the *Gabriel*, we have the first record of a cargo of fish brought from the new world—thirty-six tons of salt cod, valued at £180. This dockside landing in Bristol marks the beginning of the great Newfoundland codfishery.

England was eager to let its presence in the new world be known, and with good reason, for the Portuguese were determined to stake a claim, in accordance with the Treaty of Tordesillas. Indeed, on a map of 1502 Cabot's 'newe found launde' has been designated *Terra del Rey de Portuguall* (Land of the King of Portugal), this a result of the voyages of a second Portuguese explorer, and another native of the Azores—Gaspar Corte-Real.

Corte-Real was the youngest son of João Vaz Corte-Real, an explorer in his own right, and who, some Portuguese contend, landed in Newfoundland before Cabot. In 1500, Gaspar led a voyage northwest from the Azores that brought him to mountainous and frozen terrain, and eventually to a land that was 'very cool and green and with many trees,' in about the latitude of Newfoundland. So taken was he with the land that the following year he returned to it, leaving this time from Lisbon with two caravels and more substantial provisions. The reports of the journey make no mention of any encounter with his countryman Fernandes, or the Bristol merchant men. If they did cross paths, the meeting would not have been an altogether pleasant one.

Corte-Real explored the coastline of eastern North America for several hundred kilometres and 'never found the end.' Exceedingly impressed by what was termed 'the mainland,' he journeyed up one of its many mighty rivers. And there he discovered an 'abundance of most luscious and varied fruits, and trees and pines of such measureless height and girth, that they would be too big as a mast for the largest ship that sails the sea.' As such he may well have been the first of a long line of people to leave Newfoundland and be dumbstruck by the continent's mainland. The experience seems to have done him in, however. He didn't live to tell the tale. Only one of the ships made it back to Lisbon. Corte-Real was lost, and his brother, who went in search of him the following year, also struck the mainland and was never heard from again.

Captives before the Kings

The ship that did return in October 1501 arrived with considerable cargo. Besides great quantities of pine for shipbuilding, and a vast store of salmon, herring, and cod, it had aboard seven native men, women, and children. These people had been kidnapped, souvenirs to be presented to the king of Portugal. They would, wrote the Venetian ambassador in the court at Lisbon, 'be excellent for labour and the

Cantino's map of 1502 made Newfoundland 'Terra del Rey de Portuguall.'

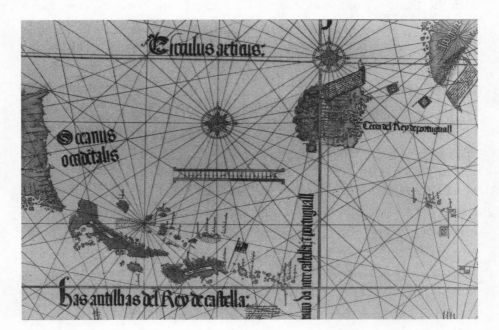

best slaves that have hitherto been obtained.' It was these natives who carried the piece of broken sword and the pair of silver earrings.

The following year, on an English boat arriving in Bristol from the Island of Newfoundland were more captured natives—three men, most likely Beothuk. They were paraded before King Henry at his newly built Richmond Palace, and he was suitably intrigued. 'These were clothed in beast skins, and ate raw flesh, and spake such speech that no man could understand them,' it was reported, 'and in their demeanour like to brute beasts . . .'

7 | Allure of Cod and Whales

In the name of God, Amen. Let it be known by this letter of testament, and last and ultimate will, that I, Juan Martinez de Larrume . . .in bed and ill but with as sound a mind as it has pleased our Lord to give me . . .

—From North America's earliest known will,

written 22 June 1577, Red Bay, Labrador

An imaginative rendering of early Basque whaling in Labrador.

The Reason to Return

With the start of the sixteenth century, 8,500 years of our human history had passed. Two aboriginal nations had come and gone; another had been terrorized by three separate groups—the Norse, the Portuguese, and the English.

The century began with the return of Europeans, but already the three main players—Cabot, Fernandes, and Corte-Real—had met untimely deaths. It was a warning that permanent European settlement would not be a predictable game.

For these foreigners the climate of the northern edge of this new world proved a disappointment. It was certainly not the land of the East, and with the cold Labrador Current sweeping past its shores, it was not even the land a few hundred kilometres to the south. If Europeans were to find a reason to hold on to it, it would not be in the rewards of the weather. Nor would it be the working of the land, as it was along the seaboard of the rest of North America. The soil was generally thin, or non-existent. Where it was sufficient, the growing season turned out to be a fraction of what the foreigners knew in their homelands. To reach any fountain of youth, such as Ponce de León was searching for in Florida, would, for much of the year, require snowshoes and an ice pick.

Once the excitement of discovery had passed, pragmatic financial considerations took hold. To keep Europeans coming back, and eventually make them want to settle here, some resource would have to outweigh the many attractions farther south. Landscape, as spectacular as it was, just wasn't going to do it.

Our sole enticement to an expansion-hungry Europe was cod. We had it, and in such wealth that it quickly captured the attention of European fishing fleets. The stream of ships was steady during the decades that followed Cabot's first dip of the fishing basket, but it would require a diehard cast of characters to sustain it. And settlement, once it did finally come, would take the toughest and most self-sufficient of that lot.

Cod Enough for All

A ranking of the work of the common man at the beginning of the century placed fishing second only to farming. Catholic doctrine forbidding meat on Fridays and during the forty days of Lent had created a ready market for fish. And now Church decrees designated many other days of saintly observance as 'meatless.' It was a gift from heaven for the fishmongers. But many of the fishing villages that dotted the coast of western Europe had reached the limit of their resource. Eager fleets ventured farther and farther offshore to meet the demands of the swelling populations, especially of Paris and Madrid and other cities inland.

Since the product didn't travel well in its fresh state, especially to warm Mediterranean markets, much of it, once cleaned and split, was salted, and then dried for long periods outdoors. *Morue seche* the French called it. To the Spanish it was *bacalao*. The finished product had the added advantage of being much reduced in weight, and so could be transported in greater quantities for less cost.

Some markets, especially the more northerly ones, preferred *morue verte*, in which the cod was heavily salted, but not dried. Generally, the longer and warmer the journey to market, the drier the product. Saltfish had become an irre-

pressible staple of the western European diet.

Once word spread of Cabot's discovery, and then its confirmation by the Portuguese, there were many quick to seize on it as a prime commercial opportunity. And, of course, the countries with the strongest and most efficient fishing fleets were the first off the mark. England might have been the one to discover the fish, but it was France, Portugal, and the Basque region of northern Spain that took early advantage of it.

In comparison with the other

In 1556 Newfoundland's deep bays led map-maker Gastaldi to depict it as a cluster of islands.

countries, England was sparsely populated and underdeveloped. After the early ventures by the Bristol merchants, its ships made relatively few trips across the Atlantic, lapsing back to dependency on the Icelandic fishery. Even a voyage of John Cabot's son, the much-favoured and smooth-talking Sebastian, failed to generate interest in the new world. In 1508 Sebastian sailed to Labrador and northward in a futile search for a northwest passage to the Orient. He returned to find Henry VIII on the throne, a new king with much more on his mind than cod. Only with a decline of the Basque and Portuguese fishery later in the century did England step in and fill a gap in the marketplace.

It was the French, setting out from ports in Brittany and Normandy, ports such as Saint-Malo, Honfleur, Fécamp, and Dieppe, who took the lead. The voyages may have begun as early as 1504, and by 1510 'new land' cod from a Breton ship, *La Jacquette,* showed up in the fish markets of Rouen. (The price of fish was a point of contention right from the start. Following the sale of the cargo in Rouen, one of *La Jacquette*'s crew quarrelled with the mate over wages, and in the ensuing scuffle, fell overboard, sinking to a briny end.)

The French were already old hands at deep-sea fishing, and once they returned with their *morue verte*, up the Seine it went to the prime markets of Rouen and Paris. The new-found lands became their Terre-Neufsve, and to their fishing harbours they gave names such as Saincte Katherine (Catalina) and Le Karpont (Quirpon). By 1519 they had more than one hundred ships making the annual voyage across the North Atlantic, to help meet the demands of a population whose calendar now had 153 meatless days.

There they were joined by Portuguese fishermen, who probably had been making regular voyages since the days of Corte-Real. There were plenty of good fishing grounds to go round. Witness the profusion of present-day place names, such as Fogo Island (y del fogo) and Cape Spear (Cauo da Espera).

The Portuguese fishery did not keep up with that of France. Its northern ports sent ships, but there is no record of the government ever fostering it as it did its other fisheries. In the summer of 1527 John Rut showed up in the harbour called St. John's. There he found only 'two Portugall Barkes,' but 'eleven saile of Normans and one Brittaine.'

Rut, under the sponsorship of Henry VIII, had set out from England in a feeble attempt to again look for a northwest passage. He reached the ice-bound coast of Labrador and 'for fear of more Ice,' quickly turned south, leaving us to wonder just what he could have been expecting. Rut eventually sailed into St. John's, did a little fishing, and set sail again, this time for the Caribbean. During the stopover in Newfoundland he penned a report on his journey in a letter that he put in the hands of the captain of one of the French ships returning to Europe. Rut's letter to Henry VIII ('in bad English and worse Writing'), dated 3 August 1527, together with a second letter about the voyage written by a fellow traveller (in Latin to Cardinal Wolsey), were the first pieces of mail ever sent from North America to Europe.

Another territory to take early advantage of the codfishery was the Basque region of northern Spain. Its fishermen were present in Newfoundland by at least 1512. Some contend it was much earlier. In the early decades of the sixteenth century, they were part of an international enterprise, with no one country laying claim to the resource. With such a surfeit of cod, there was no need to confuse matters by trying to claim it all. It was only when a number of the countries took up arms in Europe that outright ownership become an issue.

A voyage that a few years earlier was looked upon as an incredibly risky venture was by this time becoming routine. Each spring several hundred fishermen aboard dozens of vessels sailed across the North Atlantic in search of good fishing harbours. Especially attractive were those along the southeast coast, the Avalon Peninsula, and the Strait of Belle Isle. By day the fishermen caught cod from small boats, then salted and sometimes dried their catch. They slept aboard ship or in temporary dwellings on shore. At the end of the summer, their holds full, they headed back home, often with a stop in St. John's Harbour on the way.

The eventual capital city of the Island had its beginnings as a place for a little rest and relaxation, and the occasional brawl—an international port city in the making. It was here the crews came to swap stories of the fishing season (including their dealings with the 'savages') and make plans for the following year, all over food and a few bottles of stiff drink. St. John's proved 'a very popular place during summer but in winter given over to the fruition of birds and wild animals.'

Cartier Has His Fill

The French activity in Terre-Neufsve entered a new era with the arrival of Jacques Cartier in 1534. The native of Saint-Malo had been to Newfoundland as a fisherman, but this was an official voyage of exploration under the sponsorship of King François I, the first by a Frenchman in the new world.

Cartier's knowledge of Newfoundland led him directly from his landing in Catalina to the Funk Islands. There the crews killed enough of the great auks that, salted away, filled close to ten casks. A trip to the Funks became commonplace for visiting Europeans, until the early nineteenth century when the great auk had been slaughtered to extinction. Cartier and crews were no eco-tourists. Before reaching the Strait of Belle Isle, they added more birds (gannets and tinkers) to their store, and even chased down in longboat a young polar bear. 'His flesh,' said Cartier, 'was as good to eat as that of a two-year old heifer.'

The Strait was a definite destination, leading us to speculate he already knew there was something of interest beyond it. Among the sights to confront Cartier was a large French fishing ship out of the port of La Rochelle in the Bay of Biscay. The vessel had sailed into the Strait, well past Blanc Sablon, a clear indication of just how knowledgeable the French had become about the Gulf of St. Lawrence.

Cartier wasn't much impressed by the landscape, dubbing the rocky Labrador coast 'the Land God gave to Cain.' The 'wild and savage' Cainites he encountered were there to hunt seals, having arrived from 'warmer countries' in birchbark canoes. They were most likely Innu from the interior, or possibly Beothuk from across the Strait. It wouldn't be the only group of natives that Cartier would meet

It was in caravels like this one that the French sailed to the fishing grounds off Newfoundland.

that summer. The reaction of the Mi'kmaq and Iroquois to him, with their eagerness to trade, confirmed Cartier was far from the first of his kind to have ventured
into the Gulf.

But he was the first to record such a voyage of exploration, including passage
down the west coast of Newfoundland. Here he found the landscape more impressive. Who wouldn't be stirred by the sight of the Long Range Mountains, or the
Bay of Islands? He explored the angular Port au Port Peninsula and sailed as far
south as Cape Anguille, before heading west.

In the Gulf he discovered islands with more seabirds, this time adding 'more
than a thousand murres and great auks' to the ships' store. He declared Îles de la
Madeleine the best land he had seen so far, adding, rather hastily, 'two acres of it
are worth more than the whole of Newfoundland.'

These islands were eventually settled by the French. Had our own landscape
been more genteel, who's to say the French might not have fought harder to lay
claim to what its fishermen were so keen to exploit. No doubt Cartier's view of
Labrador and Newfoundland played a part, though it didn't stop him from returning a second and a third time. Again he saw it as a food supply and a gateway to
what eventually became New France. Obviously filling the man's stomach was not
the way to his heart.

His voyages did, however, lay the basis for a more thorough understanding of
the marine geography of the region. The last weeks of his voyage of 1535–36
brought him through the Cabot Strait and along the south coast of Newfoundland,
proving Newfoundland to be an island. He spent time with other French ships in St.
Pierre, and in Renews he took on wood and water, before setting course for Saint-
Malo. He wrote in his journal, 'Thanks be to God, whom we implore on bringing
our voyage to an end, to give us His grace and His paradise hereafter. Amen.'

The Basque Whaling-Works

As Cartier sailed into the Gulf of St. Lawrence in 1534, one of the sightings he dutifully recorded in his journal was Hable de la Ballaine, Whale Harbour. Another was
Buttes, later known as Red Bay. These sites on the Labrador side of the Strait of
Belle Isle were well-known to fishermen, not just for their abundance of codfish
and seals, but equally for the vast number of right and bowhead whales channelled past its shores each year, drawn there by the plankton-rich Labrador

Current.

Neither the French nor the Portuguese saw much of commercial interest in the whales. It took the newly arrived Basque fishermen to turn this shoreline into the first industrial complex in the new world. By the middle of the sixteenth century, Basque merchants were sending upwards of thirty galleons and two thousand men and boys a season to this one region of southern Labrador, for the sole purpose of hunting whales and rendering their blubber into oil for the markets of Europe.

Whaling was an enterprise the Basques had perfected in their own Bay of Biscay, where for centuries they pursued the giant mammals in small open boats. Whale oil was a much-prized commodity, used mainly for lighting and lubrication, and in clothing industries. The quality of the oil extracted on the coast of Labrador turned out to be particularly good, and at the peak of production the ships were returning to Europe each year with cargoes totalling twenty thousand barrels, each weighing 180 kilograms. The Basques were soon referring to this stretch of the Labrador coast as if it were an overseas territory, La Provincia de Terranova.

Amazingly, this vibrant segment of our history has only come to light in the past few decades. For that we are indebted to the work of historical geographer Selma Barkham, who spent years searching Basque archives, mostly notably in the Spanish town of Oñate, near Bilbao. The first land sites in Labrador were uncovered in 1977, their investigation spurred on by surface evidence of fragments of the red roofing tiles known to have been used by sixteenth-century Basques. Over the next several years, Red Bay and nearby harbours yielded a remarkable picture of the whaling operations.

The spring of each year saw the great exodus of whalers from Basque ports to a region of the Labrador coast they called Gran Baya. Their ships arrived loaded with provisions—dried beans and peas, bacon, ship's biscuit, sardines, cider, and sherry among them. It was enough to last several months, to late December, when the impending freeze-over of the bay forced them back across the Atlantic.

The underwater excavation of the San Juan *at Red Bay revealed this Basque whaling harpoon.*

Once in the harbours, those who did not sleep aboard ship settled into make-shift shelters on shore. Only the coopers' dwellings were substantial, for theirs were workhouses as well as living quarters. Under their tiled roofs the *barricas* were re-assembled from the rough-cut oak staves brought from Europe. These leakproof barrels, bound securely with split alder branches, were invaluable to the success of the whole whaling expedition.

From lookouts word of whale sightings were relayed to the beach shelters below, where crews, usually six in number, boarded eight-metre boats called *chalupas* and headed out on the open waters of the Strait. They manoeuvred to within a metre of the mammal and the strongest of the men sank a harpoon into it, to which was attached a bulky drogue, a drag to slow and tire the beast. At every chance the whalers flung their lances into its vital organs, as other *chalupas* converged on the scene for the final kill.

Before beaching it, the men hacked off its flippers and tail. They rolled it on its back. With long flensing knives, sheets of the blubber were stripped away, and then hoisted to shore to be hacked into chunks and dropped into huge copper cauldrons. Fire beneath the vessels, often fuelled by the leftover skin of the whale, rendered the blubber to oil.

As the liquid was ladled into vats of water, the impurities sank, and the cooling, precious oil floated to the top. Filled barrels were sealed and rolled aboard ship, stored in its hold until the Basques closed down their operation for the year and sailed home.

A storm in 1565 threw the planned trip home into chaos. It snapped the mooring of a three-hundred-tonne galleon at Red Bay, crashed it against the rocks, sending the ship and its cargo of a thousand barrels of oil into twelve metres of water. The *San Juan* (now excavated but kept in the cold-water environment that has preserved it so well) is the most complete sixteenth-century working galleon found anywhere.

Excavated, too, at Red Bay are burial sites whose bones and fragments of clothing give us a glimpse of the health and physical appearance of these Basque whalers. Most were short, muscular, robust young men, who dressed in dark blue pants drawn together at the knees, topped by a collared shirt, long-sleeved and dyed brick red. Death came often from scurvy or natural causes, but multiple burials suggest that some may have died from disaster during the whale hunt itself.

From one site were counted eleven men in a shallow grave. Most likely they had lingered too long in Gran Baya. Trapped by ice, forced to overwinter, the men fell victim to the scarcity of food and the dreadful cold. By this time the Basque whaling in Labrador was in decline, for no whalers returned the following spring to give them decent burials.

By the early decades of the seventeenth century the Basque expeditions had ended. The disastrous results of the Spanish Armada sent against England in 1588 had drastically cut the number of ships in the fleet. And with piracy on the rise from the English, the French, and the Dutch, even fewer ships were willing to risk the trip across the North Atlantic. In the end the financial hazards proved too great. Commercial interests turned elsewhere, especially to Spitsbergen, off the coast of Norway.

In the decades that followed, the tiled roofs of Labrador whaling stations, once home to thousands of men, gave way to the elements and collapsed. Evidence of their bustling enterprise was gradually covered in sod, except for the fragments of tiles among the shore rocks and the mountains of whale bone bleaching in the sun.

8 | Staking Claim

. . . as they seized the woman she took her stand as if she were completely raving and mad because of her child whom she would have to leave behind . . . as though she would rather lose her life than leave her child . . . Because she was so mad, they let her alone a bit; she went to the spot where she had concealed her child, then she was calmer than before, then they took the woman and her child and brought them away . . .

—From a handbill advertising the exhibition of the Labrador Inuit mother and child. Its woodcut is the earliest known portrait of the Inuit from life.

The 1567 woodcut of an Inuit woman and her daughter brought to Europe.

At Gran Baya

Every Basque whaler arrived with a crossbow, a sword, or an arquebus, and in ships bearing heavy cannon. And when the financial risks increased and the number of whales dwindled, they were gone, without reason to return.

At Red Bay a few Inuit artifacts have been unearthed, but these are likely no more than evidence that the Inuit visited the site during the winter months, or after the whaling had come to an end, likely scavenging for a few bits of iron to fashion into tips for their arrows and harpoons.

In contrast, the Innu had sustained direct contact with both fishermen and whalers. At times it swelled to friendly relations. Some of the Innu 'talk and associate with our men and help to prepare the fish on shore in exchange for a little bread, biscuit and cider,' we are told in documents of the day. They worked side by side with the Basques 'with great labour and patience' in all aspects of whaling. The Basques thought them 'better people' than the natives farther down the St. Lawrence, whose arrows had slain many of Cartier's men. In winter the whalers stored their *chalupas* in Labrador, without fear of damage, proof their culture and the Innu's lived in mutual trust.

The Ways of Christian Men

Such an alliance between natives and Europeans was the exception. The first thoughts of the newcomers were of conversion, of saving the 'savages' from the bonds of their heathen existence. And, in leading the natives to the Christian God, the Europeans saw themselves as rightful landowners in the new world.

The doctrine behind this attitude evolved in medieval Europe. Unknown lands were the property of the Christian God, to be assigned to countries at the will of the pope. The pope, in turn, bestowed on European monarchs their right to grant charters to would-be explorers and colonists to the new world.

Such skewed application of the tenets of Christianity rested on a more fundamental question. Were the natives of the new world human? Common was the belief that 'they should be treated as dumb brutes created for our service.' Pope Paul II, in his *Sublimus Dei* of 1537, took the opposite view, and decreed 'the Indians are truly men.' The pontiff went further—'They may and should, freely and legitimately, enjoy their liberty and the possession of their property.'

Many of the Europeans who landed on the other side of the Atlantic ignored their reform-minded pope. Even among those who accepted the first pronouncement were many who dismissed the second. The Protestant Reformation proved a convenience to still others eager to disregard the pope's edict altogether.

These European perspectives shaped the turbulent history of aboriginal peoples. The native view of land as the source of life to be shared, without any concept of personal 'ownership,' was given no credence. Many were the Europeans who, in fact, turned it to their own advantage.

Civilizing the New World

This attitude of Europeans is exemplified by the 1536 voyage of one Richard Hore of London. What might best be described as the first sightseeing cruise to the new world was undertaken by this 'man of goodly stature and great courage' and six score of his compatriots, mostly eager young barristers with an eye out for opportunities abroad. Duly 'mustered in warlike manner,' they showed up to board their ships, and 'after receiving of the sacrament,' all embarked for the new world.

Following the mandatory stop at the Funks for their fill of great auk, they roamed the coast of Newfoundland, eventually sighting a boat 'with the Savages of

The flesh of fellow lawyers made for a sorrowful meal.

these partes.' The Beothuk raced ashore and escaped inland, leaving Hore and his gentlemen friends to ponder a side of bear meat roasting on a spit.

Several weeks passed. It seems the adventurers had not happened upon enough fish or wild game to keep body and soul alive. More to the point, they were not sufficiently clever to capture any. One gentleman resorted to eyeing the flesh of his fellows, and so 'by this meane the company decreased.' Those left alive blamed the Beothuk, of course, until finally, in a confrontation over a particular piece of boiled meat, the gentleman blurted out that it 'was a piece of such a mans buttocke.'

The sight of lawyers devouring themselves proved too much for the more civil among them. The blasphemers were severely rebuked. They fell into prayer and 'such was the mercie of God, that the same night there arrived a French shippe.' Master Hore and his famished crew seized the ship and headed for its galley, after which they set sail for fair England. The French were left with nothing but the empty English vessel in which to ply their way back home.

In the years that followed came numerous other reports of encounters between natives and those who deemed themselves more worthy. Many resulted in the capture of native people. In Europe in 1567 an Inuit mother and her seven-year-old daughter, captured on the coast of Labrador, were put on exhibit. The curiosities from the frozen wastelands of the new world were displayed in several cities, including Augsburg, Antwerp, and Nuremberg. Their captors assured the gawking citizens that the mother ('yellow brown like the half Moors') was the equal, in her heathen, cannibalistic nature, of her husband who had been killed during the capture, a man they declared to be no less than twelve feet tall. The woman, garbed in seal skins, lived 'almost more wickedly than the beasts.' They all thanked God for the favour He showed them, that they weren't 'such savage people and man-eaters as are in this district.'

The paternalistic Europeans, fortified by their religion, shaped the footprints of everyone who staked a claim to the new world. In 1583, it was the turn of Sir Humphrey Gilbert.

The Hapless Gilbert

Gilbert was born of privilege, and of stout Devonshire stock. A half-brother to Walter Raleigh, he came from a long line of marine merchants and adventurers, many with a roguish bent. His love of the sea led him to counsel his boyhood friend Elizabeth I that England reclaim parts of the new world, and set its sights on settlement. Gilbert's voyage, and proclamation in the Harbour of St. John's on behalf of his queen, marks the colonization of Newfoundland, and what some claim to be the very beginning of the British Empire.

Gilbert's formal education took place at Eton and Oxford, but he thought it lame preparation for his life ahead, a life marked by a courageous, if often misguided, pursuit of greatness. His notions often outstripped his abilities, but never did he lack an eagerness to see them through. He wasted much of his wife's money in the process, a state of affairs that peaked when an alchemical enterprise failed to turn lead into antimony. He was known to erupt into wild rages, yet he dreamed of building a placid utopia on foreign soil. Wrote Gilbert: 'He is not worthy to live at all that for fear . . . shunneth his countries service; seeing death is inevitable, and the fame of virtue immortal.' The new world could not have wished for a more eloquent trustee.

It was eloquence ofttimes overshadowed by ruthlessness. Gilbert had been knighted after four years of fighting rebels in Ireland, who branded him 'more like a devil than a man.' It was said that he had the heads of the enemy dead lined up outside his tent at night so the Irish who wished to confer with him would have to walk past the bodiless faces of their slaughtered relatives.

Elizabeth I, merciless herself when she felt the urge, continued to find something in Gilbert to admire when his attention turned back to the sea and to the relatively unknown worlds beyond it. (No doubt the queen's fondness for his half-brother had more than a little to do with it.) Gilbert's ambitions came to a head in 1578, at a time when John Cabot and his son were all but forgotten. Elizabeth granted him a charter to go in search of 'such remote heathen and barbarous lands, countries, and territories not actually possessed by any Christian prince or people.' Her Majesty had been stirred to action by Spain's zealous and profitable dealings abroad. It irked all Englishmen to hear of Spanish ships laden with plundered gold from the new world, while the few English vessels that ventured across the Atlantic returned with holds full of salt cod.

Gilbert was taut with the urgency of setting off after reading accounts of colonization in Richard Hakluyt's *Divers Voyages* of 1582, especially the part about there being 'in small running brooks divers pieces of gold as big as his finger, others as big as his fist.' Among his recruits was Daniel, an expert in minerals from Saxony. With him, too, would be Stephanus Parmenius, a Hungarian poet who would duly record the embarkation in three hundred hexameters of Latin verse. When Gilbert's financial backers finally mustered enough faith in the expedition, five ships set sail from Plymouth. The crews were an unhealthy combination of hardened pirates and 'shipwrights, masons, carpenters, smiths . . . mineral men and refiners,' as well as musicians, morris dancers, a hobby horse—'Maylike conceits to delight the savage people.'

Little wonder Gilbert had trouble from the start. The lateness of the season forced him to abandon his hope of sailing south, and instead take the well-known and shorter route to Newfoundland. After just two days, the two hundred-tonne bark *Raleigh*, the largest of his ships, turned back to Plymouth with the rather dubious claim that there wasn't enough food aboard to last the trip.

Just prior to the voyage, Elizabeth had sent Gilbert her anchor brooch as a sign of faith in his seamanship. Now she was forced to conclude he had 'no good hap at sea.'

The truth of her claim intensified. Gilbert was weeks longer at sea than such a voyage should have taken. Then in the fogs of the Grand Banks he was separated from two more of his vessels, the *Swallow* and the *Squirrel*. The only

Sir Humphrey Gilbert. His motto:
Quid Non *(Why Not?).*

encouraging sign was the squawking gulls that thronged amid the fish offal cast overboard from the fishing fleets. It was Gilbert's first hint of landfall.

His sight of the new world—'hideous rocks and mountains, bare of trees, and void of any green herb'—came on 30 July. For a crew who had signed up thinking they were bound for the West Indies, the sight that greeted them lacked charm, not to mention warmth. Not even the Funks and auks held their attention for long.

At the place 'the vulgar sort called the bay of Conception,' they were reunited with the *Swallow*. Its crew had fallen back on their pirate ways, plundering a fishing vessel of food and clothing. An enraged Gilbert steered for St. John's. Near the port he came upon the *Squirrel* at anchor. The four ships, reunited for a grand arrival, prepared to sail past the Narrows and into the harbour.

Gilbert promptly ran his vessel onto Cahill's Rock. He had to be towed off by a few obliging foreign boats—a rather more ignoble arrival than he had envisioned. It didn't seem to diminish the feasting that followed, however, and the sense of pageantry two days later. The ships at anchor (thirty-six in total, of which only sixteen were English) proved sceptical of Gilbert's intent. They recalled how a year earlier two armed English vessels had gone on a pirating spree in Renews, not far to the south. Gilbert assured them that his purpose was honourable. That, in fact, he was on official business for the English queen.

A pavilion was set up on shore. Gilbert 'summoned the merchants and masters, both English and strangers' and read to them a proclamation. By the power of Elizabeth he took possession of 'the harbour of St. John and 200 leagues every way.' It was 5 August 1583.

He declared three laws immediately—that the religion was to be the Church of England, that anyone who opposed the queen's right to the land would be executed, and that anyone who uttered a word dishonouring Her Majesty would lose his ship, his goods, and his ears. A tree limb and piece of turf were handed to Gilbert to consummate the deed, and later, not far from the spot, was erected 'the Arms of England ingraven in lead, and infixed upon a pillar of wood.'

Newfoundland was officially English. But Gilbert had no means to enforce the laws, let alone collect the rent he had designated as owing to himself, and 'his heires and assignes for ever.' There was more than one indulgent smile, kept under control only by the sight of firearms in the hands of Gilbert's crew.

Gilbert sent his man Daniel off to look for minerals. The Saxon struggled through the underbrush and climbed the surrounding hills. He returned with an ore he declared to contain silver. Gilbert would deliver to his queen a sign of wealth to rival the riches of Spain! He was ecstatic, though forced to keep it all to himself and his closest confidants, 'here being both Portugals, Biscains, and Frenchmen not farre off.'

He led his men to the countryside, and although the poet Parmenius could find little to his liking save the profusion of sweet wild strawberries, Gilbert was charmed with the place. He now regarded himself as 'a Northern man altogether.'

As fortune should have it, Gilbert did not encounter any Beothuk. (Nor any Irishmen.) He left St. John's harbour with the smell of 'roses . . . , wilde, but odoriferous,' and the taste of freshly cooked fish and 'plentie of rasp berries, which doe grow in every place.' The thought of sailing south, to present-day New England, had lost its allure.

He would not have a chance to compare the two places. Off Sable Island, the *Delight* ran aground, sending Parmenius and Daniel to their deaths, and all Gilbert's cherished notes and maps and ore samples to the bottom with them. He set sail for England, broken-hearted.

He took to his tiny frigate, the *Squirrel*, refusing to cross in a larger, safer vessel. Near the Azores Gilbert ran into a fierce storm. The last recorded sight of the man who claimed Newfoundland for England had him sitting in the stern of the *Squirrel*, a book in his hand, calling to another of the ships, one fated to survive. 'We are as near to heaven by sea as by land!' he bellowed. At midnight, Gilbert, and his dream of returning to Newfoundland with colonists to reap its wealth, sank into the Atlantic.

9 | Shiploads of Cod

The diseases of this country are: breaking out of the arm wrests, cold and coughs, and the scurvy, of which they have two sorts, the one an acute scurvy, soon caught, soon cured . . . their gums rot, thick-breathed, swollen, black, indurated hams and thighs, tumors of the legs, yielding to the touch, extravasation of the blood, a disease not curable by all the medicines which can be carried here, but easily by a few vegitives of the country.

—Journal of James Yonge

The land-based dry codfishery was a precisely organized endeavour.

Not for Elizabethan Ears

When Gilbert sailed out of St. John's Harbour on 22 August 1583 no one was happier to see him go than the foreign captains. They were eager to get back to fishing, in the manner they had been doing for decades. Gilbert had overstayed his welcome.

Among the mementoes he left behind was a handwritten 'passport' for each of them. That issued to Tomas Andre, captain of one of the Portuguese vessels, gave him 'free access to and liberty in the fishing and trade of Newfoundland.' It is surprising that this testimony to Gilbert's arrogance has survived, because to Andre it must have amounted to a pointless, laughable scrap of paper.

Elizabeth I was not about to back up the English claim to Newfoundland. Nor was she willing to entertain the notion of settlement there, despite the efforts of those who argued for it in the wake of Gilbert's voyage. The assets of Newfoundland were loudly proclaimed by, among others, Edward Hayes, the captain of one of the ships that accompanied Gilbert on his ill-fated voyage across the Atlantic.

'In the months of June, July, August and September, the heate is somewhat more than in England,' he declared. There was not only cod, but 'incredible quantitie, and no less varietie of kindes of fish in the sea and fresh waters.' And 'foule both of water and land in great plentie and diversitie.' And much, much more. 'The grasse and herbe doth fat sheepe in very short space,' he asserted, but no one cared to pay any attention.

English settlement in Newfoundland would have to wait. The queen was preoccupied with the Spaniards and the glitter of their wealth as she plotted a halt to their empire building (which in 1580 included the annexation of Portugal). In 1585 news reached Elizabeth of Philip II's embargo of English ships in Spanish ports. She acted swiftly and decisively. Within a month Bernard Drake (the brother of Sir Francis) was on his way to Newfoundland to warn English fishermen not to take their catches directly to Spain, as was their normal practice. Moreover, Drake was directed 'to cease and take into your possession' any enemy ships he sighted.

In the waters of the Avalon Peninsula Drake attacked and captured nearly twenty vessels, all of them Portuguese. He arrived in England with six hundred prisoners, and half their ships. The rest had been sunk at sea. Drake was knighted and the prisoners were marched to the jail in Exon castle and 'there cast into the deepe pit and stinking dungeon.'

The filth and overcrowding led to an outbreak of typhus. It spread through the jail, and when the prisoners not yet dead were dragged to trial at Exeter, it infected the many unfortunates in the courtrooms. In the end typhus claimed the lives of the judge, several justices of the peace, and Sir Bernard Drake himself.

Drake died knowing his actions had altered the course of the Spanish involvement in Newfoundland. The fishing fleets of the Iberian Peninsula curtailed their voyages and joined forces with the ships of war in an Armada bound for the shores of England. Drake's brother would be the one to save the day for Elizabeth, and in doing so set the stage for English expansion across the Atlantic.

Surge in the English Fishery

England came to value the codfishery of Newfoundland as it never had before. Not only did it provide food for its navy, it was good sea training, turning green men and boys into potential recruits. The French fishing boats held to the southern coast (including the islands of St. Pierre and Miquelon) and the northeast coast, from La Scie to Cap Dégrat at the tip of the Great Northern Peninsula. The remnants of the Portuguese and Basque fleets were scattered in other parts of the Island, including the west coast and the Strait of Belle Isle, near the Basque whaling stations. This left the English with the eastern Avalon Peninsula to themselves. It was here, over the final decades of the sixteenth century, that they established, not by Gilbert's vacant declaration of ownership, but by a tradition of continuous use, their foothold in Newfoundland.

The fishery remained a migratory one. No fisherman was about to spend his winters here, idle and cold, when his wife and children and the taverns were an ocean away in Europe. When fishing was over for the year, he needed to find work back home to feed his family. More to the point, it was considerably cheaper for the ship owners to transport the fishing crews back and forth since all the supplies and the markets were on one side of the Atlantic.

The English venturers sailed from the ports of the West Country—especially those of Devonshire, Dorset, and Hampshire. Early each year the ship owners disbursed their agents into the ports and market towns to sign on crews for the upcoming summer. March and April found the fishermen congregating in Plymouth and Dartmouth, where the docks were piled with gear and supplies. They stowed it all aboard ship, found leftover space for themselves, and

*The prized codfish (*Gadus morhua*).*

off they sailed, in pursuit of the prevailing easterlies that would take them across the Atlantic.

Weeks later, relatively shallow soundings told them they had made it to the Grand Banks. The sighting overhead of a few blunt-headed 'noddies' confirmed that land was not far off. All eyes were peeled for the first sight of Newfoundland and some landmark to show where on its coast they had struck.

The competition for the best section of shoreline (or 'fishing room') turned intense. 'Those mad Newfoundland men are so greedy of a good place they ventured in strangely,' was one way of looking at it. The vessels weaved their way through fog and ice and shoals, the last few kilometres often covered in longboats dispatched from the ships. A single ship might send several boats into fishing spots up and down the coast, and then later choose the best of the lot.

And, just as had been the custom when many fishing nations were competing, the captain of the first boat to arrive in a harbour took the title 'admiral,' and had first choice of the fishing rooms. To the fishermen he was the 'lord,' and the second to show up in the harbour, though officially 'vice-admiral,' was dubbed the 'lady.' In later years, the third in line was accorded the title of 'rear-admiral,' though we can only speculate on what the fishermen might have tagged him.

This chain of command decided the fishing rights of every other ship to show up in the harbour—who fished where and what section of the shoreline each could claim. It was the first court system in Newfoundland. As wild and unruly as it might have been at times, it does show that from the start there was at least the attempt to bring some civil order to the fishing business.

With the last season's shelters repaired and any new ones erected, fishing started

in earnest. The methods of production of salt cod would remain relatively un-
changed for centuries, and for much of that time, the stacks of dried fish were the
one product synonymous with Newfoundland. (My father and other fishermen
four centuries later would still talk of 'arm wrests' or 'water pups'—skin ulcers
brought on by oil-clothes chafing the wrists in salt water.)

The fishing was done by three men from large open boats, using handlines
baited with herring, squid, or capelin. Two others of a crew, lads often of no more
than eleven or twelve, remained on shore to deal with the fish once it was landed.
Back from the fishing grounds, loaded down with several hundred cod, the boat
drew up to the head of the 'stage,' the processing plant that extended over the
water as a wharf. There, with long-handled prongs, the fish were tossed ashore,
and into the hands of the boy whose job it was to set them on the cutting table, in
reach of the header.

The fellow slit the belly of the fish, twisted off its head, and gutted it, directing
the liver through one hole in the table, and into a great vat, and the offal through
another, where it fell into the sea. The fish was then slid along, and into the hands
of the splitter. With a few quick strokes of his knife, the second fellow had the fish
split abroad, and the backbone removed. The fish dropped into a 'drooge barrow,'
where it was covered with salt.

'A salter is a skilful officer, for too much salt burns the fish and makes it break,
and wet, too little makes it redshanks, that is, look red when dried, and so is not
merchantable.' The drying process was executed on 'flakes' (raised wooden frames
covered by boughs) or directly on beaches if they were blessed with broad
expanses of stones. A good sense of the weather conditions was crucial. Knowing
when to gather in the drying fish, how to make it into a 'prest pile' so some of the
salt would sweat out of it, even knowing how to store it aboard ship, were all skills
that called for the know-how of many men.

It was no easy labour. In mid-summer they were working eighteen to twenty
hours a day. The flies ('muscetos and garnippers') proved especially vexing. The
young boys, so exhausted that they would fall asleep in the woods, would wake up
hours later swollen blind by flybites.

And generally all for a one-third share of the trip, split among the crew, with
two-thirds going to the owners. The captain took the greatest portion, of course,
and the 'boys, lurgens, and such' were left with the least. The amount tallied up at

the end of the trip varied from year to year, depending on the run of fish, and the market conditions.

The good years seemed to offset the bad, and by the end of the sixteenth century, the English fishery in Newfoundland had grown to nearly two hundred vessels a year. In 1593, Sir Walter Raleigh described the codfishery as 'the stay of the West Country.' So much had production been perfected and expanded that more salt cod was being cured than could be carried to market by the vessels which transported the fishermen back to Europe. It became common practice for the English merchants to send large 'sack ships' to Newfoundland near the end of the fishing season, vessels whose purpose was to transport the dried cod directly to the markets of southern Europe, including their old enemies, Spain and Portugal. There the English traded fish for the oranges, spices, and gold bullion, and for the white wines of Malaga and the Canaries, *vino de sacca*, which gave the ships their name.

And with the rise of the sack ships, there grew up a new class of fishermen. These were entrepreneurial sorts who migrated each spring as passengers aboard the West Country ships. In Newfoundland they took part in the inshore fishery with their own boats and sold the season's catch to the sack ships and merchant traders. They came to be known as by-boat keepers. Over time, instead of storing their boats and returning to England at the end of summer, some chose to overwinter. It was settlement, but only of a semi-permanent sort.

But the French Lead All

While the English fishery increased in size, that of the Spanish declined further. Only the Spanish Basques continued to come to Newfoundland to fish for cod, that despite the fact their whaling fleets were disappearing from the shores of Labrador. We see the lasting evidence of the Basques' yearly expeditions in the string of place names along the west coast of the Island. Today we can point not only to Port aux Basques, but to the others that are corruptions of original Basque names—New Ferolle (Ferrolgo), Port au Port (Oporportu), and Port au Choix (Portuchoa) among them.

However, it was the French fishery that took the lead. Twice the size of the English enterprise, it saw more than fifty ports sending ships to Newfoundland by the turn of the century—Saint-Malo, Nantes, La Rochelle, and Bordeaux foremost

The French fishery on the Grand Banks.

among them. The French had the added advantage of a natural supply of salt from the salt marshes of Brittany. While some of their fishermen preferred the inshore dry cure, from mid-century the French greatly expanded the lucrative *morue verte* fishery directly on the Grand Banks.

The fish were caught from the windward side of ships that drifted, sails furled, over the Banks. The vessels averaged about fifty tonnes and each carried a crew of roughly a dozen men. Along the port side was constructed a *bel*, a long wooden platform that projected over the railing. Secured to it were barrels, from inside which *lignotiers* cast out their baited lines. Covered in tarred, waterproof coats extending over the outside of the barrels, these fishermen went about their business without fear of falling overboard or getting soaked by the icy salt spray.

To keep count of the catch, each codfish hauled over the railing was first hooked on an iron spike and had its tongue cut away by an *élangueur*. From there the fish went to the header and the splitter, and eventually into the hold of the vessel, to be drained, salted, and stacked. It would stay that way until the catch was landed back in France.

The first fish would strike the prime markets north of the Loire in late August. This *morue nouvelle* was eagerly anticipated and came with a high price, turning the competition between the bankers to be the first to market into an intense race. The fishing expeditions to the Newfoundland Banks were quick and efficient, the crews never sparing a moment, not even to set foot on the land they sighted beyond their fishing lines.

Trading in Mistrust

Crew members of the inshore fishery often brought a personal store of provisions, some for their own consumption, some to barter with any natives they might encounter. The object was trade in furs. But mistrust on both sides gave way to increasing hostility. 'Fighting with the savages of Terra-nova' brought the death of one Basque fisherman in 1574. In the 1580s French fishermen from Saint-Malo had anchored near Quirpon, at the tip of the Great Northern Peninsula, only to discover that Inuit who had crossed the Strait from Labrador were camped nearby. During the night watch a French crewman, in fear of being attacked, fired his gun in the direction of sudden noise. The shot killed the wife of one of the elders of the band.

For several years after, the Inuit regularly crossed the Strait in their kayaks, armed to attack the French in retaliation for the woman's death. A rampage in St. Julien's, in which sixteen French fishermen were murdered while piling up their fish, was the result. The assailants dressed up in 'the apparell of the slayne French' and proceeded along the coast to Croque where, sighting more fishermen, 'they surprised them at their work and killed twenty-one more.'

European fishermen and natives came to avoid direct contact, even though each wanted the goods of the other. Near Port au Choix the Inuit and the Basques remained separated by a narrow body of water. To initiate trade the Inuit would load furs in a boat and thrust it across to the other side. Removing the furs, the Basques loaded the boat with goods (including clothing, needles, thread, pipes, and tobacco) and pushed it back. For the fisherman, such trade added to the potential profit of their arduous voyage across the Atlantic. For the Inuit, it continued a practice, which, though it had its risks, was one they had grown used to and upon which they had come to depend.

The Beothuk often avoided all contact with Europeans. Scared away by their initial encounters, they chose to live without foreign goods. For much of the second half of the sixteenth century there is no record of any contact.

In the early summer of 1594, the *Grace* out of Bristol arrived in Bay St. George on the west coast of Newfoundland. There the crew came upon a circular dwelling place, made of poles and covered with bark. Nearby were 'the tracks of the feete of some fortie or fiftie men, women and children.'

The Beothuk had seen them coming. They hurried off, leaving behind 'Deeres flesh roasted upon wooden spits at the fire, and a dish made of a ryne of a tree, sowed together with the sinowes of the Deere,' as well as cormorants plucked and ready 'to have dressed.' It was typical of the reaction of the Beothuk. Though they outnumbered the twelve-man crew of the ship, their dread of what firearms could do sent them scurrying into the woods. For the ten days the *Grace* remained in Bay St. George, the English saw nothing more of them.

A few weeks later the ship arrived in Placentia Bay. There, under the cover of night, 'the Savages came' and cut the ropes that had secured three of their boats. These furtive encounters, and the fear and mistrust they engendered, would forever mark relations between the Beothuk and Europeans.

10 | That First Colony

Presentlie after, the shalloppe landed Mr. Whittington with the flag of truce, who went towards them. Then they rowed into the shoare with one canoa, th'other standing aloofe of, & landed two men, one of them having the wolfe skinne in this hand, & coming towards Mr. Whittington, the savage made a loude speeche, & shaked the skinne, which was answered by Mr. Whittington in like manner, & as the savage drew neere he threw downe the wolfe skinne into the grownde. The like was done by Mr. Whittington. Where upon both the savages passed over a litter water streame towards Mr. Whittington daunsing, leaping, & singing, & coming together . . .

—John Guy, 1612

Matthaus Merian's fanciful seventeenth-century woodcut of the Beothuk encounter with John Guy and his crew.

Different Beginnings

With an end to England's war with Spain and more capital available, interest in the new world widened. The 1580s saw Walter Raleigh's failed bid to colonize Roanoke Island in North Carolina. An expedition in 1607 to Jamestown in Virginia did meet with success. And soon after, Samuel de Champlain sailed into the St. Lawrence to initiate the settlement of New France.

The time was ripe for a permanent presence in Newfoundland. If England didn't act forthwith, King James was told, France would soon lay claim to it; in fact, there had been an aborted attempt by some French fishermen to overwinter there. It would only be a matter of time before they would try again.

John Guy, a prominent member of the Bristol Society of Merchant Venturers, paid a visit to the Island in 1608 and upon his return promptly composed a tract to elicit the support of Bristol and London merchants in the establishment of a colony there. He had even chosen the spot in Conception Bay where an eager band could take root.

The first settlers were markedly different from those who had set sail a few years earlier for Jamestown and those who would soon colonize New England. To begin with, they were much more knowledgeable about their destination. Newfoundland had seen a steady seasonal population for more than a century. To many fisherman born to the Atlantic ports of Europe, Newfoundland was a second home, where they spent almost half of each year.

And rather than the gentry and ex-soldiers who lacked trades, those who landed in Newfoundland were a skilled lot, well able to tackle the basic construction tasks needed for settlement. Yet, in the end, it was the other colonies that took hold more strongly and those in Newfoundland that struggled, some eventually fading away. Climate was a factor, and the lack of arable ground, but the causes ran much deeper. They shaped the course of our development, and perhaps, in the end, for the better, considering what it took for the colonies to the south to reap their prosperity.

The settlers in these mainland possessions quickly realized that to survive they would have to create their own sources of wealth, that mining and trading with the natives were not activities on which they could thrive. And so they turned to agriculture. In this they had a substantial advantage over Newfoundland, and in tobacco they soon found the cash crop that would support them. But of greater consequence was the system of subservient labour they set in place. Many of them brought boatloads of slaves from Africa. These colonies succeeded, but for many it came with a severe price to their societies, one which Newfoundland, as poor as it remained, never had to pay.

Colonists in Conception Bay

On 2 May 1610, King James I had stamped his seal on a royal charter. A bevy of merchant speculators, which included Sir Francis Bacon and the diehard believer in Newfoundland, Sir Percival Willoughby, formed a charter company—the Newfoundland Company—with shares selling at twenty-five pounds. By July Governor Guy and his colonists were on their way across the Atlantic, thrilled at the prospect of life in a new world amid unpopulated tracks of land.

In the late summer Guy and thirty-nine men—masons, carpenters, blacksmiths, and apprentices of all kinds—came ashore at Cuper's Cove, present-day Cupids on the Avalon Peninsula. The first winter would be the trial, and if all went well, their wives and other women would follow, and a true settlement take shape.

The Newfoundland Charter made it absolutely clear that the settlers were not to interfere with the operations of the migratory fishery. Indeed, the West Country fish merchants would not have it any other way. To Guy it was no obstacle. Besides the fact that Cuper's Cove was removed from the centre of the migratory fishery, his men had the winter months to prepare their gear and would be first to the fishing grounds each spring.

Of course, there were the other resources of Conception Bay to exploit, its timber and minerals in particular. Cuper's Cove offered a sheltered harbour, a good supply of fresh water, and what was thought to be land to support livestock and bring forth a steady supply of grain and vegetables. All in all, the colony could hardly fail.

At the end of the first winter (an unusually mild one) the report back to England was entirely optimistic. The men had cut timber and erected not only living quarters, but a smithy and enclosures for boat-building and storage. They had built no less than six fishing vessels and a twelve-tonne bark. They had even fortified themselves with three guns mounted on a palisade of 'railes, and great Poles sixteene foot [five metres] long set upright round about.'

John Guy

The livestock they'd brought from England all thrived, and added to their numbers with 'one lustie Kidd' and 'eighteen young Chickens, besides others that are a hatching.' In his first letter back to the shareholders, Guy couldn't say enough good about the place. The notion had been that the Newfoundland winter would be much worse than anything England ever had to endure. Guy set them straight, declaring ' . . . men may safely inhabit here without any neede of Stove.'

Only four settlers died during that first winter, a better rate of survival than that experienced by any of the mainland colonies. None were lost because of climate, or the strange terrain. 'The feare of wilde Beasts we have found to be almost needelesse,' wrote Guy. When crews of migratory fishermen showed up in the spring, their talk quickly turned to how soon they, too, would be spending their winters in Newfoundland.

Guy credited the colony's health to plain hard work. Of the few complainers he asserted, 'if they had had as good will to worke, as they had good stomackes to their victuals, would long since have bin recovered.' Under Guy the disgruntled either shaped up, or found themselves on a boat back to England.

No one was excepted, not even the son of Sir Percival Willoughby. The unruly lad, the black sheep of the family, found himself in Newfoundland after he stole the family silver. His idleness was repaid with a ducking in the icy waters of a Cuper's Cove brook. The ordeal must have done him good, for he wrote to his father with the resolve to 'leaue aside idel vices' and turn into 'a newe man.'

As fortune would have it, Newfoundland did not have such redemptive power over all its men. Many of the crop of apprentices that arrived in 1612 grew woefully disenchanted with the place, despite the fact that arriving with them were sixteen women. The apprentices whined about the hard work. Those in charge countered that too many of them 'scorned to torne a Fish.'

That reluctance turned into a major problem. Many of the colonists had been lured to Newfoundland with the understanding that there would be much more than the relentless toil of the fishery to occupy them. Hadn't they been promised other ways of earning a wage, together with a piece of agricultural land all their own? Not enough of them had the interest or the skills to properly prosecute the fishery. The financial base of the colony grew more and more shaky.

And in the third year of the colony came the brunt of a more typical Newfoundland winter. By March, twenty-two of the settlers had taken to their sickbeds, mostly with scurvy. The snows were too deep to reach the 'scurvy grass' or the turnips, the only food to offer any relief. Many of the livestock went without fodder and succumbed to the cold.

The colonists struggled on. That same spring of 1613 saw the delivery of the first English child born in Newfoundland. But then John Guy, the one person many of the colonists looked to for leadership, quit the colony and sailed back to England, apparently in a quarrel with the merchants in charge of the company. His authority had been undermined by a treasurer unwilling to pay the wages needed to hold the workers or to grant them land in lieu of earnings.

By the fall of 1613 only thirty settlers remained. The colony was doomed, and within a few decades had turned to pastureland. Guy's original colonists gave up on Cuper's Cove. But some of them, with no intention of forsaking Newfoundland altogether, migrated to a place farther along the shore of Conception Bay. In present-day Harbour Grace, long the scene of a summer fishery by Channel Islanders, they built the foundation of a colony they named Bristol's Hope. Unlike the first attempt, it endured, holding on to its meagre roots after the ships and men of the migratory fishery disappeared each fall.

A Shaky Beginning

The reasons for the failure of Cuper's Cove are many. The much-hailed resources that drew the colonists to Newfoundland quickly faded in importance. Some of the settlers took to the country to trap animals, but the few otter, beaver, and fox pelts they secured were hardly worth the effort. Neither were there minerals to be mined. A survey of Bell Island brought great excitement at the discovery of iron deposits (with no one with more sustained enthusiasm than Willoughby), yet the technology did not exist to make its recovery practical. The bid to sell timber and

This German storeware 'bellarmine,' salt-glazed and with a bearded face on its neck, was found at the Cuper's Cove Plantation site. It once held wine or beer, or perhaps aquavitae.

masts came to a halt when it became clear the migratory fishermen would rather cut their own. Even the efforts at growing simple grains came to naught; the only crops that seemed to take hold were root vegetables. The promise of trade in pitch and turpentine, whale oil and sealskins, languished, as did the hope that the Cuper's Cove settlers might supply some of the needs of the plantations of Virginia. The countryside of England, as crowded as it was getting, looked more and more appealing the longer the settlers hung on.

The colony's failure started and ended with a dependency on the fishery. It was the one resource that could have sustained settlement, yet it was not given the attention it required. Not only did many of the colonists lack the interest in it, but the migratory fishermen stood in their way, eventually leading to open hostility. They refused to share any of the privileges that would have made it easier for the colonists to survive. The migratory fishermen had the experience to profit from the fishery; the colonists, weighed down with the additional living costs that came with settlement, did not. And when the company's private backers in England failed them, the government of the day was not about to step in to help. It had given firm support to the West Country fish merchants. Profit, not concern for the few settlers, ruled the day.

As the number of the colonists in Cuper's Cove dwindled (a few hung on until at least 1624), the southern mainland colonies grew stronger, though often on the backs of the slave labour. In desperation, the merchants controlling the Newfoundland Company went so far as to suggest that an answer for the fledgling Island colony was to bring iron ore as ballast in the fishing ships arriving from England, with the intention of building a smelter in Newfoundland. It was a proposal that passed the Privy Council of the day, but not unlike many such proposals in the future, it failed to take hold anywhere but in the imagination of politicians.

Song and Dance with the Beothuk

The petition of the Newfoundland Company in 1610 made no mention of the natives of Newfoundland. The omission helped speed it through the Privy Council. The brief reference in the Charter itself came with the understanding that the ultimate goal of contact with natives would, of course, be to convert them to Christianity. (For that reason the English king proclaimed that any person suspected of adhering to 'the superstitions of the Church of Rome' would not be allowed to set foot aboard the ship to Newfoundland.)

But if John Guy's time in Newfoundland had a measure of success, it was in his contact with the Beothuk. Although he assumed they had abandoned Conception Bay, Guy also knew they were not far away. One reason for constructing the bark *Indeavour* during that first winter in Cuper's Cove was to explore nearby Trinity Bay and establish trade with the natives.

In the fall of 1612, having failed in two attempts to make contact with the Beothuk overland, colonists from Cuper's Cove boarded the *Indeavour* and one of their fishing boats and set off. In the bottom reaches of Trinity Bay they came upon a Beothuk band. Guy's account of the event is our earliest first-hand description of the native group. 'They are broad breasted, and bould, and stand very uprighte!' he wrote in his journal. In contrast to the conduct of other Europeans, Guy's approach showed an admiration for the Beothuk and a genuine interest in learning about their culture.

The meeting took place in Bull Arm (where, centuries later, the great feat of engineering, the Hibernia offshore oil platform, would be built). Bull Arm in 1612 knew only the Beothuk, it being too far removed from the best of the codfishing grounds to see much of migratory fishermen. The natives had chosen it because it is at the narrowest point of the isthmus of the Avalon Peninsula. Just three kilometres along their broad path through the forest brought them into Placentia Bay on the Island's south coast.

On the day before the meeting, Guy and several of his men had waded across the Come-by-Chance River and ascended the highest hill in the area. From there, once the fog lifted, they had a panoramic view of both bays. It was a feast of land-scape. On one side the long narrow inlet of Bull Arm leading into Trinity Bay; on the other the inner reaches of Placentia Bay, broken by a host of islands—among them Woody Island, Long Island, and the imposing Merasheen. Guy must have stood charmed by the sight, and its potential for settlement. Had it not been his vision that one day this vast stretch of the Avalon Peninsula spread out before him would be settled by his countrymen?

Yet, curiously, his journal records none of that. It would seem he was acknowl-edging the fact that the land was already inhabited. After spending the night camped on the hill, he returned to Bull Arm and came in sight of the Beothuk. A fire burned on the shore a mile away, and 'presentlie two canoaes appeared, & one man alone comming towards us with a flag in his hand of a wolf skinne, shaking yt, & making a lowde noice.'

The Beothuk wanted to meet with them. Guy and his men took to their bark and fishing shallop, and raising a white flag, headed toward the canoes. The natives fled. Guy quickly drew a halt to his advance. His men anchored the bark and waved the white flag again. The Beothuk responded in kind.

On the nearby shore the captain of the bark, George Whittington, came face to face with two of them. They exchanged gifts. Whittington was given a feather to stick in his hair. One of the Beothuk was handed a linen cap, which he stuck on his head, and 'hand in hand all three did sing, & daunce.' Another of Guy's men joined the group and all four together 'daunced, laughing, & making signes of joy, & gladnes, sometimes strikeing the breastes of our companie & somet-ymes theyre owne.'

It was a frightfully unrestrained occasion, especially for Englishmen. Guy and another crewman rowed ashore to join the merrymaking. More Beothuk showed up, more gifts were exchanged, and eventually they all sat down, to dine on bis-cuit and raisins, 'beer and aquavitae.' One of the Beothuk, perhaps a little heavily into the aquavitae, blew on the top of its bottle and made a sound 'which they fell all into a laughture at.' The Beothuk offered dried caribou meat, and some plant root which Whittington washed and shared among his crew. All agreed 'it tasted very well.'

It was nearly dark by the time they dispersed, exchanging flags before taking to their boats. In the days that followed, Guy and his men came upon a display of furs that the Beothuk had put out for trade. Guy took three of the skins and left a hatchet, a knife, and some threaded needles. They waited several days, but as the winter was closing in, left for Cuper's Cove without seeing any more sign of the Beothuk.

It had become clear to Guy that this was not the first time that these people had traded with Europeans, not surprising in view of the fact that migratory fishermen of many nationalities had used Trinity Bay for much of the sixteenth century. The Beothuk showed caution, yet fully embraced the opportunity 'for a parlie,' as Guy put it, once they saw that the intentions of the Englishmen were honourable.

The colonists of Cuper's Cove planned to return to Trinity Bay the following year for more trade with the Beothuk. The natives gathered there with their furs that summer in expectation of Guy showing up. But by that time the governor of Cuper's Cove had returned to England.

And when a migratory fisherman, who knew nothing of Guy or his intentions, happened by, disaster struck. His first reaction was to 'let fly his shott from aboard amongst them.' The Beothuk fled, certain they had been betrayed. 'From that day to this,' a report of 1639 regretfully concluded, the Beothuk 'have sought all occasion every fishing season to do all the mischief they can.'

In a few years Guy's colony ceased to exist. It was a sad end to what could have been a flourishing relationship between the Beothuk and English settlers. Instead, the natives found themselves dealing with migratory fishermen. Many were brutish men whose animosity could only lead to retaliation.

11 | Princess, Pirates, and Poets

I will not omit to relate some thing of a strange Creature that I saw there in the yeere 1610, in a morning early as I was standing by the water side, in the Harbour of Saint Johns; which I espyed very swiftly to come swimming towards me, looking cheerefully, as it had been a woman . . . having round about upon the head, all blew strakes, resembling hayre . . . such a strange Creature that was seene at New-found-land, whether it were a Maremaid or no, I know not; I leave it for others to judge, &c.

—Richard Whitbourne, 1620

*Alas, no longer are the bubbles of St. John's Harbour a sign of mermaids,
as they were in the time of Richard Whitbourne.*

Perfection in a Sheila

Newfoundland had been cursed by pirates since the raids of the Frenchman Jean Ango in the opening decades of the migratory fishery. By the 1600s the Island's waters were rife with them. And none roused greater dread than the nefarious Peter Easton. For his fortification Easton chose Harbour Grace, north along Conception Bay from John Guy's colony, though his first rendezvous with Newfoundland took place several years before any sign of settlement in Cuper's Cove.

Easton had been one of the English navy's privateers, under the approving eye of Elizabeth I. In 1602 he accepted orders to escort a convoy of fishing vessels to the waters of Newfoundland. Not long out of the Channel Easton crossed paths with a warship belonging to the Dutch, allies of England's arch enemy, Spain. Easton boarded the ship to find its hold crowded with Irish prisoners, captives from a vessel scuttled just a few days before.

Thus begins the long-standing, and intensely romantic, legend of Sheila Nagueira, the 'Irish Princess.' Aboard the vessel was a young woman who had been sent from Ireland to France to escape the Irish Freedom Fighters. Her father, a Celtic nobleman and supporter of the English, had arranged for her to live in a French convent under the protection of an aunt, an abbess there. But her life's journey took an abrupt and unexpected change of direction—first as a prisoner, and then as a captor herself, of a young gentlemen's heart. Smitten by her on the way to Newfoundland was the ship's handsome young navigator, Gilbert Pike.

The rest, many Newfoundlanders are convinced, is history. At the least it is our interpretation of the same. For hard facts are hard to come by. Of Gilbert's first view of Sheila, it has recently been written: 'From the tips of her tiny satin shoes to the mane of raven hair that cascaded over her shoulders, she was perfection. Her deep blue eyes seemed to penetrate his very soul.' She was obviously made for legend. And legend has it she and Gilbert were married aboard ship by Easton, and that once in Newfoundland, they settled in the part of Conception Bay afterwards called Bristol's Hope. (Its original moniker, 'Mosquito,' though perhaps truer to the physical realities of the place, is hardly in keeping with the romance of the tale.)

Gilbert took to the fishery, while Sheila, most likely the only woman on the coast, cared for the sick and the unfortunate, of which there were many. It is told by some that it was she (not a settler at Cuper's Cove) who gave birth to the first non-native child born in Newfoundland since the days of the Norse. And that she lived to be 105.

Such is the fabric of legend. Blended as it is with the documented life of Peter Easton, it is more than worthy of its modern-day re-enactment each summer. Exactly how much of the tale could ever be authenticated is hardly the concern. For the charm of legend is its enhancement of fact over time. There was indeed a beautiful Sheila, daughter of a nobleman, who, according to Irish scholars, was 'a noted figure in popular lore . . . probably from the Connaught area . . . ' She was the subject of song, and so fair a maid was she that her name became 'Nagueira,' a Gaelic word for 'beautiful.' In Newfoundland she became a Pike, and many are the good-looking Pikes in Conception Bay and beyond who today trace their family lines back to hers.

Rogue in Harbour Grace

Peter Easton turned pirate when England's war with Spain ended in 1603. The new monarch, James I, took away the navy's authority to plunder, so Easton commandeered his own fleet and continued unabated his thieving ways. By 1610 he had charge of forty ships and controlled the shipping lanes of the English Channel. Not content with domestic villainy, Easton headed to Newfoundland to establish a base from which to attack ships destined for Europe from the Americas.

When he set up operations in Harbour Grace, Sheila and her law-abiding man escaped up the shore to Carbonear Island. Easton was a plague to the newly arrived John Guy and his colonists. Though he never struck the colony at Cuper's Cove directly (Guy having bought him off with two 'rosting pigges'), the colonists were forced to spend valuable time and energy building a fort in case they were attacked.

In the summer of 1612 some of Guy's men attempted to start a second colony in Renews, on the southern shore of the Avalon, but there they were confronted by Easton's gang. Having 'liked well' their first taste of pork, they 'had a mynd unto some of our goats cowes and great pigges.' Guy's men, from the deck of their bark, were able to fend them off and retreat back to Conception Bay with their livestock. Perhaps it was the keenness of Easton and his cohorts for a supply of fresh meat that saved Cuper's Cove itself from destruction. That and the fact Easton had his eye on much greater prizes.

Easton plundered whatever ships he wanted in Newfoundland waters, taking his fill of its fish and wine, and its crewmen, many of whom were more than willing to trade the drudgery of the migratory fishery for a promise of high-seas adventure. Easton's gaze shifted south, and came to rest in Puerto Rico. There he led an assault against Maro Castle, a fortress that even Sir Francis Drake had failed to penetrate. He came away with heaps of gold, loaded it aboard a Spanish ship, the *San Sebastian*, and sailed back to Newfoundland.

He arrived in Harbour Grace to find Basques in control of his stronghold. The only recourse was to do battle with the wretched curs. It cost him fifty-seven men, but Easton proved the victor. He regained the fortress, buried his dead (in a place still known today as the 'Pirate's Graveyard'), and retired to his living quarters to count his gold. His fortune, and his reputation, had risen considerably.

Easton kept the fortress in Harbour Grace, but decided to move his personal residence to Ferryland, whose geography made it virtually impossible to attack by sea. At the entrance to the harbour stood Isle aux Bois, easily fortified, and from the Gaze on Ferryland Head any ship within miles could be sighted.

The English king had never been amused by Easton's antics. Years earlier James had sent the Oxford-educated navy man Henry Mainwaring in pursuit of him, after Bristol merchants complained about his relentless disruption of their trade. Mainwaring's strategies for capturing Easton proved useless, though he must have learned a few things from his nemesis, for he himself turned to pirating. He spent the summer of 1614 terrorizing the coast of Newfoundland. In his beloved vessel the *Princess*, Mainwaring struck at will, for there was nothing to match the agility of his ship and the array of cannon on her decks. He even took over Easton's fort at Harbour Grace.

But he never did encounter his fellow pirate. While Mainwaring was in Newfoundland, Easton was in the Azores ambushing the fleet of ships returning from Central America laden with gold for the Spanish treasury. By 1615 Easton had ceased his pirating ways, had settled in Villefranche on the French Riviera, and bought himself a residence befitting his wealth, and the title of Marquis of Savoy. Newfoundland, its remoteness once a great convenience for his piracy, was put out of his mind.

Though perhaps not completely out of his mind. Many are those who contend that somewhere beneath Newfoundland's rocky soil lies a portion of his looted treasure.

Governor Mason, Map-maker

John Guy was followed as governor of the colony at Cuper's Cove by the naval commander John Mason, some said as a reward for his work in the Hebrides, where he helped bring the 'barbarous . . . untamed generation' into the Christian fold. In comparison, dealing with the pirates of Newfoundland must have been a trifling matter. He arrived in Conception Bay with his wife in the spring of 1616, and stayed in Newfoundland for more than three years.

When not dealing with pirates and irate migratory fisherman, Mason spent much of his time surveying the coastline. He sailed around the south coast to Placentia, and perhaps as far to the west as Bay St. George, though to what extent he was willing to venture into the territory of the French and the Basques is certainly open to question. The result of his excursions was the first reasonably accurate map of the Island to be drawn by an Englishman from direct observations.

Mason published *A Briefe Discourse of the New-found-land* in Edinburgh in 1620, in an attempt to convince the Scots that settlement in Newfoundland would be a wise and profitable thing. The cod, he announced, were 'so thicke by the shore that we heardlie have been able to row a Boate through them . . . ' There wasn't the anticipated rush to investment.

John Mason's map of 1625 (though inverted by today's standards)
would not be surpassed in accuracy for a full century.

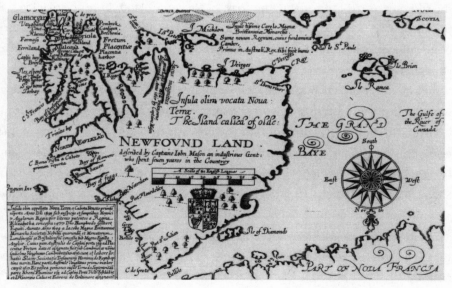

Mason succeeded in defending the fishing rights of the Newfoundland colonists before the court of James I, though in the end Cuper's Cove still failed. By 1621 piracy was such a problem for the whole of English fishery in New-foundland that Mason was back again, this time with royal authority to do what-ever he could to put an end to the pillage. But within a few years his own attention had turned to New England. In 1629 it was John Mason, former governor in Newfoundland, who founded the colony of New Hampshire.

Whitbourne Lauds the New-Found-Land

The year 1620 also saw the publica-tion of Richard Whitbourne's *Dis-course and Discovery of New-found-land*. Again it was an attempt to encourage settlement, but Whitbourne's treatise was by far the more practical (despite its account of a mermaid in St. John's Harbour). The man knew the Island intimately, having made the first of his numerous trips to Newfoundland more than forty years before. He was witness to Sir Humphrey Gilbert's sojourn in St. John's. He was present when Bernard Drake plundered the Portuguese, and found himself a pris-

An astrolabe, navigational instrument dated 1628, found off Isle aux Morts.

oner of Peter Easton when the pirate showed up in 1612. Three years later, at Trinity, Whitbourne held the first Admiralty Court in North America. And in between it all he commanded four ships in England's battle against the Spanish Armada.

Most of his countrymen knew Newfoundland only as a supplier of fish and cod liver oil. Whitbourne set out to convince them it should no longer be just the domain of the migratory fishermen. That settlement, rather than hinder the fish trade, would bolster it. What dried fish lacked in glamour compared to gold and silver, he argued, it more than made up for in profit and employment. Indeed no other resource did Britain reap at so little cost.

He saw Newfoundland's strategic importance in the context of the whole of America. For Whitbourne it was a place were the idle 'superabounding multitudes' of his native land could be relocated and set to work. He argued that Newfoundland's climate was no harsher than that of many populous countries in Northern Europe, and to think otherwise was giving in to unfounded rumours spread by fish merchants bent on protecting their own interests. He set out to counteract such propaganda as spread by Captain John Smith, who declared of his New England cod: ' . . . each hundred is as good as two or three hundred in the New-found Land.'

Whitbourne's was one of the first in a centuries-long stream of voices to rise up against the view that Newfoundland was a wild outpost to endure while cramming ships with its fish. If England was going to exploit the resources of the Island, ran the undercurrent of his text, then it was deserving of investment as a place to inhabit.

Whitbourne's case received a wide hearing. His book was twice reprinted and distributed to parishes throughout England. Some members of the Privy Council, in particular, seemed to be paying attention, for in the years that followed, two of them, Sir Henry Cary and Sir George Calvert, initiated plans for colonies in Newfoundland.

When Poets Govern

The original land grant by James I to the Newfoundland Company included the whole of the Avalon Peninsula. John Guy chose to settle in a cove in Conception Bay, with the notion of starting other settlements once the colony was on sound footing. That first attempt, a move of some men to Renews, ended at the hands of Peter Easton. In 1617 a second move was initiated, though not as had been originally planned.

After John Guy returned permanently to England, the Company's Bristol merchants broke away from their London partners and launched their own alliance. It was their Bristol Society of Merchant Venturers who transplanted several of the colonists to a place farther north along Conception Bay and started, appropriately enough, Bristol's Hope.

The settlers were led by Nicholas Guy, whose wife, five years earlier, had been the one to give birth to the original colony's first child. By the time of the move the pirates Easton and Mainwaring were long gone, so it would appear to have been a safe place to raise their little one. Bristol's Hope and environs held on to its settlers in the succeeding years to become the oldest continuously settled region of Newfoundland.

As the colony at Cuper's Cove floundered, the Newfoundland Company searched for ways to help revive it. One obvious means was to sell off other sections of the land granted in its charter. The first person to avail himself of the company's offer turned out to be a Welsh writer, lawyer, and visionary. It was not a good combination.

The gentleman, William Vaughan, confessed to having been saved by divine intervention on no less than three occasions, including one terrifying episode when he fell overboard in a storm off the coast of France. He had been saved, he reasoned, for 'the Publicke Good,' to serve some greater cause. Unfortunately for some, that cause proved to be the colonization of Newfoundland.

Vaughan came to view Newfoundland as the saving grace for the many Welsh who were landless and living in poverty. He looked to Devon and saw the prosperity brought on by the Newfoundland fishery, and so purchased title to a section of the southern Avalon, which he named 'New Cambriol,' in honour of his homeland.

And in 1617 he sent several of his chosen people to one of its harbours, Aquaforte. The unfortunates had given up poverty in Wales for a winter in Newfoundland, shivering in the cold of the sheds the migratory fishermen had built for use during the summer months, all the while wishing the Lord had left Vaughan to wash up on a beach in France.

In 1618 Vaughan made the acquaintance of the stalwart Richard Whitbourne and hired him to take charge of the colony. Whitbourne arrived to find the settlers in a wretched state. He sent some of them back to Wales, and decided to move the rest to Renews where living conditions would be much improved. Even that turned into a disaster. One of his two ships was attacked by pirates, deserters from Sir Walter Raleigh's expedition to Guiana.

In the end a few men spent the winter of 1618–19 in Renews, somewhat more comfortable than before, but no more enthusiastic about their lives in the new world. By 1619 'the welch Fooles' had all quit the colony. Eventually Vaughan sold off his stake in the Avalon, though he did write about it a few years later in the fanciful *The Golden Fleece*, when not, in the same breath, ranting about the evils of Roman Catholicism. Some have claimed he wrote this oddity in Newfoundland, but that is very unlikely. The Newfoundland landscape needn't be held accountable.

Our first true and resident poet was an acquaintance of Vaughan's at Oxford. He was Robert Hayman, for a time governor of the colony of Bristol's Hope. His stay there may even have improved his verse. Certainly anyone who penned this two-line 'Antidote for Drunkards'—'If that your head would ake before you drinke/ As afterwards, you'd ne'r be drunke, I think'—could not be said to have been wholly out of touch with reality.

Like Vaughan, Hayman seemed an implausible candidate to lead colonization in Newfoundland. Yet Bristol's Hope met with 'good and hopeful success,' unlike most other Newfoundland colonies. That was due largely to the fact that the Bristol merchants who backed it were long established in the fish trade. They knew the markets and seemed to have reached an understanding with the migratory fishermen on how to share in them. Some would say that Hayman, who spent his time in Newfoundland writing verse and translating Rabelais, was rather inciden-tal to the colony's prosperity. (Others would argue that setting such an intellectual and cultural tone can lead to an enriching of the pocketbook as well as the mind. Present governments take note.) His days ended in a death befitting a poet—in 1629 in Guiana, of 'a burning fever' while venturing up the Amazon. In Hayman, at the very least, we have the beginnings of our fertile and varied literary heritage. He left us this lasting tribute in *Quodlibets*, the first English book written in North America:

The Aire, in Newfound-Land is wholesome, good;

The Fire, as sweet as any made of wood;

The Waters, very rich, both salt and fresh;

The Earth more rich, you know it is no lesse.

Where all are good, Fire, Water, Earth and Aire,

What man made of these four would not live there?

The Newfoundland Falklands

Another of Hayman's quodlibets of 1628 bemoaned the attempt of a fellow gradu-ate of Oxford, Sir Henry Cary, to colonize a part of Newfoundland. Cary, confidant of James I, was otherwise known as Viscount Falkland and Lord Deputy of Ireland.

The title page of Robert Hayman's Quodlibets.

Unfortunately, his numerous titles proved no indication of his ability to manage an overseas colony.

In 1620 he received title to a huge tract of land that included the Bonavista Peninsula and much beyond it, to be called North Falkland. And from Vaughan he purchased what he called South Falkland, a narrow strip of land on the southern Avalon that included the harbours of Fermeuse and Renews. To help organize the colony he solicited the sound advice of someone who, by this time, must surely have thought himself a Newfoundlander—Richard Whitbourne.

A tract was published outlining the scheme for settlement of the Falkland territories. A site, Renews, was chosen. A governor, Sir Francis Tanfield, assumed his place. And in 1623 a group of able settlers, mostly Irishmen, landed in Newfoundland.

The colony lasted three years at the most. In 1626 Viscount Falkland was to be found disposing of his Newfoundland investment. And although the purchaser, Sir Henry Salisbury, didn't proceed with an initiative to settle there, it was not for lack of planning. Or, presumably, discussion around the dinner table. For the gentlemen was the brother-in-law of William Vaughan. And for advice on settlement he went in search of John Guy. It seemed that for a select group of family and friends Newfoundland had became a preoccupation that was not about to go away.

12 | Colonies Upon the Avalon

Be True in Hart

—Inscribed on a seventeenth-century ring found at Ferryland

Lord and Lady Baltimore would not linger long in Ferryland.

Lord Baltimore's Haven

At the same time that Henry Cary acquired his strip of Newfoundland that he called South Falkland, another Oxford chum and colleague on the Privy Council, Sir George Calvert, acquired his own piece of Newfoundland. Calvert hired an agent and dispatched him to set up headquarters in Ferryland, the beginnings of what Calvert termed 'The Colony of Avalon,' in honour of 'old Avalon . . . the first-fruits of Christianity in Britain.'

In 1625 Calvert's own fruits of Christianity were not faring well in Britain. He had taken the scandalous step of declaring himself a Roman Catholic. Fortunately, he'd had the forethought to first resign his position as secretary of state to the king, James I. (There he had been central to the negotiations that would have seen the prince of Wales, later Charles I, marry the Spanish Infanta, leading to accusations from the Archbishop of Canterbury that it was fraternizing with the Spanish that corrupted his soul.) The king remained loyal to Calvert, however, rewarding him for his long service with the title of Lord Baltimore, in recognition of the lands Calvert owned in Ireland.

But it was to Newfoundland that Lord Baltimore turned his attention. His choice of Newfoundland came from the prevailing medical opinion that Englishmen who chose to colonize other parts of the world would be wisest to seek climates close to that of their own country. Colonies too far south 'is unto our boddies offensyve, Which cannot prosper in dry and scalding heates, more naturall to the Spaniards than us.' Becoming like the Spaniards (that quarrelsome and unprincipled lot) was to be avoided at all cost. Newfoundland, situated in latitude just south of London, was looked upon as ideal land on which to settle. Unfortunately, little was understood of the effects of prevailing winds and ocean currents. A quick lesson in the unpredictability of Newfoundland's climate would soon be forthcoming.

George Calvert's Colony of Avalon was firstly a commercial venture. But Lord Baltimore brought to it the vision of a haven for Roman Catholics in the new world. In 1627 Calvert, together with two seminary priests, spent the summer in Ferryland, and the following year he returned with his family and forty more Catholic colonists.

The Calverts set up residence in the elaborate stone mansion that had been built for them, overlooking the sheltered innermost reach of the harbour called

'The Pool.' Lady Baltimore and her children were to live the life to which they were accustomed. That summer they walked the Ferryland Downs and sampled its wild berries. They breathed the refreshing salt air and learned the ways of the fishing business that was to be the source of their livelihood.

Meanwhile, Lord Baltimore was busy dealing with French privateers and a resident Protestant priest indignant at the sight of so many Catholics and their clerics who 'every sunday sayth Mass and doe use all other ceremonies of the church of Rome in as ample a manner as tis used in Spain.' Not to be outdone, the opposing camp declared: ' . . . in one area Mass was said according to the Catholic rite, while in another the heretics carried out their own.' Religious tolerance was having trouble getting a foothold in the new world.

And then came the Newfoundland winter. The cold and the scurvy sent over half the colony to their sickbeds. By the following summer Calvert and his family had had more than enough. They quit the colony, 'after much suffrance in this wofull country, where with one intolerable wynter were we almost undone.' They were not up to winter along the Avalon, nor its 'spring' tinged with the chill of icebergs. Calvert's agents had obviously lied to him about what to expect. He abandoned Ferryland to the fishermen, and in August 1629 his stiffened chin and sailing ships turned south, toward Virginia.

There, at Jamestown, he was met with a citizenry who expected him to swear the oath of Supremacy to the Church of England. He turned sail for Ireland, on the way drawing up a petition to Charles I for a new grant of land in the Americas. He died waiting for it, though a grant did eventually receive royal approval. With it his son Cecil set off for a piece of territory north of the Potomac. The winters proved less chilling in Maryland, and there the new Lord Baltimore was able to plant his colonists in a land unsullied by religious allegiances.

The Colony of Avalon (with 'the coldest harbour of the Land,' according to William Vaughan) needed someone with rather more fortitude. Settlement of the site would endure, and in time the colony would show a profit. But it would take a woman of a rare determination to show just how it was to be done.

The Kirkes of Ferryland

When the colony at Cuper's Cove saw the birth of its first child ('a lusty boy'), the identity of the mother was not recorded. When Richard Eburne, in 1624, published his guide to encourage colonization of Newfoundland, *A Plaine Path-Way to Plantations*, he wrote about the women who might be unwilling to venture forth, pronouncing that they be 'put in mind of their duty, which is to forsake father and friends and to cleave unto their husbands.' Women were wanted and needed in the Newfoundland colonies, but given the tenor of the times were expected to dutifully follow the call of the men, not forge ahead on their own. For a quarter century, in the windblown outpost of Ferryland, Lady Sara Kirke proved the exception.

Sara Kirke arrived in Ferryland, of course, with her husband. He was David Kirke, a well-known military man and wine merchant. When war was declared between England and France, Charles I sent him off to attack the French in Canada. His astuteness in the game of war resulted in the surrender by Champlain of Quebec in 1629. It wasn't restored to the French until the Treaty of Saint-Germain-en-Laye three years later.

It is thought that Kirke visited Ferryland during his voyage to Canada and saw that the Calvert family had deserted it. In 1637 Charles I passed the commercial rights to the colony to 'The Company of Adventurers to Newfoundland,' of which the now-knighted David Kirke and a number of his brothers were leading partners. Kirke became the governor at Ferryland, and ostensibly the whole of Newfoundland. He arrived with Lady Sara and about one hundred settlers, appropriated the Calvert mansion and moved into it with his family. The colony was renamed 'Pool Plantation.'

Kirke even arranged for the designing of a coat of arms. And in 1928 that same coat of arms, after having been lost for centuries, was made the official emblem of Newfoundland. (Unfortunately, the artist's direct knowledge of the place would seem to be lacking. The central shield bears the cross of St. George, two lions to represent England, and two unicorns to represent Scotland, though very few Scots ever settled here. Flanking the shield are two natives, supposedly representations of the Beothuk, though stick armour is not something ever known to have been worn by them. And atop the shield is a proud elk, unknown in Newfoundland or Labrador, but apparently the closest the artist could get to a caribou.)

Kirke governed his territory for thirteen years, and made Ferryland what could

David Kirke's Coat of Arms of 1628. 'Seek ye first the kingdom of God,' it reads.

be considered the capital of the Island. Though the migratory fishermen retained their rights, Kirke had been authorized to collect a tax of 5 per cent on all fish and oil taken by foreign vessels. He fortified St. John's and Bay de Verde, as well as Ferryland, and exercised broad control over the English Shore, that part of the east coast of the Island frequented by the English. He dispatched ships to collect the tax as far north as Trinity Bay.

Kirke expanded his authority further, presiding over courts of law in Ferryland. (One could hardly expect otherwise from the man who in his previous expedition to the new world had held control of Canada for three years.) He won no friends among the migratory fishermen, though the animosity might have been eased somewhat by the liquor served at the string of 'tippling houses' Kirke set up along the coast. It was the West Country merchants who complained the loudest. Kirke's taverns, they said, were taking fishermen away from the long hours needed to carry on the fishery. The protests reached a crescendo when the Civil War broke out in England and Kirke, a long-standing ally of Charles I, threatened to capture their fishing ships and use them in support of the royalist cause.

The Civil War was the undoing of Kirke. In 1651, in the wake of the victory of Cromwell's Roundheads and the beheading of Charles, Kirke was summoned back to England. He was accused of withholding taxes due the government, and from the heirs of Lord Baltimore resurfaced charges that he had illegally taken over the

Ferryland property. Sir David was thrown in prison (probably the infamous 'Clink' in Southwark), and there he died in 1654.

Lady Sara held strong in Ferryland. It can rightly be said that she was the first woman entrepreneur of British North America. Although the Baltimores won back their rights to the colony, they never bothered to exercise them. (Presumably they had plenty to keep them busy in the heat of Maryland.) Until 1679 Lady Sara ran the enterprise started by her husband. While her sons built up businesses of their own, expanding to other parts of Ferryland and on to Renews, the census figures of the day reveal that her fishing operation was the largest on the entire English Shore. She directed the work of sixty fishermen and their dozen boats. The Pool Plantation, besides the thirteen-by-five-metre stone Mansion House, included a forge, storehouses, and servant quarters. And what could be termed the first flush toilet in North America, a stone privy constructed to take advantage of the twice-daily heave of the ocean tides. Lady Sara and her family dined on fine Mediterranean wines, she wore silk embroidered with gold thread, and on her furniture rested *terra sigillata*, elegant Portuguese ceramics highly prized among the nobility of Europe.

Together with her sister, Lady Frances Hopkins, she saw the plantation through a

The waterfront at Pool Plantation.

raid in 1673 by the Dutch, who were out to avenge the loss of their colony at New Amsterdam (now New York) to the British. Four ships (aboard one of which was Dudley Lovelace, the former governor of New Amsterdam) 'plundered, ruined, fired, and destroyed the commodities, cattle, household goods . . . ' They burned forty fishing boats in the harbour, and made off with as much fish as they could carry, together with hogs and cattle, on their way to further raids along the coast.

Lady Sara retired from the fishing business in 1679, and died a few years later. She is thought to be buried somewhere beyond the Mansion House, on the wide expanse of the Ferryland Downs. She left behind a healthy plantation, a colony as secure as any as yet established in Newfoundland. The ongoing archaeological excavations at Ferryland may one day uncover the gravesite of Lady Sara Kirke, and make of it a lasting memorial to the woman who demonstrated the sustained and strong-willed enterprise needed to maintain settlement on this Island.

Along the English Shore

The English Shore of the 1670s, stretching from Salvage in the north to Trepassey in the south, had about 1,700 settlers, or 'planters' as they were called. During the spring and summer months they were vastly outnumbered by the thousands of migratory fishermen, but for the remainder of the year they had the coastline to themselves. The Beothuk, who were to be found in places like Ferryland when the Europeans first arrived, had long since withdrawn to other parts of the Island. Now, reports of contact were coming only from the salmon fishermen and furriers of the northern reaches of the English Shore.

In some coves and harbours lived just a single family. In the most populous, St. John's, were 250 people or more, lured by one of the best natural harbours to be found anywhere in the world. Like St. John's, many settlements had sprung up without organized colonization. Decades of use by West Country fishermen led to some of the boat owners and their workers overwintering, probably to safeguard the fishing premises and keep them in good repair, though one suspects Kirke's drinking houses were an added incentive. Not many cold winters went by before wives and families joined them. 'The inhabitants . . . build houses and make gardens and orchards in places fitt for cureing and drying fish,' whined some seasonal fishermen, but by this time they must have grown used to the fact they would no longer have the place to themselves.

Others of them welcomed the change, and turned a tidy profit by providing the settlers with the goods they needed. One enterprising Bideford supplier of fishing gear had a warehouse built near Ferryland to better serve that part of the coast. Ships from Ireland showed up with food and clothing (and a steady supply of servants). Other vessels sailed north from New England, laden with livestock, grain, rum, and molasses.

On their return trips these ships became suppliers of Newfoundland salt cod to the West Indies, as well as convenient passage for Newfoundland settlers wanting to move on to the New England colonies. More often than not the settlers who came to Newfoundland stayed for only a few years, resettling in other parts of British North America, or returning to England.

Some might have thought it not a fit place to rear their children. It was true that the Kirkes of Ferryland led the life of the gentry, on a plantation where workers were more likely to warm themselves with wine and brandy than drink the ales common to their class elsewhere. One young servant named Mary, brought from Ireland to work at the Pool Plantation, even married Lady Sara's son, David, Jr. (and subsequently laid claim to the estate after her mother-in-law and husband were both dead). But for most inhabitants, especially with the influx of the migratory fishermen, the Newfoundland of the late seventeenth century was no tranquil outpost.

Records for 1677 show that at least 160,000 litres of alcoholic drink were landed in St. John's Harbour alone. In the course of a six-month season fishermen could expect to make upwards of twenty pounds, that at a time when the wages for a comparable class of worker back in England were less than ten pounds for a full year. The Newfoundland society was a relatively prosperous one. The fishermen had money, and it appears they chose to spend much of it on alcohol.

'The people, being all seamen, are of a hasty temper, carried on with a licentious mirth whereby they allowe themselfs such freedom of Spirit, that doth not Conflict with modesty, or distinction,' penned one observer, albeit a man of the cloth. When not fishing the men were given over to drink, or 'jollities with a Woman,' all of which led to some rowdy times, given the fact that the licentious young men vastly outnumbered the eligible women. One suspects that Newfoundland had much in common with New England, where in 1664 a royal commission was led to note 'as many men may share a woman as they do a boat, and

Iron cross bearing traces of gold, found by Jim Tuck and his archaeological team at Ferryland.

some have done so.' No wonder calls went out to England for 'a Governor and a Minister.'

Ministers they'd had from time to time, perhaps as far back as the days of John Guy in Cuper's Cove. There was even a visit by Richard James, the 'learned and religious Minister' who went on to become the first librarian of London's famous repository, the Cotton Library. His stay, however, was very brief and his impression of Newfoundland ('upon the land nothing but rocks, lakes, or mosses, like bogs') anything but learned.

The early days of the Calvert's Colony of Avalon had seen a formal proposal to the cardinals in Rome to turn Ferryland into a great Roman Catholic sanctuary and mission. A Carmelite acquaintance of Calvert's had envisioned it as a missionary stepping-stone to the Americas, and (through the Northwest Passage) to the Orient. The grand scheme never materialized, in part because not enough Carmelites could be found willing to sacrifice themselves to the challenges of life in Newfoundland.

To Calvert's credit, his own vision was greater still, that of a religion-tolerant colony, where the adherents of his own Roman Catholic faith would live in the harmony not found in the England he had left. It was the first such colony in British North America, initiating a concept eventually carried on to the Calvert settlement in Maryland.

But when Calvert arrived in his Colony of Avalon he was met by someone more than a little sceptical of his intentions. Erasmus Stourton, though he wasn't the first Protestant minister to the scattered flocks of settlers in seventeenth-century Newfoundland, was undoubtedly the most vitriolic. 'That knave Stourton,' as Calvert called him, accused the 'popish' governor of forcing the child of a Protestant colonist to be baptized 'according to the orders and customs of the Church of Rome.' By August, Calvert, tolerant or not, had Stourton on a boat back to England.

Thus were the beginnings of organized religion in Newfoundland. For the decades that followed visits from preachers were sporadic at best. In Ferryland in

1659 arrived the Congregationalist preacher Richard Blinman, escaping contro-versy in New England and setting up pulpit for the summer under the watchful eye of Lady Kirke. 'People flock from neighbouring harbours to heare the word of God, & attend diligently,' Blinman wrote with obvious satisfaction to his friend John Winthrop, the governor of Massachusetts.

At the same time, up the coast in St. John's had arrived two leading Quaker missionaries of the day—Esther Biddle and Mary Fisher. The women were giving Blinman some competition in the quest for souls. 'There they vent their opinions,' he wrote, quickly adding, 'I heare 2 or 3 masters of ships are perverted by them.' The fervour of the conversions (many of the saved must have had a noisy climb out of their lawless, drunken pits) so alarmed some of the other ships' captains that they sent word to Ferryland for the more conservative Blinman to come at once.

By fall all three preachers had gone back to England, not to return, leaving the settlers to sort out the consequences. Sustained missionary work would have to wait for more permanent settlement. And the Newfoundlanders (as they must now be called) would eventually see Calvert's goal of a religious-tolerant society take hold, even if at times they would seem to do so grudgingly.

The other call that went out from Newfoundland—for a governor—met with a more baffling reaction. An Order-in-Council of 1675 commanded that all planters along the English Shore remove themselves, either back to England, or on to other parts of British North America. 'The country is barren and rocky, is productive of no commodies as other Plantations, or affords anything of food to keep men alive,' the fish merchants continued to harp from their estates in Devon and Dorset.

The planters of Newfoundland protested, the most vocal being those who had the most to lose, including John Downing of St. John's with his farm, five boats, and two stages, and twenty-five workers. The order was eventually withdrawn, though it was probably less in response to the planters' pleas than it was to some-thing much more ominous. Word had reached the English king that the fiendish French had founded their own colony in Newfoundland. It lay on the eastern shore of Placentia Bay, and they were calling it 'Plaisance.'

13 | The Fearsome French, the Unenviable English

On the 28th we burned Carbonear, and left again for Heart's Content. On the 1st of March M. D'Iberville sent MM. de Montigny and de la Peiriere to go with all the prisoners (about two hundred) to Bull Arm, in the bottom of Trinity Bay. He left . . . a detachment at Heart's Content, with orders to keep a strict watch on Carbonear, and he himself, with nine men, set out across the woods for Plaisance. The road is not quite as good as between Paris and Versailles.

—Diary of Jean Baudoin, 1697

Sieur d'Iberville.

More Than the Avalon

It is the English settlement of the Avalon Peninsula that has received most of the attention from those looking back on seventeenth-century Newfoundland and Labrador. That's to be expected, given the English dominance of our history in the centuries to follow.

Yet, if a lost soul were to have drifted down the coast of Labrador and circled the Island in mid-century, he would have likely concluded he had arrived in French territory, not English. True, there were Basque fishermen still to be found, especially along the west coast, and the English were entrenched in their own corner of the Island. And he might even have run into a few New Englanders or Dutchmen out for trade or privateering. But by far the majority of people to cross his path would have been fishermen from France. At the peak of the summer fishery they numbered close to twenty thousand. And each one of them, no doubt, thought of Terre Neuve as their part of the new world, in the very same way that others of their countrymen viewed the territory of New France.

In what was called Le Petit Nord (an area comprising the coast of southern Labrador and that of the peak of the Northern Peninsula) vessels of New France and those of Terre Neuve would likely have come in contact. Pushing eastward, along Quebec's Côte-Nord, fishermen from New France were determined to get a foothold on the inshore fishing grounds of Labrador, now that the Basque whalers had disappeared. They successfully petitioned the king of France for the right to fish along the coastline from Mingan to the Strait of Belle Isle.

A particular attraction was the seal fishery. In December of each year a couple of hundred fishermen from New France would spread themselves as far along the coast as Cape St. Charles, in wait for the herds of seals heading for their winter sites near Île d'Anticosti. And of increasing interest was the possibility of trade with the eastern bands of Innu. The Frenchmen were joined on Le Petit Nord by the seasonal fishermen who came each year directly from France to fish for cod.

If there was a deterrent to their plans, it was the Inuit and the Beothuk. While contact with the Innu is likely to have been amicable (with reports as early as 1633 of a Jesuit priest wintering with one of their bands), the Inuit and Beothuk were increasingly suspicious of foreign incursions into their territory. Inuit hunters had attacked the explorers who went ashore in Labrador as part of the search for the

Northwest Passage. Both groups raided the vacant premises of the fishermen and made off with any iron they could find. In 1610 the fishermen of Saint-Malo were so fearful of attack that the merchants of their port petitioned the French king for two armed vessels for protection from the *'sauvaiges de Terre neuffve.'*

Plaisance

Meanwhile, in the southwestern part of the Avalon Peninsula, the French were making preparations for a year-round colony in Newfoundland. They had witnessed the English settle in several other parts of the Avalon, and decided that the time had come for a permanent presence of their own. They set in place plans, not for a commercial venture, but for fortification. They had fished in Terre Neuve continuously for more than 150 years, longer than any other nation, and with much of their nation's marine fleet. Of all the nations of Europe, they were the strongest and most prosperous. To their minds the English were but upstarts on the open seas.

To their fortification, they gave the name 'Plaisance.' It was blessed with an ice-free natural harbour and with long stretches of beach for drying cod. It was close to the English settlements on the Avalon, and close to the Grand Banks. And the cod in its bay was said to be of a quality *'plus délicat et exquis qu'en aucun autre endroit.'* Music to the ears of the *poissonniers* of Paris.

Plaisance was a cornerstone of a grander scheme of expansion in the new world set in place by the resolute Jean-Baptiste Colbert, Louis XIV's minister for the colonies. Fortifications were to be erected, not only to protect the codfishery, but to establish a decisive military presence at the entrance to the Gulf of St. Lawrence. From the moment ships from Europe ventured past the prime English settlements of St. John's and Ferryland and rounded the southern headlands of the Avalon, they were meant to feel the threat of Frenchmen more than willing to defend the gulf and the territories of New France beyond.

Such were the plans. In reality, for most of the first thirty years of its existence Plaisance was a poorly maintained outpost struggling to survive. Its problems echoed those of the English colonies—an ocean-wide gap between the policies of the home country and the realities of Newfoundland, and a resident population forever at odds with the migratory fishermen.

The latter even threatened the start-up of the colony. In 1655 merchants from

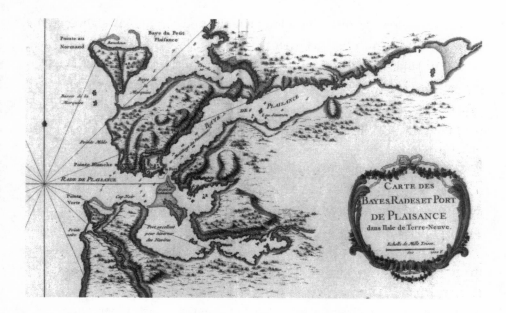

Plaisance, engraved by J. N. Bellin, Paris, 1764.

Saint-Malo protested the appointment of a governor for Newfoundland. Nothing more was heard of the appointee, and five years passed before a second attempt was made. Again the fish merchants twisted a few influential arms at Versailles, and again the governorship was revoked. It wasn't until October 1662 that a governor, the young and ill-prepared Thalour du Perron, set foot in Plaisance. He arrived aboard the *Aigle d'or* with two dozen men.

When a supply ship and a new contingent of soldiers and settlers showed up the following spring, what they laid eyes on was a gruesome sight of mutiny and murder. Besides the slaughter of du Perron, his brother, and the chaplain (done in with an axe), another ten of the men were dead. The murderers were near dead themselves, of starvation.

It was not the start the French had been counting on. But they were determined that they would follow through on their original plan. They set to work, expanding on the meagre start du Perron had been able to make on fortification. Plaisance, with the commitment from Versailles of supplies and colonists, began to take shape. For a time it even attracted settlers from some of the English colonies on the Avalon.

But then, after ten years, the administrators under Louis XIV tightened the purse strings, with the expectation that Plaisance would survive on its own. With little land worth planting, the colony floundered, unable to subsist on fishing alone, even after the settlers began hiring workers (*engagés*) from France to help them at the fishery. A succession of governors were all appallingly weak and corrupt, more interested in filling their own pockets than in setting the colony on a firm course.

The two sectors of the population fought at every turn. The settlers accused the seasonal fishermen of trying to take over the stretches of beach they had traditionally used for drying fish. The fishermen countered that the settlers ransacked their sheds during the winter when they were home in France. The settlers denounced the owners of the seasonal vessels for buying up the merchant goods intended for them. The same owners refused to transport any more *engagés* from France. And through it all the governors were weak and indecisive, though whether they could have done anything, given the sorry state of the military force, is doubtful.

Plaisance was saved in 1689 by the outbreak of war. In Europe the War of the Grand Alliance pitted Louis XIV of France against a coalition of countries determined to put an end to his territorial incursions. The following year the hostilities spread to North America, and in Newfoundland a band of English privateers crossed overland from Ferryland and attacked Plaisance. The colony was easily overrun, and six weeks later, when the English finally returned home, they took with them all the colony's provisions.

By the fall of 1690, new fortifications were being built, and the following year ships arrived from France with two dozen soldiers and a stockpile of ammunition, together with a new governor. Construction of Fort Louis was started immediately, and Plaisance went from a defence of eight worthless cannon to a formidable array of twenty-three.

More soldiers and even stronger defences followed, and in succeeding years Plaisance successfully repelled two more attacks by the English. Then, in 1696, the French in Plaisance went on the offensive, charged with the mission of routing the English from the Avalon. To lead them they were sent from New France no less a soldier than the young and brilliant Pierre Le Moyne d'Iberville.

D'Iberville on the Move

Under the commission of Louis XIV and with orders from Frontenac, governor of New France, d'Iberville sailed into Plaisance on 12 September 1696. There he was to meet the colony's governor, Jacques-François de Brouillan, and with him devise a strategy for the offensive. Instead, what he faced was word that de Brouillan, with hundreds of seamen from Saint-Malo as reinforcements, had taken the war into his own hands and three days before set off by sea to raid the English settlements on the eastern Avalon. De Brouillan would later contend that d'Iberville was late in arriving, that any further delay would have been imprudent. D'Iberville would charge that de Brouillan, ten years his senior, was unwilling to share in the plan of attack. It was the start of a steady round of bickering between the two.

In any event, de Brouillan returned to Plaisance in October with a partial victory and plenty of captured English, including David Kirke, Jr., who would die a prisoner in Plaisance. De Brouillan had plundered and burnt several settlements, Ferryland among them. In Bay Bulls the frigate *Sapphire*, rather than be captured by the French, was set afire and sunk by her captain. (What is left of the thirty-two-gun, 346-tonne ship still lies at the harbour bottom.)

But the biggest prize, St. John's, eluded the governor. And for his inept tactics de Brouillan garnered the scorn of d'Iberville. The soldier was doubly vexed, for the English now had been warned of the French intentions. De Brouillan held his ground, unwilling to let the upstart from New France take charge. In the end, the two reached a compromise. They would wage a winter war, de Brouillan by sea, d'Iberville across the land of the southern Avalon.

On the first of November d'Iberville set off with the contingent of 124 men he had brought with him—Abenaki Indians and 'many gentlemen, four officers, and other people of distinction,' together with hardened coureurs de bois, d'Iberville's sixteen-year-old brother, and Jean Baudoin, a Récollet priest who would keep a meticulously written account of the ensuing battles. Their nine-day trek over half-frozen bog and through thick clumps of stunted spruce was unlike anything the Canadians had ever experienced. Chilled to the bone by the November winds off the open Atlantic, and 'quite frequently up to the waist in water,' they came in sight of Ferryland miserable and out of provisions. To satisfy their hunger they slaughtered roaming horses, animals that, weeks before, had been part of a thriving Pool Plantation.

D'Iberville, terrorizer of forts, proved no match for the natural barricades of Carbonear Island.

D'Iberville gave his men time to recover, and to loot what was left of Ferryland. He met up with de Brouillan, who had arrived by sea just to the south in Renews. There sprang up a fresh spat, and this time swords cut the air. The Récollet priest forced himself between them. Finally, d'Iberville resigned himself to the governor's demands, knowing that after St. John's he would be done with him. The soldiers took to the boats, sailing and rowing on to Bay Bulls. They struck out overland in the direction of St. John's, halting long enough to capture Petty Harbour, killing thirty-six English in the process.

Word had spread to the people of St. John's that the French forces were heading their way. Though the residents far outnumbered the French, they were neither trained nor equipped for war. Eighty-eight of them (fishermen turned soldiers) took to the Southside Hills to fend off the oncoming troops. The French, over two hundred strong, came marching up the Waterford Valley. They took sight of the English behind the cover of the huge boulders that dotted the hills.

'After having received absolution, each man dropped his pack and attacked . . . D'Iberville threw himself on the left of the enemy . . . ' killing many of them and, sword in hand, chasing down those who ran away, 'fighting as far as St. John's . . . where he arrived a good quarter an hour ahead of the main body led by M. de Brouillan.'

This was d'Iberville in his glory. The English who were neither dead nor captured held up in King William's Fort, built just three years earlier after numerous petitions by the citizenry for some line of defence against just such an attack. Unfortunately, the fort was ungarrisoned. And for the already terrified occupants the devious d'Iberville had in store another of his tactics honed in the wilderness of New France. One of the captives, William Drew, was hauled in view of the fort. The French 'cutt all around his scalp and then by the strength of hand strip his skin from the forehead to the crowne and so sent him into the fortification, assuring the Inhabitants that they would serve them all in like manner if they did not surrender.'

For the peace-loving Newfoundlanders, it was an ugly exhibition of what being Canadian was all about. And there was to be no arguing with the man. By the last day of November all of St. John's was in his bloodied hands. The arch-soldier from New France could relish the victory, lame as it was, given that the residents were so ill-prepared.

De Brouillan, much to d'Iberville's annoyance, was the one to put his signature to the declaration of surrender. After one final squabble, de Brouillan marched off with his share of the spoils. He and twenty of his men made their way back to Bay Bulls, and there re-embarked for Plaisance.

For d'Iberville there were more English settlements to deal with, the anticipation of victory infinitely sweeter since it would be all of his own making. First, though, was the matter of the hundreds of English prisoners—men, women, and children awaiting their fate at the hands of the dreaded French. Some were shipped off to Plaisance on the heels of de Brouillan, but most found themselves on two overcrowded ships, one destined for England, the other France. More than two hundred of the destitute English reached Dartmouth on the tenth of January. Eighty others were shipwrecked off the coast of Spain. Of what happened to the remaining prisoners, the wounded and near-dead, there is no record. What we do know is that St. John's was left in smouldering rubble as d'Iberville and his fellow Canadians took to the snow-clogged woods, on their way to Portugal Cove and the English harbours of Conception and Trinity Bays.

A Wall of Rock

D'Iberville's plan was to lay waste to the remainder of the English Shore, as far to the north as Bonavista. The relative ease with which he brought St. John's to ruin had made him all the more presumptuous of victory. But the residents of Carbonear, raised on the fiendish habits of Peter Easton, had a plan of their own. At the centre of it was something even the wily d'Iberville should not have thought he could outmanoeuvre—the geography of Newfoundland.

When he reached Carbonear (having ravaged Harbour Main and Port de Grave en route) d'Iberville discovered an abandoned settlement, if a notably prosperous one, with houses that were 'the finest built in all Newfoundland' and 'some folk worth 100,000 livres.' In Carbonear lived descendants of John Guy's original colonists from the now-abandoned Cuper's Cove, including some who had never dwelt in any other place but Newfoundland. They were the long-lived core of settlement on the Avalon and they were not to be easily driven from their land. They took to Carbonear Island, out from the mouth of the harbour, together with planters from Harbour Grace and Bristol's Hope, and others who had escaped the pillage of St. John's. The Newfoundlanders had erected shelters and stocked them with provisions.

The island was fortified with a few 'six-pounders.' But its greatest defence was its sheer cliffs and scarcity of beaches suitable for landing. The best of these beaches the men on the island had barricaded with their own vessels. As for the others, any amount of tide and surf made getting ashore a job for only the most skilled fishermen, especially in January when ice coated the rocks. Woodsmen from New France were left bobbing in the swell.

What riled them further was the discovery that the planters had taken all their valuables and, weeks before the French arrived, 'hidden them in the woods and islands of this bay before the snows.' The French rowed off in frustration to Bay de Verde. They crossed overland to Old Perlican and marched down the shore of Trinity Bay, pillaging settlements as they went, scattering what English they failed to capture. Ending in Heart's Content, they crossed the Barrens and arrived back in Carbonear to a situation worse than what they had left.

In their absence, some of the men holed up on Carbonear Island had ventured off and seized four of the soldiers d'Iberville had left behind. The champion fighter of New France flew into an even wilder rage. He sent half his men off to burn Port de Grave and Brigus and whatever other places had any sign of English settlers. Legend has it that so exasperated were the French that after raiding one settlement and taking their leave, 'the barking of a dog brought them back' to finish the job by burning seven more houses.

And in the end, the attempt to strike a deal with the planters on the Carbonear Island for the return of the prisoners only brought d'Iberville to the very last strand of his rope. The Récollet priest was left to record in his journal, rather abashedly, that 'no one should mock the officers of the King.'

Carbonear was torched. D'Iberville and his men quit the place for Heart's Content, dragging what prisoners they could with them. D'Iberville made for Plaisance, hustling over eighty kilometres in four days, displaying the mettle of a man with other battles to fight. There he awaited the arrival of the ship carrying another of his brothers, with new orders from France.

D'Iberville had been forced to give up on his plan of making one last raid, on Bonavista. As spring arrived, ships of the migratory fishery returned to the destroyed harbours of the English Shore. The holdouts in Carbonear ventured off their island, revived by the provisions aboard the ships from England. On May eighteenth d'Iberville's brother and five ships of war showed up in Plaisance, and with them orders from Louis XIV for d'Iberville to proceed immediately to Hudson Bay and there recapture Fort Bourbon from the English.

On 8 July 1697 d'Iberville left Newfoundland, much of it in ruin, its settlement barely holding on. Late that same year, the Peace of Ryswick put an end to the war between England and France. The seventeenth century ended with the English picking up the charred pieces of their attempts at settlement. The fishermen were back for the cod, which had been in no way diminished by the terrorizing French. The cod would keep them coming back, settlers would rebuild, and new ones arrive . . . all until war in Europe broke out once again.

14 | No Peace for the Weary

The island called Newfoundland, with the adjacent islands, shall, from this time forward, belong of right wholly to Britain . . . But it shall be allowed to the subjects of France to catch fish and to dry them on land in that part only, and in no other besides that, of the said Island of Newfoundland, which stretches from the place called Cape Bonavista to the northern point of the said island, and from thence running down by the western side, reaches as far as the place called Point Riche.

—Article XIII, Treaty of Utrecht, 1713

Detail of French map, 1756.

Defenceless Still

There was a lesson to be learned from the French raids on the English Shore—the need for ample, year-round defences. Newfoundland might have been prized as a training ground for England's seamen and a critical source of wealth for its West Country, yet the crown's only nod to any military obligation had been a few navy ships cruising the waters of the Avalon during the months of the migratory fishery.

In the spring of 1697 a newly arrived contingent of soldiers counted the English losses along the Avalon. They came face to face with nothing but 'destruction and Ruine.' D'Iberville's ruthlessness had been a rude awakening for the English. Their lot would be a supremely tenuous one as long as the *troupes de la Marine* were peering out from their posts atop the thick stone walls of *Fort Royal* in Plaisance.

And continue to peer they did—with a lustful eye on the rest of the Avalon. They didn't have the numbers to make good on their claims of sovereignty over the Island, but the governor wasn't about to hesitate in sending word down the St. Lawrence for reinforcements. All he was waiting for was a legitimate reason to fight.

It came in the form of Queen Anne's War. It was known, more palatably in England, as the War of Spanish Succession. In Newfoundland the English fishing ports had barely rebounded from the havoc of d'Iberville's winter campaign when they were set upon again.

This time there was at least some show of military strength from Britain. In the wake of the overland war of 1696–97, the English settlers attempting to rebuild in Newfoundland had argued vehemently for proper protection. If their homeland was going to be a battlefield for the countries of Europe, they asserted, they had a right to garrisoned fortifications. When the fishing merchants of the West Country added their voice to the call, the Crown finally paid heed. The merchants of the migratory fishery, in their self-centred wisdom, admitted that a force of settlers and soldiers would oversee their own fishing rooms during the winter months . . . and protect their investments. It was tacit acknowledgement by the merchants of the usefulness of a settled population in Newfoundland.

Yet the military measures taken by Britain were no more than half-hearted. Batteries were constructed on the hills that flanked the entrance to the harbour at St. John's. Soldiers cut thirty-centimetre timbers from the shores of nearby Deadman's Pond and Long Pond and hauled them by horse for the rebuilding of King William's Fort (later renamed Fort William). But the military force, which at first numbered 1,500, was quickly reduced to a mere 80 men and their superiors, all stationed in St. John's. The remainder of the English settlements, the ones with the majority of the population and including those who had escaped the first round of French devastation, were left to do what they had always done—fend for themselves.

Even the English navy was of little help. In 1702, at the start of the war, came a report that 'a French man of war hath been off St. John's all summer and hath taken seven ships in sight of the harbour.' That same summer '40 or 50 armed Frenchmen came over by land . . . to Sillicove,' a track of death and destruction following them to Bonavista. The navy's response was to send Rear-Admiral John Graydon to capture Plaisance. He proved a weak, incompetent choice.

Graydon arrived, via Jamaica, for a council of war in St. Mary's Bay. Some of his captains pointed out the wretched condition of their vessels. Others complained that many of their men had fallen sick and were hardly up to the task, given what they could expect of the French at Plaisance. Others whined about the thick fog shrouding the bay. In the end the attack was called off 'since it might tend to the dishonour of Her Majesty's arms.'

Graydon was either displaying a streak of cowardice or acting on lame advice. Word of the strength of the garrison at Plaisance was no more than rumour. And in Placentia Bay no one puts off the business at hand because of fog. If they did they'd be hard pressed to ever get much accomplished.

For whatever reason, Graydon failed the settlers of Newfoundland. He sailed back to England, leaving the French in the fog, polishing up their arms and reinforcing their foot gear. Though it was no consolation to the English settlers on the Avalon, when Graydon arrived in England he was soundly reprimanded for his inaction. He was cut from Her Majesty's navy, and the House of Lords even took away his pension. Still, he had his life and his freedom, more than could be said of many of the settlers he left behind on the Avalon.

Only rarely during Queen Anne's War did the shoreline settlements manage to stave off the French attacks. In August 1704, visiting New England trader Michael Gill boldly led Bonavista in the repulsion of a French onslaught by sea. 'When the inhabitants who had fled into the woods and rocks saw Captain Gill's courage, they came down and appeared in a body in arms, which when the French saw, they immediately weighed and set sail . . .' The following year the inhabitants of

A Canadian colonist of the sort who was game for warfare in Newfoundland.

Carbonear again took to their island, under attack from Canadians and Abenaki Indians, led this time by Jacques Testard de Montigny (back for his second taste of war in Newfoundland, having served under d'Iberville eight years earlier). He fled Carbonear as humbled as his former commanding officer had been, and just as vengeful. This time the French reached Bonavista. 'The very name of Montigny made the arms fall from the hands of the most resolute' it was said. The terror-struck folk of Bonavista chose not to test his limits, and conceded defeat before blood had chance to flow.

In St. John's the garrison, under the command of Lieutenant John Moody, had holed up in the new fortifications at Fort William. He outlasted the French . . . while the town surrounding him was plundered and burned. Only four houses were left standing.

St. John's was attacked yet again, on New Year's Day 1709. This time Fort William fell within a half-hour. The French commander, Saint-Ovide de Brouillan, and his men (Canadians and their Indian compatriots once more) had stolen through the snow-covered woods under moonlight, lain in wait within sight of the fort, then stormed it at daybreak. The revellers of the night before were caught completely by surprise, no one more slack-jawed than the chief carouser and officer in charge of the garrison, Thomas Lloyd. The French commander, face to face with Lloyd in his dressing gown, 'took him by the hand . . . and said that he thanked him for his New Year's gift.'

To the Loser the Spoils

Again the French destroyed St. John's, and again they marched back to Plaisance in triumph. English settlement of the Avalon seemed now to exist only at the whim of the French. Not that their control had a lasting effect. In Europe the English had gained the upper hand, and talk of peace was simmering. It was there, an ocean away, that the fate of Newfoundland would be tossed back and forth across the negotiation table before being handed to the inhabitants of the Island as a *fait accompli*. And had those negotiations taken another turn, had the fishery in Newfoundland not been such a crucial bargaining lever for both countries, today we might well be Terre-Neuviens, francophones speaking our own patois, preferring red wine to tea, *pâté de foie gras* to marmalade.

The Treaty of Utrecht of 1713 put a halt to the French domination of Newfoundland. Newfoundland and the offshore islands, the treaty made clear, belonged to Britain. Plaisance changed hands, to be promptly renamed Placentia. St. Pierre became St. Peter's. And all French fishermen were forced to retreat to the part of the coast that stretched from Cape Bonavista to Point Riche.

It was the inception of the infamous French Shore. There the French were to erect nothing more than fishing sheds and stages, nor were they to linger on shore beyond the end of the fishing season. Many chose to shift their fishing operations to Cape Breton, which the French had managed to hold on to and where they now began construction of the mighty Fort Louisbourg.

For a nation on the losing end of the war, their right to fish along such a broad expanse of Newfoundland's northeast and west coasts was a substantial consolation prize. Almost from the moment the signatures were dry, the French Shore turned into a source of irritation for both the English in Newfoundland and the French fishermen who arrived on its coasts.

Just what, for example, was meant by the term 'fish'? Codfish, as the English in Newfoundland generally think of it? Surely a few lobster for the aristocracy of Paris are not in violation of the treaty. And where exactly is Point Riche? A third of the way down the west coast of the Great Northern Peninsula, where it has always been, or a few hundred kilometres farther south, as it began to appear on some French maps?

To the English the French right to the coastline was not an *exclusive* right. In fact, Bonavista Bay, included in the designation of the French Shore, had seen continuous use by the English long before the signing of the treaty. Captain Russell's *Accompt of the English Inhabitants in Newfoundland* of 1676 listed sixty-six men, women, and children for the headland of Salvage, and by 1698 the English had settled into Greenspond on the north shore of the bay, with a population of fifty-one pursuing the summer fishery. By the mid-1700s, with England and France at war again, they were making regular use of Notre Dame Bay, and heading where no English fishermen had dared go before—into the long-standing French domain beyond Cape St. John.

The French were not impressed, and declared as much at every diplomatic turn. The English would hold up for scrutiny the wording of the treaty, and inch their way along the French Shore while doing so. The disputes returned to the negotiation table time and time again, and it would be another two hundred years, in 1904, before the question of the French Shore was finally put to rest.

Go Hungry or Go Elsewhere

With the Treaty of Utrecht the English in Newfoundland had the freedom to rebuild without fear of the merciless tactics of the French. But then came ten long years of extraordinarily low fish landings. The codfishery lapsed into such a poor state that one visitor claimed the settlers were 'worse off than negroes and slaves.' A petition by some Bristol merchants warned that without relief the settlers 'must starve or go to the Plantations.' It drove a desperate population either to leaving or scraping together an existence any way they could—an ugly attribute of settlement on this Island that would show its face again and again.

In 1720 the census of the white population of Massachusetts counted close to a hundred thousand people. Newfoundland's totalled fewer than five thousand . . . and was falling. Many inhabitants had no choice but to move. They gave up on Newfoundland, sailed off, and indeed added to the numbers in Massachusetts and other parts of New England. By one estimate, 1,300 left in 1717 alone.

The few thousand inhabitants remaining in Newfoundland were not much to show for more than two hundred years of European exploitation. And those who did try to make a home here did so without any of the encouragements found in the thriving mainland colonies—a clear set of laws with a governor and court system to enforce them, established churches, medical services, a school system, roads. Theirs was a primitive, isolated existence, made worse by an unpredictable climate, and a severe lack of defences.

A dandified 'Black Bart' struck terror in Trepassey.

Pirate Pursuits

It is little wonder then that in 1720 there showed up on our shores the infamous pirate 'Black Bart' (known to his better friends and relations as Bartholomew Roberts). With the end of the war in 1713, legitimate work for cut-throat seafarers had waned. Those left with a taste for blood led a resurgence of piracy. In the case of the swarthy Welshman, it was also revenge for the fact that his humble birth had prevented him from climbing the ranks of the Royal Navy, despite his long years of unerring service. His well-honed skills as a seaman, turned to diabolical ends, made him one of the most dreaded marauders afloat. He is said to have seized some four hundred ships before his new career came to an end. This man, who 'made more Noise in the World' than most of his fellow pirates combined, cut a striking figure, dressed as he was 'in a rich crimson Damask Wastcoat, and Breeches, a red Feather in his Hat, and a Gold Chain Ten Times round his Neck, a sword in his Hand, and two pair of Pistols hanging at the End of a Silk Sling . . . '

Trepassey, on the southern coast of Avalon, was hardly prepared for such a spectacle. In a clever ploy, Bart and his crew sailed into the harbour 'with Drums beating, Trumpets sounding, and other Instruments of Musick, English Colours flying, their Pirate Flagg at the Topmast-Head, with Deaths Head and Cutlash . . . ' The fishermen of Trepassey fled in desperate fear of their lives, forsaking some 'two and twenty' of their boats. It was just as Bart had hoped, since he was commanding a mere sloop of ten tonnes, having lost his regular vessel the previous year off South America.

The fishermen's fear proved to be somewhat unwarranted. Bart was intent not on meting out death and destruction (at least not immediately) but on finding himself a bigger ship, on refitting it with an array of arms more in keeping with his reputation, and on enticing some of the local lads to join him in his exploits. He seized a 'Bristol Galley . . . and mounted 16 Guns on board her.' And what with the sad state of the fishery, he had no trouble filling his crew list.

It was off, then, to the Banks, to cross paths with the French and English vessels fishing there. He spied 'nine or ten Sail of French Ships' destroying them all 'except one of 26 Gun.' He promptly rid himself of his Bristol galley and took charge of a new prize, renaming her the *Fortune*. At her helm he seized several English vessels and commandeered what men he wanted to further augment his mob. He departed the Banks for the Caribbean, delighted with the consequences of his cruise north to Newfoundland.

His brief sojourn on our shores seems to have given some residents of Newfoundland a few ideas of their own. In August 1723 one John Phillips, ostensibly employed as a fish splitter in St. Peter's, led four others in the seizure of a schooner, and a voyage into treachery. They escaped under the cover of darkness and aboard their *Revenge* drew up nine articles of pirate conduct, then 'swore to 'em upon a Hatchet for want of a Bible.' The rules were severe, though probably somewhat standard for the circumstances. Article Five, for example, warned 'that Man that shall strike another . . . shall receive Moses's Law (that is, 40 Stripes lacking one) on the bare Back.' The five 'fishermen' meant business.

Before heading south to the prime scene of piracy, the West Indies, they took a detour to the Banks and convinced several more men to forsake their honest toil and join with them in their quest. One, as luck should have it, had once been a crewman of the dreaded Blackbeard. The fellow was immediately assigned the position of quartermaster. It was Phillips's first mistake. It brought dissension within the ranks; one of the original crew, 'Thomas Fern, the

Carpenter,' was especially vexed at being passed over for promotion in favour of the newcomer.

After several months of plundering and general debauchery in the West Indies, Phillips headed north again, back toward Newfoundland, most likely with the intention of refitting his ship in quieter waters. But before reaching here, the carpenter Fern, still smarting from his lack of authority, attempted to strike out on his own, going off in a captured sloop. Phillips took after him, crossed bows with the renegade, and murdered him forthwith (as per Article Three).

But Fern, from his watery grave, had the last laugh. For a short time later Phillips himself was murdered, not far from Newfoundland, at the hands of a prisoner of a sloop he had captured. Captain Phillips, cod splitter from St. Peter's turned pirate, had his jaw smashed with a carpenter's mallet, and his brains bashed in with a carpenter's adze.

15 | More Than Profits

The Island . . . is neglected by us, being desolate and woody, and the Coast and Harbour only held for the Conveniency of the Cod Fishery, for which alone they are settled.

—Daniel Defoe, 1724

Captain James Cook

The Irish Make a Home,
the French a 'Petite République'

The year 1699 saw the first act of the English Parliament directed specifically toward Newfoundland. It had been a long wait, yet hardly a worthwhile one. Its title alone—*An Act to Encourage the Trade to Newfoundland*—betrayed its intentions. King William's Act, as it came to be known, was put in place to safeguard 'the beneficial trade to this kingdom' and the resultant 'increase of revenue.'

Obviously, Newfoundland was still a place to do business, not a viable and developing colony. But we must be wary. It makes for a tidy scenario to be thinking that the lawmakers in London were forever banding together with the West Country merchants to thwart settlement. It is the foundation of that vision of ourselves as a people forever having to squirm from under the thumb of the rich and influential. The truth is, we weren't hiding out in the deepest recesses of the bays, furtively clinging to a few squares of turf. Sparse though it was, settlement had taken hold. The merchants and their migratory fishermen were not blind to its value, especially in times of war. If the Island were ever to recover from Queen Anne's War and see itself through to the day when the fish catches rose again, then the two factions had no choice but tolerate each other. And let economics take care of the rest.

By the second quarter of the eighteenth century fish catches were on the rise again. And so, too, was the population. The English, once confined to the Avalon, were pushing into new territory. They moved into that part of the south coast where the French had lost their rights—Placentia, Fortune, and Hermitage Bays— and farther north into Twillingate and Fogo in Notre Dame Bay, where the French had supposedly gained them.

The toughest times had passed, in some measure because the English seized the opportunity to profit from other resources. For the first time they fished offshore, on the Grand Banks. And many of them (especially the settlers in Bonavista and beyond) moved away from sole dependence on cod, and into new resources such as salmon and seals.

By the 1740s the picture had brightened considerably. The new bank fishery, based out of St. John's and the Southern Shore, had taken hold. Pursued mainly by merchants from South Devon, the enterprise brought a new influx of workers. But this time, because of the bleak state of the Newfoundland fishery in the past, many West Country fishermen no longer had any interest in crossing the Atlantic. Instead, the majority of workers came from Ireland.

Cork and Waterford on the south coast of Ireland had been the traditional victualling ports for many of the ships of the migratory fishery, stopping points where they would pick up supplies at prices cheaper than in England—salt meat, cheese, woollens, and beer. Now they were supplying men to the fishing trade as well. Irish 'youngsters' they were called, in the old sense of the term: unmarried young labourers (in this case landsmen with an added bit of pluck to stave off seasickness).

Most made a go of it in the foreign land, many as part of the by-boat fishery. Even when they found themselves abandoned by bankrupt merchants, many stayed on and laid down their Irish roots, especially along the Southern Shore, where today the lilt and legend of their homeland still dominates.

The presence of the Irish was not confined to one stretch of the coast, however. Irish servants showed up wherever they were needed—in Placentia, and as far along the south coast as Cape Ray and Codroy, which now, despite the Treaty of Utrecht, were in the hands of the French.

Some of the French living in and around Placentia at the end of the war had no intention of relocating to Île Royale in Cape Breton. They dismissed the lure of the more crowded mainland (rational people that they were). A few agreed to swear allegiance to the English monarch and were allowed to stay in Placentia. Others, their allegiances less pliable, chose instead to secrete themselves in the remote, but strategic, area around Cape Ray, far to the west. There they were away from the meddling habits of the authorities and could carry on their fishing businesses free of nasty tariffs and regulations.

The English navy in Newfoundland had neither the ships nor the will to root them out, in part because the lieutenant-governor at Placentia, Samuel Gledhill, was not immune to a little illicit money-making himself. The French authorities at Louisbourg did come up with methods of pressuring the renegades to mend their ways, among them forbidding priests in one Cape Breton community to perform marriages between his female parishioners and Newfoundland men from Cape Ray. But any reprimands generally fell limp. As it turned out, the Anglo-American trading at Cape Ray was triangular in nature, and helped to line the pockets of the French at Cape Breton as well as those at Cape Ray.

A blind eye encouraged two decades of relative prosperity in *'cette petite République.'* Fishermen were employed by merchants from France, most notably the four brothers of the Chenu family of Saint-Malo. By 1740 Codroy and the surrounding area could boast more than a dozen families. Their presence even warranted a visit by a Récollet priest from New France. And they may even have traded with the Mi'kmaq, who by this time had started to make seasonal visits from Cape Breton in search of game, frequenting the sparsely populated coastline west of Fortune Bay.

In summer the inhabitants of Codroy fished for cod and salmon; in winter they trapped furs and cut the thick stands of timber in the fertile Codroy Valley. Their enterprise led to illicit trading with nearby New England, and indirectly with Spain. After the outbreak of war between Spain and England in 1739, fish buyers in Spanish ports such as Bilbao and Cadiz were secretly acquiring the much-favoured light-salted cod, cod that had been caught and cured in New England. It had found its way across the Atlantic in ships of the Chenu brothers of Codroy, covered in the holds with French fish to disguise the forbidden trade.

In 1744 France entered the war against Spain. The Chenu family knew it spelled the end of their tidy enterprise in southwestern Newfoundland. They abandoned it, leaving the French and Irish settlers no choice but to move on to Île Royale. Within a few months what was left of their lucrative but illegal operations had been sacked by English privateers.

The Cobhams: Pirates with Potential

The French were able to seclude themselves in this corner of Newfoundland because the Island's coastline, except for that of the Avalon Peninsula, was largely uncharted. Past surveys had been sporadic and imprecise. There were hundreds of kilometres of the south and west coasts still rarely sighted by Englishmen.

And those who did know it may well have been of dubious character. Legend has it that from 1740 to 1760 Sandy Point in Bay St. George was home to the notorious husband-and-wife pirating duo of Eric and Marie Cobham. It is said they attacked ships heading out of the St. Lawrence, and were especially keen on any bearing cargoes of furs from New France. They were known for massacring all on board and then scuttling the vessels, with Marie often taking the lead in the heinous goings-on. 'She poisoned one ship's crew, had others sewn into sacks and thrown overboard alive, still others tied up and used for pistol practice,' says one modern account. Newfoundland seems to have brought out the worst in her. Unfortunately, as tempting as it is to embrace the story, there is no documentary evidence from the eighteenth century to support the notion of the pirating pair ever having lived on the west coast of Newfoundland—no insurance claims, no reports from other ships, no reports from the authorities. (Nevertheless, if there is a musical starring Eric and Marie coming next tourist season, you can be certain it will be a hit, especially with Marie looking stunningly demonic in beaver pelts.)

The Incomparable James Cook

There is, however, one striking figure who sailed into the waters of Newfoundland at this time, for whom we have a vault full of formidable records—Captain James Cook. The empire builders of England realized that if they were going to safeguard their territorial interests, and defend them against the designs of other nations (and, some would say, discourage pirating), then it was imperative that detailed hydrographic surveying be undertaken.

A CHART
OF THE
STRAIGHTS of BELLISLE
WITH PART OF THE COAST OF
NEWFOUNDLAND and LABRADORE
FROM ACTUAL SURVEYS
Taken by ORDER of
COMMODORE PALLISSER
GOVERNOR of NEWFOUNDLAND, LABRADORE &c
BY
JAMES COOK
SURVEYOR
1766.

Detail of chart engraved by Larken, from the surveys of James Cook.

To recruit the famed cartographer and explorer just as his talents were coming to maturity was indeed a fortuitous decision. Not that he needed much persuasion. Cook had been coming to North America for several years as a naval officer, and it was along the St. Lawrence and the coast of Nova Scotia that he had mastered the techniques of surveying. In the late summer and fall of 1762, before returning to England, Cook had charted several harbours in Newfoundland. His work in Conception Bay proved particularly useful. 'Hitherto we have had a very imperfect knowledge of these places,' it was reported to the Admiralty Board, 'but Mr. Cook . . . has discovered that ships of any size may lie in safety both in Harbour Grace and the Bay of Carbonear.'

But it was his exacting and uncompromising work over the next five years that would prove to be an outstanding contribution to the development of New-foundland, at the same time that it set new standards in hydrographic charting. His distinguished biographer, J.C. Beaglehole, contends: 'Cook was to carry out many accomplished pieces of surveying, in one part of the world or another, but nothing he ever did later exceeded in accomplishment his surveys of the southern and western sides of Newfoundland from 1763 to 1767.' Cook's *Collection of Charts of the Coasts of Newfoundland and Labradore, &c.*, later consolidated into *The Newfoundland Pilot* (surveys using land-based instrumentation rather than those of the more common, but inexact, running survey), would not fall out of use for a full century. Their added detail on topography, currents, and tides, as well as asides detailing animal and plant life, proved invaluable to the spread of population. And in a broader context, they confirmed the position of disputed points of land. The French no longer had a case for changing the position of Point Riche, the limit of their French Shore. And when the French ambassador claimed rights to Belle Isle on the basis of it being closer to the French Shore than to Labrador, Commodore Palliser of Newfoundland reported, ' . . . a chart constructed on those surveys hav-ing been published, I referred him to it, and so this subject ended.'

All this and the study of a solar eclipse as well. In 1766, on one of the islands off Burgeo (still called Eclipse Island), Cook stood witness to such an astronomical event, precisely as he had forecast it. Using his brass telescopic quadrant, he obtained exact measurements of longitude, and transposed these to determine the longitude of several other points of land along the south coast, something that he had not been able to do during the normal course of his surveying. The following spring his observations were presented to the Royal Society in London, whose members were duly impressed that 'Mr James Cook, a good mathematician, and very expert in his Business' could have made such accurate calculations in the far-off reaches of 'New-found-land.'

In a remarkable six weeks of his final summer in Newfoundland Cook surveyed nearly the whole of the west coast of the Island, from the cape just north of Codroy, where the renegade French settlement had once been, all the way up the Great Northern Peninsula to Point Ferolle. (Included, at the end, was a pair of mounded islands in St. John Bay his journal records as 'Our Ladies Bubies,' though he had the islands engraved on his chart as 'Twin Islands.' It had been a long six weeks.)

Along the way, in Bay St. George, he encountered 'a Tribe of Mickmack Indians,' some of the first to settle on the Island. Exploring what he named the 'Bay of Islands' led him to a five-day excursion up the laudable Humber River and into Deer Lake, recording that 'on this river has formerly been a very great salmon fishery,' most likely seasonal use by the French. At Bonne Bay he observed the grandeur of the Long Range Mountains, then dutifully noted to mariners that 'small vessels must anchor just above a low Woody Point.' It was one of hundreds of place names assigned to his charts that remain in use today. Some of these names would stay with Cook when, a few years later, he undertook his famous voyages to the South Seas. New Zealand, too, now has a Bay of Islands and a Hawke's Bay. And following his brutal death and dismemberment in Hawaii in 1779, it would be a deep scar to Cook's hand received while surveying the New-foundland coast that would be used by his grief-stricken companions to identify his remains.

The Inquisitive Mr. Banks

Cook's was not the only scientific mind detailing the attributes of Newfoundland and Labrador in 1766. Another belonged to the twenty-three-year-old Joseph Banks, at the start of a career that would see him become an acclaimed naturalist, long-serving president of the Royal Society, and key figure in the development of Kew Gardens. His support of such a broad range of scientific endeavour (sheep breeding in Australia, geological mapping in Britain, exploration in Africa, etc.) was to make him one of the most significant men of science in the eighteenth century.

The youthfully curious Joseph Banks.

On 27 October 1766 both he and Captain Cook were at anchor in St. John's. Both were on their way back to England, each having spent the past six months in this part of the world, Cook surveying the south coast, Banks exploring and gathering specimens along the Avalon, the northeast coast, and Labrador. Although there is no record of it, most likely the two encountered each other. In any event, at the end of Cook's surveying season the next year, he had aboard his ship a curiosity that had been secured for Banks—a Beothuk canoe. (Unfortunately, the canoe washed overboard and was lost en route to England.) And in 1768 it was Banks who was aboard the *Endeavour* with Cook on the way to the Pacific, the start of their renowned three-year journey of surveying and nature study. (Banks and his botanist assistants returned with thirty thousand specimens, increasing by nearly 25 per cent the number of known plant species.)

In Newfoundland in 1766 Banks was also adding substantially to the understanding of the natural world. In what is considered 'the first extensive and properly documented scientific collections' from the area, Banks, working alone, gathered or documented 'at least 340 plants, 91 birds, many fishes and invertebrates.' And not forgetting a few mammals, including a porcupine, brought to him at Chateau Bay in Labrador, and which he attempted to transport back alive to England. His summer of investigation was an incredible achievement for the time and the conditions under which he had to work. When he arrived in England he arranged for many of the species to be painted as permanent records, including the Eskimo curlew (*Numenius borealis*), once so plentiful throughout the Americas, now near extinction. They were to be found, he wrote to a friend, 'in amazing multitudes,' adding of them: '& every body here agrees most excellent eating.'

Banks's investigations (including the sight of great piles of whale bone left from the days of the Basque fishery) serve as a plaintive reminder of the profusion of wildlife before European settlement.

The Fight for the Labrador Coast

The *Niger* on which Banks had found passage to Labrador was not a ship on a scientific mission. It was a navy patrol vessel that sailed into Chateau Bay with a military purpose. It carried a contingent of marines assigned to construct a block-house, fortified living quarters they would name York Fort. When the *Niger* sailed off, it left behind a lieutenant and twenty men, a garrison for the protection of the fishery against attack by the Inuit. The animosity between the Inuit and the encroaching Europeans had reached unparalleled heights and turned southern Labrador into a battleground for access to its resources.

Distrust and rivalry along the Labrador coast went back a long time, well before any English fishermen had made an appearance. It was there in the early days of the Basque whaling enterprises and the French migratory fishery. At the beginning of the eighteenth century Labrador had come to be considered a largely unexplored continuation of New France, and the Treaty of Utrecht of 1713 did nothing to change that. It was a colonial view, of course, one that dismissed any thought of

The Eskimo curlew, as drawn by Sydney Parkinson after Banks returned to England.

a native right to the territory. And, while the Innu seemed willing to establish working alliances with the French, the Inuit did not.

As far back as 1661 residents of New France (chiefly Quebec City) had been given the right to apply for land concessions along the Labrador coast. The largest of the grants had been issued to Augustin Le Gardeur de Courtemanche in 1702. It extended from Rivière Kegaska, not far from Île d'Anticosti, to Kessessasskiou River (today, Churchill) at the head of Hamilton Inlet, a vast expanse of coastline, and one, as Courtemanche had seen for himself, teeming with wildlife. He had a fort built in Baye de Phélypeau (Bradore Bay), and sought out the southern Innu, whom the French called Montagnais. Eventually thirty to forty Innu families agreed to settle there. 'He has made them very sociable,' it was reported a few years later. Together with the settlers from New France, they fished for seal, cod, and salmon along the coast, and trapped wild game inland. Even though the codfishery had to be shared with the migratory fishermen who still showed up each spring from France, the Canadians and the Innu working together made for a flourishing community. At its peak it held two hundred houses.

But all this activity did not sit well with the descendants of the Thule Eskimo, the Inuit. Their trade with Courtemanche, as much as he wished it otherwise, was infrequent and unprofitable. This was not what the authorities in France were expecting, although they were willing to concede that Courtemanche had tried his best.

French trade with the 'Esquimaux,' early 1700s.

King Louis XIV, on the heels of the Treaty of Utrecht of 1713, was quick to serve notice of French intentions to expand the number of concessions: 'the new settlement (Île Royale) would not provide enough work for all the boats of the kingdom engaged in the commerce of fishing and, thus, it would be necessary to take advantage of the fishing off the Coast of Labrador.' But because more Quebec City merchants had their eyes fixed on the potential profits there, the grants were increased in number, and now comprised much shorter stretches of coastline (generally four or five leagues [nineteen to twenty-four kilomentres]).

By this time the original concession to Courtemanche had expired. But for him alone Louis XIV made an exception. In view of 'the pains and cares which his establishment had cost him,' the king now granted Courtemanche lifetime rights to Baye de Phélypeau, and at the same time appointed him as the Crown's official representative on the coast of Labrador, endowing him with the power to 'settle and adjust the disputes which arise between His Majesty's subjects.'

The Inuit hardly thought of themselves as 'His Majesty's subjects,' and when eight hundred of them showed up a few months later and overran the fort, pilfering whatever they could, it was obvious that Courtemanche wouldn't be able to do much settling of disputes. He and his settlers drove them off. And although the king's representative and some others again attempted to establish friendly relations with the Inuit, many of the French thought of them only as 'savage animals' whose 'presence all along the coast is to be feared.' Some even captured Inuit and carried them off to Quebec City, where they were made to work as slaves. Several of the captives died, often at an early age, in the city's Hôtel Dieu.

The Inuit of southern Labrador were following the migration route of the seals, and when they arrived at their traditional hunting grounds to find them occupied by the French (often in consort with their traditional rivals, the Innu), hostilities erupted. From the fishermen at La Forteau, L'Anse-au-Loup, Sainte-Modet, and other places along the coast came reports of looting and damaged property, vain attempts by the Inuit to stop the operations of the fishermen. In many cases the fishermen reciprocated, with firearms. Killing of Inuit became commonplace. Counterattacks ensued. The French could only come out the winners, what with the Crown supplying them with firearms and ammunition to protect the fishery. In the case of Courtmanche it amounted annually to two dozen guns and 90 to 135 kilograms of gunpowder.

In 1743 another Quebec City merchant, Jean-Louis Fornel, seemed to be having more success in building friendly relations with the Inuit. He set out to establish a trading post in what the French called Baie des Esquimaux (Hamilton Inlet), venturing deeper into Inuit territory than any trader before him. By schooner Fornel reached present-day Rigolet, where he and his men erected two large crosses and raised the French flag. They sang hymns and shouted 'repeatedly "Long live the King,"' declaring the land theirs, 'a land never before occupied by any nation.' They renamed it Baie Saint-Louis, in honour of their king. It was Cabot and Cartier all over again.

Fornel left behind 'a man named Pilote and his son,' thought to be the first Europeans to ever have wintered there. Several Innu families stayed with them, and together they explored the deeper reaches of the bay, setting up a winter trading post, most likely near what is now the community of Sheshatshiu. Fornel had warned the two Frenchmen 'not to expose themselves on the sea-shore for fear of the Eskimaux,' though he himself had no such apprehension. On his way home he traded with several groups of them at what he concluded was 'a meeting place, from whence they intended to go plundering along the coast.' Not surprisingly, his journal is rife with opinions about how to reform the Inuit, and turn them from their practice of pilfering the vacated premises of the seasonal fishermen. Unfortunately for Fornel, he was not around long enough to see any of his ideas take root. He died suddenly two years later.

His business initiative lived on, however. It fell into the hands of Marie-Anne Barbel, his wife, and mother of their fourteen children, seven of whom survived infancy. She could be viewed as the Labrador equivalent of Ferryland's Sara Kirke, although she never actually set foot in the concession, conducting her business from New France through her agents. The Labrador operation was expanded and it flourished, providing a steady supply of furs, chiefly marten and beaver. 'Widow Fornel has a company . . . ' said the intendant in defence of his grant of Baie Saint-Louis to her, 'and . . . the King will be well paid each year.' Much of the profits went toward the building of a very successful *briqueterie* for the manufacture of pottery in the Lower Town of Quebec City.

Her businesses all came to a sudden end with the outbreak of the Seven Years War. In Labrador violence erupted as it never had before. Fierce clashes pitted the

French and their Innu allies against the Inuit. Battle Harbour saw the worst of it, and from a final bloody confrontation it is said to have acquired its name.

The Inuit ceased coming so far south. They had been forced to give up their hope of driving away the French. But at the end of the war, it was no longer the French they faced. The English had gained control of Labrador. And it was the English merchants with businesses already established in Newfoundland (in St. John's and a few of the bigger outports) who were now showing up on Labrador's southern shores.

The British quickly put in place military protection (including the blockhouse at Chateau Bay in 1766), and when that didn't work they resorted to encouraging a new group of people interested in making contact with the Inuit of Labrador— the Moravian Brethren (Unitas Fratrum) from Saxony. Perhaps, the British were forced to conclude, religion might work where firearms had failed.

16 | A Home and Native Land

Oh! I am tired; here are too many houses; too much smoke; too many people;
Labrador is very good; seals are plentiful there; I wish I was back again.

—Attuiock, Inuit man in London, England, 1772

Mikak and Tutauk, as painted by John Russell, 1769.

The Woman behind the Portrait

In the early months of 1769 an Inuit woman, Mikak, was ushered into the drawing room of the English portraitist John Russell. By then she had become the talk of London's high society. The élite were astounded at her attractiveness, her ease of movement among them, her obvious intelligence, and charm. She was not at all the 'brute savage' they were expecting.

Mikak, together with her young son, Tutauk, and an older orphaned boy, Karpik, had been taken across the Atlantic at the insistence of the naval governor of Newfoundland, Hugh Palliser. His intent was to have her experience the 'power, splendour and generosity of the English nation' so she would carry back word of it to Labrador, and thus aid him in his mission of establishing friendly relations with the Inuit. Now, as Russell painted her, she was wearing an elaborate outfit that included leather boots, velvet breeches, and an embroidered hooded jacket trimmed in gold lace, all presents from Augusta, Dowager Princess of Wales. To the jacket was pinned a coronation medal of the new king, George III. From her wrist dangled a bracelet presented to her by the Duke of Gloucester. Even Russell, painter of princesses and future kings, seemed to have been enthralled. The portrait that would later hang in the Royal Academy captured a self-reliant and penetrating gaze, as if the subject knew more about the viewer than the viewer would ever know about her.

Indeed, Mikak had learned a great deal about the English, of how their ways clashed with those of her people. The year before they had killed her husband, one of twenty men slain by soldiers from York Fort in Chateau Bay in a revenge attack for the Inuit destruction of fishing premises at Cape St. Charles. The women and children had been captured and forced to spend the winter in the fort.

There, when her grief subsided, Mikak began to learn English. Second in command at the post was an Irishman, Francis Lucas, and her quickness to grasp the language captured the lieutenant's attention. (And his heart, it appears, was not far behind.) Mikak's aptitude and confidence had fascinated other Europeans who had come in contact with her, most notably a pair of Moravian missionaries who landed on the coast of Labrador two years before. These men had come in a cautious attempt to establish friendly relations with the Inuit, following the disastrous expedition of 1752 when the first Moravian missionary to set foot in Labrador, John Christian Erhardt, together with the crew of his ship, was slaughtered.

In London, under the care of Lucas, Mikak again encountered one of the Moravians she had met in Labrador, Jens Haven. He was there seeking permission from the British Crown to make another attempt to establish a missionary outpost in Labrador. Whether Lucas liked the idea or not, a dual role for Mikak began to emerge in the eyes of the English. Once back in Labrador, not only could she publicize the good nature of the English, she could also encourage her people to follow the Moravians and establish their own Christian community to the north. Perhaps, the governor was reasoning, it just might put a stop to the Inuit raids on his fishing stations.

Under orders from Palliser, Lucas escorted Mikak and her son back to the coast of Labrador, while the older boy remained in London. They were put ashore on an island north of Hamilton Inlet, together with the Inuit who had remained captive in York Fort. It was August 1769.

A year later Lucas, having quit the navy to go into business as a trader, arrived back on the Labrador coast. But Mikak was nowhere to be found. Into the fall he searched the coastline, without success. Nor did his anticipated trade with the Inuit prove fruitful. By late October, he was in command of a ship on its way from Newfoundland to Portugal with a load of salt fish. Reports say he was in a foul mood, and it was predicted that 'he will scarce know how to pass the winter without Mikak.' He would not have to try, for the ship he commanded was never heard from again. It was lost in the open Atlantic, taking the rueful Francis Lucas to his death.

Meanwhile, in Labrador, Jens Haven and a fellow Moravian had arrived on the coast also looking for Mikak, with the hope that she would help them establish a mission. Haven met her as she was travelling south to reunite with Lucas. For Haven she put on her rich English outfit, the king's medallion pinned in place. At her side stood her son, whom she had chosen to rename Palliser. Yet Mikak, though she relished her taste of English society, appeared content to be back with her people. For in company with her was a new husband.

Haven was able to persuade the pair to abandon their plans to meet Lucas, and instead guide him to where he might find a site for his mission. They boarded the Moravian ship and headed north. Their journey came to an end at a summer settle-

Moravian missionary conversing with the Inuit at Nain, watercolour by Maria Spilsbury, 1809.

ment of the Inuit where there had congregated, by Haven's eager count, five hundred people. To name the location of his mission he studied his Bible, where in Luke 7:11 he read, 'And it came to pass the day after that he went into a city called Nain.'

It was the start of the Moravian Church in Labrador. Palliser, though no longer governor, would soon hear of the benefits of his plan. Granting 100,000 acres (40,000 hectares) of land to Haven had been well worth it, even if for the Moravians the agreement had been a compromise. While their Christian teachings took hold, they were obliged to set up trading posts to satisfy the Inuit thirst for European goods.

As for Mikak, she and her family stayed in Nain for only a short time. The rest of her life proved to be turbulent, caught as she was between the Moravian wish to see her settle into the submissive life of the mission and the lure of the wilder side of European traders to the south. Her streak of independence did not suit the male polygamous tradition of her people. With a husband quick to abandon her for other wives, and a people jealous of the 'treasures' she had acquired during her stay with the English, Mikak found herself an outsider.

On hearing of the death of the princess in London who had given her the outfit that she still so liked to wear, Mikak was said to have displayed 'excessive grief,'

George Cartwright heads to his fox traps.

declaring, 'No! I no longer wish to go to England.' In her final days she came to Nain to seek the help of the Moravians. Before she died in 1795, she had given herself over completely to their teachings.

Thirty years later another missionary, a Methodist one, met an elderly Inuit man named Palliser near Hamilton Inlet, who told of a boyhood voyage to England, and of the strange things he had seen there. And when the man's wife appeared to the missionary she wore an outfit of velvet and of rich, embroidered cloth, trimmed with gold lace.

Lured by Labrador

Labrador has always attracted the nomadic gentry, the restless adventurers who seemed ill-content in their native lands. Its wild terrain and profuse wildlife, its relative closeness to both America and Europe has lured them with a power they seemed helpless to subdue. Many came and went. Of those that stayed for any substantial period, none had more impact than the Englishman George Cartwright.

Cartwright first came to the coast of Labrador in 1770, having made previous trips to Newfoundland, one that included an expedition led by his brother John up the Exploits River to the interior of the Island, in an attempt to establish friendly relations with the Beothuk. Although they didn't find any natives, they did learn much about their living conditions, leading Cartwright to predict their extinction. It may have been this experience that sharpened his interest in native cultures and brought him to Labrador, the start of a sixteen-year period of trading with the Inuit.

Unlike the Beothuk (or for that matter the general population of Newfoundland), the number of Inuit had grown considerably over past centuries. The Moravians had estimated an Inuit population of three thousand at the opening of their mission, representing as much as a six-fold increase since the Inuit first arrived from Canada's Arctic in the fifteenth century. This, in part, is the reason they were so bold in their attacks on white traders. As they told Cartwright many times, 'they could cut off all the English with great ease, if they thought proper to collect themselves together . . . ' Yet they always held back from an all-out assault. Their need for European goods was too strong, a situation Cartwright well understood.

Cartwright had little worry about any threat to his own life. Like the Moravian missionaries, he arrived in Labrador with an honest regard for both the Innu and the Inuit. When his years in Labrador were drawing to an end he would say of his main trading partners, the Inuit: ' . . . they are the best-tempered people I ever met with, and the most docile: nor is there a nation under the sun, with which I would sooner trust my person and property.' The openness of his dealings with them was not what the Inuit had experienced from the traders who came before him. There had been constant clashes with the lawless workers of Nicholas Darby, whose abandoned premises at Cape St. Charles were taken over by Cartwright.

Cartwright renovated one of Darby's winter buildings into a house for himself, naming it 'Ranger Lodge.' Situated in what is now Lodge Bay, it was the centre of his operations. Cartwright had come to make a living from the business of trading, but also was there, as he readily admitted, to satisfy his 'insatiable appetite for shooting.' He arrived in Labrador with 'three couple of foxhounds, one couple of bloodhounds, a greyhound, a pointer, a spaniel . . . ' He must have cut a commanding figure snowshoeing across the frozen marshes, a hound at the ready. Often he traversed the country in the company of the Inuit, eager to learn the secrets of their hunts. And when not in the chase or trading for baleen, fish, and furs (the polar bear was, of course, a favourite), he was there to take up the other duties that fell to him, be it midwife, preacher, or surgeon.

As a businessman, George Cartwright had been the one to form a trading partnership with Francis Lucas before Lucas's ill-fated voyage to Portugal. He had first

Attuiock, as drawn by Nathaniel Dance, London, 1773.

learned about Mikak from Lucas and must have traded with her during her family's frequent trips to southern Labrador. From Lucas, Cartwright learned of Mikak's sojourn in London, and it may well have been that story which prompted him to initiate a similar expedition in November 1772 for five of his Inuit friends. The woman Caubvick, her husband, Tookla-vina, and their young daughter, Ickeuna, together with her husband's brother, Attuiock, and the youngest of his wives, Ickcongoque, were all aboard the *Mary* as it set sail for England.

From Cartwright's account the stay in London proved a fine success. He took great delight in the attention they received, and perhaps even more in their reaction to the sights of the city. At the opera, sitting in the king's box, 'their pride was most highly gratified at being received with thundering applause by the audience . . . ' At discovering that St. Paul's Cathedral was man-made, 'they were quite lost in amazement . . . and insisted that it must be at least as high as Cape Charles.'

Attuiock found it all too burdensome and longed to be back in Labrador. Cartwright decided that country air and some exercise would remedy his confusion. He took Attuiock and his brother for a nineteen-kilometre dash on horseback, on a fox-chase through the countryside near his family home in Nottinghamshire. Although the Inuit 'had been on horse-back only three times before,' he wrote with obvious pride, 'they were both in at the death.'

In May, by then desperate to get back home, they all prepared for the return voyage to Labrador. The Inuit had barely settled aboard the vessel when Caubvick took sick. Her illness persisted and Cartwright arranged for a doctor to examine her. The diagnosis was smallpox.

Caubvick was not the first of her people to fall victim to the disease after being brought to England. Three years earlier, Karpik, the young boy who had remained behind in London when Mikak returned to Labrador, had contracted smallpox and died. This Cartwright had known. Why he would choose to risk his Inuit friends' meeting the same fate is difficult to surmise. Certainly the diagnosis overwhelmed him. It was, he wrote in his journal, 'as if he had pronounced my sentence of death.'

Death came not to Cartwright or Caubvick, but to the four other Inuit. Caubvick, though 'reduced to a skeleton,' her hair falling out and 'matted with the smallpox,' survived. As they neared the Labrador coast Cartwright prevailed on her to shave her head in order to prevent the spread of infection, but the hair she 'angrily snatched' away and locked in her trunk, never letting him near it.

As the ship reached the coast five hundred of her people had gathered in Lodge Bay to greet their returning relatives. When word spread of what had happened, there erupted 'violent, frantic expressions of grief.' Many of the women 'snatched up stones, and beat themselves on the head and face till they became shocking spectacles.' Yet, such was their respect for Cartwright that they did not blame the Englishman, even when, a year later, the bodies of Caubvick and her whole family were discovered at an Inuit encampment, dead from the spread of smallpox contracted from the contents of Caubvick's trunk.

Caubvick, as drawn by Nathaniel Dance, London, 1773. Inscribed on back: '. . . her name . . . in her language signified Wolverene.'

Cartwright went back to his hunting and trading. He lasted another dozen years on the Labrador coast. In the end he gave it up, not because he had lost interest in Labrador or its people, but because he was driven to bankruptcy by the attack of an American privateer. Following the outbreak of the American War of Independence, Captain John Grimes, in the *Minerva* out of

Boston, showed up sporting 'twenty nine-pounders' and 160 men, a crew that included several former servants of Cartwright turned informants. Grimes, the 'lying rascal,' and his troop, 'as great villains as any unhanged,' pillaged his premises up and down the coast, sailing off with £14,000 of traded goods, and leaving only enough provisions to keep Cartwright from starving during the winter.

'May the devil go with them!' raged Cartwright in his journal. 'As soon as they were gone,' he wrote, 'I took up my gun, walked out upon the island and shot a curlew.'

It was not the last Cartwright would see of skulduggery from the American colonies. Sharing the Atlantic passage, as well as some fine wine, with him in a brig out of St. John's was a traitor of larger dimension. Benedict Arnold, turncoat American general, was making his way to England to fetch his family and return with them to New Brunswick where, after quitting America, he had set himself up as a merchant. Partway across the ocean the brig fell victim to a violent storm. It tore most of the rigging from the ship and washed from the quarter-deck a sizable portion of the ship's fresh water. What water remained was quickly and scrupulously rationed.

The brig finally saw an end to its frightful journey, and in English waters Cartwright and the general parted company. Only then, with Arnold long gone, did Cartwright discover how his wine-drinking companion had increased the odds of his own survival. 'At such times as I was upon deck,' recounted the vexed Cartwright, 'general Arnold . . . had stolen most of the wine, which belonged to us both.' Arnold had then dealt the wine to the sailors for water, keeping all the precious liquid for himself, not telling Cartwright a word about it.

All confirmation that Benedict Arnold is only too deserving of his place in history. It may have been of some cheer later in life for George Cartwright ('Old Labrador' as he was known by then) to realize that although he had lost the battle, his reputation was still intact, unlike that of the well-watered general.

Beothuk Lament

By the time George and John Cartwright had made their trip up the Exploits in search of the Beothuk in 1768, the natives of Newfoundland were already in a desperate state. They could no longer find a part of the Island where they would be left in peace. Fishermen were taking over more and more of the salmon rivers, and furriers venturing farther and farther inland, both depriving the Beothuk of access to their traditional food supplies. Worse yet was their treatment at the hands of some of the white settlers. They 'are much greater savages than the Indians themselves,' he wrote, 'for they seldom fail to shoot the poor creatures whenever they can . . . '

Combined with the spread of disease to which they had little resistance, the Beothuk were set on an irreversible path to extinction. Why was this the case when other native peoples in North America, equally mistreated and equally susceptible to disease, were able to maintain a population level strong enough to bring them into the modern era? The Newfoundlanders of the day were no more barbarous than their counterparts in other parts of the continent. It would seem the answer may well lie in the pattern of non-Beothuk settlement, and in the natives' reaction to it.

The Beothuk population in the last decades of the eighteenth century had shrunk to a few hundred individuals. Other groups were constantly expanding into territory the Beothuk had once occupied. By then they were left with only Notre Dame Bay—a fraction of the coastline and interior they once knew. The Beothuk, rejecting the use of firearms, had invariably given way to the newcomers.

To the south, after a lengthy tradition of seasonal visits, Mi'kmaq from Nova Scotia arrived with a plan for permanent settlement. It came on the heels of the fall of the fort at Louisbourg, where the British had routed the French in 1758. The Mi'kmaq were particularly drawn to what was to become the centre of their population in Newfoundland—Conne River, at the head of Bay d'Espoir. They also established themselves along the southern end of the west coast at Bay St. George, and it was here they came face to face with the Beothuk. Oral tradition has it that for a time the two groups lived in harmony. But when conflict did arise, the Mi'kmaq, having long ago learned the use of firearms from the French, won out. The Beothuk retreated, some say for a time to Bonne Bay, farther north along the coast.

But by then the west coast was no longer the little-known shoreline it had been just a few decades before. Cook's surveys had brought new interest from the British fishery. Innu from southern Labrador were venturing across the Strait of Belle Isle once more, and before long the Mi'kmaq were moving up the coast from Bay St. George. The French, of course, had firmly established themselves within the

boundaries of the French Shore, bringing the Northern Peninsula under their control through much of the year.

From the other direction, the British fishery had moved farther and farther from
its traditional base on the Avalon Peninsula. This expansion was driven by the
thirst for other resources, ones the British said were not open to the French. Salmon
and seals were now being netted in their thousands. In comparison to the early
decades of the century, the tally of salmon taken by the English in Newfoundland
had risen more than five-fold, to an average of 3,400 tierces (550,800 kilograms) a
year. Add to that an annual harvest of thirty thousand seal pelts, and it becomes
obvious why the Beothuk were hard pressed to stay clear of Europeans.

The only territory that remained for them was part of Notre Dame Bay. There
they traversed its long waterway, called by the English 'The Exploits,' leading to a
body of water that for centuries had been a sanctuary of their people. On this 'Red
Indian Lake' they thought they were safe.

This pattern of continuously pulling back to seek uninhabited territory, of
never gathering in large numbers to overrun an enemy, is difficult to understand,
especially in light of how quickly other native groups had adopted the weapons

A Beothuk camp, from John Cartwright's map of 1768.

brought by Europeans. Why didn't the Beothuk trade furs for guns and in the end use them to defend themselves?

In the earliest days of contact, when the Beothuk did attempt to trade, they found themselves victims of unwarranted and savage attacks from fishermen. The deaths that resulted made them forever wary of the motives of Europeans. To get the goods they needed—the axes, the fish hooks, the nails to fashion into tips for hunting tools—they fell into a pattern of pilfering from the premises of the migratory fishermen after the fishermen had returned to Europe for the winter. The Beothuk had, in fact, all they wanted of Europeans, without having to come in direct contact with them. It was much safer than being shot at for no reason.

This is clearly evident in the early occupation of several sites, such as the one at Boyd's Cove. Here the Beothuk had planted themselves between two areas of European contact, the French migratory fishery to the west, and that of the English to the southeast. They thrived because they had the immediate coast and interior to themselves, and because during the winter months they could steal what they needed from the vacant premises up and down the shore.

There grew an intense distrust between the Beothuk and the other inhabitants of the Island. As the decades passed, any contact they had was fleeting and fraught with danger. Trade was insignificant. In any case, firearms were certainly not among the items Europeans would have been willing to make available to the Beothuk.

Neither was there any intermediary to interpret the actions of Europeans and mollify the reactions of the Beothuk. No missionaries had been sent to establish relations with the Beothuk in the early days of contact, in the way Roman Catholic priests had been sent to minister to the Innu and the Mi'kmaq, and the Moravians to the Inuit. When sympathetic officials did finally intercede, it proved too little too late.

With their range of habitation narrowed, and access to their food supplies increasingly denied, the Beothuk were forced to become bolder and bolder in their actions in order to fend off starvation. In a sense, they had nothing more to lose. They resorted to stealing salmon and nets, and cutting loose the settlers' mooring ropes. Fishermen and servants, themselves flogged if they were ever caught stealing, were quick to find ways of punishing the Beothuk. At times the conflicts escalated to outright warfare, and in some cases to murderous revenge attacks. There were several reports of the Beothuk subsequently attacking, then beheading, fishermen.

But the settlers maintained the upper hand, and the Beothuk grew terrified of them, especially certain individuals who had gained reputations as killers of Beothuk. As it turned out, the most notorious of these were not ordinary fishermen or servants, but a pair of men who should have been leaders in settling disputes in a civil manner. John Peyton, Sr., and his partner, Harry Miller, had started a salmon and fur-trapping business at the mouth of the Exploits River. In 1781, in retaliation for the theft of goods from their premises, they formed a raiding party and headed inland in pursuit of the natives. After about fifty kilometres they came upon a cluster of dwelling places—mamateeks—occupied by Beothuk. 'They immediately fired upon them with long guns loaded with buckshot; they killed and wounded several, the rest made their escape into the woods, some naked, others only half clothed . . . ' When Peyton spied one of the wounded holding a trap that had been stolen from his property, he 'wrested the Trap from him & and beat his brains out with it.' By some accounts sixty people were killed by gunshot, or died of starvation, left as they were in the snows of the surrounding woods by raiders who plundered their mamateeks and then burnt them to the ground.

Out of the range of what meagre law enforcement there was in Newfoundland at the time, the guilty went unpunished. And though there were some who treated the Beothuk with a measure of decency, the pervading notion, left unchecked by authorities, was that the 'Red Indians' were deserving of their fate. 'Why,' said Harry Miller years later, 'if we were not to shoot at 'em, others wou'd . . . Now wou'd not you kill any man that you found robbing your house or vessel?'

17 | Law Makers and Breakers

Patrick Knowlan, for stealing a counterpane, value 10d., from Peter Prim, sentence: That you P. Knowlan be whipped by the common whipper with a halter about your neck, that is to say you are to receive on your bare back twenty lashes at the common whipping post, then to be led by the halter to the Publick Path just opposite Mr. Peter Prims door and there receive twenty lashes as before, and then led as before to the Vice-Admiral's Beach and there to receive twenty lashes as before; to forfeit all your goods and chattels; to pay the charges of the Court, and to depart this Island by the first vessel bound for Ireland never to return on pain of having the same punishment repeated every Monday morning . . .

—Court proceedings, St. John's, 1777

St. John's in the mid-1700s.

Inadequate Admirals

The turmoil that enveloped the Beothuk world resulted not only from a moral failure of the individuals who held the guns, but equally from the inaction of the nation laying claim to the Island on which these horrific deeds were carried out. With one hand the British Crown penned a scattering of laws to keep order in the place, and with the other it cast aside any workable mechanism for their enforcement. The residents of Newfoundland were left to police themselves. And all the while the British treasury reaped the benefits of trade in cod, and the merchants of the West Country grew richer and richer.

Well into the eighteenth century the only semblance of law enforcement was the insufficient patrols of the Royal Navy and the antiquated, corrupt system of fishing admirals. Put in place for the migratory fishery two centuries before, this system was as self-serving as ever. In King William's Act Britain had made the barest of nods to the need for something more by instituting the right of appeal for decisions made by the admirals. 'If any party shall think themselves aggrieved they can appeal to the commanders of His Majesty's ships of war appointed as convoys,' reads section 15. And a few years later these naval commanders had, on paper, even more authority to administer government regulations.

In practice, their rulings fell to the wayside. Whatever they decided had no hope of ever being enforced if it didn't get approval from the fishing admirals, who were, after all, much more numerous and widely dispersed. The admirals had no intention of co-operating, especially in any decisions (such as the allocation of the prime fishing rooms) that might jeopardize their profits. They were in Newfoundland to serve the interests of their masters, not for whatever glory there might be in fairness. Or, to add a more earthy tone to the debate, we can take them for how they are often portrayed—as coarse and dim-witted louts. D.W. Prowse, our foremost historian writing in the nineteenth century, in one of the most eloquent of his many fiery moments, described a fishing admiral thus: ' . . . clothed . . . in his ordinary blue flushing jacket and trousers, economically besmeared with pitch, tar, and fish slime, his head adorned with an old sealskin cap, robbed from an Indian, or bartered for a glass of rum and a stick of tobacco.' And as for an evaluation of the man's work: 'Justice was freely dispensed to the suitor who paid the most for it . . . Sometimes, alas! the dignity of the Bench was diminished by the sudden fall of the Court prostrate on the floor, overcome by too potent effects of new rum and spruce beer.' We would like to think that Prowse exaggerated. But, alas, we fear, if he did so it was not by much.

What it all came down to, of course, was money. If a proper legal system were to be put in place (in which individuals resident in Newfoundland were employed solely to enforce the laws), how was it to be paid for? Ideally, with money raised from the commerce of the Island. Yet there was a long-standing agreement chis-

Governor Henry Osborn

elled in the minds of the merchants and the British Crown that the fishery was not to be taxed. And if not on the fish trade, what else was there on which to impose a levy?

The root of the problem was the fact that a legal system with year-round enforcement might just encourage more settlement. And who among them could foresee what that might lead to? Hand out money directly from the treasury for a proper legal system, the thinking went, and the next thing they'd be expecting is schools, and doctors, and roads. Where's the profit in that?

And Now, Governor

Occasionally, the luck of the draw brought Newfoundland a senior naval officer willing to inject some moral order into the place. When Captain Joseph Crowe showed up in St. John's in 1711 he was so appalled at the widespread drunkenness and the torrent of 'oaths, curses, blasphemous expressions and horrid impreca-tions' that he rounded up the ship captains and leading citizens and gave them all a stiff piece of his mind. He nailed up public proclamations declaring that the laws of England were to be enforced. No taverns open on Sunday, no profanity from the lips of anyone but a common seaman. But even Crowe realized that none of his efforts would survive without the appointment of a properly empowered magistrate, someone who preferred 'the Publique before his own private interest.'

Such unsparing moral lapse took place in later years that a few of the more decent citizens decided to take matters into their own hands. In 1723, with the fishing admirals and the naval commanders back in England for the winter, fifty-one of the townsmen affixed their signatures to a document declaring a right to hold court and punish the 'wicked and malicious men' loose in the streets, to put a halt to the 'Burglaries . . . Cattle Stolen, Merchants insulted, Servants cajoled to leave their Masters without just cause or Grievances . . . ' Still fresh in their minds was the murder five years before of Torbay planter Thomas Ford, by a servant never brought to justice.

These citizens were inspired to action by their reading of the English philosopher John Locke. His *Second Treatise* on civil government they quoted in a preamble to their declaration. If the fishing admirals were indeed as 'illiterate' and 'ignorant' as Prowse would have it, there were many under their jurisdiction who were not. Locke's polemics were being soundly debated in Newfoundland, albeit within a small group, and on safer ground since the Crown was so little in evidence. Nevertheless, this express use of his treatise as the basis for the framework of a governing body is the only such incidence known prior to the American Revolution.

The British masters weren't long getting wind that there was an unsanctioned scheme afoot in Newfoundland. Authorities in London made 'diligent enquiry.' It is not known if the good citizens of the city were called to task; we only know there is no record of any court being held the following year.

What did happen, however, was that it nudged the British toward taking some initiatives of their own. While some members of the Council on Trade (no doubt the dullards among the lot) recommended that the settlers all ship themselves off to Nova Scotia, in the end more conscious minds prevailed. Still, they couldn't decide exactly what to do. From citizens of Bonavista came complaints that in winter the town was rife with 'ill minded men who, knowing they cannot be punished in Newfoundland, commit many outrages, robberies and murders.' Then, in 1728, a boatload of Irish convicts on its way to Virginia made an unscheduled stop in Bay Bulls. When some of the ne'er-do-wells escaped and terrorized St. John's, it proved to be the decisive prod. Authorities in London finally made a decision.

In 1729 it was declared that the chief naval officer would become 'Governor and Commander-in-chief in and over the Island of Newfoundland.' The coastline from Placentia to Bonavista was divided into districts and authority granted 'to appoint Justices of the Peace and to erect Court Houses and Prisons.' The purse strings holding the money the British treasury had culled from their fishstore on the other side of the Atlantic were finally loosening, a little.

The first governor was Henry Osborn. He quickly toured the English Shore and 'out of the Inhabitants and Planters of the best characters' he appointed 'winter' justices of the peace, and constables to help them enforce the law. (Regrettably for the Beothuk, the division into districts had ignored the areas of English settlement beyond Bonavista.) The new appointees were to hold quarterly court sessions, and for each of them Osborn ordered a copy of Joseph Shaw's *The Practical Justice of Peace*, the name of their respective districts stamped in gold on the front covers. He ordered the construction of courthouses, stocks, and whipping posts, and, in St. John's and Ferryland, jails. To pay for it all he took the unheard of step of levying a tax: 'half a quintal of Merchantable fish per boat, and half a quintal for every boat's room . . . with like proportionable rate upon persons in trade . . . ' The inevitable protests to the Crown were ignored, and the tax held.

Of course, King William's Act (cherished defender of West Country interests) had not allowed the Crown to suspend the authority of the fishing admirals or that of the commanders of the navy's patrol vessels. And now that the admirals had competition, some of them were suddenly dashing about holding court, where they had languished in indifference before. But the governor was not deterred. A less irksome course of action might have been to show his colours only in the winter months when the admirals were long gone, but instead Osborn had the justices hear cases year-round. And, in an even bolder step, the justices not only ruled on petty criminal offences (as they had been officially empowered to do), but they also began acting on matters of civil law. The fishing admirals were under threat. And though they cried foul and the state of affairs in Newfoundland was once more vehemently protested in London, again little was done about it. It was the beginning of the end for the judicial role of (to let Prowse have at them one last time) 'the bullying old ship-fishermen.'

Governor George Rodney, in Newfoundland for an all-too-short three years, was known for dispensing justice in equal measure to the rich and the poor.

English Justice

Succeeding governors brought still more changes. By mid-century the right to try criminal cases and sentence felons had been sanctioned. With it came the establishment of a grand-jury system, and the appointment of sheriffs to ensure that the decisions of the court were carried out. This brought an end (except for cases of treason) to the ridiculously inept practice of transporting the accused and witnesses to England for trial. Newfoundland was finally deemed worthy of dealing with its own criminals. A fundamental right, but a mixed blessing.

On a note of morbid irony, one of its first cases of murder to go to trial was that of a justice of the peace who had worked tirelessly to get the new court system for Newfoundland. Dead was William Keen, a New Englander turned merchant in St. John's. In September 1754, nine men, and a woman dressed up as a man, had entered his house, some say in a conspiracy to revenge one of Keen's court decisions. In the course of scouring his house for money, they roused him from his bed. (They could hardly have thought that ten people in a house would do otherwise.) Ridding themselves of the eye-witness proved to be a tougher job than they expected, and in a last resort they smashed in his brains with the butt of a musket.

It was not a pleasant sight. Nor were the hangings shortly afterwards of four of the culprits. The body of the woman was spared public exhibit, unlike those of two of her fellows left for all to ponder on the gallows at the end of Keen's own wharf.

The murder had caused a greater sensation than usual, for all ten of the accused were Irish. Fear surged through the English populace, who took the murder as an indication of widespread looting and violence to come. The Irish, for their part, had grown justifiably incensed by their inferior treatment, especially the intolerance for their religion. None were allowed to own property and if discovered taking part in mass, the owner of the building where it was held was by law fined and the offending building burnt to the ground.

The French Call Again

The situation was exacerbated by the outbreak of the Seven Years War. In 1762 the French showed up in Newfoundland again. On landing they had at their sides 161 Irishmen. By some accounts they were Whiteboys, part of the fearsome resistance movement that had grown up in Ireland in reaction to the Penal Laws, brought to Newfoundland to encourage the Irish Catholics to take the side of the invaders against the repressive English.

Several hundred soldiers, led by Charles-Henri-Louis d'Arsac de Ternay, came ashore unchallenged at Bay Bulls on June twenty-fourth, and recruitment from the Southern Shore doubled their number of Irish. In St. John's d'Arsac de Ternay found a decrepit Fort William manned by a few ill-prepared soldiers. The garrison commander surrendered with hardly a second thought. A contingent of French and Irish, in cocky fine form, set off on a course of destruction through Conception and Trinity Bays.

In Trinity itself their warring ways were somewhat moderated by the taste of good brandy and the aroma of roast chicken. The French found a thriving outpost well stocked with provisions. Their diet of horsemeat gave way to 'Beefs, Calves, Sheep, and Fowls.' And when it came time to plunder and destroy, the enemy didn't seem to have the heart to do much on a full stomach. Any burning of ships and fish flakes that did take place came to a sudden halt when a message reached the troops that the British were under sail and heading to Newfoundland for a counterattack.

On the twelfth of September fifteen hundred men, some from New York, others out of Halifax and Louisbourg, and all under the command of William Amherst, dropped anchor off Torbay. Within three days d'Arsac de Ternay was running scared through the thick fog that had enveloped St. John's. He slipped past the Narrows, only his Fort William troops with him. His 'shameful Flight' had left nearly eight hundred more of his men behind, with no sane option but surrender.

The Treaty of Paris that ended the war put Labrador in the hands of the English. But the treaty was not particularly favourable to Newfoundland, a vexing deduction given that the French had lost the war and had inflicted considerable havoc on the Island in the process. 'The Newfoundland fishery is absolutely necessary for the support of the Kingdom,' ran the French argument at the peace talks. And, in western France, 'thousands of families would be reduced to beggary' if they were denied access to Newfoundland waters. Their right to the French Shore in Newfoundland was reconfirmed, and, in a moment of unfathomable generosity, the islands of St. Pierre and Miquelon given back to them. The Newfoundland fishery was a prime bargaining chip, the people who inhabited it still a minor consideration. (The more cynical would have it that England's chief negotiator took a bribe of £300,000.)

A Foothold in War

Over the next two decades new fortifications—Fort Townshend, Fort Amherst, and Chain-Rock Battery—were put in place in St. John's. By 1778 there were 426 troops

General William Amherst's plans for the fortification of Carbonear Island.

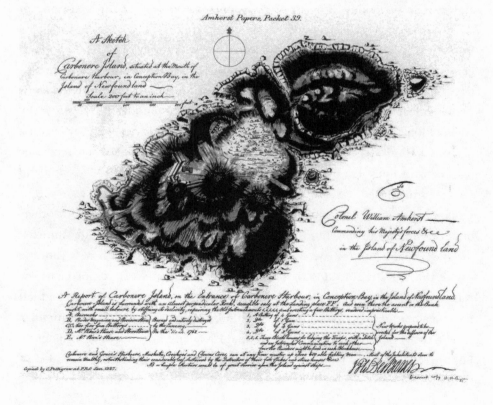

standing guard in the city, and two years later they were joined by three hundred of the Island's own men, its first-ever military contingent—the Newfoundland Regiment of Foot.

The American Revolution stirred things up again. In southern Labrador, the Yankee privateer *Minerva* put a quick and nasty end to George Cartwright's decade of work. On the unpatrolled south coast of the Island, fishing ships proved hopelessly easy targets for the Americans, as did the scattered vessels of the Grand Banks fishery.

With the entry of France into the war came the possibility of something more than a few patrol vessels heading off in a fruitless search for privateers. New targets emerged. The British in Newfoundland, under John Montagu, sailed off straightaway and captured St. Pierre and Miquelon.

That put a decisive end to its use by the French in transporting war supplies between Europe and America.

It was a much-needed show of strength, to which the English navy finally paid attention. Before long Newfoundland was being sent more frigates, some of which could boast three dozen guns. Even more batteries were being added to the fortifications in St. John's. And (hard to believe) batteries were being erected in outports around the Island, readied with small arms supplied by the Crown. (It had been not many years before that the secretary of state in London had pronounced, as he looked down his nose and across the Atlantic, 'The protection of the Inhabitants settled on the Island is neither practicable nor desirable.')

Prior to the American Revolution, Newfoundland had developed a healthy trade with New England—fish for essentials such as flour and livestock. (Given England's treatment of Newfoundland, it's too bad they hadn't traded in a few more political ideas at the same time.) In 1774, for example, some 175 vessels were making the annual trek from Boston, New York, Salem, and several other northeastern ports. Some of the Yankee traders also had on board sugar and rum from the West Indies. Their goods were cheaper than what English ships could supply, and the populations of both Newfoundland and Labrador had come to rely on them.

Then, with outbreak of war, came quick and drastic changes. The Tea Party shenanigans so outraged the British they shut down Boston Harbour. The other ports up and down the New England coast joined forces and retaliated where they thought they could inflict the most harm to the British. They banned all trade with Newfoundland.

It was a consequence the British had never considered. The fishing boats had already left England for the season, and when they arrived in Newfoundland they had to turn around and head straight back across the Atlantic for a supply of food. What they were able to secure on short notice wasn't much more than enough to supply their own men. That winter, and several succeeding ones, the settlers of the Island were left in a desperate state. 'There is a raging famine,' it was written of Conception Bay. 'None can express the heart felt woe of Women & Children mourning for want of Food.'

By 1783 the war had came to an end, though Newfoundland and Labrador had still another price to pay. With the Treaty of Versailles the English handed St. Pierre and Miquelon back to the French yet again, and the boundary of the French Shore was realigned. The coast from Cape Bonavista to Cape St. John, which the French had rarely used, was traded for the stretch from Point Riche to Cape Ray, thus giving the French access to the whole of the west coast of the Island. And, to add insult to injury, any English settlers who lived there were promptly expelled. The Americans were given the right to fish the Grand Banks, and 'all the other banks'

Two men of leisure look out on the 'seven islands of Placentia Bay,' 1786.

as well as any coastal waters used by the British. In the unsettled areas of Labrador they were even given the right to cure and dry their catches. Britain had lost more than its American colonies.

Yet some of the measures people had taken to make it through the war proved, in the end, to have economic benefits. Some settlers had managed to became more self-sufficient as agriculture expanded, the production of root vegetables more than tripling in some places. The war opened the markets of the West Indies to Newfoundland merchants, establishing partnerships with merchants in Bermuda to act as middlemen, the beginning of a long-term connection between the two islands. This, in turn, encouraged shipbuilding in Newfoundland.

As the economy became more diversified, a new merchant class arose, independent of the West Country. Substantial economic ties developed between Newfoundland and Canada as the Island sought much-needed food and fishing supplies. For the first time Newfoundland was looking west to Canada to see what trading alliances could be struck, rather than south to America as had been the tradition. From the frying pan into the fire? An answer would take a few centuries to formulate.

And something even more significant had happened. At long last the population of Newfoundland had started to take hold. It rose—to twenty thousand at the turn of the century—in part because of restrictions placed by the British on dealings with the new United States. In times of poor fishery there was no longer the option of moving on to New England. And now the migratory fishery, having lost many of its men to the navy during the war, was quickly being supplanted by the fishery of the residents. And with an economy less dependent on a single commodity—cod—the population found more reason to stay.

By the last decade of the century a full 90 per cent of the summer population stayed on for the winter, and some settlements could boast that almost half their residents were Newfoundlanders born and bred. As the migratory fishery faded, the proportion of single men lessened. The number of families rose, and with it the stabilizing influence of women upon the communities. There were schools and churches being built. There were even medical practitioners to be found, including a friend of Edward Jenner, John Clinch of Trinity, who in 1800 gave the first inoculations against smallpox in the new world.

For the ambivalent, it was time to settle down or move back to England and Ireland. All it took was a walk along the shoreline cliffs during the first warm day of spring (albeit May), a few lungfuls of air pungent with the scent of the salt water, and the sight of fishing boats, codfish to the gunnels, being rowed to shore . . . and was there really any choice? It was beginning to feel like home.

18 | In Spite of Mother England

Newfoundland has been peopled behind your Back.

—John Reeves, chief justice, to the British Parliament, 1793

A winter outing, as depicted by Margaret LeMarchant, governor's wife, St. John's, 1848.

Mansions and Tilts

Although things were looking up, the Newfoundland and Labrador of the latter part of the eighteenth century was not the prosperous place that some sojourning Englishmen had expected. Granted, if visitors stepped ashore in Trinity and tarried at the three-storey Georgian-style mansion of Susannah Lester and her merchant husband, Benjamin, they would have found themselves in luxury uncommon to much of the England they had left behind. And had they the good fortune to sup at Ranger Lodge in Southern Labrador, on a meal prepared by Mrs. Selby (George Cartwright's housekeeper), it's likely they would never taste such fine fresh game again. Or if by chance they had attended the Governor's Ball in St. John's in 1766, as did Joseph Banks, they would have danced and made merry before sitting down to an 'Elegant Supper Set out with all Kinds of Wines & Italian Liqueurs.'

But for most visitors the sights that did greet them were hardly worthy of a place whose fishery had been deemed (during negotiations to end the Seven Years War) more valuable 'as a means of wealth and power' than Canada and Louisiana combined. Even so, some writers were rather prone to extremes when trying to convey to their countrymen the flavour of it all. Joseph Banks, who so enjoyed himself at the ball given by Governor Palliser, in his next breath said of the town: 'for dirt and filth of all Kinds St Johns may in my opinion Reign unrivaled.' The town was assuredly no worse than the squalor to be seen in parts of London and Dublin, and the outports a darn sight healthier than much of rural Europe of the day. At least the air was fresh and the properties of a size and location that the sewage could be kept at a distance or washed away with the tide. The beauty of the landscape more than made up for any odoriferous moments among the fish offal, or (something on which many visitors were prone to dwell) the recurrent fog.

Of the general inhabitants, opinions varied, depending on the upbringing of the writer and his mood once he struck our shores. If he was willing to look beyond the roughened countenances (they were pioneers in an untamed land after all), then there was much to appreciate in them. 'They are a people of very bright genius,' said the missionary Lawrence Coughlan in 1780. 'I have known a man, who could not read a letter in a book, go into the wood, and cut down timber . . . and build a boat, rig it, and afterwards go to sea with the same boat.' Theirs was a

A winter tilt of the mid-eighteenth century.

coarse and plain existence, and most people of eighteenth-century Newfoundland had little energy (or money) remaining for even modest luxuries.

The earliest outport homes of the fishing families (for that in the main was who they were) were humble affairs of rough-cut timber nailed together upright and 'chinsed' with moss to keep out the draughts. These 'tilts' were not always success-ful in holding back the weather, even with the addition of tree bark or extra board. 'Several times this winter I have been snowed upon both as I sat in the house and lay in bed,' wrote William Thoresby of his time in Conception Bay.

Merchants could afford something more substantial, and the wealthier classes of St. John's might dwell in one of its 'many elegant homes . . . ' These well-to-do residents knew of tilts only as shelters for winter outings. 'Drawn in Sledges by one or two Horses or by Dogs . . . Lapped up in Furrs and warm Cloathing,' off they went to the Twenty Mile Pond (now Windsor Lake), 'a Rendezvous for Gentlemen and Ladys who go a Tilting,' by which was meant they took their sleds onto the frozen lake to 'skim o'er the glittering surface with all the security of a Bird.' Such playfulness was an early indication that life in St. John's was not what it was in the rest of the Island. (Might the long-standing rivalry between 'townie' and 'bayman' be setting roots?)

In Labrador the contrast in meaning was even greater again. There a tilt might be made of sealskins or a trapper might build a tilt line, a series of tilts as stopping points along his winter route. Of course, in Newfoundland there were summer tilts in places where people moved to the coast for a couple of months of seal hunting, and winter tilts for those who moved inland for a few weeks of snaring game. A permanent home might have a storage shed attached to it, a tilt-back. (That was only in places where, of course, it wasn't called a linny. Not to be confused with linnet, which is something altogether different.) If an inhabitant was a constant user of tobacco, he might be said to 'smoke like a tilt' and if he failed to provide for tomorrow, he would 'sit in one end of a tilt and burn the other.'

With a settled population was emerging a distinctive use of English. The inhabitants held to many of the words and phrases brought with them from England and Ireland, some of which would eventually fall out of use in their place of origin. The people made a point of adding new meaning to other words or devising variations to suit their needs. And where there was no word to be had, such as that needed to denote the shoreline between high and low tide, they invented one—'landwash.'

Food was simple fare for the most part. From the sea came fish of several kinds, seal, and seabirds—the staples of their diet—and from the land came small game and berries, to add variety. Even those living on the barest of rock tried to scrape together enough soil for a vegetable plot. Much was imported—salt pork, flour, molasses, hard biscuits, and other items easily preserved. Their combinations saw the evolution of some time-honoured recipes, such as boiled salt cod and hard biscuit, topped with rendered salt pork—fish and brewis. Joseph Banks in 1766 thought well of it: 'Luxury that the rich Even in England . . . might be fond of.' A more sound indication of its worth is its longevity in the place where it originated. It is still eaten today with great relish, and in both St. John's and the outports. On food we can sometimes all agree.

Drink, on the other hand, has not always outlived the centuries. The prime beverage of the early settlers was spruce beer, a fermented drink made from the boiling of black spruce boughs and molasses. It prevented scurvy, but in excess led to drunken stupors, which the single males (who made up the majority of the population in most places) seem to have been especially prone to. It had its unwavering champions, however. Aaron Thomas, writing in 1794, was especially keen on the brew. Even the moderate drinker, he claimed, found 'his facultys vigorous and strong, a mind Cool and Easy and an understanding comprehensive, capacious and intelligent.' One wonders why its usage ever waned.

Royally Brash

To judge by many a commentator's dispatch and governor's report, the moral welfare of Newfoundland in the eighteenth century was adrift. Governor Palliser wrote of 'our wild ungovernable people' living around the Strait of Belle Isle. Some residents of Trinity (one presumes not the wealthy Lesters) were said to be 'in a manner in an original state of nature, or if you please, little better than savages.' The folk of Trepassey fared no better. In summary they were but 'drunken Irish fishermen.' Though most writers were careful to note that there were exceptions, in general it was their considered opinion that the place was in need of a little taming, a little moral uplift.

Enter His Royal Highness, the Prince of Wales, the future 'Sailor King,' William IV of England. The young royal visited Newfoundland during the summer of 1786, and in his capacity as commander of the frigate *Pegasus* executed the duties of surrogate judge. How fine an undertaking—to bring some propriety to the island, by the hand of a future monarch, no less.

The prince was not known for his restraint. Eager to prove himself, he dispensed justice with swift excess. He was especially keen on the cat-o'-nine-tails, as his time in Placentia attested. There he seized the alleged leader of a riot, and immediately bore him to court, ordering a hundred lashes, 'which punishment was immediately inflicted with the utmost severity.' At eighty lashes the sentence was halted because the man

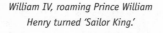

William IV, roaming Prince William Henry turned 'Sailor King.'

could endure no more. The following day more facts of the case came to light, and in the process it was discovered that 'they had whipped the wrong man.'

And if William's public life had its miscalculations, his private fared no better. The prince passed his twenty-first birthday while in Placentia. In keeping with his 'wildness,' as he himself called it, he got royally drunk. The celebrations took place aboard the *Pegasus*, below deck, though 'by some means . . . His Royal Highness contrived to crawl up to the main-deck . . . ' There he was recognized by other members of his crew, in an equal state of inebriation. In a late-night romp they 'mounted him on their shoulders and ran with him violently from one end of the deck to the other.' His head skimmed the beams several times. He barely escaped alive for 'one blow at the rate they were going would inevitably have killed him.'

William established a reputation for poor judgement early in his voyage to Newfoundland, and kept finding ways of adding to it as the weeks went by. The naval governor of the Island had sent him to the south coast to keep him away from the French, and out of harm. What he hadn't counted on was the loose-tongued prince pitting himself against the Roman Catholic cleric in Placentia.

William's own religion had fallen on hard times. Placentia had not seen an Anglican missionary for thirty years, nor had its church been replaced since it burnt years before. Many of its congregation, for want of an outlet for their faith, had taken to attending the services provided by the newly arrived Catholic priest, Edmund Burke. This did not sit well with the most resolute of Placentia's Anglicans, and in Prince William they finally found an influential ally. The prince promptly evicted the Catholics from the courthouse where they had been holding service while their new church was under construction. He forbade Burke to baptize or marry any Protestants, even if they requested it. He ousted any Catholics holding public office. And generally left Placentia feeling very good about what he had done to re-establish the Church of mother England.

In St. John's five days later William encountered the head of the Roman Catholic Church on the Island, James Louis O'Donel. When O'Donel protested to the governor that his flock in Placentia had been mistreated, the Prince of Wales was roused to new heights of indiscretion. 'He insulted me with obscene language and with great violence he threw a heavy iron file at me,' wrote O'Donel sometime later. Fortunately, the file only glanced his shoulder, though the episode did send O'Donel into hiding. There he remained, until twelve days later the prince boarded the *Pegasus* and 'ran thro' the Narrows' on his way to Halifax, much to the relief of O'Donel, the governor, and a generally indulgent population. By this time, the future king of England had learned a few of the many things Newfoundlanders already knew about civility.

Law in the Hands of the People

A fair appraisal would conclude Newfoundland and Labrador upheld law and order much better than anyone could have expected, given the meagre support it received from England. Governor John Campbell in 1786 went so far as to claim that there were 'fewer crimes and gross misdemeanors committed on the whole island than in the smallest county in England.' Whether or not we choose to take him at his word, this ragged stretch of coast was doing reasonably well for an underpopulated, half-remembered place without any elected officials, or hint of them for some time to come.

In fact, in some cases, rather than any laxness in the judicial process, the courts might legitimately be accused of overreacting, as with their judgement of the Ferryland 'riots' of 1788. One hundred and fourteen men were found guilty of unlawful assembly, of causing 'great and manifest danger' to person and property. A trio of judges slapped them with £640 in fines, sentenced five ringleaders to flogging, and ordered eleven more deported.

One suspects the so-called riots weren't a great deal more than a bunch of young Irish bucks having their annual punch-up at the end of a long idle winter.

Little St. Lawrence by J. S. Meres, from the log of the Pegasus, *1786.*

Some said what started as a 'hurling' match (an old sport not unlike field hockey) gave way to faction fighting, fisticuffs roused by the county rivalries brought with them from Ireland. And one has to question whether the Protestant élite that made up the judiciary weren't trying to contain what they saw as a Catholic threat to their authority, to rein in the Irish on the pretext that drunken males smashing in each other's skull on the Ferryland Downs was a danger to the few families and property owners.

The Irish who chose the Southern Shore seemed forever to be dealing with incidents, real or enhanced, that lurked outside the boundaries of the law. Legend has it that in mid-century a band of escapees from the Royal Navy took to the Butter Pot Barrens and there, as 'Masterless Men,' survived by hunting and raiding, and confounding the authorities who had nerve enough to come in pursuit of them. Rather like the antics of Sherwood Forest, without the moderating influence of Maid Marian. The story goes that after several years a-roaming, only four had eluded capture and the noose, and these dauntless souls eventually slipped back into society and settled, married, and raised families. (And, it is tempting to add, became lawyers and entered politics. But that would be adding rumour to an already nebulous story.)

Far from nebulous was the sight in Bay Bulls and Petty Harbour in July 1789 of the brig *Duke of Leinster*, its crew herding ashore 12 women and 102 men and boys, Irish convicts arriving unannounced in the dead of night, and with the compliments of the lord mayor of Dublin. Their original destination was supposedly Australia, but, shipping costs being what they were, it was decided that some barren fishing outpost on the other side of the Atlantic was a more economical dumping spot and potential penal colony.

Once 'those wretches' (as the governor, Mark Milbanke, called them) had made their way north to St. John's, 'open and professed Villainy' took hold, sending the town into a state of panic. Burglaries abounded, with 'the lower order' of permanent residents enthusiastically joining in. Worse still, the typhus the convicts brought with them spread like mad, eventually causing the death of two hundred of the townspeople.

The judiciary in St. John's stepped in to put a swift end to it all. Their action was certainly not the response of a lawless backwater, and was well beyond what might have been expected, given the limited statutory law at the time. Taxes were levied so the convicts could be confined (in a large isolated house a distance inland) and fed, while a ship was being contracted for their expulsion. Within three months most were back on the doorstep of his lordship in Dublin.

It was not a cheap undertaking. Nor was it a simple one, since many of the residents openly disputed that they should be the ones to pay for someone else's skulduggery. But its success was also a clear sign that co-operation for the common good, independent of outside support, was needed to carve out an existence on this Island. Some things, by their size and risk, would only ever be accomplished if the populace pulled together. Such tasks would be a recurring feature of our society, and proved to be a major component in shaping a country and an identity. Let it be said that Newfoundland and Labrador was built from within, and grew in spite of, rather than with the blessing of, its masters in England.

19 | Mixed Blessings

. . . in this part of Newfoundland they never had a Minister, till the Providence of God sent me there . . . As to the Gospel, they had not the least Notion of it: Drinking, and Dancing, and Gaming, they were acquainted with; these they were taught by the Europeans who came annually to fish . . .

—Laurence Coughlan, 1776

The inscriptions on this pair of chalices read simply,
St. John's Church, Newfoundland, 1785.

Naked before God

Among the many exquisite pieces of church silver in Newfoundland are two chalices: one, made in London and inscribed 'Given by His Royal Highness Prince William Henry to the Protestant Chapel at Placentia in Newfoundland 1787'; the second, made in Dublin and inscribed 'Fr. John Broe for the Franciscans in Wexford 1768,' was brought by Bishop Fleming a few decades later for the Catholics in St. John's. Both are for the service of Communion, but serving two Church communities often at odds with each other.

That friction, and the eventual measure of harmony, played an extraordinary role in the shaping of Newfoundland and Labrador. Religious stripe was a person's defining feature, more often than class or occupation. It would come to determine not just how individuals spent a Sunday but what school their children went to the rest of the week, with whom they socialized, who would hire them, and how they would mark their ballots on election day.

The Church of England, Anglicanism as it is now known, had remained the official denomination of Newfoundland and Labrador through the 1700s. In Labrador, England had relented, for the sake of peace with the Inuit and harmony in the fishery, and allowed Moravian missionaries to go where Anglicans had no desire to tread.

Prince William, staunch anti-Catholic that he was, in 1786 gathered all Placentia's male residents over the age of twelve and made them swear allegiance to the king, and by implication (at least in his own mind) to the Church of which the monarch was the head. When he commissioned the Communion silver for the yet-to-be-completed Anglican chapel, it was with the firm belief that it would help stave off the tide of Catholicism. That would prove to be a luckless endeavour, particularly in Placentia, but also through much of the Island.

For although the Anglican Church had official recognition, and filled the ranks of the judiciary, it lacked the very thing that the people most wanted—enough missionaries to live and preach among them, to baptize their children and give their dead proper burial. 'Placentia, St. Mary's, Fortune Bay, and Trepassey are inhabited by the English, and very populous: and yet the Word has not been preached in that part of the island for thirty years,' it was said in 1784. And, except for a few pockets of Quakers (in Trinity and Placentia, and Bay de Verde), religious leaders weren't rising from the ranks of the local population. As much as it galled him, it shouldn't have been any surprise for Prince William, when he arrived two years after that, to learn that residents of Placentia ' . . . carried many scores of their Children . . . to St. Peter's [St. Pierre] to be baptized by a French Priest.'

You would think the English would have realized that faithful subjects cannot live on cod alone. Yet, throughout the eighteenth century the spiritual needs of the population were only haphazardly addressed. It was true that Newfoundland's reputation as snow-bound and desolate did little to entice would-be missionaries, but because their presence didn't bear directly on the profits of the fishery, the Crown wasn't about to offer much encouragement.

At the beginning of the century King William's Act had let it be known that 'all the inhabitants shall strictly keep every Lords Day.' And that 'none keeping taverns shall sell wine &c. on that day,' as if everyone would pay attention to laws governing their intake of alcohol once the navy vessels set sail for England in the fall. Some of the more sober residents of St. John's petitioned the Crown for a minister and received the support of the bishop of London (who, from the comfort of Lambeth, called for 'a good man to live there and make them good Christians'). A naval chaplin, Reverend John Jackson, was appointed to the garrison at Fort William, most likely the first Church of England missionary stationed in Newfoundland since Erasmus Stourton was unceremoniously ousted from Baltimore's colony at Ferryland.

Jackson, his weary wife, and their eight children arrived in 1701, on the strength of a commitment of fifty pounds per annum, to be augmented each fishing season by the value of several quintals (hundredweight) of cod. It was an obligation the citizens were quick to shirk, despite the fact that within a few years Mrs. Jackson had three more little ones scampering among them. In 1703 came relief—in the form of a stipend from the Church of England in London, from its newly formed Society for the Propagation of the Gospel in Foreign Parts (the SPG). The citizens finally anted up some fish as their part of the bargain, then cut and sawed timber to erect a modest church. Jackson lasted two more years. His stay in St. John's ended in the wake of a series of confrontations with the underhanded and brutal commander of Fort William, Thomas Lloyd. The minister pointedly accused Lloyd of playing the flute and revelling in the streets on the Sabbath in order to divert attention from church, though the commander's indifference to Christian teachings had wider limits, to judge from Jackson's choice description of him: 'a great promoter of whoring and Adultery among the people.' Somewhat the carnal Pied Piper, Lloyd was said to entice his companions 'to dance stark naked together to the shame of all modest people.' The city had never seen the like before, nor has it seen such raunchy goings-on since (though some would argue that latter-day George Street on a Saturday night has its moments). Lloyd was to receive his comeuppance, however, for he was the same wilful slacker who was found racing around in his dressing gown trying to mount some semblance of a defence as his Fort William was overrun by Saint-Ovide de Brouillan in the early hours of New Year's Day 1709.

Anglican Inroads

Reverend John Jackson's few years in St. John's were the start of a long relationship between the SPG and Newfoundland. Though most communities on the Island never laid eyes on a minister throughout the century, Anglican missionaries did turn up in several places along the east coast from Placentia to Bonavista. Not surprisingly, the least remote, St. John's, proved the most inviting. Many who came, like Jackson, and Robert Kilpatrick in Trinity, discovered few citizens willing to turn over any of their meagre wages in support of a church. After sixteen months Kilpatrick had himself removed from 'this unpleasant corner of the earth' and shipped off to New York (though within two years he had seen the light and was back on the Island, having found the American colonies even more unpleasant than Newfoundland).

It took a particular breed of the ecclesiastic to forgo the rolling pasturelands of Kent and Devonshire for the winter barrens of Newfoundland. And no doubt a few of these preachers were prompted to take up the quest overseas by a mother Church eager to be rid of them. Once they were in Newfoundland, their excitement at bringing God to the grateful heathen was often overshadowed by the realities of day-to-day living. And rather than finding themselves privileged, as they might have expected, they ended up doing what most everyone else was doing—struggling to get enough food to keep body and soul together.

Needless to say, the settlers who petitioned for a minister were not always thrilled with who was sent their way. And confrontations often led to a whirlpool of controversy, as the reports to the SPG make clear. Nevertheless, it was by the

Laurence Coughlan

presence of these missionaries that the foundation for the Church of England in Newfoundland was laid. And, curiously enough, that of Methodism as well.

Into relatively populous Conception Bay came Laurence Coughlan in 1766, under the sponsorship of the SPG and preaching as the ordained Anglican that he was. Underneath the vestments, however, beat the heart of a Methodist, a follower and one-time associate of John Wesley. In due course Coughlan began going house to house with a more fervent message. Discouraged by the initial response, he persisted and eventually discovered his words taking hold 'like Fire'—a Methodist 'awakening' manifesting itself in great outpourings of faith where 'some were cut to the Heart, and others rejoiced in loud Songs of Praise.'

The Anglicans hardly knew what hit them. Great numbers of young women were embracing Coughlan's damnation of drinking and wantonness. There were numerous impassioned deathbed conversions. 'The People at Harbour-Grace and Carbonear are going mad,' the non-followers avowed. Then Coughlan's attacks turned personal—from his 'Anglican' pulpit he accused one merchant of adultery, and physically intervened to put a stop to his labourers working on Sunday. He contested the moral standards of a second merchant, then in an open confrontation, refused him permission to act as godparent in baptism.

It proved the preacher's undoing. The merchants shot off a letter to the governor, scorning Coughlan as 'a Person of no Education,' as 'ignorant' and 'very unfitt' for his duties. He accepted bribes, they said, and, worse still, interfered in the fishery. The governor was John Byron (grandfather of the poet Lord Byron), himself no stranger to onerous circumstance. But by then Coughlan had anticipated the inevitable. He departed Harbour Grace and returned to England, eventually breaking his ties with the SPG.

But Laurence Coughlan had planted the seed of Methodism in Newfoundland. In Conception Bay had been built a church to seat four hundred, the first

Methodist church in what is now Canada. Through the work of the lay preachers Coughlan had left behind, word spread north to Trinity and Bonavista Bays. The Anglican ministers who came in his wake, such as James Balfour, who transferred from Trinity in 1775, felt the sting of 'hot headed Enthusiastic people.' And soon to arrive in Newfoundland were more so-called Dissenters—Congregationalists, and later, Presbyterians, in numbers high enough to eventually warrant their building their own churches. And like Dissenters everywhere, they were not only at odds with Catholics, they were at odds with each other.

Popery and Bigotry

What they did agree on, however, was that they would rather share the souls than have them turn to the Church of Rome, the 'Popery,' as they were fond of calling it. Yet the fact remained that nearly half of the population were now Irish Catholics, and if they continued to be denied basic religious freedoms, it would only be a matter of time before they took matters into their own hands.

Fortunately, Britain was being forced to have second thoughts about the treatment of Catholics within its own borders. In the throes of war with the American colonies, it needed Catholics to fill the ranks of the military. Britain could hardly justify having Catholic soldiers die to defend a country that denounced their right to worship (and, if they were ever killed on the battlefield, the right of their relatives to bury them in the way they saw fit). Then there was the whole question of the Irish siding with the enemy in what looked like impending war with France and Spain. And with the American Revolution came the added fear of a massive exodus from Ireland to America, where as Irish (and, of course, white) immigrants they would be guaranteed equal rights. There was even a vocal minority of English politicians (radicals, no doubt) who declared that a basic right of all citizens was to live without fear of persecution.

The result was the repeal of the notorious Penal Laws in 1778. With it came a comparable change in policy for Britain's overseas territories. As was the case for many of the islands of the West Indies, instructions were handed to Governor Richard Edwards of Newfoundland that granted 'full liberty of conscience' to all citizens. No more 'except Papists' clauses. It was exactly what the Roman Catholics on the Island were wanting to hear.

But hear it they did not. Governor Edwards ignored the change, which he could do without much problem since there was no legislature in Newfoundland. Edwards feared invasion from the French, who had by this time sided with the Americans in their War of Independence. He feared further upheaval in a society trying to cope with the famine that resulted when the Americans put a stop to their trade with Newfoundland.

Five years later, with the war over and a new governor in place, the Catholics (and Protestant Dissenters) saw their long-awaited rights put into effect. In 1784 Governor John Campbell, himself raised Presbyterian, issued a statement to the justices of the peace: ' . . . you are to allow all persons inhabiting this island to have full liberty of conscience, and the free exercise of all such modes of religious worship as are not prohibited by law.' Long overdue, but a momentous day nonetheless.

Not everyone cheered the proclamation. Some declared it more likely than ever that the Irish and French would plot to drive the English from the Island. The prosperous Trinity merchant Benjamin Lester bemoaned the sight of Catholics walking to mass on Sunday, 'instead of attending to cure the fish . . . as usual (and necessary) . . . ' James Balfour, Anglican minister in Harbour Grace, hastily penned his predictions to the SPG: ' . . . our Church will have little footing here soon on account of Methodists and Papists.'

The edge of panic in his words was no doubt caused by the fact that into Harbour Grace had sailed Patrick Phelan, a Franciscan from Ireland. He spoke

St. John's, ca. 1770. First the fishery, then religion, would take a firm hold.

Gaelic and could perform the sacraments in the only language many of the Irish in Newfoundland could understand. Not only that, he clearly displayed his commitment to his people by undertaking risky treks to outlying areas, something that Balfour (who seemed constantly to be complaining of 'this terrible clime') was loath to do. On one such winter mission to Grates Cove in 1799, the Franciscan fell through the ice and was drowned.

To Placentia in 1785 came Edmund Burke, of the Dominican order, sent there in part to rid the Church of the fiery, renegade priest Father Lonergan, who had shown up the previous year from France, one of several unauthorized priests found to be roaming the outharbours of Newfoundland at the time. The following summer it would be the equally hotheaded Prince William whom Burke would have to confront. The priest survived and before long the parish flourished. He was said to have brought three thousand people into his flock (some from as far away as Fortune Bay), converting many lapsed Anglicans in the process. An Anglican priest, John Harries, arrived on the scene rather too late, and was left to conclude that the Catholic Church did indeed rule the day, leaving his own Church but 'within the limits of Toleration.' Burke was an affable Irishman who liked his drink, the beginning of a long line of priests to solidify the foundation of the Roman Catholic Church in Newfoundland. But he was also a keen communicator and a bit of a radical, to be noted for using English instead of Latin for much of the mass.

Burke's secondary calling, that of the fishing business, no doubt contributed to his commitment. By one estimate he was bringing in £300 a year, a very substantial sum that must have made anything the SPG could offer Harries look rather paltry. So influential was Burke that when at the turn of the century he took a position in Nova Scotia as head of all the Maritime missions, great numbers of Placentia's Catholics followed him to Halifax, forming the majority of that city's Catholic congregation.

The Catholic Pastor
The continuing success that greeted the Catholic initiatives in Newfoundland could only have further frustrated the Protestants, and by this time the SPG in London would have been growing mighty weary of the whining. The Anglican Balfour in Harbour Grace, already at his wit's end with Methodists, had summed

up his dismay: 'Popery is like to be the only prevailing principle round this island.'

In the battle for the Christian unclaimed, the Catholics took a giant leap forward. The governor had even permitted them to perform marriages, something unheard of in England. Then in 1784 the Vatican declared Newfoundland to be an independent ecclesiastic territory, the first in English-speaking North America. Pope Pius VI placed it directly under the administration of the Holy See, a decision that would have far-ranging consequences for the Island. (Two centuries later, Andy Jones, great comic actor and writer—whose most memorable send-ups are of Catholic priests—ruminated quietly on growing up in St. John's: ' . . . there was the feeling that you somehow had a connection with Rome . . . you owned a little part of that because you were Catholic.')

The early achievements of the Church were due in no small measure to the arrival of James Louis O'Donel, a priest from Waterford in Ireland, that long-standing centre of the Newfoundland trade. The pope had appointed the well-liked O'Donel to the position of prefect apostolic. The man was both a scholar (having lectured in theology and philosophy in Prague) and a pragmatist who spoke Gaelic—a healthy combination in dealing with the taut religious atmosphere of the day.

O'Donel was up to the task, rebounding not only from the barbs of non-Catholic clergy and the less tolerant governors who followed Campbell, but also the challenges to his authority from within his own Church, and, of course, the infamous iron file from the hands of Prince William. Through it all the erudite cleric maintained his sense of humour, as evidenced by his letters, especially those to the bishop of Quebec. (In one he joked about the regulation in Quebec of Catholics having to take oaths on Protestant Bibles. 'I knew a Bostonian servant here,' he recounted, 'who took his oath against drinking . . . which he did not keep for 3 days & to excuse himself . . . said

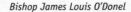

Bishop James Louis O'Donel

he only swore upon a Popish prayer Book, one word of which he did not believe.') In 1796 O'Donel's perseverance and ability to rise above the fray of petty dispute led to his nomination, and then consecration in Quebec City, as Newfoundland's first Catholic bishop.

He was especially astute in his dealings with the governors who came and went during his tenure in Newfoundland. He maintained clear and unequivocal support for the British Crown and demanded similar loyalty of his congregations. He had it written into the Church statutes, including regular and public prayers for the British monarch (though some of his successors must have choked on the words when Prince William ascended the throne as William IV a few decades later). O'Donel stilled the waters between church and state, allowing his priests to do what they did best—preach and convert, with, as the non-Catholics of his day noted, alarmingly 'active zeal.'

In 1800, with Ireland in a state of revolution, talk of uprising was afoot in Newfoundland. Pockets of the Society of United Irishmen secretly gathered support among the soldiers of the Newfoundland Regiment. An armed gathering was planned for the night of April twenty-fifth. Their exact plan was never clear, but bloodshed would certainly have been the outcome. When O'Donel got wind of it, he relayed what he had been told to the governing officials, and at the same time worked to convince his own people that such an uprising would prove useless and would only impede further gain for the Irish.

To O'Donel must go much of the credit for heading off the sectarian violence that later plagued Newfoundland, as it did to a much greater extent Ireland itself. Some contend, in no uncertain terms, that O'Donel was a weak leader who gave in too easily to the Protestant leadership of the Island. They celebrate the rebellion and condemn O'Donel for his part in suppressing it. The fact that five of the rebels were captured and hanged on the same site (now the corner of Belvedere Street and Barnes Road) where the uprising was aborted did little to endear him to future generations of Irish nationalists. They prefer the later bishops who openly challenged the governing and merchant élite. That was not O'Donel's way. Taking his inspiration from the tenets of his faith, he preferred to think that more could be gained through peaceable means, that in the end justice would win out, without bloodshed.

O'Donel eventually chose to retire, and was given a modest pension from the

British government. In some eyes it was a Protestant payoff for keeping his Irish congregations under control. Gathering for a farewell dinner in his honour were leading citizens of St. John's, both Catholic and Protestant, many of whom O'Donel could count among his close friends. He spent his final years in a Franciscan monastery in Waterford, still dealing with a slight stroke he had suffered during the delivery of a sermon in St. John's several years earlier. In 1811, while reading from his beloved collection of books, he fell asleep, and awakened to find his chair in flames, the result of a toppled candle. He died within a few weeks, never having recovered from the trauma of the event.

More than a century later, one of his successors would describe James Louis O'Donel as 'a man of plain and simple tastes, though of wide worldly experience, full of sound sense and playful amiability; a true pastor . . . ' One imagines O'Donel would surely have relished the thought that Catholics and Protestants (though it would take a very long time) would one day find ecumenical occasions to drink from the same chalice.

20 | Of Fish and Fate

As Newfoundland is subject during the summer to sudden showers, the hurry and confusion which these frequently create throughout the whole place can hardly be described . . . the flakes are then in an instant covered with men, women, and children, busily employed in turning up the fish or in making it up into faggots; the profits of the whole voyage, the means of paying the debts contracted, and of procuring supplies for the support of the family during the ensuing winter, may all depend upon the exertions of that moment.

—Lewis Amadeus Anspach, 1819

The nineteenth-century codfishery at Heart's Content.

Our Bit for the Empire

In 1770 the per capita exports of Newfoundland amounted to twelve to fifteen pounds sterling. No other territory in North America could boast anything near that figure. South Carolina's, the second highest, stood at four pounds, and that largely produced by slave labour. After the American War of Independence, the number of British fishing ships showing up on our shores each spring reached a record four hundred vessels. Each fall they shipped out nearly one million quintals of fish! To say nothing of a French fishery that sailed away with several hundred thousand quintals more.

You'd think Newfoundland and Labrador would be awash in capital, that the rich wouldn't be able to build their marble-filled mansions fast enough. They did, in fact, build several such mansions, but not in Newfoundland. They were erected in the southwest of England, and in the southeast of Ireland, where the merchants, having amassed their wealth in the cod trade, retired in luxury. Many of them had never set foot in Newfoundland.

They were called 'merchant princes' with good reason. Upton House, the lavish Georgian mansion near the harbour at Poole in Dorset, was constructed with the hefty profits the Spurrier family took from their saltfish operations in Burin and Fortune Bay, and their salmon fisheries on the southern Avalon. From his enterprises in Trinity and Bonavista Bays, the Quaker Joseph White left the princely sum of £120,000 when he died in 1771 (and that despite not carrying insurance when he lost all but one of his ships during the Seven Years War). Other Quakers, George and William Penrose in the Irish city of Waterford, grew so rich supplying salt pork to the migratory fishery that they started a glass factory, and grew even richer in the process, as the founding manufacturers of Waterford crystal.

The Lesters, and their successors, the Garlands, at least left Trinity with something to show for all its commercial activity in the eighteenth century. Several of the town's noteworthy buildings are reminders of a time these families operated dozens of fishing and sealing properties from Trinity to Venison Island in Labrador, supplying upwards of three thousand fishermen. This show of prosperity, of course, pales in contrast with what was to be found back in Poole. They sank their cod money into property, including two country estates, and what came to be known as the 'Mansion House.' (Hardly to be confused with the more modest

Upton House in Dorset was built by Christopher Spurrier. Though he reaped the profits of the fish trade, it is thought he never set foot on the Island.

'mansion' in Trinity.) It's a monument of sorts to Newfoundland's vast contribution to Britain's economy and the building of its Empire. One aspect of the mansion's architectural detail is an especially fitting tribute. The dining room's marble fireplace is adorned with a matching pair of marble cod fillets.

At the height of the fishery 80 per cent of the residents of Poole drew their income from the fish trade in Newfoundland and Labrador. Large tanneries fed more than a dozen cobblers shops, turning Newfoundland sealskin and other hides into the boots the fishermen wore to the Island and the Grand Banks. Here and in neighbouring towns were the mills that yielded the thick flannel for their clothing, the factories that turned out the hooks, rope, and nets. The region abounded in candlemakers, shipwrights, and anchorsmiths who thrived on the Newfoundland trade. And from here came the huge quantities of food needed to last thousands of men several months. What this corner of England couldn't supply, the stopping-off points in Ireland did. In Waterford, besides the hog farms and butter factories, were bakeries to fill the constant demand for ships' biscuit, hardtack, much of it made by Jacob's, another business that would rise to greater heights.

Fishing for Opportunities

Sir Hugh Palliser, former governor of Newfoundland, friend and backer of James Cook and Joseph Banks, died in his country home in England in March 1796. Champion of the migratory fishery, Palliser had worked tirelessly to personally assert British authority along the coast of Newfoundland and southern Labrador. He would have been aggrieved to know that the West Country merchants would never again have such influence as they did during his five years as governor. His *Act for the Encouragement of the Ship Fishery,* which the British Parliament passed into law in 1775, was the last great strategy for clinging to the migratory fishery. And the very aspect of it that the naval governor most wanted to protect— Newfoundland as a training ground for his fellow British seamen—would, in the end, be what felled the centuries-old tradition.

Napoleon was the culprit. Britain, plunged into a long conflict with France as the new century began, boosted the size of its navy with the ships and men of the Newfoundland trade. It was something it had always done in war, but this time there were others quick to take over the trade once the migratory ships no longer showed up on our shores. A handful of opportunistic citizens, chiefly in St. John's and Conception Bay, seized the chance to collect fish up and down the coast and ship it off to markets desperate for cod. In a sense what the West Country merchants had predicted came true: let them stay in Newfoundland year-round and before long they'll want to own the business.

It marked the rise of a new breed of merchant princes. Some of the outports hardly felt the difference. But at least some of the profits would have more reason to stay in Newfoundland. And soon the Island was developing a migratory fishery of its own. Some Conception Bay fishermen, with their coastline looking over- crowded, began spending the fishing season on the north coast, on the French Shore that was now vacant, the French having gone off to war. Before long they extended the range of their activity to the Labrador coast.

Soon they were being joined by schooners from Trinity and Bonavista Bays. And when the war came to an end, and the Treaty of Paris again handed the French the northern coast of Newfoundland, it was the Labrador fishery that held strong and expanded. An annual fleet of schooners became a common sight, their huge sails catching the wind north as the coastal ice broke up in the spring. By mid-century there were close to four hundred of them.

Growing vegetables among the rocks of Badger's Quay.

What England had been doing to Newfoundland for centuries, Newfoundland was now doing to Labrador— sailing in for the summer and sailing away with its fish. While the population of Labrador remained small and sparsely distributed there appeared to be enough fishing rooms for everyone. The Newfoundland fishermen and the native populations crossed each other's path with mutual respect. Some of the Inuit, having settled in under the influence of the Moravians, had much they could offer the Newfoundlanders, including an ability to read and write, skills many of the yearly visitors did not possess.

What Good Was Credit

The face of the fishery in Newfoundland and Labrador was changing. In more and more places it became family-based and self-sufficient. The days had gone of a spring migration to Newfoundland of thousands of fishermen, some of them passing an idle winter and getting up to no good. The resident population of the Island took a dramatic leap forward. Fishermen were arriving with their families, and with the intention of staying. By 1816 the population exceeded fifty thousand, more than four times what it had been thirty years earlier. And for the first time the proportion of women and children neared the normal range of a settled population.

Yet, new obstacles arose to the evolution of an economically sound society. A method of conducting the fish trade—the credit or 'truck' system—emerged in the outports. Some say it was the only way commerce could have evolved, given our endless coastline and small isolated pockets of settlement. Others vehemently argue that it was nothing less than systematic oppression of a voiceless people. Ultimately, neither fisherman nor merchant was well served by it.

Each spring the merchant supplied the fisherman with the goods he needed on credit, payment to be made with the cod that was landed and cured over the months ahead. He charged not only his fishing supplies, but anything else his family may have needed, from nails to molasses. At the end of the season the merchant and fisherman straightened out their accounts. A good year might see a surplus, one that would be used for more of the things that stocked the merchant's shelves, and for credit during the upcoming winter. In bad years the fisherman and his family were at the mercy of the merchant. If credit wasn't extended, it resulted in a lean winter ahead, and near starvation for many.

The key aspect of the system was the fact that the merchant set the prices, both for the fish he bought, and for the supplies that filled his store. The outport economy had turned cashless. Such a system negated any measure of independence for the fisherman, his wife, and children. They were forever beholden to the merchants. A long-standing subservient relationship could never be anything but unhealthy for a struggling society. Left to implant itself in future generations, it would become a constant impediment to their hopes and expectations.

Such a system failed to generate pride in the fish that was produced. A lifetime of debt was little incentive to delivering quality fish, especially when the culler who graded it was employed by the merchant. And for fear of losing control, the merchant himself saw little reason to refine his operations. As a result, much of the Island's fishing industry languished in the backwoods of the world's markets.

Why did this method of trade take hold, and why did it continue for so long, in some places well into the twentieth century? In part, the answer (as it does so often) goes back to our geography. Unlike much of the rest of North America, Newfoundland and Labrador had little arable land, certainly not enough to provide a second resource industry, something that might sustain an economy if the fishery failed. What meagre garden plots there were could, in many outports, barely produce enough vegetables for a family's winter. A trip down the Great Northern Peninsula today reminds us of just how much of an effort it can be for outport people to maintain a simple vegetable garden. Here, all along the highway, far from the rocky ground of their coastal houses, are small patchwork squares of semi-fertile soil that Newfoundlanders have fenced, planted, and fervently protected. Newfoundland court records of the 1800s are punctuated with fiercely contested cases of pilfered topsoil.

Isolated, forced to rely almost exclusively on the fishery, too small in population to see any buyer competition for their catch, these people found themselves at the mercy of the merchant, he himself often an agent for a company hundreds of kilometres away in St. John's. The undereducated fishermen accepted what they were told about the unpredictable price of cod. They became immobile, increasingly fearful of uprooting themselves and their families, seeing only the choice of going to another outport where the way of life was little different.

What they had was the known—the stretch of coastline that belonged to them and the promise that they would be given something in return for their catch. Many of these people had come from overcrowded, impoverished corners of England and Ireland, places where owning land was equated with wealth. Life in Newfoundland was probably as secure as any they had ever known, for indeed, they had all the land they could ever want. Unfortunately, they lived in a place where land, beyond a place to build a house and fishing premises and to cut wood, was useless. Here it was the intemperate sea, not the solid rock, that produced a livelihood.

In this scenario the merchants are often seen as the villains of the piece, quick to take advantage of the hapless fishermen. And in a good many instances that portrayal is not inaccurate. The merchants would have been quick to counter that they bore risk as well. The run of fish was not to be relied upon from year to year. Foul weather could prevent proper drying. The markets fluctuated. The merchants would say that the relationship between them and the fishermen was a mutually dependent one.

In the end, the difference lay in the fact that the merchants could control their losses by controlling their prices. They could fall back on the fat from the good

Women and men share the work on the fish flakes of Burin.

years. For the regular fishermen there was no fat. There was just credit for next season. And the only fight the merchant had was with his conscience, as he eyed the
settlers outside his premises, 'men waiting, watching, and scrutinizing the motions
and features of their supplying merchants . . . that they might find him in good
humour, then . . . present themselves to ask for a barrel of flour.'

Sharing the Strain

Despite this economic predicament, the change to family-based settlement made
Newfoundland a more sane and stable place to be living, especially for women.
Not uncommon in the reports of magistrates during the 1700s were horrific
accounts of women suffering at the hands of lawless bands of vagrant men. One
such episode from the south coast told of a mother who had been 'dragged from
her children and her bed by five men and thrown in the stern sheets of a small
boat.' The ruffians rowed her to some remote dwelling where they raped her and
left her near death. Eventually she was returned by others to her house, where, it
was said, 'the condition her mother and father described her to be in shocks
decency to relate.' By the time the magistrate was told the story the woman's
assailants were long scattered for the fishing season.

Now the fishery was very much family work, with the women's part as necessary to the success of the venture as that of the men, unlike much of North America where there was a strict separation of roles. Generally the men caught the fish, and the women cured it, but the equally laborious tasks of gutting, splitting, and salting the fish were shared between them. Any children they had, and any workers they might afford, joined them in what was an intense and back-breaking few months.

If indeed there was soil enough to hold some root vegetables, tending it, too, was the responsibility of the women. As, of course, was the cooking and the cleaning and the raising of the children. If during the fishing season it was observed of men that some of them ' . . . have not had their fishing boots off for a week . . . ,' one can be sure the women, if they did manage to remove whatever they found to put on their feet, were no better rested than their husbands.

Yet the extra work of these pioneer women did not lead to anything other than subsistence living. Women's agricultural activity in the more fertile regions of North America provided a secondary means of acquiring goods. They traded their extra grain for textiles, their eggs for household tools. Their work fostered the growth of other industries. But in Newfoundland, it was all a family could do to keep producing salt cod. And when disaster struck, be it a poor fishing season or a vicious storm, there was little to fall back on. Sometimes no more than the few potatoes that the ground grudgingly produced.

Fate Plays Its Part

One storm, that of 1775, was particularly severe. It hit the Atlantic shores south of Newfoundland, and on September twelfth it pounded the Avalon, and up the coast as far as La Scie. An abrupt rise in the wind threw up waves of nine metres, catching the fishermen offshore unprepared and desperate. It was like nothing they had ever known before—more than seven hundred vessels lost, their crews thrown into the ocean to drown. On land the storm flattened the makeshift houses, devastated the shoreline sheds and flakes. It is said that of all those fishing off Northern Bay only one young boy survived. The boat with him lashed to its helm was pitched on shore, coming to rest between two trees. 'For some days after, in drawing the nets ashore, they often found twenty or thirty dead bodies . . .' The total number to die in Newfoundland, by some accounts, neared four thousand. It is listed as the seventh deadliest Atlantic hurricane of all time.

The ocean was never to be trusted. For the new arrivals to these shores that was quickly understood. They weren't nestled in the temperate charms of the Gulf Stream as were their immigrant relatives to the west and south. They had thrust themselves into the unpredictable brunt of the North Atlantic, and it, together with weather and war, defined their world.

In 1813 the price paid for fish was its highest ever, up to thirty-two shillings a quintal, more than twice what it had been just a few years before. There was sudden prosperity. Then in 1814 the war with France ended and prices plummeted. Merchant bankruptcies abounded. At the same time immigrants, buoyed by stale news of fortunes to be had in fish, were on their way in record numbers from Ireland; six thousand of these 'wretched and miserable' souls landed in 1815 alone.

Their misfortune knew no bounds, for the winter that followed was one of the coldest ever. The Island was thrown into turmoil with thousands desperate for food. Roaming bands of men went on wild looting sprees. Merchants joined together to safeguard their properties. To add to the misery, in St. John's a February fire raged through part of the town, destroying 120 houses. In 1817 a second one destroyed 130 more, and many storehouses with them. Heavy spring ice devastated the seal fishery. Desperate for food for their families, hundreds of outport men made their way to St. John's, adding even more to the plight of a town already beset with homeless, jobless immigrants. Food riots broke out, contained only by dispersing some of the military supplies, and rationing the hungry to one meal per day. The long hungry months became known as the 'Winter of the Rals,' by implication setting blame on Irish 'railles' or vagabonds. Wrote one witness to the fire of 1817: 'The rich, awaiting the inevitable destruction of their property, were almost frantic with despair; wilst the poor (particularly the *Paddies*) were delighted beyond measure at the prospect of plunder which presented itself . . . '

By 1818, with a seal fishery that rebounded four-fold and some of the immigrants shipped back to Ireland, the worst had passed. Those that remained had quickly learned a truth about survival on this Island. It was done one winter at a time.

A Family of Heroes

Perhaps because of the hopelessness they had left behind, and the dreadful conditions of their passage here, in most years the settlers found reasons to be thankful. For some, such as Ann Harvey and her family who had settled at Isle aux Morts on the southwest coast, those reasons were more apparent than most.

Ann's father, George, had come to Newfoundland as a young child from the Channel Island of Jersey, the ancestral home of many on that part of the shore. He had married and made a home with his wife and ten children as the sole family in this isolated inlet. Theirs was a life of fishing upon a stretch of rocky coast whose vegetation was lichen and gnarled, wind-stunted conifers. It was said that Ann's father once went by boat as far to the east as Fortune Bay, and there saw his first horse and, urged to ride it, flatly refused, saying he would rather face the fiercest storm in his dory.

Where the Harveys lived there was plenty of opportunity to face storms, and, as the name of their outport implies, many who did lost their lives in the process. Isle aux Morts' razor-sharp reefs and shoals of mica and slate just offshore were notorious among the many ship captains who ventured past this coast. The fate of one vessel, caught in a fearsome gale and thick fog, should be renowned in the annals of maritime rescue. But this incident, in remote Newfoundland in 1828, passed by hardly noticed.

The ship was the brig *Despatch* out of Londonderry with a crew of eleven and two hundred woefully impoverished men, women, and children—Irish immigrants

Outport people lived by the will of the sea.

bound for Quebec City. In early June, off the south coast of Newfoundland, they struck fog and a storm of wind. Thinking themselves 'abreast of Cape Ray' and 'distant off shore 20 miles,' they steered northwest by north to round the Cape for the Gulf of St. Lawrence. An hour later the swell sucked back to reveal one of the small offshore islands and the cluster of jagged rock extending from it. The brig 'was hove almost on the top of the rock,' doomed to end its days there as it broke apart in the thundering surf.

There was no choice but to get all hands off the ship. The captain took to the jolly boat, three passengers with him, but 'after hanging on by a stern davit tackle for three hours, the boat was washed over the brig's quarter.' One passenger was rescued. The two others and the captain perished. In the hours that followed, two dozen more were swept away by the surf or died of exhaustion in their attempt to get ashore.

Eventually the first mate and several passengers took to a longboat, and though they nearly swamped it, managed to reach a beach on the mainland. The rest of the passengers and crew cut down one of the ship's masts for a bridge to the island, crawled ashore and stood 'clinging together like seabirds.'

Such was the state of affairs when Ann Harvey, just seventeen, her father and younger brother, and their dog came upon the scene in their skiff. The day before, George Harvey had sighted a keg and other debris on the beach near their home, evidence enough of a shipwreck that they set off at daybreak, the storm still raging. What they found was a trail of more debris and eventually four desperate men trudging along the shoreline looking for help.

When breaks in the storm allowed it, George Harvey directed an attempt to rescue the piteous cluster of survivors, stranded on a piece of rock 'only large enough to hold them.' Some of the men from the beach boarded the longboat, and others the jolly boat that had washed ashore. In the Harveys' skiff Ann took control of the two long oars, holding the four-metre boat clear of the rocks and pounding surf, while the boy stayed aft and worked the sculling oar. They could get no closer than a hundred metres for fear of themselves breaking up on the rocks. But her father managed to get a billet of wood to the survivors, to which they tied a rope. The dog braved the turbulent water and retrieved it, and so a lifeline was secured, and one by one the poor creatures were hauled aboard the boats. The Harveys managed to retrieve sixty of them before darkness fell. It took three days to rescue them all. In the process fourteen more, including ten children, were lost to the elements. In total 163 people had been saved.

Each night the Harveys rowed the worst-off of the survivors to their home in Isle aux Morts, returning the next morning with provisions to feed those left on the beach. With the last of the brig's crew and passengers safely off the island, and 'not a particle of food left' at the Harvey home, they began the transport of survivors to Port aux Basques, some fourteen kilometres distant. By chance the navy patrol vessel H.M.S. *Tyne* was in nearby Cape Ray. The captain made it to Port aux Basques to find some ninety men, women, and children 'in the most wretched condition, many of them barely covered with the clothes washed on shore from the wreck.' He immediately dispatched an officer and boats to Isle aux Morts to retrieve the others, accompanied, the captain reported, by 'a man of the name of Harvey . . . whose exertions I attribute to the savings of the lives of the whole.'

George Harvey set the record straight. Years later when Governor Thomas Cochrane, touring the south coast of the Island, showed up on Harvey's doorstep with a medal that had been struck by the Royal Humane Society in London to honour the amazing feat, Harvey insisted that it be presented not to him but to his daughter, Ann.

Today few of us know of Ann Harvey. Many more extol the bravery of Grace Darling, the lighthouse keeper's daughter who ten years later, in 1838, helped rescue nine people from a shipwreck off the coast of England. Wordsworth and Swinburne penned words in her honour. Victorian English hailed her in countless books and magazines. When she died they buried her in an elaborate tomb, built a museum, imbedded her story in the minds of every one of their schoolchildren.

Except for the community tribute in Isle aux Morts, our sole public acknowledgement of the bravery of Ann Harvey was to paint her name on the bow of a coast guard vessel. We choose to neglect our heroes. Then wonder aloud if as a people we have an inferiority complex.

Our ancestors should be lauded for their stamina in enduring life on a bleak, unwelcoming seacoast. And part of their story is the willingness, time and time again, to risk their lives for strangers. Imagine what would have been made of Ann if her formidable deed had taken place off Cape Cod?

21 | The Road to Reform

To crown the absurdity of every little Society wishing to govern themselves, the cod-fishers of Newfoundland are sighing after a representative government. We imagine we shall next hear of the liberated negroes of Sierre Leone petitioning to be represented by a black House of Assembly.

—*Quarterly Review*, London, 1829

Government House, St. John's. 'A plain, substantial residence of stone . . . surrounded by a moat.'

Officially a Colony

Newfoundland and Labrador were turning into a decidedly different kettle of fish for the British. There were rumblings from prominent inhabitants of St. John's about the need for more say over internal affairs. Some were bold enough to call for an elected legislature. The British Parliament thought the Island (it is doubtful if Labrador even entered the picture) rather too immature as a settled population to be granted such a right. Wasn't the court system that Parliament had put in place enough, especially with the Judicature Act of 1791 and the appointment of a chief justice? Hadn't Parliament not made the position of governor a year-round appointment in 1817? The Island received regular attention from Westminster . . . what more did these fishermen need?

Newfoundland was of no great concern now that the migratory fishery had all but disappeared. Britain's commercial interests were embracing the Industrial Revolution taking place within its own borders. And now that the Royal Navy reigned over the oceans with such size and force, it was proving to be its own training ground for seamen.

Perhaps to appease the few malcontents (among them the rich of Poole and the British officials in Newfoundland), in 1824 Parliament declared the Island *officially* a colony. It was a little late off the mark, considering the fact that the British had been fervently reaping the rewards of its resources for more than three centuries. (What the place could be called up to that point is a matter of conjecture. No one has ever been quite able to affix a label that would do justice to its lopsided relationship with Britain.)

The Island, or St. John's at least, was beginning to dress itself up in the trappings of independence, to step out with some confidence and openly debate its future. It now had more public forums, newspapers of a sort. The *Royal Gazette* appeared in 1807, and the *Newfoundland Mercantile Journal* a few years later. While they printed little of consequence other than government notices, copy from foreign papers, and shipping news, they did set the stage for the bolder newspapers that followed, such as the *Public Ledger*, first published in 1820. The *Ledger* came out in support of representative government, while the *Gazette* opposed it. And in the pages of both, between the ads for casks of porter and chaldrons of coal, began to emerge the religious tensions that had been fermenting below much of the debate.

What the rest of the Island thought of it all hardly mattered. It was not as if copies of the St. John's newspapers were showing up in most of the outports. The people in Conche and Gaultois and the hundreds of other far-flung outports were too busy in the struggle to catch and dry their codfish. St. John's was the political centre. It would lead the fight . . . and it would reap the rewards.

Much to Cochrane's Relief

Sir Thomas Cochrane arrived in St. John's in the fall of 1825, the first governor of the newly designated colony. He would stay in that position for nine years, longer than any governor before him. One of his first acts was to commission a census of Newfoundland, though, to judge by his actions, he didn't give much heed to its results.

The census revealed a population very close to sixty thousand. While more than two-thirds of these people lived on the Avalon Peninsula, only eleven thousand were residents of St. John's. Scattered beyond the isthmus, in the far reaches of the Island, were a number that exceeded by several thousand the population of the capital.

In 1825 the people in the outports found themselves victims once again of the fluctuating markets for cod. The price paid for their fish had taken a sudden plunge. On Fogo Island starving fishermen were breaking into the storerooms of the local merchants. Reports arriving from Bonavista Bay attested to the dire poverty spreading along the northeast coast. Cochrane's response was to spend £2,100 in relief. He would later note that such sympathetic response to pleas for relief in one year 'only insures their repetition in the next.'

Who in the distant bays was aware that Cochrane, in his first years in office, would spend in excess of £36,000 on the construction of an elaborate residence for himself and the governors who were to follow? And who in St. John's for that matter voiced alarm at the fact that the figure was more than four times the original estimate, itself an outrageous amount of money, given the economic state of the colony.

The building of Government House has been viewed by some as a worthy reflection of the governor's family traits. 'The Cochranes are not to be trusted out of sight,' it was said. 'They are all mad, romantic, money-getting and not truth-telling.' Cochrane insisted that all the construction workers be brought over from Scotland. One would like to think there was good reason for local tradesmen not being hired to build their own Government House. Cochrane, money-conscious man that he was, maintained that local wages were too high.

He changed the layout of the interior several times, making the residence even more ostentatious than originally conceived. 'In a climate where so large a portion of time must be passed indoors, the indulgence of rooms a little larger than might be requisite in a temperate climate may be admissible in a building intended to be permanent and durable,' he explained to the Colonial Secretary in London. It came as no consolation to anyone (least of all succeeding generations) that the exterior design of the building is exceedingly dull. Though, true to Cochrane's intent, it has become permanent and durable.

The fact that Government House was constructed on eight hectares of land on what was then the edge of the city no doubt discouraged thieves in the night and the tongues of the city's fires. And perhaps the construction of a moat might even have deterred would-be vandals . . . or snakes. Its designer in England confused Newfoundland with one of the isles of the West Indies and included the moat to ward off such reptiles as might lurk at the edge of a governor's dwelling.

Shortly after Cochrane and his family took up residence at Government House, part of its roof blew off. Repairs were done by one of the local chaps, Patrick Kough, the same fellow who shortly before had constructed the courthouse in Harbour Grace (within budget, it must be noted). Toward the end of the century, with the cost of the residence still an embarrassment, the government of the day found more economical means of adding to its appeal. A Polish artist, Alexander Pindikowsky, imprisoned in St. John's for forging cheques, paid part of his debt to society by painting the intricate frescoes that adorn its ceilings.

Government House is now the residence of the province's lieutenant-governor. It's a lavish dwelling place even in today's terms, though one assumes British royalty feel comfortable enough when they come to visit. Ordinary citizens who find them-selves there on occasion seem constantly to feel the need to look up, seeking solace in the fact that the most interesting aspect of the structure did come free of charge.

At the End of the Trail

Some portions of the Island, particularly the south and west coasts, were more than physically far removed from St. John's. Economically, they had stronger ties to parts of Canada. A visitor to Lamaline in 1839 found a Nova Scotian schooner,

The Betsy of Halifax, trading up and down the south coast, exchanging for dry fish not only 'pork, molasses, rum,' but all manner of 'shop-goods . . . including calicoes, cloths, ribbons, gloves, shoes . . . '

William Cormack also found this to be true of Bay St. George when he emerged from the woods there in the late fall of 1822, having completed his now-famous walk across the interior of the Island (the first white man to do so). In Sandy Point he discovered 'about twenty families, amounting to one hundred souls, most of the parents being natives of England and Jersey,' as well as a considerable number of Mi'kmaq. Rather than codfishing, here the dominant activities were salmon fishing and fur trapping ('martens, foxes, otters, beavers, muskrats, bears, wolves, and hares'). Some of the furs and barrels of cured salmon were transported by schooner for sale in St. John's. But the residents were just as likely to take them to Halifax, or 'barter their produce with trading vessels from Canada and New Brunswick, or with the vessels of any other country that may come to the coast.' And rather than being paid using the truck system of credit, workers were given cash. 'The principle is well worthy of imitation on the east coast,' Cormack made a point of writing in his journal. It seems there were distinct advantages to being out of reach of the St. John's merchants.

Cormack was surprised to discover the people so self-sufficient, his experience of Newfoundland farming having been limited to the Avalon. At Barachois River 'oats, barley, potatoes, hay, etc., are produced in perfection, and even wheat.' His host, a Mrs. Hulan (who was old enough to remember the visit of James Cook), had six milch cows, 'the dairy not being surpassed for neatness and cleanliness.' She made and sold butter and cheese, and showed off a cellar full of vegetables, including 'eight different kinds of potatoes.' It was a whole different world.

Audubon and His Party

The American naturalist John James Audubon liked Bay St. George so well he stayed for five days in the summer of 1833. It was a welcome change from the Quebec north shore where he had just passed several weeks collecting and drawing specimens for his monumental *Birds of America*. 'Seldom in my life have I left a country with as little regret . . . ,' he wrote upon his departure from Bradore Bay. Sailing down the west coast of Newfoundland on a warm, calm day in mid-August, with his son, John, and crewman Lincoln on deck 'playing airs on the violin and

The Great Auk by Audubon. Once the pride of the Funk Islands, extinct by 1844.

flute,' Audubon was stirred to add to his journal: 'I gazed on the romantic scenery spread along the bold, often magnificent shores . . . Now and again, the gently swelling hills came into view, rearing their heads skyward as if desirous of existence within the azure purity.'

Indeed. The sight of the Long Range Mountains can seduce even the most travel-weary. It seemed the finicky Audubon couldn't find much to fault about the Island.

Bay St. George, in particular, thawed his humanity. 'A more beautiful and ample basin cannot easily be found,' he wrote. He spent much of his time gathering and recording information on birds and mammals from the local people, and from the expeditions of his crewmen to the interior with their Mi'kmaq guides. He worked on his paintings, one morning adding a plant abundant in the area—*Kalmia angustifolia* (sheep laurel)—to the drawing of a ruby-crowned kinglet. Audubon made time to sample caribou and berries ('called here "baked apple"'), to feast on roasted lobsters, and to join in a house party at the invitation of the residents of Sandy Point. His eye for the finely feathered caught 'the belles of the village . . . flourishing in their rosy fatness . . . ' Particularly intrigued, he was, with their adornments. 'Around their necks, brilliant beads mingled with ebony tresses, and their naked arms might have inspired apprehension had they not been constantly employed in arranging flowing ribbons, gaudy flowers, and muslin flounces.'

He quit the party by eleven. His son on the flute and 'a Canadian . . . on his Cremona' kept the others dancing till daybreak.

Two days later the naturalist and his crew were on their way back to Maine. Joining them on the return sail were seven Newfoundland dogs, Audubon having purchased them for seventeen dollars as gifts for friends.

What Could Have Been

This was a very different picture of Newfoundland. And leads one to speculate on just how prosperous the Island might have become had its settlement evolved from the more fertile west coast, rather than the barren headlands to the east. Had population growth centred on Bay St. George rather than St. John's, we would most likely have become a part of Canada with its Confederation of 1867. Labrador would certainly have felt more closely tied to the rest of the province. And by now there might well have been a bridge between it and the Island, connecting the Canadian mainland to the west coast, to a million or so people . . . Warmer summers. Prime skiing all winter. The most spectacular scenery to be found on the Island. If only Farley Mowat's 'Albans' had managed to take hold in Bay St. George.

There was one major reason, of course, why the population of the west coast in no way reflected its potential. It was part of the French Shore. The French fishing rights there made extensive settlement impossible. William Cormack inquired of the coast to the north of Bay St. George and found there were but a few dozen settlers in the whole of the Bay of Islands, and only 'fifty British families' on the entire shore fished by the French.

The colonial officials in St. John's were indifferent to the situation. Despite repeated petitions, the determined souls who did cling to the coast were never given clear indication of their rights as settlers. They were left to drift in indecision by the government. And ignored by other institutions, surviving, in Cormack's words, with 'neither clergyman, schoolmaster, church, nor chapel.'

And not only was there a French Shore. By this time there was an 'American Shore' as well. With the Treaty of Ghent that ended the War of 1812, the British passed to the Americans non-exclusive rights to fish the waters of the west coast and southern Labrador, as well as to fish and dry their catch along 120 kilometres of the south coast between Cape Ray and the Ramea Islands. Along that stretch were 'scarcely forty resident families' despite its 'many fine harbours.'

Among the few would have been the Harvey family in Isle aux Morts. Cormack, as he sailed along the coast to reach Fortune Bay, noted that 'thousands of valuable lives have been lost by shipwreck . . . in consequence of the most dangerous currents and sunken rocks.' Within a few years that number would greatly increase, despite the heroism of the Harveys.

It would be 1873 before Rose Blanche had its lighthouse. The lighting apparatus was supplied by the Edinburgh family of Robert Louis Stevenson.

As Cormack pointed out, no colonial decision-makers had ever determined that a lighthouse should be erected. Incredibly, that would take another forty years. Even Sir Thomas Cochrane, who sailed the coast in 1833 in his governor's vessel (at a cost of more than £2,000 annually), must have noted the need for a lighthouse when he entered the harbours at Isle aux Morts and Rose Blanche. In the latter outport he met Ann Harvey, by then married and residing there, and in a special service presented her with a medal for her bravery in the *Despatch* rescue two years earlier. Cochrane loved ceremony and the trappings of his office. He undoubtedly enjoyed displaying the grandeur of his position to the common folk in the outports, though he must have also wanted to get back to the capital city to see just how work on Government House was progressing.

Carson and Morris

It is perhaps unfair to Governor Cochrane to dwell on his taste for the good life. Historian D.W. Prowse called him 'eminently practical' and 'the best Governor ever sent to Newfoundland' . . . while in the same breath terming Government House 'a huge pile of unredeemed ugliness.' Much of Cochrane's attention had to be taken up with other matters. Specifically, the pressure for Newfoundland to be granted responsible government.

Nova Scotia had been given the right over seventy years before, in 1758. As had Prince Edward Island and New Brunswick fifteen years after that. By 1791 Upper and Lower Canada had representative assemblies. Newfoundland could hardly be expected to be denied theirs, especially in light of the mood for reforming the

Patrick Morris

governance of the colonies that pervaded the British Parliament.

Pushing most vigorously for change in Newfoundland were two immigrants who had been part of the great influx of settlers in the early 1800s—Patrick Morris, an Irish merchant, and William Carson, a Scottish physician. In contrast to the lethargic political posture of most St. John's citizens, they emerged as a pair of dogged and outspoken reformers. They drew their inspiration not from anything their compatriots might be secretly expounding but from the words of reformers on the other side of the Atlantic. This was especially true of Morris, who, during his numerous return trips to Ireland, became an associate and vigorous campaigner for Daniel O'Connell, the famed Irish 'Liberator.' Morris's sympathy for the plight of Newfoundland's Irish Catholics would profoundly influence the reform movement. For many the movement was a means to confront the constant injustices suffered by Catholics at the hands of the Protestant upper class.

But it was William Carson who set the reform movement in motion. When he arrived in St. John's in 1808 he was appalled to discover that the place was without even a hospital to serve the civilian population, the majority of whom were living in squalor, breeding grounds for tuberculosis and cholera. The education system was paltry, consisting of a few schools, and of those only the Anglican schools could expect support from the colonial government. There wasn't even a road to connect St. John's to the nearest neighbouring settlement, Portugal Cove. That would have to wait until 1825. 'It speaks volumes for the injustice with which the colony had been treated,' said Moses Harvey, who was to write much about the Island later in the century, 'when . . . 242 years lapsed from its annexation to the British Crown by Sir Humphrey Gilbert till the construction of the first road.'

The conditions were ripe for action. While Carson continued to practise medicine, his attention turned increasingly to the goal of self-government for the oldest British territory in the empire, the Island that Britain still viewed as little more than a fishing station. Carson realized from the beginning that his first step had to be getting onside those with the most influence—the Water Street merchants. It wouldn't be easy. Change, he knew, would only come if they saw their power threatened.

Carson's brilliance was in taking advantage of the moment, of assessing situations and using them to advance his cause. He undoubtedly magnified the significance of some to suit his ends, and never held back when there was gain to be made from confrontation. In that, he set the tone for politics in Newfoundland, making it the entertaining sport of personalities it remains to this day.

In 1811 an issue presented itself that alerted his reformist instincts. The British Parliament, acting on a recommendation of the then governor, John Thomas Duckworth, had removed the right of merchants to freely use waterfront property, what had been the fishing rooms of the now defunct migratory fishery. The several merchants who had erected sheds for storing provisions and repairing their equipment had to pay rent, they were told, or vacate their premises. The proclamation struck the merchants where they felt it most.

In November, when Duckworth had gone back to England for the winter, they called a public meeting. From it came *An Address to the Prince Regent*, drawn up by Carson and some others, in which they were to 'humbly pray' that the monies collected in renting the properties be used to institute a police force, support schooling, help the poor, and undertake a program of 'paving, lighting and widening the streets . . . ' Hardly an unreasonable suggestion. And of itself probably not one to raise the ire of Duckworth when it was brought to his attention.

When Duckworth returned to Newfoundland the following summer, however, there was awaiting him a few less deferential words, in the form of an open letter to the members of the British Parliament written by Carson and in wide distribution in the town.

Carson had raised the rhetoric by several notches. 'The Inhabitants of this Island have no legislature' he pointed out by the fourth paragraph. He berated the Island's antiquated courts of law, especially its outport surrogate judges for their 'ignorance of the most common principles of law and justice, . . . their prejudices, their imperious and impetuous habits.' Justices of the peace he called 'too often men of low education and corrupt manners.' But he saved his greatest censure for the person who held the highest position in the land. 'The Governors of Newfoundland have in many instances acted illegally, and in an arbitrary manner,' Carson alleged. 'They have clothed themselves in the Juridical robe, contrary to the English constitution, and contrary to express laws.'

Needless to say, Duckworth was furious. He dashed off a letter to Lord Bathurst, the colonial secretary in London, together with a copy of what he termed the 'very mischievous pamphlet.' By the second letter to Bathurst, his evaluation of the pamphlet had become 'most indecent and libellous,' though Duckworth never pursued the matter in a court of law. Yet the swords had been drawn. Duckworth dismissed Carson from his position as regimental surgeon to the voluntary military corps. Carson, as furious as Duckworth, sat down and penned a second pamphlet.

This time he openly declared the urgent need of 'a civil government consisting of a resident Governor, a Senate House and a House of Assembly,' and warned that if the wishes of the people for fair treatment were ignored 'admiration will be converted into contempt . . . submission to revolt.'

William Carson

Revolt was not in the offing. Carson had overstated the mood of the citizens, though for good reason. In any event, Duckworth's term as governor ended. He returned to England in 1812, having been nominated as an M.P. (with time to ponder the benefits of a House of Assembly). His memory is preserved in the name given to one of St. John's wider downtown streets. Over time (perhaps even within Carson's lifetime) it came to be paved and well lit.

Surrogate Injustice

The governors who followed Duckworth were no more enamoured of Dr. Carson, though it would be several years before his influence on the citizenry peaked. In 1819 there occurred an event in Conception Bay that greatly altered the fortunes of the reform movement. In separate court cases, surrogate judges found James Lundrigan and Philip Butler (both poor fishermen and both of Irish descent) guilty of contempt. The courts then handed out sentences that had not been seen for thirty years. They ordered that each be bound and given thirty-six lashes. Lundrigan, an epileptic, was roped to a fish flake and whipped fourteen times before he fainted in convulsions. Butler, tied to a picket fence, endured twelve lashes before he agreed to turn over his property and the affair was brought to a halt.

One of the surrogate judges was a naval officer, David Buchan, who, for two winters, had been acting governor while the real one took his annual respite in England. The other judge was an Anglican priest, John Leigh. Despite the fact that Buchan was a naval officer and used to seeing men under the whip, what transpired in Conception Bay had obviously crossed the boundary of fair sentencing into something near ruthless vengeance. Just what led to it? Was contempt of court a pretence for something, from the court's skewed perspective, more loathsome?

Lashing with a cat-o'-nine-tails had made it into the nineteenth century.

Lundrigan and Butler had both mortgaged their homes to local fish merchants in order to outfit themselves for the fishery. When a bad season struck, the merchants took the fishermen to court for non-payment, and won. The debt-ridden fishermen, failing to comply with court orders, were charged with contempt and sentenced. But there was much more to the judges' rulings than appears from a simple reading of the court proceedings. Behind the deeds of Lundrigan and Butler were those of their wives.

Sarah, the wife of Lundrigan, and Mrs. Butler (there is no record of her first name) were the equals of their husbands in the fishing trade, as was now the case in most households. They shared in the defence of what meagre property they had managed to accumulate. The women weren't about to stand by and see their homes taken over by heartless merchants as payment for debt. Sarah refused to budge from the property when a constable showed up at her home in Cupids. She stood with her children and threatened to 'blow his brains out.'

As for Mrs. Butler, she was in fact the sole owner of the house in Harbour Main, having inherited it. (Mr. Butler had only his boat and fishing gear to give up.) When constables showed up at her door, she barred it shut and left them to confront her husband. He told them he would turn over the house 'if she chose,' whereupon the constables dragged him off for sentencing and a taste of the whip. Not only did Mrs. Butler not choose to give up her property, she repeatedly ignored the threats of the constables. In the end they smashed in the door and threw her out, along with her possessions.

This was not the way women were supposed to act, at least not in the eyes of Buchan and Leigh. By law these women should have been subservient to their husbands. And by law they had no economic rights. It would seem the surrogate judges had seen too many such incidents of defiance along the Newfoundland coast. With the cases of Lundrigan and Butler the judges had reached the limits of their self-control. The whippings were to be a warning to the whole population— husbands who refused to put a stop to unruliness in their wives were condemning Newfoundland society to chaos. Another century would pass before women, and new laws, set them straight.

Justice Revised

William Carson and his compatriot Patrick Morris didn't see the incidents in Conception Bay in those terms. For them the incidents were simply prime examples of the moronic rulings of surrogate judges. They seized on them and held them up to the public. 'The flagrant acts of cruelty and injustice,' as Morris called them, had the added benefit of having occurred in an outport. And the constables who carried out the court orders were themselves Irishmen. Now, perhaps, more than the Irish population of St. John's would answer to the call for support of reform.

Several of the reformers organized the two Conception Bay fishermen in taking action against Buchan and Leigh in Newfoundland's Supreme Court. It was an unheard-of step, and though they lost the case, it only increased the momentum for change to the justice system. Public meetings led to a petition to the Colonial Office in London, one in which the need for change in the judiciary was astutely coupled with a call for a legislature. Morris took an extended trip to London in 1824, pressing the Colonial Office at every turn. He fiercely defended the stance of the reformers against a band of obstinate merchants determined to undermine their position.

The matter went before the House of Commons. It rejected any notion of self-government, but in the end passed a bill to revise the Island's justice system. The practice of surrogate judges was abolished, replaced by circuit courts with properly trained and qualified judges. The Supreme Court was expanded, and a system for granting Crown land to those wanting to develop agriculture was put in place. All in all, it was a striking victory for the reformers.

Paving the Way

Two episodes eventually turned the tide in favour of a legislative assembly for Newfoundland. Both were set in motion by the 'eminently practical' Governor Cochrane, in keeping with the provisions that accompanied the new colonial status of the Island. One was his attempt to appoint a government advisory council, the other to bring a form of municipal government to St. John's. There may well have arisen a third—the construction of Government House—(especially in view of the fact that some of the paving stones intended for the grounds had inexplicably turned up at Cochrane's private summer cottage), but by the time the costs became known to the public, self-government was within reach. Perhaps the reformers deliberately chose not to raise it as an issue, but were content to watch the Treasury in London squirm with each additional bill, all the while arguing that representative government would make Newfoundland less of a financial burden.

The setting up of an Executive Council to advise the governor on matters of local concern sounded for all the world like a step toward reform. However, Cochrane's initiative began in a sea of controversy, and ended in disgrace. One of the first men he appointed was Thomas Burke, head of the military forces in St. John's. In Burke, Cochrane had chosen a Roman Catholic—a laudable decision, and a practical one, until the man stood up to be sworn into office. Burke swore allegiance to the monarch, but refused to take two of the succession of oaths standard in British officialdom. One was the Oath of Supremacy, placing the monarch ahead of the pope. The other would have had him renounce transubstantiation (the Catholic doctrine of conversion of the bread and wine into the body and blood of Christ during Eucharist). Could he or could he not still be a member of the Council?

Governor Thomas Cochrane

The controversy ended up in the hands of the attorney general in London. He ruled that the appointment of Burke, or any Roman Catholic, for that matter, had to be denied. This meant Cochrane's intended appointments of Patrick Morris and Thomas Scallon, vicar apostolic of Newfoundland, would also be disallowed. As if that weren't insult enough, following the passage of the Catholic Emancipation Act in the British Parliament in 1829, the Island's own attorney general and its Supreme Court justices ruled that the Act didn't apply to Newfoundland. The Catholic population was infuriated.

About the same time Cochrane tried to introduce municipal government to the capital city. The public was called to a meeting to discuss just how to proceed. With the mention of taxation, hell broke loose, especially among merchants. They appeared determined to find any means possible to stave off the dreaded tariffs from London. The uproar played wonderfully well into the hands of the reformers. At least, they discreetly argued, with a legislative assembly Newfoundlanders themselves would control any taxation.

Was there any debate in the minds of the merchants about just who would control such an assembly? To his credit, Cochrane warned of the consequences. Representative government, he pointed out, might turn into something more unpalatable than what currently existed. It might just become a forum for merchants. The outports, he argued, would not be able to raise their own candidates, and would, instead, see St. John's merchants manoeuvre themselves into the position of also representing the outlying districts. Merchants, that is, who already had a considerable hold over them with the fishery's system of credit. Perhaps

Cochrane, now from the comfort of his new residence, had turned finally for a closer look at the census figures.

But there was to be no stopping the current of reform. In 1832 came a final push in the British Parliament from George Robinson, M.P. for Worcester (and a partner in one of the principal trading companies in Newfoundland). After considerable waffling, Parliament declared that the Island would be granted its own assembly. William Carson and Patrick Morris, and their supporting cast of reformers, had won the day.

In recalling the course of events, we would do well to look more closely at the motivation of the reformers. Dr. Carson was part of the St. John's élite after all, and put his name forward for election to the new assembly almost before the parliamentary ink was dry. Many, like Robinson and Morris, were merchants and had much to gain. Some were even direct descendants of the West Country merchants whose neglect of Newfoundland they had been so quick to hold responsible for Newfoundland's ills. But just how many of the reformers were out to advance the lot of the impoverished outport fishing men and women?

Most were men determined to protect, above all, their own interests. Cynics would contend that as such they were no different from most politicians. But what made this situation potentially poisonous was that they were about to fill the seats in the assembly, almost to a man, from the same class in society and from the same far-eastern reach of the Island. What Cochrane had predicted seemed about to unfold.

Sir Thomas Cochrane can have the last word, for, despite his fondness for solid stonework, the man had a mind for the future. A few years earlier, in a letter to the Colonial Office in London, he had reflected on how two segments of society were emerging as the major rival forces in Newfoundland's political life—Catholics and Protestants. 'A perfect harmony, or should I rather say, tranquillity exists between them. Yet I am persuaded . . . that a small spark could excite a flame not easily subdued.'

The attainment of representative government had been a decisive victory, but the fight for it would prove the lesser of the political battles to be fought in nineteenth-century Newfoundland. That battle had kindled a much larger one, one whose flame, lamentably, still flickers almost two centuries later.

22 | Where Once They Stood

DIED—At St. John's, Newfoundland on the 6th of June last in the 29th year of her age, Shanawdithit, supposed to be the last of the Red Indians or Beothicks. . . . In Newfoundland . . . there has been a primitive nation, once claiming rank as a portion of the human race, who have lived, flourished, and become extinct . . .

—Obituary, *The Times*, London, 1829

Shanawdithit

The End of a People

In the early days of June 1829, the Beothuk woman Shanawdithit lay under the care of Dr. Carson in St. John's. She was fighting tuberculosis, the same disease that had killed her mother and sister soon after the three of them, near starvation, were taken captive. Shanawdithit had been brought into the city from Notre Dame Bay to live with William Cormack. Two years earlier Cormack had founded an organization desperate to save whoever might be left of her group, and had walked across the Island in a futile attempt to make contact with them. And now he spent several months with Shanawdithit, recording all she could tell him about her people. In January Cormack left for England and Shanawdithit was moved to the household of James Simms, the Island's attorney general.

Gathered around her were many leading citizens hopeful that she would recover from her illness. Concern for her and her people had come too late. Shanawdithit, the last of the Beothuk, died on June sixth.

There is no darker moment in Newfoundland history.

The story of what happened to the Beothuk has haunted Newfoundland ever since. Other native populations in North America had a faster rate of decline, and were also driven to extinction following European settlement. Of the twenty-four nations cited as living in seventeenth-century New England, New York, New Jersey, and Pennsylvania, fourteen had become extinct by 1907. Yet, in Newfoundland guilt for what happened to the Beothuk seemed only to grow more intense with each generation.

It peaked in recent decades with the sensational, lurid, and wildly exaggerated accounts in the popular press. Keith Winter had people believing there were fifty thousand Beothuk, when their numbers were never more than one-twentieth of that. For *Maclean's* magazine, Harold Horwood took the rumour of a massacre in Trinity Bay, embellished it, and had it stand as the apex of systematic carnage inflicted on a people 'murdered for fun.' Pierre Berton was quick to add his own equally questionable views on the issue.

And once the seal hunt controversy erupted in the late 1970s, it was all incentive for an even more sensational accusation—opponents of the hunt were eager to link the clubbing on the ice fields to what they had read as wholesale slaughter on the land. They were intent on portraying Newfoundlanders as primitives, of seeing them as killers of whatever variety suited their propaganda.

In the story of the Beothuk there had indeed been many outrageous acts of violence perpetrated on a defenceless people. And no excuse is to be made for them. But these murders were the most graphic element in a complex story. The extinction of the Beothuk came about for an intricate variety of reasons. Only one of them was the brutal attack of a settler population.

A strong memory of these people is our most important tribute to them. An image that lingers in many minds is a miniature portrait of the young woman Demasduit, upon which a later portrait of Shanawdithit was based.

In March 1819 Demasduit was abducted at Red Indian Lake by the son of the dreaded John Peyton. If we were to believe Peyton, Jr., the foremost reason for the taking of Demasduit was to have her live with white settlers for a time, in order to show her how charitable they could be. When she was returned to her people, Peyton contended, it would help to establish friendly relations.

Though Peyton, Jr., showed considerably more tolerance toward the natives

The murder of Nonosabasut and the capture of Demasduit, March 1819.

than did his father, that argument hardly seems credible. More likely, he captured the Beothuk primarily to put a stop to the constant harassment of his salmon fishing and fur trapping business. In his actions he was supported by John Leigh, newly arrived from England, later one of the magistrates who ordered the whippings in Conception Bay, but at that time the Anglican minister in Twillingate. Leigh wanted to convert the Beothuk, to 'raise these our fellow creatures from a state of darkness and wildness.'

A few months before, in September 1818, the Beothuk had undertaken their boldest raid yet on Peyton's premises. Several of them (including Shanawdithit) watched silently in the black of night as Peyton stood on his wharf, guarding a boat loaded with salmon and furs for market. When, shortly after midnight, he slipped away for a few hours' sleep, the natives cut loose the mooring and escaped with the boat to the other side of the bay. There they tore loose the riggings, discarded its cargo, and made off with a pile of goods that included cooking utensils, clothing, and a pair of silver watches.

Though he discovered the theft when he arose during the night, it was daybreak before the enraged Peyton could find the pilfered boat and what was left of its contents. In a brook nearby he came upon ' . . . the guns alone, battered and broken, and otherwise rendered perfectly useless . . . ' The image stands as a consummate summary of the relationship between the Beothuk and the men who had taken over their lands.

By March Peyton, his father, and eight others were on their way inland in search of Beothuk encampments. By that time, according to Shanawdithit, there were only thirty-one of her people still alive, sheltered in three winter mamateeks. The settlers trekked on snowshoes for five days before arriving at Red Indian Lake. There, on its northeastern arm, they came upon a small group of Beothuk. At the sight of the Peytons and their men, the natives ran off.

Demasduit, who had recently given birth, was one of them. She quickly passed the child to someone else, but still she could not keep pace with the others. Peyton, Jr., kicked off his snowshoes and chased her down. As she yelled out to her family for help she tore open her caribou-skin coat and bared her breasts in a plea for mercy. Nonosabasut, her husband and chief of the band, turned and raced back to her. He was a giant of a man, well over six feet tall and easily the physical better of any one of the white men. He stopped a few yards distant, the branch of a fir tree in his hand. He railed at the Peytons and their men for ten minutes, with increasing animation, until his eyes 'shot fire.' At the end he calmly walked closer and extended his hand. He shook the hand of each of the white men. Then he gestured for his wife to be freed.

The Peytons refused. From his coat Nonosabasut pulled out an axe, brandishing it wildly about his head. Instantly muskets were turned on him. Nonosabasut realized he had no defence and gave up the weapon. The younger Peyton again insisted that Demasduit go with them, and made a move to lead her away.

Nonosabasut lunged forward, and tried to drag his wife from her captors. He shoved away his attackers and in the melee that followed his hand went for the throat of old man Peyton. Gunfire erupted, and Nonosabasut fell to the snow-covered ice of the lake. 'Slowly and gradually he raised himself from the ice,' one of Peyton's men later wrote. He 'turned round, and with a wild gaze surveyed us all in a circle around him.' In his final moments he uttered 'a yell that made the woods echo.'

Demasduit was carried away to live with her captors. Her child died two days later.

Demasduit was not the person the white settlers were expecting. She became the one to change minds about her nation, rather than have her own mind changed about her captors. She startled the people of Twillingate and St. John's with her delicate nature and intelligence. Her 'knowledge of character showed much archness and sagacity.' Yet, she was often to be found alone in her room, sewing material into moccasins for her people. Once she refashioned a nightcap into two pairs of child's stockings.

In St. John's people preferred to call her Mary March, in reference to the month in which she had been captured. Her portrait was painted by Lady Hamilton, wife of the governor. Everywhere she went people showered her with presents. In the meantime, a jury appointed by the governor examined the death of her husband and concluded that the Peytons were 'fully justified under all the circumstances in acting as they did.'

In the succeeding weeks a committee of six men, leading citizens of St. John's and Twillingate, formed to decide how best to return Demasduit to her people, together, it was assumed, with her many stories of the generosity of her captors. To her presents they added a great quantity of other things, among them clothes, tools, food, two dozen looking-glasses, and fifteen strings of beads.

It was decided that early the following winter an attempt would be made for direct overland contact with the Beothuk. In charge was the generally level-headed naval commander David Buchan. Buchan had a long history of concern for the Beothuk, though an expedition he led years earlier to establish friendly relations with them had ended in tragedy. The Beothuk had killed and beheaded two of his marines. (Regrettably, Buchan's reputation for fair treatment would suffer as the years passed. He and Leigh were the magistrates in Conception Bay who ordered the infamous whippings.)

Buchan's concern in the fall of 1819 was how best to reunite Demasduit with her people. There was no longer a simple solution, for when John Peyton arrived from Twillingate and boarded Buchan's ship with Demasduit, she was found to be stricken with tuberculosis. It was obvious that she would not be able to undertake an arduous journey through the woods. Perhaps Buchan and Peyton would make the trip without her and return with some of her people? 'Gun no good,' were her words of advice to them.

Then on 8 January 1820 Demasduit's illness took a sudden turn. Nobody had expected it. Within hours she was dead. It had been ten months since the time of her capture.

Two weeks later, over ridged and broken ice, Buchan, Peyton, and several dozen other men began their trek inland on snowshoes. They took turns dragging the sledges and catamarans. One held the coffin of Demasduit. On February eleventh they arrived at the place along Red Indian Lake where she had once lived.

There they found the resting place of Nonosabasut—a burial chamber constructed from an unused wigwam. Around his body had been placed all his possessions. The men opened Demasduit's coffin to be sure that the body was undamaged by the journey, before closing it again and suspending it from the ground and away from wild animals. 'So little was the change in the features,' Buchan was to later write in his report to the governor, 'that imagination would fancy life not yet extinct.'

There is another image to remind us of the Beothuk, and the ends to which they were driven. It is to be found in the Newfoundland Museum—a woman's beaver-skin legging, mended in several places. Its outside had been stained with red ochre, its edges decorated with bird claws and bone pendants. It was discovered to be not a piece of clothing but a shroud encasing the body of a four-year-old child buried at Burnt Island. How desperate were the people that in their final days a mother had no other covering for her dead child but her tattered legging?

Northern Tribulation

The native peoples of Labrador fared differently. They survived, though in the case of the Innu, just barely. Both the Innu and the Inuit would face devastated populations.

With the ownership of Labrador falling into British hands in the latter part of the eighteenth century, three areas of habitation, with some overlapping between them, began to emerge. Along the southern coastline, West Country entrepreneurs (often based in Newfoundland) had arrived with their fishermen and furriers and notions of profit. Inland were the nomadic Innu, roaming over great distances, venturing to the coast to trade their furs and secure the European goods upon which they had come to depend. And to the north, the concentration of Inuit, falling increasingly under the influence of the Moravian Missions.

Not long after Jens Haven opened the first mission station at Nain in 1771, the Moravians discovered that the traditional hunting grounds of the Inuit were actually more than 160 kilometres farther north. A contingent set out by boat, in a search for a location suitable for a second station. On the return trip they ran into wind and snow, then smashed upon a reef, the roaring seas claiming two of the Brethren. Jens Haven and those who were left only just made it to shore, clinging to 'a bare rock, half dead with cold . . . without the smallest gleam of hope that we should ever leave this fearful spot alive.' Death ('if it please the Lord thus') they were quite willing to face in their quest to gather in the heathen. This stoic, uncompromised faith in the face of some of the harshest landscape anywhere made the complaints of the English gentlemen of the cloth on the Avalon seem exceedingly petty.

Haven lived to see a station at Okak open in 1776. And a third in Hopedale five years later. 'At the close of the year 1800, there were at the three stations 110 baptized converts and 228 persons in the care of the missionaries.' By 1830 those numbers had doubled and a fourth station had opened in Hebron, north of Okak.

What had started off slowly and with indifference on the part of most Inuit had grown to a 'Great Awakening,' in large measure the result of the conversions of several prominent *angakkut* (shaman). It was all welcome news to the governor in Newfoundland, who saw a period of calm fall over the region south of Hopedale where the English merchants, and soon the Hudson's Bay Company, were conducting their business.

It was common for Moravian missionaries (married couples and single men most often from Germany) to spend thirty to forty years on the coast. Many died and were buried there. They came, not only as 'workers for God,' but also as practical tradesmen. They used their carpentry skills to construct a mission's cluster of buildings, their abilities as blacksmiths and farmers to help smooth its operation. They built boats and *komatiks* to get them from one mission to the next. They set up schools in the language of the people and taught them to read and write. Elementary education was integral to mission life at a time when the rest of Labrador and much of Newfoundland had to make do without it. So, too, was music. Instruments were imported from the missionaries' homelands, some even from the hands of Stradivarius, it was said. String ensembles formed, as did brass bands. Hymns mixed with Bach chorales and the newest music of Haydn and Handel. At Christmas, under the lamplights of simple wooden churches festooned with spruce wreaths and garlands, German carols translated into Inuktitut filled a night air that had once been filled with the sounds of drums and the stories of ungodly spirits.

Today there are those who bemoan that fact that the traditional Inuit drum was never among the instruments to be heard. Playing it was one of the pagan practices

Moravian choir, Nain, 1880s.

that the missionaries had done away with. The missionaries, in their paternalistic attitudes, unwittingly eroded the self-confidence of the people they had come to serve. Add to that the continuing cycles of famine and disease that invaded these northern communities and the sometimes unjust trading practices of the mission-ary stores, and it all leads to intense questioning of the ways in which Inuit society evolved. There is no denying that the Moravians did bring a measure of stability to northern Labrador, and a moral foundation whose effects for good are still very much in evidence today. Ultimately the Inuit will decide what of their past they should retain and what of it to leave behind.

South of Hopedale

Construction of the Moravian Mission at Hopedale was meant to halt the move-ment of Inuit to the more southern inlets of Labrador, where the European traders were in command of the commerce, and where, the natives were warned, godless ways abounded. In this strategy the Brethren were never entirely successful. The Inuit were not about to be bound by foreign notions of settlement. They contin-ued to drift in and out of the mission stations at will, though taking with them their church experiences. 'Four families of Esquimaux from Hopedale . . . have come to live here,' wrote George Hutchinson, Anglican minister of Battle Harbour in 1863. 'They came here hoping to better their worldly circumstances. They . . . did not settle until they found a pastor and a church.' The rector (a nephew of William Wordsworth, with a great fondness for poetry himself) eagerly added, 'All the adults can read, and most of them write. They sing hymns very nicely. They attend church very regularly and four children come to school.' It was quite a change from the encounters of the Inuit at Battle Harbour a century earlier.

In 1810 there were but five hundred permanent settlers of European descent in the whole of Labrador. Some worked for themselves, others for the merchants who followed in the wake of men such as George Cartwright. Rather than sail off to Newfoundland or England at the end of the season as they had traditionally done, more and more decided to stay the year round. Many found Inuit partners to help them through the winter, and often children appeared before the next winter blew in. Many began to accept Labrador as their permanent home.

So the inlets of the southern coast gradually became populated with clusters of self-reliant families of mixed ancestry. The Europeans adopted Inuit ways, building their tolerance of the frigid environment. Most were forced to live by the merchants' credit system, and, as the decades passed, neglected by the government in Newfoundland, some sank into desperate poverty. 'All are very scantily clothed, the children being practically naked,' it was written of one family in Long Bight in 1893. 'In October, they had already begun their winter's diet—4 barrels of flour, 1 1/2 lbs. tea and molasses—that was to last till July.'

Yankee Know-how

Labrador had few parallels anywhere in North America. It continued to draw the curious and the adventure-seekers. In 1861 an ardent 'gang' out of the Smithsonian in Washington boarded their schooner ('long, low, and rakish, and jaunty as a coquette') for what they expectantly termed 'the most sterile land on the continent.' They came (with their crew that included 'black Dan, steward, galley slave, and general mixer and dispenser of viands') to observe the natives and take in a solar eclipse.

'Ye are Yankees, I believe,' muttered the first Labradorian they encountered. He gave them all a tour of his fishing premises and a solid whiff of his vat of rotting cod livers, swishing his bare arm through it for effect. The old fellow slid across his tongue the cod oil dripping from his forefinger. Such sights, together with the

A family of Labrador livyers at the turn of the twentieth century.

incessant hordes of blackflies and mosquitoes, did much to contort their swagger during the ensuing few months. By today's standards they were a racist lot (and by any standards, an insufferably patronizing one), but they did come with a scientist's keen eye for detail. A filtering of their observations gives a reasonably good picture of summer along the southern coast at mid-century.

Much of it was filled with Newfoundland fishing schooners and the many thousands of men and (in lesser numbers, women and boys) who made the trip 'down on the Labrador' each year. Some were 'floaters,' roving sorts always on the lookout for the best run of fish. They lived aboard their vessels and there salted and stored the catch, before racing back to Newfoundland while there was still enough of summer left to dry it. Others, the 'stationers,' set up makeshift living quarters on shore and dried their fish along the beaches there. The gang of Americans were astonished at their calculation of the number of cod—three hundred thousand—taken in one day by the fifty vessels in Tub Harbour alone. It was an immense fishery that couldn't last. But for a few months of summer throughout much of the century and into the next, the bustle swelled the population ten-fold and completely transformed the coast. When it was over each September, when the Newfoundlanders had packed up their gear and their accordions and traded a few pipes and what was left of their rum for some skin boots, the coast fell back to its old ways.

What the permanent settlers, the 'livyers' as they called themselves, thought of it all is hard to judge. They observed Newfoundland fishermen who were no better off than themselves in most ways. Both were beholden to the merchants and their markets. Privation probably enjoyed the company. Both had a few more stories to tell to get them through the winter nights.

In Tub Harbour old John Williams (a transplanted Londoner), his

Newfoundland fishermen on the coast of Labrador, late nineteenth century.

Inuit wife, and four daughters, like most others, were barely making a go of it, net-ting salmon and seals along with their share of the cod. In late fall they would all make the trip to their snug winterhouse, twenty-four kilometres away, up from the mouth of Flatwater River. There they found timber and wild game, and frozen, snow-covered terrain that could make travel overland something close to efficient and rou-tine, what it could never be in summer. Many of the Newfoundland fishermen who returned from Labrador did much the same thing. Bonavista Bay families from the barren headlands of Salvage, for example, moved 'in the bay' in winter, to the then-unsettled Eastport, to cut wood and snare game in what was a 'veritable forest.'

Unlike families in Newfoundland, though, when the snow was on the ground Williams would also take to furring and his wife to cleaning the pelts for sale. 'Lucky is he if he find a black or silver fox among them,' noted the American, 'for each is a twelve-pound note in his wallet.' Such notes were no doubt scarce and payment or credit from the Hudson's Bay Company store in nearby Rigolet noth-ing more than enough to get the family through to the summer fishery. The HBC post and its fourteen buildings (two of which were left over from the days when Quebec City merchants operated there) were in sharp contrast to the 'Esquimaux toupiks [that] dot the shore,' and the temporary dwelling place of 'Michelet, an old Canadian voyageur,' his native wife, and their seven children. All showed up at the HBC to sell their fish and furs.

And what would a Hudson's Bay post be without its Scots? 'Oliver, an Orkney-man . . . and the best dog-driver on the Bay' trekked between Rigolet and North West River, 193 kilometres in the bay and in the shadow of the noble Mealy Mountains. When conditions were at their peak he could do the return trip in eighteen hours 'changing dogs but once.'

A Scot and his Cucumbers

In North West River the contrast between life under the good graces of the Hudson's Bay Company and that of the rest of Labrador was even more pronounced. There the operations were run by another Scot, and no less a person than Donald Alexander Smith. This was a red-bearded Smith before he became the largest shareholder and eventually governor of the HBC, helped settle the Riel Rebellion, drove the last spike to complete the CPR (captured in what is the most famous photograph in Canadian history), headed up the Bank of Montreal, was made chancellor of McGill University

The Hudson's Bay Company post at Rigolet, 1861.

and founded the Royal Victoria College for women, was knighted and made Baron Strathcona. His two decades in Rigolet and North West River (1848–69) taught him a thing or two about adaptability, skills he put to use in eventually becoming 'the richest and most powerful Canadian of his day.'

Smith even managed to impress his American visitors: 'There is no other place like Smith's in Labrador, in all its area of 420,000 square miles!' That's the hefty Quebec chunk included, and though North West River is far from the barrenness of the coast (its soil and summers being the envy of most places in Labrador), what Smith accomplished within its short growing season is striking even by today's hydroponic standards. 'He has seven acres under cultivation, of which a considerable portion is under glass. There are growing turnips, pease, cucumbers, potatoes, pumpkins, melons, cauliflowers, barley, oats . . . ' Not to mention his cows, sheep, goats, chicken, and flower gardens.

By this and all other accounts Smith was an exceptional HBC factor. He encouraged settlers to cultivate their own plots of vegetables and to make handicrafts for sale. He fostered education and religious observance, and brought the people medical assistance when he could. The station became a social centre, the focus of celebrations and community mourning. Couples showed up to be married, families to revel at

Christmas and Hogmanay, relatives to bury their dead. Smith even performed his own marriage ceremony there in 1859, legally uniting himself to a Montreal woman of long acquaintance (who, unbeknownst to the wedding guests, had given him a daughter while she was still the wife of another HBC man in Rigolet).

Visitors to North West River during Smith's long tenure were surprised to find such a well-read and articulate couple, the factor dressed in 'a black shallowtail coat' for dinner and both eager to discuss the Civil War in America. To the local people Smith was a benevolent, if demanding, overlord. He expected hard work, but when the people suffered from the vagaries of weather and resources, he was not about to see them go hungry.

But as at all HBC's posts, business was at the heart of the matter. There was a rival to be found in the Moravians, especially north of Hebron. The Brethren, to offset the 'evil influence' of the Company's traders in Seglek Bay, went farther north still and set up shop in Ramah. They moved also into Zoar, close to Davis Inlet, where trade had started with the only Innu band that far north, first by an outside merchant firm, then by the HBC.

Smith had invited the Moravians to send missionaries (without their trading component, of course) to preach at North West River. They refused, arguing that not handling the day-to-day trade in furs was 'a plain neglect of the duties devolving upon us as guardians of the Eskimos in Labrador.' The Moravians might not

In Hebron, Moravian missionaries and Inuit women harvest turnips, ca. 1885.

always have had the soul at the centre of their thinking, but neither were the motives of the HBC necessarily the most honourable. Late in the century the two did find it in themselves to co-operate, in trying to put a stop to the mercantile notions of a third group, traders for fur who were showing up with the Newfoundland fishermen each summer. By 1926 the Moravians were no longer able to carry the financial burden of their commercial activities and passed them all over to the HBC. By that time Smith's governorship of the Company had passed (the icon had died fourteen years earlier at age ninety-three), but his HBC had won out in the end.

Beyond Words

While the Inuit found themselves trading most often with the Moravians, the Innu generally took their business to the Hudson's Bay Company. And it was in its deal-ings with the nomadic Innu furriers, whose travels through Nitassinan kept them out of sight of the trading posts for most of the year, that HBC's morals came most into question. Accusations flew that Company agents deliberately kept back sup-plies of ammunition so the Innu would spend more time trapping furs than hunt-ing to feed their families. This, combined with a series of forest fires early in the century and the fluctua-tion in the numbers and migratory habits of cari-bou, caused the Innu population to fall dra-matically.

When famine finally subsided, left were two

The colourful dress of 'Nascopies or Mountaineers,' engraved for Harper's New Monthly Magazine *of April 1861.*

allied but distinctive bands. One, known to non-natives as the Montagnais, ranged over the vast interior on foot and by canoe, including the high ground that fed the immense falls that we today call Churchill Falls. During the summer many would emerge with their furs at the HBC store in North West River. The Montagnais bloodlines were mixed with both French and Scots. Their belief systems had long ago assimilated those of the Catholic priests who had been struggling for centuries to keep pace with them through the wilderness.

The other band, the Mushuau Innu, known to the Europeans as Naskapi, were distinct from the Montagnais in many ways, including features and dress. They roamed at will the northern, more barren grounds of Labrador, showing less interest in European goods. Their visits to the HBC or Moravian stations were infrequent, one reason their cultural distinctions were carried well into the next century. They used bone tools to paint intricate patterns on softened caribou hide, transforming it into extraordinarily beautiful garments. 'Tall conical caps of gaudy flannel are invariably worn, ornamented with beads, and sometimes with bears' and eagles' claws,' observed the Smithsonian group, who stood somewhat in awe of men 'so passionately fond of dress,' who willingly outdid the women. 'A few have adopted the dress of the whites in part, but will wear only the finest cloth, and that of the gayest colors.'

The Americans returned to Washington, their minds fresh with the image of the Innu in their finery about to set off for the return journey north, where in winter 'they drag their effects upon sleds, by means of breast-straps, marching in single file . . . ' The romantic view of life in the northern climes was not to be denied the urban audience. It was a view that stubbornly persisted when the rest of North America paid any mind to Labrador. Few people did, of course, including the newly formed government in St. John's. The Newfoundland fishermen and the tax collectors who annually showed up on the coast had a truer view, though theirs was a summer perspective, in the bustle of the fishery. 'Oh, our Indians have been killed with liquor, strong tea and dirty tobacco. How few they are now,' wrote the old livyer Lydia Campbell in 1894.

Epidemic at Okak

For the Inuit, devastation of their numbers came from a different source. The impact on their communities of the Spanish flu of 1918 was hardly to be believed.

The Inuit lacked any resistance to the disease, and by the time it had run its course, one-third of their people were dead.

It struck the village of Okak with particular wrath. The sickness came with the November arrival of the Moravian supply ship *Harmony*. As always the ship's appearance had been cause for celebration, with 'hundreds of people . . . on the shore shouting, singing . . . ' Within hours after it sailed away, people fell sick. With each day more and more lay about their homes, semi-conscious, labouring for breath.

In some dwellings only one person remained, in others none, as soon 'the dead outnumbered the living.' Those still alive gathered together in a few houses. Outside the houses where the corpses were collected sled dogs roamed, crazed with hunger.

Martha Joshua, a girl of seven, had gone away with her grandparents for the fall seal hunt soon after the *Harmony* left Okak. Of the thirty-seven people in the camp, the sickness took all but the girl and her younger cousin. In the semi-darkness one evening dogs broke in and tore the boy apart. Martha survived, her grandfather's lead dog holding the others at bay. For five weeks she barely moved from her bed, sitting up, her head against her knees, 'always crying.' It was

A German postcard sold in support of the Moravian mission
at Okak prior to the epidemic, with a 'native helper.'

Missionsstation Okak, Labrador

Eingeborener Helfer

January by the time the Moravian missionary and the storekeeper arrived from Okak and discovered the fate of the seal hunters. At the sound of Martha's voice they burst into the shack and shot all the dogs, including the one who had helped to keep her alive.

Of the more than three hundred people who greeted the *Harmony* when it arrived in Okak, only fifty-nine, almost all women and children, were still alive by spring. The bodies had been buried in a mass grave that had taken a week to dig through the frozen ground. Okak was abandoned, the houses burned to the ground.

In the summer people still visit Okak to fish. They sometimes cut the rhubarb that grows in the missionary's garden. The flu epidemic of 1918 marked a turning point for the Moravian Church in Labrador. Never again would the missionaries hold the people as they once did. In Hebron, where many of those who survived the devastation at Okak resettled, the person in charge of the mission wrote in his yearly report: 'Since the time of the epidemic . . . if I try, in one way or another, to reach the heart of the individual, I often have the impression that I am knocking at a door that is closed.'

Schweitzer of the North

Of the rest of the population of Labrador (the non-native livyers), trader Tosten Andersen, an immigrant from Norway, had this to say: ' . . . we reap no advantage from the government. No provision is made for the starving. Little or no law is administered on the coast. Education is absolutely ignored, and our spiritual welfare is relegated to one visit from a Moravian missionary in his dog sled during the winter . . . ' The listener was young Wilfred Grenfell, a visiting doctor and self-styled social reformer. The government in St. John's had thousands of mouths to feed much closer to home, the last Great Fire having destroyed much of the city but a few years before. It was easy to ignore the very distant, mostly inaudible, voices from Labrador.

But in Grenfell, the northern coasts had finally found an advocate, someone who would not just visit Labrador and the northern tip of Newfoundland and be done with it, but make his life there, when he wasn't touring North America, that is, preaching of the injustices cast its way. His voice would be heard loud and long in St. John's, but with greater reward in Boston, New York, and Montreal (including at the offices of Sir Donald Smith, formerly of North West River).

Grenfell, a graduate of the London Hospital Medical College, first arrived in Labrador in the summer of 1892 under the sponsorship of the England-based Mission to Deep Sea Fishermen. The government of Newfoundland had for years requested help from the Mission, to augment its own pitiable medical presence in Labrador—a sole doctor in an ill-equipped vessel sent out from St. John's each summer.

Grenfell proved to be a lot more than the government ever expected. If there is a person who approaches sainthood in the annals of Labrador and Newfoundland, it is Wilfred Grenfell. The man became a humanitarian legend in his own day, recipient of the first honorary doctorate of medicine conferred by Oxford. His impact on our northern coasts was monumental, though his methods rarely without controversy.

By the end of that first summer of 1892, aboard the Mission ship that had taken him as far north as Hopedale, the limit of the Moravian territory, the twenty-seven-year-old Grenfell had treated close to a thousand people— natives, settlers, and Newfoundlanders engaged in the summer schooner fishery. Struck as he was by the 'splendid seafaring genius' of the people, what stayed with him most was the widespread poverty and neglect. He decided to devote his life to the welfare of the people holding to this inhospitable stretch of coast. Eventually he would break away from the Mission to form the International Grenfell Association, with headquarters in St. Anthony on the Northern Peninsula. By the time of his death in 1940 the IGA had erected five hospitals, seven nursing stations, two orphanages, several co-operative stores and agricultural centres, and fourteen industrial centres.

Grenfell's early efforts found support from the establishment in St. John's, especially the merchants with a stake in the Labrador fishery. But government commitments failed to materialize. And when Grenfell took his fundraising campaign to the cities of Canada and the United States, his speeches weighted with vivid description of the coastal poverty and illustrated with lantern slides, the blessings of the merchant and government élite soon abated. In St. John's Grenfell was labelled an idealist, too impatient for reform, seeking self-aggrandizement in a country where there was no need for 'itinerant, self-dubbed philanthropists.'

Neither did he have the support of the established Churches. Protestants felt the hold on their flock threatened by Grenfell's robust and forthright brand of Christianity that went hand in hand with his medical services. Roman Catholic

Forty years after he first arrived on the coast of Labrador, Wilfred Grenfell continued to bring much-needed medical attention.

Archbishop Howley pegged Grenfell an outsider misrepresenting the colony by overdramatizing the plight of the most needy. 'There is nothing in the circumstances of Labrador,' he wrote in a letter to the *Daily News*, 'that calls for extraneous help, or that our local government ought not to be able to cope with . . . the Grenfell Mission . . . is not only useless but worse than useless. It is demoralizing, pauperizing, and degrading.' In subsequent years a government-appointed commissioner showed up in St. Anthony accusing the IGA of, among other things, sectarian discrimination in its treatment of patients.

What stood out as fact was that like much of Newfoundland far from the Colonial Building, Labrador continued to be ignored. The government, while it ought to have coped with its health and welfare, never did. Grenfell and the staff he recruited from England and other parts of North America confronted a desperate situation. Howley might have countered that the streets of East London had an equal measure of filth and misery (though he need not have gone beyond the shadow of any of the St. John's churches), but that view could never stand as justification for governments neglecting the people along our northern coasts for so long.

Much of the criticism resulted from Grenfell's attempts at economic and social reform, changes that he saw as essential if people were to become healthier and more self-sufficient. He openly condemned the credit system on which the fishery was based. He termed the denominational education system regressive and wasteful, never a popular stance with any of the Churches. His efforts for change were directed toward the establishment of small-scale cash co-operatives, first introduced in Red Bay in 1896. His detractors (those who termed themselves 'legitimate' traders) were quick to take pleasure in his failed experiments, such as the introduction of Lapland reindeer to St. Anthony, brought in as an additional source of milk and protein. St. John's merchants questioned his distribution of donated clothing to the needy as undermining their business and in 1917 were still condemning his co-operative ventures as 'a menace to all other mercantile concerns on the coast.'

But the stature of Grenfell as a tireless instrument for good had risen far beyond anything the capital city could control. It reached near mythic proportions when Grenfell was set adrift on an ice pan with his dog team in answering an urgent call for medical attention, surviving the cold only by sacrificing his dogs and wrapping himself in their fur. In 1909 he married the wealthy Anne MacClanahan from Chicago. Together they worked to expand the IGA, through fundraising tours and the publication of numerous books about Grenfell's northern adventures. With *Adrift on the Ice*, a bestseller for decades, Grenfell's image—athletic Christian hero, sporting the ideal fibre of both the Empire and expansionist America—was rendered indelible.

To its credit the IGA realized from the beginning the importance of education in bringing stability to the coast. It started schools and brought in teachers to run them. Long-term dependency on outsiders, no matter how well-meaning, is not something the people ever wanted. Though still very much a supporting organization for health care in Labrador and northern Newfoundland, the IGA in 1981 turned over the last of its facilities to a regional board of the provincial government, facilities staffed by descendants of the people who a century before had so embraced the rugged young idealist.

23 | A City Arising, a City Destroyed

Water Street—Where else is there . . . any shop where one might purchase a crape-bonnet, a ham, a chimney-pot, a wedding-ring, and a bottle of Radway's Ready Relief? This, however, is more correct of the big stores on the south or aristocratic side of the crooked street. In justice to the proprietors of those on the opposite face it is but fair to say that apparently the whole of the shops there, with scarcely an exception, dispose of but six articles—old crockery, apples, lucifers, herrings, stale buns, and rum; and the greatest of these is rum.

—R.B. McCrae, *Lost Amid the Fogs*, 1869

Water Street West, ca. 1900

The Makings of a City

Any capital city raises the collective ire of the population beyond its boundaries. Generally a comparison of tax rates goes a long way in quelling the discontent, but even that can't stop all the griping. St. John's, the capital of the Colony of Newfoundland and, ostensibly, Labrador, grew to have more dirt flung at it than most such cities. Location has a lot to do with it. St. John's might have a noble harbour and a somewhat milder climate, but the place is situated at the very eastern edge of the vast territory it must govern. It took several days by boat to reach the tip of the Great Northern Peninsula, weeks to the northern tip of Labrador. Even today there are many people in less accessible inlets who pass to their eternal rest without ever having laid eyes on the capital city. If St. John's appears remote to some outport people today, in the 1800s it could just as well have been on the other side of the Atlantic. (And in its attitudes toward the outports, in many respects it was.)

By reason of settlement patterns, and some would say an innate sense of self-importance, the city grew from a collection of fishing rooms just like all the other coves and inlets on the Island. It's just that this particular one, to quote an outport phrase, grew rather 'big in itself.' And as wonderful a place as it turned out to be in its own right, every now and then it is due some reminding that at one time there were several settlements of greater importance than itself. In the early centuries Conception Bay could boast winter populations well in excess of those of St. John's. At other times in our history, Placentia or Ferryland looked and acted much more like a capital. And some places, such as Trinity, went about their fish business with the rest of the world without much thought to what St. John's might be up to.

Yet, with its back up against the broad Atlantic, St. John's held firm and gathered enough people into itself to look like a more exciting place to reside. Being roughly in the centre of the old English Shore, it grew from a stopping-off point for many of the ships of the migratory fishery to the centre of the English fishery on the Grand Banks. It acquired the fortifications, and the governors, and the court and customs houses. The large number of taverns helped. And once the migratory fishery faded, control of the Island's trade gradually passed into the hands of the rising merchant class of the capital city. Outports were now dealing with agents for St. John's firms, the likes of Job Brothers and Baine & Johnston Company.

And with this change came a relatively prosperous middle class, one that started to agitate for the Island to have control over its own affairs. That control, centred as much in the thoroughfare of the merchants, Water Street, as it was in any seat of government, would never endear the city to those people outside its boundaries. Not that St. John's much cared.

St. John's passage from fishing station to mercantile centre dates from the Napoleonic Wars. In 1811, Parliament in Britain, acting on the recommendations of Governor Duckworth, did away with the centuries-old tradition of 'fishing rooms,' that remnant of the days of the migratory fishery. Property rights were granted to the waterfront area, although only to those directly involved in fishing activities. Other businesses were removed to a street set back from the waterfront itself, and thus rose Water Street as the commercial centre of the colony. Along its length collected the artisans and shopkeepers, where new regulations transformed the town 'hitherto remarkable for a confined and unwholesome atmosphere' (to

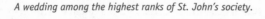

A wedding among the highest ranks of St. John's society.

choose one of the more restrained depictions) into something more livable. Just how livable depended on the part of town and the time of the year. Some parts remained 'of a very wretched description,' made worse each spring 'in consequence of the effluvia from seal oil vats.' When it rained, streets were 'rendered impassable, by mud and filth.' Winter freezing and its blanket of snow may well have been a welcome sight.

So, it would appear, Water Street was the best of it. It was here that some small businesses grew to take a hefty share in the commerce of the Island. In 1811, Benjamin Bowring (whose ad in the *Royal Gazette* termed him a 'Working Watchmaker, Silversmith, and Jeweller') arrived in the port and set up business. The following year he brought his wife and children. Charlotte Bowring opened a dry goods store in adjacent premises and soon her business was outstripping that of her husband. It was such a success that the watchmaker's trade was put aside in favour of expanding his wife's enterprise of importing and retailing the soaps, fabrics, china, and other goods to which the townsfolk had taken a shine. By 1823 Bowring had purchased three schooners and had also become an exporter of saltfish. It was all the foundation for one of the Island's most prominent business enterprises, one that would in the next century carry the Bowring name and its chain of gift stores across Canada and into several parts of the United States.

The Fire Knew No Bounds

Of St. John's in 1837 it was written: 'There are some good shops or stores in the line of street along the water's edge . . . and very nasty, ugly paths too.' The conditions of the streets aside, the city could now boast several fine churches, a few schools, and even an Amateur Theatre with its 'Dramatic Representations' both local and imported, the proceeds from the many performances 'for the benefit of the Poor.' A few years later it was reported that Duckworth Street was 'improving . . . by the addition of stone and brick houses,' a significant accomplishment considering the cost of importing such building supplies.

But it would be the lack of fireproof materials and the preponderance of 'thickly crowded little wooden tenements' that would prove to be the city's undoing. St. John's had survived major conflagrations in the early years of the century, yet clusters of more wooden dwellings, with their adjacent sheds and outhouses, reappeared, all turning to tinderboxes in the heat of summer. Nearer the harbour these

Fire rages through the city.

residences gave way to merchant stores and warehouses crammed with combustibles— oils and tar, canvas and animal feed. It is a wonder that the few merchants who did look for insurance were ever able to secure it.

The George Street of 1846 was as congested as it is today, though for different reasons. Here, in the core of the city, workshops shared the narrow street with tenements. Early in the morning of June ninth, a glue pot on the stove of a cabinetmaker named Hamlin overheated and set his shop ablaze. It was twenty minutes before fire brigades arrived, and by that time a stiff northwest wind had set Queen Street aflame. The fire headed southward to Water Street. To the west the firefighters managed to put a stop to it, saving the premises of Newman & Co. Of all the merchant stores, it would be the only one to survive. The flaming debris carried by the wind set a destructive course through the centre of the city, fuelled by the vats of seal oil.

As the fire raged Governor John Harvey ordered a house at Beck's Cove, on the south side of Water Street, to be blown up, its destruction to act as a fire break. The military misjudged the amount of explosives needed for the job. The blast killed a man and flaming timbers spread the fire even farther, destroying everything in its path, including the Bowring premises. The sails of several ships tied to the nearby wharfs caught fire and burnt the vessels to their waterlines.

When it finally burnt itself out, ten hours after it had started, the fire left close to 60 per cent of the town's twenty thousand residents homeless. Destroyed were the majority of the public buildings, including banks and churches, the Customs House, the courthouse, and even the much-loved Amateur Theatre. Just a few months earlier, in addition to its regular dramatic fare, it had been the site of a special showing of wax figures from Madame Tussaud's in London.

Queen Victoria, whose likeness had been among those to grace the stage in St. John's, was one of many to support the massive relief effort needed for the city. She gave her name to a petition for funds that was sent to all church parishes in Britain. Money arrived from British North America and the United States as well, though most of the cost of the reconstruction was borne by the Island itself. A great debate arose about who should pay. The outports complained about so many funds coming out of the colony's general revenue. The city's property owners, close to half of whom were absentee landlords living in England, continued to condemn assessments as a way of raising money.

Neither would the imperial government in London back the loan needed to undertake the full extent of the reconstruction. In the end a smaller loan was secured on the basis of general revenue, and a 10 per cent tax imposed on goods imported into St. John's. The untaxed landowners were happy enough, especially when they counted the money handed over as compensation for land taken in the widening of Water and Duckworth Streets, and for the creation of new intersecting streets to act as natural fire breaks. Those among them sitting in the comfort of their homes in England might no longer be able to count on the migratory fishery, but Newfoundland (whether shrouded in fog or ablaze) was still proving to be a dependable source of income.

The new regulations straightened the two downtown streets. They had been irregular and twisted, with widths that varied as much as six metres. The regulations also called for stone and brick construction of all merchant premises. But with less money available for reconstruction, the plan was abandoned for the north side of Duckworth Street. Temporary wooden sheds were allowed to rise throughout the downtown core of the city. The hills behind, the property of indifferent landowners, were soon filled with clusters of wooden tenement dwellings, looking very much as they did before the fire. The grand plan for the city, with more orderly, less crowded streets and adequate room for the embellishment of properties, had given way to something much less, something that again resembled a firetrap.

The Shadows of Poverty

St. John's wasn't the only city in British North America to suffer the ravages of fire, of course. The century would see huge conflagrations in Saint John, Montreal, and Quebec City. But of all the cities, St. John's was slowest to learn from its mistakes. The need for more stringent building codes was ignored. Fire companies remained poorly trained. The steam fire engine (which could discharge much more water over a greater distance and with half the manpower) reached St. John's thirty years after it had become commonplace in other North American cities.

The sense of fatalism that greeted each new blaze reflected the impoverished state of many of the inhabitants. The majority of them were renters crowded into ramshackle properties. They were not about to invest their own money in these 'fetid dwellings' that were as likely as not to succumb to fire. The landlords, many of whom never laid eyes on the city, ignored the situation except to make sure their agents collected the rent money on time.

Some of the more conscientious citizens in St. John's at least made an effort to improve the circumstances of those in poverty. A 'Committee of Ladies for establishing a Factory for the purpose of giving useful Employment to the Poor of the Town' had been formed in 1832. The factory was soundly endorsed by the political leaders who saw it as a way of instilling the work ethic in the lower classes. It would provide wages at the same time as it worked 'to improve and elevate the mind.' The workers, mostly women and older children, worked at 'carding, spinning, and net making' and earned little more than enough to ward off starvation, though the advocates of the program would have the general public think otherwise. Still, in view of the fact that so many of the Island's basic goods (including almost all the gear for the fishery) were imported, the program had its merits.

It was charity that soothed the conscience of the well-to-do, but clearly upheld the distinctions of social class. There were a number of such programs by which the more prosperous attempted to cope with the daily sight of so much hardship in the city, hardship often compounded by poverty-stricken men showing up from the outports each fall. The situation was especially grave in years when the fishery failed and the merchants refused to advance the provisions necessary to get families through the winter. The year of the great fire, 1846, also saw a widespread potato blight in the outports. Men rushed to St. John's hoping to find relief. Instead they found thousands of homeless in makeshift 'camps' and the new governor, John Gaspard LeMarchant, desperately trying to deal with the immense suffering the fire had caused. He dispersed some money for a program that saw more than a thousand of the able-bodied poor reconstructing the downtown streets.

Eventually, relief for the poor throughout the Island became tied to the building and repairing of roads, including those needed when Newfoundland became the terminus for the new transatlantic telegraph cables. A committee report of the colony's Legislative Council suggested that such road workers could be had 'at rates a degree lower than their ordinary rate of wages.' Decisions as to who would qualify for relief were put in the hands of magistrates. It was agreed that the clergy should be spared the decision-making since it was too disturbing a process.

The Churches helped out in other, more questionable, ways. As the rebuilding of the city after the fire of 1846 continued, five monumental edifices were under construction in St. John's—the Colonial Building and four churches. Great controversy arose over the fact that half of the money raised through the parishes in England as relief for the city was given over to the construction of the new Anglican Cathedral. Work on the equally imposing Roman Catholic Cathedral took place in the shadow of the 'camps' at Fort Townshend, which housed in wretched conditions the burnt-out poor from the fire. One assumes that some of the poor were employed in the construction, and that the wood shavings on which they were forced to sleep came free of charge from the site.

In 1855 fire struck again, this time leaving homeless two thousand of the poor in the area of Gower Street and Queen's Road. The *Public Ledger* declared that 'the stench emitted from the blazing mass offered full evidence of the filthy condition of the place.' The *Ledger* and other local newspapers thought the fire a godsend. It was said that construction workers on the nearby cathedral were especially thankful.

It is little wonder then that when the cannon atop Signal Hill sounded to alert the fire companies and the military that a blaze had broken out in the city, the reaction of the impoverished was less civic-minded than what the richer classes would have liked to see. But these merchants and landlords were reaping what

The fire of 1892 destroyed much of St. John's. The Roman Catholic Cathedral escaped damage.

they had been sowing for years. It was to protect their property that four fire companies had been established in 1833, and, rightly enough, it was through property assessments issued to them that the companies were funded. Yet, many of these prominent citizens had trouble parting with their money, especially given the fact there were no legal consequences if they did not pay. So when a fire as aggressive as that of 1846 broke out, the firefighters and their rudimentary equipment were quickly outpaced. Many of the poor saved what they could of their few belongings and ignored the calls for help in fighting the blaze. And it could have surprised only the rich that in the chaos following the end of the fire, looting became widespread. On the day the fire of 1846 was put out a naval ship was ordered to search every vessel that left the harbour to thwart those trying to make off with the 'considerable property which had been feloniously obtained.'

Fire Yet Again

It took the events of 1892 for the city to rise out of its complacency. That year another fire, even greater than half a century earlier, ravaged the city. This time a full two-thirds of St. John's was left in rubble, only a few stone and brick walls and the charred spires of chimneys remained. Twelve thousand people were left homeless. It was a catastrophe almost beyond belief. It was a scene, one observer wrote, 'which not even the pen of a Dante could describe.'

Whiteway's store at 10 Charlton Street, ca. 1920.

The fire started at about 4:30 in the afternoon on July eighth. The temperature had risen to 87 degrees F (30 degrees C) and a strong wind blew from the northwest. It had hardly rained for the past month. In a stable at the junction of Pennywell and Freshwater Roads, a labourer stumbled and dropped his lit pipe in a pile of hay. To his horror there was no water to be had, and when the fire companies arrived, with the stable and adjoining building ablaze, they found themselves equally powerless. The water mains had been shut off earlier that day for repairs and, though they had been turned on again, there was no pressure to the higher levels of the city. Even more inconceivable was the fact that a nearby reservoir of water had been emptied sometime previous in a fire drill, and had never been refilled.

The fire raged until the early morning of the next day. It cut an uncompromising swath through the centre of the city. Filling the parks and open grounds were 'groups of men, women, and children, with weary, blood-shot eyes and smoke-begrimed faces, standing over their scraps of furniture and clothing . . . ' It was a sight the city would never forget.

Besides the many homes, gone were the merchant premises along Water Street (including some, such as Bowring's, for the second time), the Masonic Temple, the ornate library and lecture hall, the Athenaeum, the courthouse, several banks, and a heart-rending long list of schools, including St. Patrick's Hall and the Methodist College. The Catholic Cathedral had been left untouched, though the houses in front of it easily succumbed to the flames. Gone, too, were the Gower Street Methodist and St. Andrew's Presbyterian churches, and the Stone Chapel of the Congregationalists on Queen's Road. The great gothic cathedral built by the Anglicans following the fire of 1846 was but a burnt-out shell. In the stone walls left standing, only one stained-glass window remained. It portrayed the Resurrection. It was said that on the human faces depicted in the glass had come to rest tears of molten lead.

Up from the Ashes

St. John's would rise from its smouldering ruin, of course. It would reinvent its old self, with a little more care this time. Proud it would remain, if not still a little smug to those beyond its limits. Pushing past the pressures of religion and class, its citizens found an admirable degree of harmony.

In all the Island St. John's would stand as the only genuine piece of cityscape, and an inordinately distinctive one at that. A thoroughfare of old world mercantile charm ended in a cliffside fishing village. A mélange of quirky-coloured rowhouses gave way to the sedate manors of the wealthy. Architectural treasures re-emerged among the knots of downtown streets . . . in a city where Merrymeeting Road still meets Bonaventure Avenue, before it plunges down Garrison Hill just west of Rawlins Cross. The visitor has always had lots to write home about.

The renowned travel writer Jan Morris would call St. John's 'one of my favourite cities anywhere,' and allow it to stir a string of adjectives: 'windy, fishy, anecdotal, proud, weather-beaten, quirky, obliging, ornery, and fun.' St. John's is all of these and genuinely more.

Even in the mid-twentieth century the downtown looked as if it could be out of the nineteenth. Not content to let well enough alone (where such a visage could only be a magnet for sightseers), the business vulgarians brought in the wrecking balls and raised something they called 'Atlantic Place.' With the profile of a brick box and a personality to match, it's a blight at harbourside, only to be redeemed with the return of the wrecking ball. Such architectural idiocy along Water Street is not now without competition, of course (the prerequisite mirrored tower of Scotia Bank its stiffest rival). City councillors (and no city has had a more curious lot of these) seem forever prone to err on the side of commerce. St. John's claims to be the oldest city in North America. At times it has looked bent on destroying all evidence to support that claim.

24 | The Lessons of Religion

In Newfoundland . . . the newspapers have adopted the American custom of virulent diatribes. Every adversary is the lowest of scoundrels, every supporter . . . the noblest of heroes . . . It is mandatory that so-and-so should be a black-hearted monster, first because he is a Protestant or a Catholic, and then, but only in second place, because he would like to see a wharf built where it is not considered necessary, which is contrary to all laws, both human and divine.

—Arthur Jean de Gobineau, French diplomat, 1861

Outport life called for strong faith.

X

The coast of Labrador was certainly not the only place to find the woefully poor. The capital city had more than its share. And at the end of its road to Portugal Cove in 1842 was the sight of a sod-roofed hut of 'extreme wretchedness' where 'in every part . . . was the light of heaven visible.' A woman and her seven children had been left squatting around a scanty fire, with the father off scouring the countryside for wood. In Bonavista could be found an aged widow 'destitute of every earthly comfort, and individuals in the meridian of life with families of naked and starving children.' In the inaptly named 'Merry Harbour' in Placentia Bay, the geological surveyor J.B. Jukes took tea and fish in the home of a family of eight—'but a miserable hut, with half the roof burnt off, and the people too careless to mend it.'

Not all were as destitute as they first appeared. Squirrelled away in North Harbour, Jukes discovered two ragged Irishmen, who, despite their crops and cows and pigs, and income from the salmon fisheries, were residing in a home with 'no window in it, no floor but the ground, one stool and a log of wood.' The Protestant governing class would protest that the Irish knew no better. 'Easily led, but difficult to drive' was the assessment of one pontifical observer. But as any Newfoundland woman of the nineteenth century would avow, the reason for the slovenly living conditions of the pair in North Harbour was not their income, but their bachelorhood.

Single or married, isolated or in the shadow of Government House, the poor of Newfoundland and Labrador were in larger numbers than one would expect of a North American society of the mid-1800s. This is not to deny the fact that some areas, such as the string of settlements along Conception Bay, looked to have 'most of the comforts and conveniences of civilized life,' (including two newspapers and a 'Book Society'), and that in St. John's the more well-to-do could busy themselves with dinner parties enlivened by 'quadrilles and dancing,' perhaps in one of the 'many very pretty little villas' springing up along Waterford Bridge Road. But the dichotomy between rich and poor, with a small and well-educated segment exercising most of the fiscal and political power, was not about to advance the society to any great degree. Much of it, dependent on a single and fluctuating resource, would settle into economic stagnation.

This state of affairs is closely tied to a general lack of good schooling and the resultant high rate of illiteracy. 'The register of marriages,' a clergyman in Greenspond reported in 1863, 'shows that still very few persons are able to write their names compared with the number of those who . . . make their x.' If this was true of Greenspond, a relatively large settlement and one more prosperous than most, it could only be doubly true of the hundreds of more isolated outports.

The census of 1836 showed that only 26 per cent of school-age children were spending any time in school. Most would not have had any school to attend even if they had wanted to. By 1871 the figure was only 42 per cent. And in terms of the labour force, by century's end a mere 56 per cent of men and women had a capacity to read. Not surprisingly, the greater the distance from St. John's, the higher the rate of illiteracy, except for those northern Labrador communities that fell under the influence of the Moravians. Newfoundland—that chunk of territory the erudite English had claimed before all others—had an illiteracy rate three and four times higher than any other part of British North America.

Schooling the Lower Ranks

The place with the loudest claim to John Cabot's landfall can also lay claim to the first school in Newfoundland. In Bonavista in 1727 came a school mistress (the name of 'ye school Dame' is not recorded) and the beginnings of a Christian charity school for young Bonavista paupers, opened with the support of the Society for the Propagation of the Gospel in Foreign Parts (SPG), the same group that sponsored Church of England missionaries in Newfoundland. Literacy became a by-product of moral enhancement. To this end arrived (together with the Dixon's Spelling books) 250 copies of *The Obligations Christians Are Under to Shun Vice and Immorality*. Study of the tenets of the Church of England became the means through which the skills of reading and writing were to be imparted. But, lest we become too cynical, it must be remembered that there were plenty of the upper classes who would deny even that much education to the poor, for fear their steady supply of cheap labour might be diminished. Where their approval did come, it was with the provision that such learning would keep the poor in their place, and not 'qualify them for a rank to which they ought not to aspire.'

As more missionaries arrived, several such schools were opened, though only in the more populated areas of the Island. St. John's had its first SPG school in 1744, 'for the want of which,' according to the missionary William Peaseley, 'a large number of children attended a papist one.' It would seem that concern for education had already been afoot for some time. Informal, less structured, schooling was

Well-attended rural schools were the exception.

likely found in any settlement that had someone literate among them. Such was the case on Swain's Islands in Bonavista Bay, where a fishing servant who could read and write was bade by his master to 'stop ashore and teach the children . . . and I'll pay thee thy wages as though thee went in the boat.'

The rich sent their children away to be educated, often to England, or they hired tutors. Advertisements for 'private tuition' were common in the first newspapers of St. John's in the early 1800s. The children of the poor, where there was no charity school for them, might get to attend one of the day-long Sunday schools, if there was a minister, lay reader, or catechist available to conduct the class. Of course, even that much opportunity for education presented itself only in the larger communities. Of the seventy-nine schools of all types that existed in Newfoundland by 1836, three-quarters were in St. John's and Conception Bay. There were hundreds of far-flung inlets that held but a few families, without any adults possessing an ability to read or write, and without any hope of their children ever growing up differently.

And the changes that saw the rich aiding the establishment of schools for the poor were not the altogether altruistic endeavours they might have appeared at first glance. The first such initiative, started in 1823, was the Society for Educating the Poor of Newfoundland, commonly known as the Newfoundland School Society. The NSS was started in Britain, by merchants with a vested interest in

Newfoundland. Its founder, Samuel Codner, had been flung near death in a raging storm on his way back home from a summer in the Newfoundland trade. An impassioned evangelist, Codner promised his God that he would put himself forever in His service if spared an end upon the stormy seas. The winds abated and Newfoundland became the unsuspecting beneficiary of Codner's vow.

In Lord Liverpool, the British prime minister, Codner found a zealous supporter (and self-appointed vice-patron), and in the colonial secretary, the governmental clout needed to get action on his proposal. Governor Charles Hamilton preferred his religion a little less fervent than that of evangelist 'dissenters,' and rumours of money in support of the schools coming from (of all misguided people!) Wesleyan Methodists did little to win his enthusiasm. Nevertheless, with a little pressure from merchants passing through the office of the colonial secretary, Hamilton found himself handing over £600 for the Society's first school. Soon, on their way from England aboard a ship of the Royal Navy, were the first contingent of teachers, the scent of fire and brimstone still fresh on their slateboards.

The convictions of Codner and his merchant supporters were about to be instilled in the minds of the children of the working poor. As with the charity schools, the children would rise up from illiteracy, but not from their proper place in the lower ranks. Give them some moral fortitude to go with their seatwork, the thinking ran, and it would make them more efficient workers, as well as law-abiding and respectful of their superiors. In the merchants' view, an all-round better society was the object, that being one in which the merchants themselves could feel rather more secure.

These schools claimed to be non-denominational, but by the charter of the Society all teachers had to be ardent members of the Church of England. In essence they became missionaries whose rote teaching of the Scriptures eclipsed any secular content in the curriculum. In this, of course, they had their counterparts throughout the expanding British Empire. Sound Christian ideals, hand in hand with good returns for the British mercantile interests, were the vision of their superiors. One day, God willing, all corners of the Empire would be drinking British-traded tea from British bone china while reciting the King James Version of the Bible. It was not quite the picture of Newfoundland society that the other half of its population had in mind.

The Roman Catholics of St. John's had started their own charity school in 1823 when the Benevolent Irish Society opened the Orphan Asylum School. While it was officially accessible to all denominations, there were very few Protestant children passing through its doors. It quickly became the biggest school in the city, with its own strong measure of religious bias. But, whereas the other schools were recipients of government support, the Orphan Asylum School was denied any request for funds by the governing Protestants, most of whom were swallowed up in the general hysteria claiming that 'popery' was threatening the well-being of the British Empire. Politics in Newfoundland, with an equal population of Catholics and Protestants (and a greater proportion of Catholics in the city where the essentially Protestant government was conducting its business), became a battle shaped by religious bigotry. And the schools quickly turned into one of its battlegrounds.

Election Fires

In 1832 Newfoundland took on its new, representative form of government, with an elected fifteen-man House of Assembly. However, Britain had also deemed there would be an Executive Council made up of six men appointed by the governor. The Council and Assembly would share the legislative powers. Control of both remained in the hands of the governor, for it was he who could appoint and dismiss Council members, and delay any sitting of the Assembly, or dissolve it altogether. And ultimate control rested with the British Parliament, which retained the right to veto any bill passed in Newfoundland. Britain had concocted a tonic for disaster. In a society defined by religion and class, with factions no more willing to share power than they were a pew or a meal, it couldn't help failing.

The first election for the Assembly was held in the fall. The Island had been divided into nine districts. Some areas, because they were part of the French Shore or had few settlers, were thought not to warrant representation. Labrador was still all but forgotten. No wonder the calls for the simple necessities, such as lighthouses, were never heeded.

The franchise was a generous one by the standards of the day. Women were not even considered, of course, but included were all male British subjects, twenty-one and older, free of criminal conviction, and who had occupied a house in Newfoundland for at least a year. Indeed, from the vantage point of the upper classes the franchise was far too wide. In the Province of Canada, they were quick to point out, voters were required to be property owners, or at least be paying a minimum in rent.

The issue reared its head with the candidacy of John Kent, a twenty-seven-year-old rabble-rouser, an impetuous and articulate upstart, and a Roman Catholic at that. He was all the things members of the merchant establishment did not want in the new government, and the *Public Ledger*'s editor, Henry Winton, was only too willing to vent their frustration. Two months before the election Kent was painted as an 'inflated schoolboy' by the newspaperman. Kent returned the insult in a rival paper, asserting there was a distinct 'prejudice' in Winton's mockery. The merits of restraint were tossed aside. Kent, declared Winton, was 'on the verge of becoming a fit subject for a lunatic asylum.' Soon the issue of the candidate's religion took the stage. Into the fray was dragged (or jumped, if you took Winton's perspective) Bishop Michael Fleming, leader of Newfoundland Catholics, ardent champion of Irish nationalism, and not one to sit back when there was a public scrap involving his Church.

Fleming chastised Winton for suggesting that his priests were bringing undue influence to bear on the election, and went further, several steps further. He declared his own right to an opinion about who should be elected to the St. John's districts and proceeded to name all three of his choices, one of them being the Catholic Kent, and the others being Protestants. His boldest statement, however, came not from his words but from the sign of the cross that he affixed next to his signature at the bottom of the letter. It is perhaps the most provocative stroke of the pen in Newfoundland political history. The ecclesiastical gloves were off, and now the ink really began to fly.

Fleming, asserted Winton, had 'stooped to prostitute' his office. In a relentless series of attacks he bemoaned the 'baneful influence of Priestcraft' and called for the bishop to rein in his clerics. Governor Thomas Cochrane's 'small spark' had blazed out of control. Soon Kent was shouting from the campaign platforms: 'Irishmen and Catholics! . . . stand up for your country and creed! . . . The

Bishop Michael Fleming

merchants are opposed to me—they have determined, if they can, to put me down, because I am an Irishman and a Catholic!'

Kent was elected, but the sectarian bitterness the campaign unleashed left an imprint on Newfoundland that has never been fully erased. Winton himself paid dearly. Three years later, while he was travelling on horseback along a road in Conception Bay, he was attacked in broad daylight by five men in disguise. They stunned him with a rock to the head, stuffed his ears with gravel, then with a knife notched one ear and sliced off the other. They left him 'weltering in his blood.' The identities of the assailants were never discovered, despite the offer of a £1,500 reward. The merchants had found out that there were some things over which their power and money had no control. Winton continued his editorial ranting (wearing 'a pair of artificial ears, made of velvet') until his death two decades later. It was the same year that Newfoundland elected its first prime minister, a Catholic.

At times the name-calling during that first election campaign escalated into near riots. Some merchants threatened to stop the practice of allowing Catholic fishermen to contribute a portion of their catch to the Church. Anglican archdeacon Edward Wix, rector of St. Thomas's Church, went to bed each night with a loaded pistol. (It was a bizarre state of affairs, considering that his church had been built by a Catholic, Patrick Kough, the same fellow who worked on Government House, and who was now a member of the House of Assembly!) All in all the goings-on amounted to a very un-Christian waste of energy, at a time when the fledgling government should have been spending its time in advancing the welfare of its citizens. And nowhere did the disagreements have a more long-lasting and negative effect than in the education system.

Education by Denomination

In 1836 the Assembly introduced an *Act for the Encouragement of Education,* which would provide support for non-denominational schooling. It was based on the Irish National System, and seemed a wise choice for Newfoundland, given its split into religious factions and given what little money was available to deal with the shameful lack of schools across the Island. The Protestant merchant class set out to sabotage the Act by making it unworkable. Even though Catholics were 50 per cent of the population, the merchant-dominated Executive Council appointed them to only 15 per cent of school board positions. Some school boards passed by-laws making the Authorized Version of the Bible used by Protestants a standard reading text. Outraged Catholics refused to send their children to school. Even among Protestants themselves there were disagreements, the Methodists not seeing eye to eye with the NSS Evangelicals, and neither of them seeing eye to eye with the traditionalists in the Church of England.

Eventually, after years of one group trying to outmanoeuvre the other, a bill was introduced in the Assembly to provide for a split in the education grant along religious lines. Thus, in 1843 was born the denominational education system, with its duplication of services, and abysmal waste of money for the next 150 years. If the move had any redeeming feature, it was the fact that a push for more schools could finally begin in earnest.

Bishop Fleming, though in support of the initial efforts of the government toward a non-denominational system, was quick to embrace this new direction. All-Catholic, single-gender schools became the standard for his parishes, and to that end he actively recruited Irish teaching orders. The Presentation Sisters were the first to arrive, followed by the Sisters of Mercy. Later in the century came the Irish Christian Brothers. Together they provided the core of Catholic education on the Island. Needless to say their influence extended far beyond the classroom, much of it for good. It is doubtful if the standards they brought to Catholic education could have been initially achieved by seeking out lay teachers. Yet, the wisdom of Fleming's continuing to choose both his educators and his priests from Ireland, rather than training interested Newfoundlanders, has to be questioned. It undoubtedly added to the perception that outsiders were better equipped to solve the Island's problems. The Catholic parishes grew to place enormous trust in their Church, something that brought a steadfastness to a people continuing to confront discrimination from the governing élite, but, as the visiting French diplomat Arthur Jean de Gobineau noted, 'To find an analogy with such a situation in European history one has to go back to the twelfth century at least.' That unfailing trust, nurtured in its early days by foreigners better educated than the local Catholics, carried over to the next century, sometimes with heartbreakingly disastrous results.

Far and Beyond the Call

In the Anglican communion the predominant figure was Bishop Edward Feild, who arrived in Newfoundland in 1844. His influence, too, would be profound and far-ranging. He was as intent on denominational education as the Catholics, if not more so, pressing to have Anglican schooling separate even from that of other Protestant denominations. Feild set up a theological college and insisted that his congregations pay to help support the clergy, rather than remain beholden to the mother Church in England. He was opinionated and, in matters of morality, unyielding. This is not surprising when one considers the reports of licentious living and drunkenness that came from the missionaries who had preceded him. 'Women, and among them positively girls of fourteen, may be seen . . . habitually

Bishop Edward Feild

taking their "morning" of raw spirits before breakfast,' wrote one, adding, 'I have seen this dram repeated a second time before seven o'clock . . . '

Feild was 'high church' through and through, and was constantly at

odds with Evangelicals, and especially Methodists, whose success in gaining converts sometimes far outstripped his own. But, like Fleming, he was an individual of tremendous energy. His congregations were less concentrated than those of the Catholic Church, and he could be found each summer and autumn travelling the coasts of Newfoundland and Labrador, often logging 2,500 kilometres a year aboard his Church ship *Hawk*. Through some curious working of the colonial mind, his diocese also included Bermuda. He complained to his superiors about the difficulty of serving two places over 1,600 kilometres apart, though that other island must have offered a measure of relief from the weather and the politics of St. John's in January.

Feild came away from his coastal trips to the outports with a far more penetrating view of their people than was held by the scattering of government officials, and he wasn't afraid to speak his mind on what he saw as the reasons for their 'wide-spread, and it may be feared, wider-spreading, pauperism.' He condemned the credit system forced on fishermen and the great drain of wealth out of the

Colony. 'It would only be just and right, if a portion . . . be detained for the support of our men worn down in earning it, and of, alas! our many widows and
orphans brought to that state by the frequent wrecks and disasters in conveying
well-insured produce and merchandise from shore to shore.' For many outport
people contact with a clergyman of whatever faith became a lifeline to an outside
world they knew little about. Throughout the nineteenth century and far into the
next it would be the priests and pastors who most often led the fight for schools,
roads, and health services.

Doubly Blessed

For both Feild and Fleming, the temporal monuments to their service in
Newfoundland lie in the grand churches they worked so hard to construct— the
Roman Catholic Cathedral of St. John the Baptist and the Anglican Cathedral of St.
John the Baptist. Their names perhaps hint at an unspoken competition. Whatever
the motivation, the results were spectacular, though hardly a reflection of the eco-
nomic conditions of the time. The Roman Catholic Cathedral's twin sandstone
towers rise forty-two metres above a hill overlooking the city, with a statue atop its
archway entrance of John, holding a baptismal cockleshell in his right hand, pon-
dering, perhaps, if he should fling it at the editorial offices of the *Ledger* down
Duckworth Street. The building was Fleming's open declaration of the import of
Roman Catholicism to Newfoundland, in defiance of the governing Protestants.
When completed, the church was the second largest on all the continent, and its
architecture was said to have played a part in the design of St. Patrick's Cathedral in
New York City. All rather impressive for a town of nineteen thousand souls. Its
grounds had been yielded to Fleming after 'nearly five years of vexation and annoy-
ance' with the Colonial Office in London, by a grant of the young Queen Victoria.

Not surprisingly, Protestant tradition tells a different story. Fleming was said to
have only been given rights to as much vacant land as he could fence in one hour.
The wily bishop, asserts the tale, called all the able-bodied Catholics of the city
into action, and with time to spare was able to enclose the full four hectares he
wanted, enough for not only the church, but a convent, a school, an episcopal residence, and a couple of football fields on the side. That all may be legend, but this
much is certain: in May 1839 thousands of people, both Catholic and Protestant,
turned out to excavate the eighty thousand cubic feet of earth that needed to be

cleared in order for the foundation to be laid, some of the women carrying away earth in their aprons. The job took but two days.

Bishop Michael Fleming lived long enough to celebrate mass within the cathedral's as yet unfinished interior on 6 January 1850. He died six months later, his death largely attributed to the strain of securing the land and building the church. He is interred under its high altar. In his memory a statue of the dead Christ lying in the crypt was created by the famed Irish sculptor (and, equally important to Fleming, ultra-nationalist) John Hogan, for which purpose Fleming had willed £600. The exquisite Carrara marble is titled *The Redeemer in Death*.

Four months later the Anglicans were consecrating their cathedral. For their part, they showed no more restraint in the edifice they had raised. Designed by the celebrated Sir George Gilbert Scott (whose works include the Albert Memorial in London), it has come to be considered the best example of Gothic Revivalist church architecture in North America. Inside, the distance from the stone floor to the ceiling at it highest point measures twenty-four metres, towering above an array of carvings and gargoyles, some of which bear the likenesses of prominent St. John's Anglicans of the day. Its exterior height, needless to say, is comparable to the towers the Catholics had erected, although it doesn't take architectural command of the city by crowning one of its higher elevations as does the Catholic church.

In 1876 Bishop Edward Feild died while in Bermuda trying to recover from a serious illness contracted during his rigorous parish work in Newfoundland. Work on the cathedral continued. For a week in March 1880 hundreds of sealers, waiting in St. John's for their vessels to leave for the hunt, volunteered their time in hauling tons of stone from quarries in the Southside Hills to the site of the Cathedral. As on the day the site of the Catholic Cathedral was excavated, Anglicans and Methodists mixed with Catholics to get the job done. There were most likely a few Congregationalists and Presbyterians among the lot. There were men from St. John's and men from the bays working side by side, as the leader of their respective Churches would have wished it.

Of Wood and Stone

These buildings are but the two most prominent of the many venerable churches to be found in Newfoundland and Labrador. With roads contorting to accommodate them, they rose in the centre of St. John's (many for a second time, following the

Great Fire of 1892). Their stern, weathered, shed-like forms covered the rocks along the Moravian coast of Labrador. In any of the hundreds of other coastal communities with enough inhabitants to shoulder the work, rose white, clapboarded structures, for generations the defining architectural features of these outports.

In St. Paul's Anglican Church in Trinity in 1827 was heard for the first time the strains of the famous hymn 'We Love the Place, O God,' composed for the consecration of the church by the rector, William Bullock. In 1892 St. Paul's was rebuilt, and stands today as a masterful example of Gothic Revival architecture. Holy Trinity, built by the Catholic congregation in 1833, is the island's oldest standing church. And both came to share the landscape with a prominent edifice built by the Methodists.

Some congregations preferred stone to wood. In the case of the Catholic Cathedral in Harbour Grace, some of the stone was marble shipped from Italy, the birthplace of the bishop, Enrico Carfagnini. In the early 1850s Carfagnini had been recruited in Rome to come to Newfoundland as the first principal of St. Bonaventure's College, the Catholic boys' school in St. John's. Before long, at odds with the Church there, he was relieved of his duties. He soon found himself in Harbour Grace, and eventually was chosen to be its new bishop. He must have had that semblance of foreign know-how, for he certainly didn't have much in common with the Irish Catholics. They eventually turned against him, despite his

The church and parsonage at Greenspond, mid-1800s.

work in building their noble cathedral modelled on St. Peter's in Rome. In the midst of a dispute with the Benevolent Irish Society, he refused its members the Sacraments—not a good plan of action considering how well-connected many of its members turned out to be. He met his match in Mary Xavierus Lynch, the mother superior of the Presentation Convent. Before long, Carfagnini was on a boat back to Italy.

Harbour Grace Affray

On 26 December 1883, St. Stephen's Day, five hundred Orangemen assembled for their annual parade through the streets of Harbour Grace. For decades this ritual celebration of the Battle of the Boyne, and sanctioned opportunity for taunting Catholics, had been postponed to this date from the traditional July twelfth because the latter came at the height of the fishing season.

The sectarian tension was stronger than it had been in years. Catholics were still at odds with each other following the fight to oust Bishop Carfagnini. The arrival of his replacement, Bishop Ronald MacDonald from Nova Scotia, hardly calmed the waters. (In welcoming him the band of the Anglican Church Lads' Brigade had inadvertently played 'The Campbells Are Coming,' the tune that commemorated the massacre of the MacDonald clan at Glencoe!)

In the spring of 1883 MacDonald brought to Conception Bay from Boston several Redemptorist missionaries. Their message of eternal damnation for the spiritually sluggish was meant to unite the Catholic flock. The preachers ridiculed the origins of Protestantism. Anyone who fraternized with its adherents was condemned to an extra rough fall down the bottomless pit. For their part, the Protestants were no less vehement in their reaction to being damned by 'the papists.'

It was within this straitjacket of religious bigotry that the Loyal Order of the Orange slowly made their way toward the Catholic enclave of Riverhead. There to meet them were about 150 men, some of them armed. It was said 'the smell of strong drink ascended with the smoke of the murderous guns.' The details of what ensued have been lost in the accusations and counter-accusations that followed. What is indisputable is the count of five men dead and seventeen wounded. This bloody shameful 'Harbour Grace Affray,' and the shoddy trials that followed, in which no one was ever found guilty of the murders, had all the potential of turning Newfoundland into a second Northern Ireland.

The new railway line to Harbour Grace did nothing to quell sectarian feuding. Five men died.

In the years that preceded the riot it was looking as if the Island had managed to step beyond the sectarianism that for decades had retarded its development. This relapse in 1883 left the political and religious leaders in a daze, straining to keep their consciences clear. Their countrymen were killing each other. And it would only continue unless the leaders did away with their narrow-minded rhetoric.

Unjust Lives

Carfagnini should have realized that it was not in buildings that the denominations had their greatest effects. He might have learned the lesson from Alexis Bélanger, who arrived in Sandy Point from Lower Canada in 1850. He was typical of the clerics who gave their lives to their missions. Bélanger had to be much more than a parish priest. He was doctor and dentist, wood-cutter and carpenter. He set up a school and built a church, and made regular visits north to the Bay of Islands and south to Codroy. He served for eighteen years, and when he died his body cavity was filled with coarse salt, and as was his wish, it was shipped back to Canada to be buried.

In many places, people were not fortunate enough to see any sign of a minister. They worshipped as best they could, though at least they were spared the confrontations that scarred the society in St. John's and other parts of the Avalon. And while massive cathedrals were being erected there, many people in the more remote regions were left in ignorance, such as the man on Venison Island in Labrador who cherished his Bible presented by a missionary seventeen years before, a book found to be 'carefully preserved, and . . . not likely to be worn out by use, as none of the family can read.'

As the missionaries knew only too well, religion without education was not going to take the people out of their poverty. By the end of the century Newfoundland and Labrador had some 783 Church-affiliated schools, including several secondary academies in St. John's (the Methodist College, St. Bon's and St. Bride's for the Catholics, Bishop Spencer and Bishop Feild Colleges for the Anglicans), and a couple of smaller ones in Conception Bay. A few well-to-do families who lived outside these places would send their children to board at the schools in St. John's, and to be instructed by a steady stream of headmistresses, headmasters, and teachers recruited from England and Ireland.

For the children of poor families there was no educational advantage to living in St. John's. If your home was on Gower Street and your father worked at the Nail Manufacturing Company, you had no more hope of attending St. Bon's or Bishop Spencer College than if you lived in Battle Harbour on the Labrador coast. (In fact if you were a fourteen-year-old boy you might well be shearing sheet metal side by side with your father at the foundry.) These academies were for the upper levels of Newfoundland society, those who weren't still sending their children to England, or to Canada. (For people who did live on the coast of Labrador, it would be 1964 before they'd see a school built solely for high school students.)

In 1898 students of the prestigious Methodist College gathered to celebrate 'Junior Jubilee' scholarship winner Richard Squires (seated at left). He would eventually bring his intellect to bear on the office of prime minister of Newfoundland.

As the economic historian David Alexander has said, 'Newfoundland was like a workman sent out to do a job without his toolbox.' It's been estimated that in 1901 the number of people with sufficient education to run the country amounted to 8 per cent of the population. Further, it's said that during the last half of the nineteenth century it would have taken $13 million to bring all children in Newfoundland and Labrador to a level of basic literacy. Governments spent less than half that amount on education. (But spent in excess of $30 million building and maintaining a railway.) It would not be until 1942 that school attendance was made compulsory, a full fifty years behind most of Canada, the United States, and Great Britain. One must question whether merchants had despaired at the thought of losing the child labour force on which the family-based fishery had come to depend. My own father, growing up in Bonne Bay in the second decade of the twentieth century, left school at age twelve to go fishing with his father, my mother a little later to work in a lobster cannery.

Contrary to what we might think, the outrage at what the governments of the day (and, by implication, those who accumulated wealth from the fishery) were doing to the people of the outports was hardly deep-seated. Left isolated and in ignorance, most fishing families didn't think to expect anything different. ''Tis a hard life—the fishin',' the writer Norman Duncan said to one man in Indian Harbour when he visited there about the turn of the century. 'Oh, no,' came the reply. ''Tis just—just life!'

And it's no wonder then when Duncan asked a boy, 'What are you going to work at when you're a man?', the boy found the question incomprehensible. 'Some men have never seen the sea,' he told another lad. The boy only laughed, declaring, ''Tis hard t'believe. Terrible hard.'

25 | What Characters!

Did you not see, as we rode past
*   The houses of the poor,*
Some children running onward fast
*   To reach their parents' door?*
And now, no doubt, they've gathered there
*   In love, and peace, and glee,*
Around their father's oaken chair,-
*   The young ones on his knee,-*
All thanking God that even they
Have such a happy Christmas Day!

—from *Poems, Written in Newfoundland,* 1839, Henrietta Prescott,
daughter of Governor Henry Prescott and
Newfoundland's first published woman poet

Nineteenth-century mummers crowd the streets of St. John's.

Governing Chaos

Mary Travers, hotel owner at King's Place (near present-day Duckworth Street), rented meeting space to the government prior to the construction of the official government chambers, the Colonial Building. After several months and repeated requests, the government failed to deliver the rent money, so Mary Travers took matters into her own hands. She confiscated the Speaker's chair, the mace, the sword of the sergeant-at-arms, together with a deskful of government papers, and threatened to auction them off. An ad in one of the newspapers offered the chair as 'elegantly upholstered and finished in black moreen . . . ' Despite its embarrassment and several years of wrangling, the House of Assembly never did come up with the £108 due her.

The first sessions of Newfoundland's new representative government were thick with other strife. The governor, the Council, and the House of Assembly quarrelled continuously over who held what powers. They stopped long enough to pass a piece of legislation that instituted a savings bank, and another that abolished the court system in Labrador in order to save money. When a by-election was called in 1833 the sectarian tinder flared again. Bishop Fleming renewed his pulpit bluster and Winton spewed more of his bigoted views onto the front pages of the *Ledger*. On Christmas Night, with alcohol numbing what limited good judgement they had, a mob gathered in front of Winton's Water Street house, pelting it with insults and snowballs. Officials called out the garrison, and when soldiers surrounded the house and charged the crowd, several people were left wounded. Eventually Fleming showed up and talked the mob into dispersing, before tending to those whose blood was spilling onto the snow.

You might think all sides would have come to their senses. But with the passing of Fleming in 1850 and the consecration of a new Catholic bishop, John Thomas Mullock, the tensions and name-calling only escalated. The Catholic Church pushed its political leverage to unparalleled heights. 'Religion is supreme over politics,' pronounced the Catholic newspaper, the *Pilot*. To which a letter in the *Ledger* replied, 'Liberty and the Romish faith are incompatible.' It was merely the start.

With Mullock publicly calling the government 'irresponsible drivelling despotism, wearing the mask of representative institutions, and depending for support alone on bigotry and bribery,' and the *Pilot* declaring it against the will of the

Church to cast an election vote in favour of anyone but the candidate endorsed by the priests, the stakes were set too high for anything but political mayhem. The culmination was a riot near Harbour Main a decade later, in the midst of a particularly nasty election campaign. One person was killed. And when another riot raged through the streets of St. John's for four hours following the opening of the House of Assembly in 1861, three more lives were lost. The violence in the capital only came to an end when Bishop Mullock ordered the ringing of the Cathedral bells, and his parishioners among the mob wound their way up Church Hill to hear his admonishment and partake of the sacraments.

Of Butterflies and Giant Squid

To confine ourselves to viewing nineteenth-century Newfoundland and Labrador only through the lens of its political/sectarian pugilists would be a torturous prospect indeed. Thank God there were more engaging, less self-important men and women about. The religious duelling was, in fact, a reason that one of them—the naturalist Philip Henry Gosse—left Newfoundland for good in 1835. Gosse, by the time of his death in 1888, had authored several important and widely known books dealing with ornithology, Lepidoptera, and lower marine fauna (he was co-inventor of the saltwater aquarium). For a time the interest in his work equalled that in Darwin's. And it was Gosse who might be held responsible for the hordes of young men and women chasing each other with butterfly nets through the meadows of mid-Victorian England under the guise of scientific investigation.

Such behaviour had its roots in Carbonear, Newfoundland. Gosse was a rather puritanical and naïve young man of seventeen who came

Philip Henry Gosse

over from England to work as an indentured clerk in the Poole firm of Slade, Elson, and Company. From a collection of books being auctioned off by a Conception Bay missionary, Gosse purchased for ten shillings a copy of George Adams's *Essays on the Microscope*. He was without female companionship in his own scientific pursuits, however, the flame of his youth (and daughter of his employer), Jane Elson, having up and married a young merchant from St. John's. Gosse turned to Methodism and collecting insects. Though his treatise on the latter, *Entomologia Terrae Novae* (wonderfully illustrated with his own drawings), remains unpublished to this day, it is still a much valued systematic investigation of that branch of our lower fauna by one of the few men of science at work in nineteenth-century Newfoundland.

Ours was the loss when Gosse abandoned Carbonear, for he was also a great promoter of the local book club and Debating Society, as well as Methodist sermonizer. When he left the island he had 'pretty well exhausted Entomology in Newfoundland' it is true, but he had also grown tired (and fearful) of the incessant religious rancour. 'Protestants went in mortal fear,' he later wrote, 'for the Irish vastly outnumbered us, and everywhere dark, threatening glances and muttering words beset us.' Of course, Gosse had good reason to be fearful, employed as he was by the Protestant merchant class whose credit system suppressed many of the 'Irish Papists,' few of whom ever had the opportunity for schooling. Gosse was in Carbonear when attackers took the knife to Henry Winton's ears, and was later given to believe he was acquainted with the fellow who did the deed. 'Newfoundland,' in Gosse's opinion, 'was becoming a very unpleasant place to live in.' So he left for Upper Canada (which proved not to be the greener pasture he anticipated), and eventually returned home to England.

One man of science who didn't leave was Moses Harvey. Born in Northern Ireland of Scottish ancestry, he came to Newfoundland in 1852. Over the next fifty years he juggled several outstanding and varied careers—minister of St. Andrew's Free Presbyterian Church, lecturer, writer of innumerable articles (nine hundred for the Montreal *Gazette* alone), fisheries commissioner. He was also a tireless promoter of Newfoundland. However, he is best remembered for his involvement with what he liked to call 'the great devil-fish.'

In October 1873 there surfaced from the waters between Bell Island and Portugal Cove that rarely seen creature of mythic dimension—the giant squid. Two men and a boy of twelve were out fishing for herring when they came upon a bulky floating mass. Thinking it part of a wreck, they gave it an innocent poke with their boat hook. Suddenly the object of their curiosity 'reared itself above the waves . . . ,' and the fishermen confronted 'huge green eyes gleaming with indescribable fury, and the parrot-like beak that suddenly leaped from a cavity in the middle of the head, as if eager to rend them.' Two tentacles (one no less than twelve metres in length) latched themselves to their boat and was about to drag them to a briny end. The quick-thinking lad seized a hatchet and hacked off the tentacles where they crossed the gunwale of the boat, the squid all the while clouding the waters with a great glut of black ink. The demon retreated, the severed portions of its tentacles left to verify the tale.

Soon after the incident, the boy, carting a tentacle, was knocking at 3 Devon Row in St. John's looking to find the man who, he had been told, was 'crazy about all kinds of strange beasts and fishes.' Harvey was overjoyed, for, as he wrote later, he was now 'the possessor of one of the rarest curiosities in the whole animal kingdom . . . ' And with it would 'admonish the savants, confound the naturalists and startle the world at large.' Which, indeed, he did.

In November 1873 a second giant squid showed up in Newfoundland waters. Caught in the nets of a Logy Bay fisherman, this intact specimen eventually found its way to Harvey's home, where he dragged it inside and draped it over his sponge bath (woe to Mrs. Harvey!) to be photographed before being shipped off in a rum cask to a professor friend in England.

What was for decades known in the scientific world as *Architeuthis*

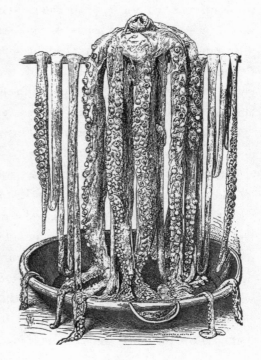

A giant squid hangs over the Harveys' bath.

The rages of the North Atlantic bred heroes.

Harveyi became the focus of dozens of articles and essays, the earnings from which were a welcome supplement to his stipend at the Kirk. Captain Nemo's nemesis in Verne's *20,000 Leagues Under the Sea* (published three years earlier) had, in short order, been turned into something rather more fact than fiction.

Two Heroes of the Deep

No people had grown to appreciate the dangers of the North Atlantic more than the settlers of Newfoundland and Labrador. When it took lives it could do so with a tremendous ferocity. When lives were saved it was often against unbelievable odds.

In early October 1867 Labrador was taking the brunt of a savage gale, surpassing anything even the oldest of its residents could recall. Forty lives were lost. It devastated the coast, wrecking countless vessels gathered there to pursue the cod fishery. Among them was the *Sea Clipper*. It had run upon a reef near Spotted Islands with a total of twenty-seven terrified souls aboard.

Their plight was witnessed on shore by two men, one of them the thirty-year-old Captain William Jackman, out of Renews, who had taken his own vessel into the shelter of Spotted Islands to wait out the storm. A distance of 182 metres lay between the beach and the stranded vessel. With his companion gone for help, Jackman took to the raging sea. The strength and stamina of the man was nothing short of astounding, for, one by one, he rescued eleven people by swimming out to the *Sea Clipper* and back again with the passengers clinging to him. By that time help had arrived, and with the aid of a rope tied around his waist, Jackman rescued the remaining sixteen. The last one was a woman near death who had no hope of surviving the ordeal of getting from the ship to the shore. Though she died, legend has it that when Jackman related the story to his father, himself a famed sea captain, the elder Jackman said to his son, 'If you had not brought that woman ashore, I'd never have forgiven you.'

The hero of the 'October Gale' of 1867 lived but ten more years, his premature death often attributed to the strain of his amazing feat. His funeral in St. John's was one of the largest the city had seen. But about such rugged and selfless individuals (of which every coast had its share) too little is remembered today.

Include in that number the deep-sea diver out of St. Mary's Bay—David Dobbin. It was the era when diving offered more risk than reward, and the underwater suit was an ungainly apparatus with an iron helmet and long hoses to the surface. As for work, there was never any shortage of it, for the frigid Newfoundland waters were littered with wrecks.

Dobbin donned a diving suit for the first time in 1849 off St. Shott's along the Southern Shore, in that region justifiably called 'the graveyard of the Atlantic.' Over the next fourteen years 'Dobbin the Diver,' as he was quickly tagged, did salvage work on hundreds of wrecks. His work aboard one in particular would make him famous among mariners.

In 1854 there showed up in Burin Harbour a ship's boat with several men and a woman aboard. According to their story, they were the captain and his wife and the surviving crew of a ship en route to America with Dutch immigrants, a ship that ran aground and sank during the night, taking all seventy-six passengers to their death. Those few who made it to shore eventually found their way to St. John's and from there took passage back to England.

But over the next weeks the residents grew increasingly suspicious of their story. Why wasn't there any sign of wreckage? Why hadn't any bodies floated to the surface and washed ashore? Word of the incident reached Dobbin and he agreed to investigate. He discovered the site of the wreck without much problem, but what greeted him below the surface was far from anything to match the story the survivors had told.

Tied to the main mast, in morbid motion with the ocean current, was the battered corpse of a woman. To the rails were tied the bodies of four men. And when Dobbin went below deck he found the door to the passenger quarters nailed shut from the outside. He forced open the door only to confront a chamber of death. Over the next few days the bodies were brought to the surface, and today they lie in an unmarked gravesite not far from Burin.

When word reached the authorities in England the captain and his accomplices were arrested and sent to the gallows. During the course of the trial the true story came out. The wealthy Dutch immigrants had taken with them on their voyage to America all their money and jewels. As the ship neared its destination, the captain and a few others carried out their morbid deed, thinking no one in the far-flung reaches of this desolate fishing isle could ever be the wiser. Certainly, never did it cross their minds that there would be among that isolated lot a dauntless man with a diving suit, whose mission it would be to walk the decks of the ship they had sent to the ocean floor.

Living in Hope

A missionary of the 1850s, Julian Moreton, pointed to a proverb he heard more often than any other in his travels among the fishing families of Bonavista Bay— 'We must live in hopes, supposing we die in despair.' There wasn't much chance for prosperity, for a good season's fishing was as likely as not to be followed by a poor one. Macabre as it may seem, the only windfall many outport families were ever likely to get was debris from a shipwreck washing up on shore (such as the 'beautiful old China plates and pieces of a more modern elegant breakfast set of dragon china' which Edward Wix found gracing the kitchen shelves of a woman in Burnt Islands in 1835).

These fishing families lived and died under the perils of isolation. The visit of someone to tend to their medical needs was as uncommon as the visit of someone to administer to their spiritual needs. When the writer Norman Duncan came into Little Harbour in the early 1900s, the first people to greet him were a fishermen and seven of his children. An eighth child was at home seriously ill. 'Be you a doctor?' the fisherman asked him. The nearest doctor was a hundred kilometres away by sea, in Tilt Cove. 'We do be too poor t'send for un,' the fisherman said. At the man's home were to be found the mother, and the young girl lying on the floor, quivering beneath a ragged covering. She had taken sick four months before, and was now near death. Her father stood nearby in tears. 'I wish you was a doctor,' were his words to Duncan. 'I wish you was.'

Near Broom Point on the west coast today you will find a cemetery of small white crosses on a windswept marsh very near the open sea. A plaque is filled with the names of those buried there—a few adults and eighteen children under the age of six years. Four of the children, born to Eliza and John Gilley, died in the space of two months in the fall of 1896. Diphtheria had swept through the community. It would be years before the government even acknowledged the fact there were English settlers along these western shores, and years beyond that before the first nurse—the indefatigable Myra Bennett—would arrive on the coast.

It is amazing to many that settlers didn't forsake Newfoundland and Labrador in droves, that people held to such isolated coves and inlets. There seemed always to be the hope, though never the expectation, of something better. The most neglected by government, such as Sandy Point on the west coast, existed without 'magistrate, or constable, or officer of any degree.' Yet they didn't disintegrate into anarchy. Far from it. They lived 'without any law,' as the French diplomat Gobineau observed of the British living along the French Shore in 1859, 'but . . . not . . . without faith, for they are the most honest people in the world.' Gobineau thought of St. George's and Conche and the other settlements as 'a kind of Utopia' with inhabitants, against all expectations, 'skilled in exercising absolute liberty without indulging in excesses, and in showing tolerance towards each other.' These indeed were laudatory attributes of the outports. However, for a people trying to raise families without the services of a doctor or teacher, such tributes wore successively thinner with each generation.

And it is amazing outport people kept an affable disposition through it all. 'A good deal of wit and repartee is common,' said the same missionary Moreton with some surprise. Much of the drollery was at his expense, though 'innocent of any ill-feeling.'

Humour offered a refuge, a way of making it through when there was little to be cheerful about. Humour was the great leveller of class and fortune. A merchant might be able to outspend the fisherman, but he was not about to outwit him. A clever tongue could sometimes ease the burden of an eye that couldn't read or a hand that couldn't write.

Fine Times

The people had their diversions. A wedding turned into revelry for the whole community, a grand reason to take the mind from whatever hardship lay ahead. Any outport wedding had at its centre, not the blushing couple, but as great a store of food and drink as the parents could afford, or the luck of the hunt would provide. The tables at one wedding feast in northern Newfoundland, recounted by an astonished visitor in the late 1800s, held 'twenty-seven enormous puddings, seven beavers, several hares and ptarmigan, a corresponding supply of vegetables, some rum . . . and cake ad infinitum.' And every man, woman, and child in the place showed up, invited or not.

At any wedding a suitable ceremony did, of course, take place, performed by a cleric, if there was one to be had. Just as often someone willing to take on the part had to be found among them, to be 'decked out with clothes resembling those of an English curate in full dress' to which was added 'mock gravity for the occasion.' The exchange of vows was often followed by a 'great firing of guns.' For the Methodist missionary William Wilson they rang out just as the couple emerged from the church, a custom still in practice today in some places in Newfoundland (much to the dismay of the RCMP).

Then it was down to the real business of the wedding—the food and drink and general revelry. Since the houses tended to be small, the guests were usually served in shifts. One assumes the many with 'alarmingly prodigious appetites' were also fast eaters. With the feasting over (at least the initial round), 'a fifer struck up a tune, and reels and jigs began.' The dancing and drinking would certainly last until daybreak, but could just as well be kept up (off and on) for days, or 'sometimes a week . . . '

The charming couple were somewhere in the midst of it all. Or, if they attempted to retire from the affair, were likely at the mercy of pranksters, a few of the intoxicated who were game for a little sport. In 1838, one American onlooker, though he frowned on the custom and the 'rude people' who partook in it, was full of details. 'They burst into the room, and dance around the bridal bed, shaking their bags of peas, and sometimes beating them with sticks, and singing coarse and vulgar songs.'

That hint of paganism stirs the minds of modern-day folklorists no end, though such a scene was probably not commonplace. And most couples who were first married in a homemade ceremony renewed their vows in front of a proper man of the cloth whenever one next visited their stretch of the coast. Still, everyone did eat a lot, and if there is a custom that has continued into modern times undiluted, it's that of consuming vast quantities of food at times of celebration. The modern fare of the insipid 'cold plate' (sliced ham flanked by limp lettuce and beet salad) might have replaced the 'cod's head chowder, or boiled salmon, or roasted venison' at the formal wedding reception, but it's only a prelude to what appears on the table once the party moves back home to the parents' kitchen.

The twelve days of Christmas (St. Stephen's Day, December twenty-sixth, to 'Old Christmas Day,' January sixth) was the celebration most steeped in tradition. It fell at a time when the fishing season was over, accounts were squared with the merchant, and there was time on hand before the prime days of winter wood-cutting and the seal hunts of March. Central to it all (and here folklorists are really in their glee) was the ancient practice of "mummering" (sometimes called "mumming" or "janneying"), a relic of the Middle Ages brought over from West Country England, and still practised in many parts of the Island, though not with the same unbridled relish it was in the 1800s.

Mummers went about in disguise, often in a troupe. In the larger places they danced and sang through the streets, and sometimes house to house as was the custom in the outports. 'Men . . . some in women's clothes, with gaudy colours and painted faces, and generally with a bladder full of pebbles tied to a kind of stick,' described the St. John's variety. The townies flounced about 'playing practical jokes . . . performing rude dances, and soliciting money or grog.' In many places the tradition was accompanied by a 'mummer's play,' a farcical entertainment with a bizarre assortment of characters, including a hobby horse (a homemade contraption with a person inside, and sometimes with a real horse's head!), good King George, a wily Turkish Knight, and the sage-like Father Christmas.

The Conception Bay crowd got out of hand in 1860, when a Protestant man was killed in Bay Roberts, supposedly at the hands of some Catholics disguised as mummers. Sectarian tensions flared once more, and the law stepped in to ban the

Fun on the Greasy Pole at the Quidi Vidi Regatta.

practice of mummering in public without a licence. The threat of a fine curbed the practice in larger settlements, but mummering continued to be a common sight in the outports, in part because they were often out of the reach of the law, but perhaps, too, because the people there only ever did it for the fun, with women as much a part of the merriment as the men.

The residents of St. John's found other ways of relieving their winter boredom. One was the custom, as Bonnycastle related in 1842, of clearing paths by 'throwing the snow . . . from the pavement or side walks into the street,' no matter how narrow the thoroughfare. It's a sadistic entertainment that continues unabated into the present era (and, indeed, was embraced with more gusto than ever during the record-breaking six-hundred-plus-centimetre winter of 2000–01). The sleigh drivers of the nineteenth century were no more amused than the car drivers of today. In earlier times it at least proved useful to the sledding buckos who used the steep city streets for 'practising the "Russian Mountain" from morning to night.' Though that, too, was a practice fraught with danger in Bonnycastle's mind, especially to 'walking females.' It, he suggested, 'like many other things in St. John's requires a little local legislation.'

With March came the Catholic call to rum and rhetoric—St. Patrick's Day. Almost invariably there showed up, too, a mild blizzard, to help prolong the return to sobriety. So dependable was that final (in the good years) bout with winter that it acquired its own name—Sheila's Brush, in honour of the good saint's partner. (Conveniently for the carousers, the female Sheila could be handed some of the blame if they didn't make it all the way home, as was their honourable intention.)

For the Protestants there was St. George's Day, a month later. They failed to endow it with the same charm, however, not being Irish, and not having the same thirst for the fiddle and the tin whistle.

Both sides came together in the summer, on the shores of Lady Lake for the Harbour Grace Regatta, and on the shores of Quidi Vidi Lake in what is the oldest continuous sporting event in North America—the annual St. John's Regatta. One reason the oarsmen returned year after year was that it took class and religious rivalry off the street and onto a more neutral arena, one less given to bloodletting. It also allowed any and all enterprising vendors a chance at making a few extra pounds. The 'day at the races' became a cherished symbol of sportsmanship and mercantile fair play, a chance for new generations to see they had more in common with other denominations than they ever thought possible.

The regatta gained increasing prestige, enhanced by a visit from the Prince of Wales (the future Edward VII) in 1860. Newfoundlanders have always been keen on royalty (Catholics as well as Protestants), and when the prince made a circle of the lake by carriage, he was met with prolonged and lusty cheering from the assembled crowds, capped by the presentation of a Newfoundland dog (which by this time was probably better known than the Island itself). This fine representative of the breed wore a silver chain, imported from Tiffany & Co. in New York. He was presented as 'Avalon,' though the prince chose to rename him 'Cabot.'

The appearance of royalty seemed to set a tone for the years that followed. 'Thousands of persons were present at Lakeside and a large number of private and other carriages were filled with fair ladies and gallant gentlemen,' reported one of the St. John's papers in 1871. Yet, that hardly did justice to the rigour of the event in the glory days of its sideshows, such as the *Exhibition of Rattlesnakes and Nova Scotian Toads,* or the famed *Greasy Pole,* which extended fifteen metres out onto the Lake, the object being to walk its length and retrieve the prize at the end without slipping off. Nor had the 'good deal of grog imbibing' yet reached the level it did in later years when influential merchants threatened to cancel the regatta altogether because so many men never made it to work the following day. Fortunately for tradition, its defenders (protesting that it was the one true 'poor man's holiday') won the day.

As the decades advanced the rowing rivalries intensified, with teams showing up from other parts of the Avalon. In 1877, a six-man crew came all the way from Placentia, walking and shouldering their boat for the last several kilometres, and then proceeded to take the championship race. By the turn of the century the most intense match-ups were between two nearby fishing communities—the strapping fishermen of Torbay going at it stroke for stroke with the dauntless lads from Outer Cove. In 1901 the Outer Cove crew set the legendary course record of 9:13:8 in the famed shell the *Blue Peter*. The record stood for eighty years.

Any attempt to bring in sliding-seat shells (like those used in every other modern-day rowing competition) has never succeeded. (It is said that on the first attempt a well-known sporting figure had his testicles crushed in a trial run, putting a quick end to the debate.) Now the *Royal* St. John's Regatta, it carries its own personality and is not about to look elsewhere for inspiration. In what other city would you find a civic holiday (usually the first Wednesday in August . . . but not necessarily) declared only after a committee meets at 6 a.m. to study the intensity and direction of the wind? More power to them. And how about a return of the Greasy Pole?

The Professor of Octagon Pond

Toward the end of the century St. John's was able to cast off some of the sectarian ugliness that had tarnished its society. It regained its sense of humour, and there began to emerge the distinct amalgam of the practical and the improbable that it wears so well today. St. John's 'characters' of one sort or another could be found on its streets, uncommon types who flavoured the daily life of a port struggling to find a place for itself as part of North America rather than a colony of Europe.

One was a native of Baltimore, who first disembarked in St. John's in the 1860s, announcing himself as 'Charles Henry Danielle—Costumier and Dancing Master.' If there was ever a man to cut a singular figure in the capital city it was 'Professor' Danielle.

Professor Danielle in performance.

His first order of business was to set about creating a demand for his varied talents. He rented a rink in Bannerman Park and converted it into a salon for dance instruction and a venue for fancy costume balls. He took his wares to the shifting social circles of Harbour Grace and Carbonear, leaving the newspaper reporters straining for words beyond 'a scene of eastern splendour had suddenly burst upon their astonished gaze.' Not many in the town would have ever witnessed anything quite like the professor in his full-costumed glory as 'The Prince of the Orient.' The men just back from the seal hunt must have gazed with particular intensity.

The professor's crowning accomplishment, however, came several years later. He acquired property on the shores of a pond just outside the capital and on it had built a combination guest house and banquet hall, which he christened 'Octagon Castle.' As was the professor's intention, it became a conversation piece from the moment it was conceived. The finished architectural bijou that graced the shores was a multi-sided, multi-dormered affair, accented with a rack of caribou antlers over each window of its first two storeys.

The interior was no less a feast for the unknowing eye. The front entrance opened to a rotunda with a nine-metre ceiling, its windows hung with the plushest draperies, its walls with richly patterned wallpapers and elaborate hand-stitched satin banners. A giant staircase led to a group of rooms where, to quote the professor, 'hundreds of yards of satin, thousands of yards of tinsel, and hundreds of thousands of spangles have been worked up . . . ' The highlight (even one better than the bridal suite) was the 'mortuary room' where the professor proudly displayed his future casket. Of his own making, it was 'Egyptian in shape,' the inside lined with 7,425 (by the professor's count) scallops of white satin, while the exterior was encased in black satin embroidered with gold thread in a pattern of flower heads flowing from a pair of Grecian lyres.

Of course, the real attraction of Octagon Castle was the flamboyant professor himself. His insults to the uncouth who dined at his establishment were legendary and in his promotional booklets he ranted at 'ignorant, brutish jealousy,' which he claimed thrived among the other hoteliers. At his death in 1902, as his will specified, an open hearse carried his casket through the city, its plate-glass top providing easy viewing of the remains amid the satins. Thousands lined the route to view the grand spectacle, before he was laid to rest in the Forest Road

Cemetery, in a tomb of his own design. He kept the inscription on the marble slab uncharacteristically simple: 'To the memory of Charles H. Danielle.'

Octagon Castle was lost in a fire a dozen years later. The city was never quite the same without the professor and his unforgettable abode.

The Bard of Prescott Street

Another turn-of-the-century figure of renown was Johnny Burke. A shopkeeper and auctioneer, the podgy little man with the bright-eyed smile was also a poet of the people. He had an insatiable appetite for the theatrical, producing talent shows and musical comedies, writing and acting in numerous 'entertainments.' Best of all, he composed send-ups of local events, satirical ballads that have become one of the cornerstones of Newfoundland's rich musical heritage. He was a bowler-hatted troubadour at the height of his comedic talents during a golden age of local concerts, between the Great Fire of 1892 and the start of the First World War. With his own press he ran off his compositions as broadsides and 'slips.' Sold on the street corners of the city for pennies, these were often more talked about than the event itself.

His best-known composition is that irresistible litany of feast and frolic at Betsy Snook's . . . 'boiled duff, cold duff, apple jam was in a cuff / I'll tell you, boys, we had enough at the Kelligrews Soiree.' It poked relentless fun at the social élite and their snooty rendezvous 'around the bay,' replacing the upper crust with such lower-class notables as Flipper Smith and his wife, Caroline (known to 'marl' through the streets of St. John's bedecked in ribbons). And who of the day would quickly forget that spoof of Gilbert and Sullivan's *Geisha*, that Japanese set piece with a Conception Bay accent—*The Topsail Geisha*? Johnny Burke launched a tradition of musical lampooning that has prevented St. John's from ever taking itself too seriously.

The Twillingate Diva

One Newfoundland voice extended far beyond the shores of the Island— that of Mademoiselle Marie Toulinquet. Her greatest triumphs were not in the concert halls of St. John's, but those of New York, Paris, and Milan. For a brief period she commanded some of the major opera stages of the world—a glorious accomplishment for the young woman who grew up Georgina Stirling in Twillingate, Notre Dame Bay.

Mademoiselle Toulinquet

A young 'Miss Georgie' had so enthralled the churchgoers of Twillingate with her singing and organ playing that her father, the local doctor, encouraged her to seek professional training. She spent two years in Toronto and then went on to Paris, where she was given an audition with the famed vocal teacher Mathilde Marchesi. Her voice drew immediate praise— 'A true mezzo-soprano of the highest order . . . a voice the world is waiting for.'

Two years later she was singing in Verdi's *Il Trovatore* in Milan, and in 1893 made her grand opera debut in Paris, now under the stage name of Marie Toulinquet (the original French name of Twillingate). She eventually joined the New Imperial Opera Company in New York, touring as prima donna soprano to great acclaim, and in 1898 was on stage at the Metropolitan in its production of *Faust*. The singer stayed in touch with her relatives and made time to visit Newfoundland during her travels between Europe and America. She gave numerous recitals in Twillingate, and in the fall of 1896, before leaving Newfoundland for New York, stopped first in Whitbourne for a church performance and then in St. John's, where she sang at the dedication service for the new Gower Street Methodist Church. The audience of 1,700 that crowded the imposing structure were said to be especially enraptured by her rendition of 'Hear Ye, O Israel.'

Mademoiselle Toulinquet's greatest triumph came in Italy, at the performance of a new mass staged in Chioggia in 1898. At a special night organized in her honour, the tributes culminated in a lavish bouquet from which emerged live doves and canaries. The singer who 'with intelligence and love . . . steals the hearts of the public,' now at the height of her fame, toured Italy for much of the next two years.

At the age of thirty-four her career came to a sudden end. Her operatic repertoire had permanently damaged her voice (a voice that some had said was more suited to oratorio), leaving her no choice but to withdraw from the stage. She sank into a depression, and turned to alcohol to relieve her anxiety. She retired to London to live with two of her sisters, intermittently seeking help at a women's treatment centre in rural England. In 1929, with both sisters dead, Georgina Stirling returned to the family home in Twillingate. There she lived her final days. The sight of Miss Georgie in the midst of her glorious garden fragrant with lavender and lilac, her hair held back with a scarlet kerchief, her cat, Marchesi, at her heels—this was the final memory most residents had of the woman who once held spellbound the audiences of the great opera houses of the world.

26 | Confederation Off the Rails

The acquisition of the Island itself is of no importance to Canada . . .

—John A. Macdonald, 1869

*Potential Fathers of Confederation, Frederick Carter and Ambrose Shea
(standing to the left of Sir John A.) at the Quebec Conference of 1864.*

The Antis Face the Wolf

In 1855 Newfoundland was granted responsible government. Approval from the British Crown was still needed for legislation to become law, but the new structure brought a Legislative Council responsible not to the governor, but to the House of Assembly, with the Council's members appointed by the prime minister. A new district was added— 'Burgeo and LaPoile' on the southwest coast. The west coast and Labrador remained a political wilderness.

The leader of the Liberal party, Philip Francis Little, was a native of Prince Edward Island, a Duckworth Street lawyer, and a Catholic. It proved a winning combination for the times. He became Newfoundland's first prime minister, and leader of a Catholic-dominated House of Assembly. Bishop Mullock's elation at that particular turn of events was somewhat tempered by the fact that in a few districts people had the temerity to elect a candidate of a minority religion. Matters really came down to earth when, months later, it became clear that some of the Catholic winners in the election were just as prone to corruption as the Protestant incumbents they had replaced. Catholic road construction, as it turned out, had no fewer potholes than Protestant road construction.

In the decades that followed, the more enlightened leaders saw that governments could not continue down such a path. One such person was Frederick Carter, first elected in 1855, and who at forty-two was Speaker of the House. Carter, a Protestant, and Ambrose Shea, Opposition leader and Catholic, had been the two men to represent Newfoundland at the Quebec Conference in 1864, which eventually led to the British North America Act and the union of Canada East and Canada West, New Brunswick, and Nova Scotia.

Carter was much taken with the atmosphere of co-operation and pragmatism he discovered among the delegates, to which he added his own voice: 'We come here representing all shades of politics . . . We break all distinctions of party down for this occasion, and I hope forever.' Carter returned from the Quebec Conference determined that Newfoundland should be part of this new union. But, unlike Charles Tupper in Nova Scotia, he saw it as a decision of the people rather than the legislature.

The affable Carter became prime minister in 1865, and formed a coalition-type government with Shea and other Catholics, a significant step forward in healing sectarian wounds. Catholics and Protestants would make room for each other at the cabinet table, and there would be a sharing of government's public works jobs and patronage appointments. As blatantly restrictive as it might seem, it is this agreement that is responsible more than anything for a cessation of sectarian turmoil. Religious feuding would not cease, of course. That would be too much to expect of a country where divergent roots of religion ran so deep. But there was a new, more substantive calm over the political affairs of the Island. (With the Harbour Grace Affray two decades later would come a short-lived return to sectarianism. Uglier than ever, a campaign slogan of the time was 'no truck or trade' with Catholics. But not long after, government leaders would rediscover a spirit of co-operation, even if their true motive was retaining political power.)

In 1869 Carter was prepared to test the political spirit of co-operation and put confederation with Canada to a vote. But the debate that ensued was far from the reasoned exchange that he had been counting on. It drew to politics a merchant workhorse whose style sharply contrasted with Carter's statesman-like approach. In a place where political debate had a tradition of being deafeningly emotional, Charles Fox Bennett filled up most of the stage.

The arguments in favour of confederation were not strong to begin with, and Bennett saw them flounder in his patriotic rants. 'For a few thousand dollars of Canadian gold, / Will you let it be said that your birthright was sold?' became the relentless refrain. What birthright? To scraping a livelihood under the thumb of merchant credit, in an outport without schools or health care? No one seemed to be asking the question. Instead, Bennett thickened the air with rhetoric about the French invasions of d'Iberville, Ireland being swallowed up by Britain, even the threat of Newfoundlanders having to join mainland armies and 'bleach their bones on the desert sands of Canada.'

And, as if that wasn't enough to stir the masses, the Antis (as they became known) hauled out the old standby—threat of taxation. The 'Canadian wolf' would slap a tax on every piece of fishing gear a family had, Bennett warned as he steamed from bay to bay in his electioneering vessel. And on every quintal of fish caught and cured!

If Bennett had let the case against confederation stand or fall without distortion, it is still doubtful if Carter could have carried the day. For many of the arguments that favoured the union of 1867 held very little weight in Newfoundland.

The Island's per capita debt and the interest rates charged on its loans were both lower than those of any of the provinces, all of whom were shouldering the burden of railway construction. There would be no new markets for Newfoundland fish since Quebec and the Maritimes already supplied all that was needed. Neither did Newfoundland feel any threat from the United States. In fact, ties, both familial and economic, were generally stronger to the United States than they were to Canada. And the issue of French-English relations was of absolutely no relevance.

Against the nebulous, intellectual notion that Newfoundland would benefit from being part of a larger political whole, that its economic state would improve as a result of joining forces with a more diversified and stable mainland, the anticonfederation arguments could hardly fail. They provided easy answers for an isolated population with no first-hand knowledge of the relative prosperity that had emerged to the west of them. Fear of the unknown and pride in standing apart—these as much as anything resulted in massive defeat for the confederates. When the ballots were counted, they held but nine seats. The Antis took a resounding twenty-one. The Canadian wolf would have to wait another eighty years before daring to show his face again.

Railway Fever

If the vote had come a quarter century later Newfoundlanders might well have sung a different tune at election time. For by then the Island was as burdened with railway debt as any of the Canadian provinces.

The latter part of the nineteenth century witnessed a fervent push for railway construction throughout North America. The iron road was seen as the great tool of progress, the way to uncover the vast riches to the west. Sandford Fleming, its greatest promoter, held up a grand vision of railway building that would speed the traveller from London to New York in less than a week! A steamship to St. John's, followed by a cross-Island railway to St. George's, were two of its key components. It all sounded wildly speculative, but that didn't stop it from stirring the Newfoundland government to action. If the Island were not to miss out on the lunge to prosperity, the thinking went, then it had better start planning for a railway.

There had already been strong signs of new wealth far from its centre of population on the Avalon. The Island's first mine opened at Tilt Cove in Notre Dame Bay in 1864, following the discovery of rich outcroppings of copper ore. What other

Copper miners (housed in the more meagre dwellings) swelled the population of Little Bay to over two thousand by 1891. A decade later the mine closed.

mineral wealth lay undetected? And what of all that land for farming and lumbering? With an annual influx of men into St. John's seeking poor relief, the government was only too aware of the need to broaden the island's economy, to move away from a sole dependence on the codfishery. Before long politicians began talking as if we had an untamed West of our own, where one day there would be vast 'homesteads' supplying the agricultural needs of the great city to the East. Moses Harvey, the Island's unrivalled promoter, saw the railway leading the way for a 'conversion of the country into a hive of industry' . . . no doubt with its fair share of cattle ranches and gold mines.

Fleming liked the rumblings he heard from Newfoundland. He had termed his grandiose railway scheme 'The All-Red Route,' in reference to the red orb that never seemed to set on the British Empire. According to his immodest vision, one day his rails and ships would link all Victoria's dominions, with the first and last spike being as one. So enthusiastic was he about Newfoundland's part in it that in 1868 he sent a surveyor to the Island at his own expense. The man reported that a railway through the interior was more than feasible, that in fact the cost would be nothing more than 'moderate.'

The first estimates to appear on paper eight years later came in at just under

$24,000 per mile, with a total cost from St. John's to St. George's of $8.5 million. 'Moderate,' still, though hardly realistic.

Now on the scene was a new prime minister, William Whiteway, with an eagerness for a railway unmatched by any politician before or since. However, his proposal to Britain for funds in support of the project hit a very high brick wall. Britain would have nothing to do with a railway that ended on the French Shore, considering the sensitive state of negotiations that were underway with France. In fact, there would be no funds forthcoming in support of a railway of any sort. It was perfectly clear that if there was to be a rail line in Newfoundland, the government would have to go it alone. Whiteway was forced to rework his dream to a trunk line that ended (for the time being at least) in Halls Bay, within quick reach of the Tilt Cove Mine. And to further cut expenses (down to $4 million), he agreed to make the railway the non-standard, so-called narrow-gauge. That particular decision, which would put it out of step with practically every other line in North America, would be one to regret for the life of the railway.

Whiteway pressed ahead, despite opposition from the fish merchants of St. John's. They viewed the ocean as all the transportation route they needed, and in the outports saw men willing to desert the fishery for railway jobs that paid them cash. Nor did the merchants share any of Whiteway's enthusiasm for agriculture or mining, and failed to invest their money accordingly.

They were left to proclaim their opposition to the scheme in the editorial pages of the newspapers. In the summer of 1880 a British team of surveyors arrived to undertake preliminary work for a first stage of construction. It would see tracks from St. John's to Whitbourne, with a branch line to Harbour Grace.

With Fish Prongs at the Ready

About thirty-two kilometres from St. John's, just outside Foxtrap, the surveyors met their first snag—a mob of several hundred, mostly women, armed with everything from broomsticks to fish prongs to stones gathered up in their aprons. Rumours, set in motion by Water Street merchants out to sabotage the railway, had worked them into a frenzy. Their land would be confiscated, they'd been told, their beds taken for taxes, and a tollgate erected outside St. John's, with 'nobody allowed to go in or out except by rail.' All the doings of a conniving Canada out to force Newfoundland into confederation!

The mob looked ready to take on the devil. They drove the surveyors into retreat and forced the government to send Judge D.W. Prowse and a squad of eleven policemen from St. John's to calm their fears. The leader of the mob would hear nothing of it. With 'hair streaming wildly behind,' brandishing her fish prong, she threatened to 'let daylight into their stomachs.' And the judge having just eaten his dinner, at that.

By this time the police learned that the rabble-rousers had seized the surveyors' instruments and hidden them in their homes. It was time to act like policemen and take charge. They fixed their bayonets and faced down the leaders of the pack. By the end of the day they had arrested 'three middle-aged women' and carted them back to Topsail as prisoners. The instruments were found and the survey started up again.

The good people of Foxtrap eventually accepted the fact that there wasn't any devil at work except for the one who lurked behind the fish buyers in St. John's. But it was far from the last of the railway troubles. Much larger ones, with dollar signs surrounding them, loomed ahead.

With Stops and Starts

Needless to say, 'The Battle of Foxtrap,' as it came to be called, brought a swift con-clusion to any debate between Whiteway and the merchants on the issue of the railway. Bids were solicited for its construction and a contract awarded to an American syndicate headed by H.L. Blackman. The contract was for thirty-five years, with the line up and running to Halls Bay in five. The first tracks were laid on 16 August 1881 in St. John's, near where the Belvedere Cemetery meets Empire Avenue. By the fall nine hundred men were at work, each drawing eight cents an hour, many providing their own shovel if they had one.

Fewer than three years later Blackman was bankrupt. Much of what his com-pany had built was substandard, and it fell forty-three kilometres short of Harbour Grace. A shame-faced government was left to quietly encourage the bondholders in their task of completing the connection to Harbour Grace in order to see some return on their investment. On 11 October 1884 a last spike of sorts was driven sixteen kilometres outside the Conception Bay community, as workers ballasted the remainder in time to have trains running the following spring. (The fall of that same year would see the silver-bearded Donald Alexander Smith, formerly HBC factor in Labrador, drive the last spike of the CPR.)

Newfoundland now had a partial rail line to serve a section of the Avalon Peninsula. Halls Bay and those fertile western shores were still a long way away. A new contract and the job of completing the trunk line westward fell to Robert Gillespie Reid, a Canadian. Reid's eventual monopoly on communications in Newfoundland, and the vast amount of land handed over to him as part of this railway deal, would cause the man and his heirs to loom large across our landscape for many decades to come.

Reid was a Scot who came to Canada as a stonemason and bridge builder. He did stone work for a time on the new Parliament Buildings in Ottawa, before going on to establish a considerable reputation in both Canada and the United States in railway construction. He was just the man Whiteway was seeking. Reid set to work with a determination that reawakened confidence in the government. A generous contract was signed, which, when revised in 1893, gave Reid five thousand acres of Crown land for each mile of track laid down, much of it of his own choosing.

Newfoundland fell into an intense period of railway work. That first year a crew of a thousand or more men made their way out from Whitbourne, working ten-hour days, sleeping in temporary tarpaper shacks of their own hasty construction. Darkness brought hundreds of open cooking fires along a few kilometres of railway bed. This was a new breed of pioneer and the camaraderie that grew up laid the foundation for a great romance with the interior of the Island and with the railway, holding many of the men to it for the rest of their working lives. It was a Newfoundland that didn't require sea legs, and was relatively unconstrained by wind and weather, welcome attributes to many who as fishermen had failed to support their outport families.

Robert Gillespie Reid

By 1897 Reid's cross-Island railway was complete. It ended not in Halls Bay as originally planned but in Port aux Basques, the closest port to

Canada, a route that brought the line through the infamous Gaff Topsails. That particular stretch of stark and rocky highland, with its snowdrifts that seemed to grow more mountainous with each winter, would forever take precedence in Newfoundland railway lore.

But with the completion of the railway came an acute financial crisis. By 1894 the public debt stood at $9 million, having more than quadrupled in ten years. A bank crash sent the colony to the brink of collapse, with much of the finger pointing in the direction of the contract with Reid. The government even went to Ottawa to explore the possibility of Newfoundland joining Canada, a scenario that politicians there quickly spurned. With our treasury books now red with railway debt just like the provinces', we were not much of an attraction. Only a last-minute loan from Britain saved the Newfoundland government from total ruin.

And now that the construction was completed, what was the government to do with more than eight hundred kilometres of rail line and Reid's contract to maintain it due to run out in a few years? Reid had a proposal.

For a land grant of an additional five thousand acres for each mile of track, he would agree to operate the railway for the next fifty years. He would purchase the drydock in St. John's, and, under subsidy, take over control of the telegraph system and the ferry to Nova Scotia, as well as operate a fleet of steamships to service the Newfoundland coast. For an immediate payment to the treasury of $1 million, the railway would become the property of his heirs when the agreement terminated.

Viable tender until the bank crash of 1894, a crash precipitated
by borrowing to pay for railway construction.

With this proposal Newfoundland would unleash an economic overlord, with all the potential for government at the mercy of at his wishes, just as a half century later New Brunswick would be at K.C. Irving's. The opposition to it was relentless. 'Immoral and dishonest,' decried the new Liberal leader, Robert Bond. There could be no justification for bartering the 'destinies of the country.' One St. John's paper summarily dismissed the government as 'rotten from the centre to circumference.'

In spite of the collective anger the contract was signed in 1898. Only then did it come to light that A.B. Morine, the colony's minister of finance, had been working as Reid's lawyer while at the negotiation table on behalf of the government. The public was outraged. The Tories fell on a vote of confidence in the House of Assembly.

Amid the turmoil that continued, Bond, as the new prime minister, entered prolonged negotiations for a revised contract. Reid and his three sons (who by now were all involved in the running of the business) would relent, but only to a limited extent, and for a price. A return of the $1 million, plus interest, saw an elimination of the clause on reversionary rights. Another $850,000 bought back the additional lands acquired in the 1898 deal. Through arbitration, $1.5 million was paid to regain control of the telegraph system. The other clauses of the 1898 deal remained the same, though the Reids no longer held the promise of becoming the economic barons of Newfoundland. Development of forest and mining resources would await other hands.

By 1908 R.G. Reid had died. The Reid Newfoundland Railway, never able to turn a profit in the way that its mainland counterparts did, lasted until 1923, at which point the government bought all title to it for $2 million. Despite the economic turbulence it caused, the railway had its benefits. By means of its branch lines, it united the pockets of the Island's scattered population, and forced the Avalon to acknowledge the rest of the Island in a way it never had before. And with a ferry to Nova Scotia at its western terminus, suddenly Canada didn't seem all that distant.

The train ride itself took on mythic dimensions. It was an all-day, all-night exercise in cultural bonding, often aided by a little rum and accordion music. Known with affection as 'The Bullet,' it lived up to its reputation to the very end, taking twenty-two hours (on a good day) to wind its way from Port aux Basques to St. John's, down from the twenty-eight hours when the railway had opened at the turn of the century. But by 1969 the Bullet was no more, replaced with a fourteen-hour bus service on the newly constructed Newfoundland section of the Trans-Canada Highway. Within two decades even the freight trains had stopped, and shortly after that crews had taken up the last of the Reid narrow-gauge tracks. Now across the Island only the rail beds remain, forming Newfoundland's contribution to that country-wide footpath, the Trans-Canada Trail.

Sir Robert

Of all our prime ministers, Robert Bond is the most admired. The impassioned, erudite career politician conducted himself like a statesman, a demeanour rare among those who preceded him, and non-existent among those who would follow.

Bond expected Britain to treat his country as the equal of any of the other territories that had once been part of British North America, Canada included. In 1890, as colonial secretary under Whiteway, he negotiated a trade agreement with the United States without first consulting Canada or considering its interests. When word of the Bond-Blaine Convention reached Ottawa (via the troublemaker A.B. Morine), a furious Canadian government dashed off a spate of telegrams to London. It vehemently protested that its Maritime provinces would be pounding the doors in Ottawa to demand nothing less than what Newfoundland had received.

Bond suspected another reason—that Canada saw a self-assured Newfoundland with closer ties to the United Sates as less likely to be drawn into the fold of confederation. Not only that, but perhaps Canada detected a richer, more accommodating American wolf lurking about the Atlantic waters. The idea of a Canada wedged between Alaska and the state of Newfoundland and Labrador sent a shudder through Parliament in Ottawa.

Under pressure from Canada, the Colonial Office in London refused to ratify the Bond-Blaine Convention. Bond was outraged, declaring interference in Newfoundland's right of self-government. Newfoundland retaliated by passing an act that forbade Canadian fisherman to take bait and supplies in its waters. An angrier Canada jacked up its duty on Newfoundland fish. The colony answered by forbidding the importation of Canadian flour and potatoes. The game threatened to get nastier, until Britain stepped in and pressed the two sides into negotiations. The tariffs were dropped and a grudging peace was made. Newfoundland's

Robert Bond

interests had been forced into line once more.

Yet, only four years later, in 1894, when two of the Island's banks collapsed and the colony fell to the brink of bankruptcy, Britain was the first to say no when the colony went looking for help. ' . . . the Mother Country's reply?' asked an indignant editorial in the *Evening Telegram*. 'We refuse to help you in your difficulties; but we will send Marines and Blue Jackets to shoot you down, in your need and desperation, raise a hand against the bank thieves who have ruined you.' Only when it saw that Newfoundland had been forced to once again consider union with Canada did 'Our Stepmother, Mrs. Britannia' come around to thinking financial aid might be a reasonable idea. It would be, in the words of the Colonial Office, 'a cheap price to pay for getting what has been our wish for nearly 30 years.'

But Bond wasn't about to go to Ottawa with cap in hand. Some Newfoundlanders were arguing that approval of the Bond-Blaine Convention might have prevented the bank crash. Bond left an Island with the Stars and Stripes prominent on several of the capital's buildings, unfurled following the arrival of relief supplies from ex-Newfoundlanders living in New England. The *Evening Telegram* had reprinted several editorials from newspapers in New York and Boston. 'American sympathies should be with Newfoundland in her contest with Britain and Canada,' said one. 'It is a battle of the strong against the weak . . . against government of the people, by the people, for the people.' Could statehood be far behind?

The Canadian government, under the less-than-inspired leadership of the less-than-memorable prime minister Mackenzie Bowell, mounted a high horse, seemingly unfazed by such a possibility. Even in Britain's eyes, Canada drove an unnecessarily tough bargain. It agreed to assume only part of Newfoundland's public debt. Britain, it insisted, should pay off the remainder. The cost turned out to be much higher than the Colonial Office had anticipated, and (to no surprise from Newfoundland) the Motherland backed off. It would rather that its first territory in the new world fall back to being a Crown colony.

Without any flexibility on the part of the Canadian government, negotiations collapsed. Bond moved on, determined to find a way out of his country's problems, without compromising its dignity. He took a train to Quebec and secured a small loan from the Bank of Montreal, using his own personal wealth as collateral. From there he went on to Boston and New York and met with Americans who had been promoting the possibility of political union with Newfoundland. But with the secretary of state ill, and other urgent matters pressing the agenda of his department, Bond's inquiries in Washington went unattended.

At the eleventh hour, Bond secured a second, and larger, loan from merchant bankers in London, working through their Montreal agents. The two loans together were enough to rescue the country from bankruptcy. Regrettably, the management of Newfoundland's finances had now been delivered into the hands of the foreign Bank of Montreal. Construction began almost immediately on an appropriate stone edifice on Water Street. The Canadian dollar became our legal tender.

But Bond returned to Newfoundland a hero, a saviour who had risked his personal fortune when the British and Canadian governments failed him. The populace had never witnessed such a commitment in its merchants or politicians. The man stood apart, was secured on a pedestal, and would remain there for much of his life.

Beyond the French Shore

Bond's assertiveness had rewarded him. A deeper strain of it surfaced once he became prime minister. In 1904 he tackled the thorniest of international issues affecting his country—the French Shore.

In Newfoundland and Labrador the hatred of the annual fishing fleets from France transcended even religion and politics. (The fact that there was an issue that did, might, in itself, be viewed as positive.) Everyone agreed that the French fishing rights were a hindrance to the development of the west coast of the Island. Every prime minister before Bond had laid that argument before the British government, but without success. Britain was not about to ruffle French feathers over a matter that concerned only the fishing colonials. The French Shore, after all, had been the stuff of war.

But by the turn of the century, in light of friendlier Anglo-French relations, there seemed a need to bring a final resolution to what had been a sore point for close to two hundred years. The construction of several French lobster canneries in Newfoundland brought matters to a head. Bond pressed the Colonial Office for action. What resulted was agreement that the French would give up the rights granted by the Treaty of Utrecht in return for a closely monitored offshore fishery and the transfer of some British territory in Africa. Bond insisted that Newfoundland's claim to the shoreline be explicit and absolute, a fine point that the Colonial Office looked upon as petty.

But Bond had his reasons. On 21 April 1904 he was able to rise in the House of Assembly and declare that Newfoundland was now 'freed from . . . the blasting influence of foreign oppression.' The Island was 'ours in entirety, solely ours.'

Henceforth, Newfoundland would no longer be able to point to the French Shore as one of the reasons for its listless economy. The new century, in fact, held great promise. Fish catches were up and prices were high. The mining industry was expanding. And in central Newfoundland construction began on the Island's first pulp-and-paper mill. The Harmsworth brothers of England had scouted the area around Grand Falls looking for a secure supply of newsprint for their newspaper

French fishing premises at Conche, 1880s.

Interior of the newly constructed newsprint mill at Grand Falls.

empire, which included London's *Daily Mail* and *Daily Mirror*. The mill would transform the region, and through the century bring it a level of prosperity unknown in most of Newfoundland.

Years later the Bond era would be looked upon as a 'golden age' of sorts. When he left politics in 1914, retiring to a life of reading and experimental farming on his estate in Whitbourne, there was still a great deal of optimism about the future of Newfoundland and Labrador. Then came the outbreak of the Great War. World economic forces would turn against the Dominion, and perhaps not even Bond could have saved the day. But the downward financial spiral that eventually swallowed up the country was only accelerated by the breed of leaders that now fought for office. The country's welfare would take second place to private gain, public life turning into, in Robert Bond's words, 'dirty business.' That it could lead to political self-destruction became a sad commentary on what ends leaders would go to for power and money. And, ultimately, a sadder commentary on how centuries of economic and educational suppression would instill in a citizenry the lack of will and confidence to rise up and rid the country of such parasitic men.

27 | A Berth to the Ice

It's jest dog's work while it lasts, but somehow there's an excitement in it that sets young fellers kind o' restless in the spring . . . Man'll go for a swile where gold won't drag 'un.

—Bob Saunders, quoted in *Newfoundland and Her Untrodden Ways*, 1907

Four sealers gather on deck, ready to take to the ice.

Ice Hunting

Salt cod was still the mainstay of the Newfoundland economy. With the invention of the cod trap by William Whiteley in 1860 more fish could be taken with less effort, though the fishery remained at the mercy of the elements. Good seasons were invariably mixed with lean ones, and the most stable communities were those that came up with other sources of income. Parts of the south coast, where temperatures were milder and harbours ice-free, initiated a winter fishery. In Conception Bay and along the northeast coast, it was a burgeoning spring seal fishery that kept poverty away from the door.

Sealing (or 'swiling' as Newfoundlanders called it) had started in the late 1700s as a modest inshore supplement to the cod fishery. Within a few decades it had grown into a vast enterprise that saw hundreds of schooners loaded with outport men heading to 'the Front'—the fields of ice with their herds of seals that had drifted south from Greenland to lie off our northern coasts. Striking a large herd brought the sealers 'into the fat,' for the quest was driven by a demand for the oil rendered from the seal blubber. It was oil to fuel the newly invented Argand lamp, which had revolutionized home and commercial lighting. Other uses for the oil quickly followed, in machine lubrication and the curing of leather. Much of the

A trail of sealers out for 'swiles.'

demand followed in the wake of the Revolutionary War in the American colonies, when Britain's supply of oil from New England whalers came to an end.

The product derived from the fat of newly born 'whitecoats' proved particularly valuable and by the 1840s in excess of half a million animals were being taken annually. At its peak the fishery drew four hundred ships to the ice floes, and, incredibly, nearly half of the adult male population from Notre Dame Bay to Trepassey. It was a vital economic boost for a people who had always dreaded the long and hungry days of March, and it proved a perfect match for the summer Labrador fishery since the same ships could be used for both enterprises.

Rough and dangerous, sealing became a passage to manhood. Every outport son aspired to a 'berth' aboard one of the ships heading to the ice. All that was required was a gaff—a wooden pole of about two metres tipped with an iron hook and spike, a knife for cutting away the pelt with the fat attached (what sealers called 'sculping'), a length of rope for hauling the pelts back to the ship, a tolerance for cold and a nimble pair of legs for jumping the ice pans.

A bloodied ice field wasn't a pretty sight, but neither was a family gone hungry. As it stood, the hardships that the sealer endured far outweighed what money he could hope to make. If herds of seals were not to be found, perhaps because he had shipped in with an inexperienced captain, his pockets might be emptier when he returned than when he left. In an average season, after the crew's share was divided among the forty men, and the sealer paid off the credit the owners had advanced him, he might take home $50. All this after several weeks aboard an overcrowded schooner that was 'inconceivably filthy . . . saturated in oil,' with the living quarters consisting of 'a narrow dark cabin of the smallest possible dimensions.'

And, of course, there was the ever-present possibility that the sealer might never return. Many of the wooden vessels were lost when a sudden change of wind turned the ice against them. Still more sank when storms struck on the voyage home, and caused their cargoes of oily pelts to shift. Men habitually risked their lives, and accepted it without question. Yet the experience of a trip to the ice was not to be missed. The lure of it was as strong as ever when the 'wooden walls' were replaced by bigger ships, iron-clad steamers, in the early 1900s.

I could see it still in the eyes of eighty-five-year-old Alf Squire of Bonavista Bay, who in 1977 recalled for me his nine springs at the hunt. 'I liked ice huntin',' he said. 'I liked anywhere where there was sport, although 'twas hard.' Alf was only seventeen when he made his first trip, aboard the *Neptune*, a ship crammed with 275 sealers as cold and eager as himself. It was a rough initiation. The owners, Job Brothers of St. John's, fed them on the cheapest food that would fill a man's stomach. 'No potatoes,' just bread and butter, duff (boiled pudding made of flour and water), boiled 'brewis' (hardtack), and tea. The only protein came when they struck into a patch of seals, and could bring back a few flippers with the pelts.

That year they came home from the ice with a paltry seventeen thousand pelts, and a vessel ravaged by typhoid fever. One man died aboard ship, another three in the hospital after they landed in St. John's. The rest were herded off to 'the quarantine ground' for three weeks. Alf Squire was one of the men who eventually came down with the fever. Though he recovered, it put a stop to his plans for a summer trip to the Labrador fishery.

In fact he was doubly lucky to be alive. Heading to St. John's from the ice, the *Neptune* ran into a savage storm and lost its bearings near the headlands of Conception Bay. Everyone aboard was called on deck, the ship pitching in the swell amid the blinding snow, everyone trusting to the one man aloft in the crow's nest. 'Not a man spoke, just like a crowd o' sheep . . . just trustin' to that one man . . . All you'd do is put yer hand on one another's shoulder and just watch 'er.' Only a last-minute call to 'bear off' saved them. 'There'd 'a been lots o' people went down in that one as sure as you'm born,' Alf Squire concluded, with no more emotion than when he told how one spring in the *Bloodhound* he cleared $102. 'That was me biggest trip. Went away next spring and I made 40.'

Led or Leading?

That stoic acceptance of whatever came to pass, of being led into danger without confronting the reason for it, was a trait for which we must account. For it bears on many of the calamities that were to befall Newfoundlanders, not only at the seal hunt, but in other, equally perilous, arenas. It is something that drew the attention of surveyor-writer J.B. Jukes in 1842, when we had only just begun to feel ourselves a nation. Jukes greatly admired the courage and hardiness of Newfoundlanders, yet he was despairing of certain other attributes he thought all too common among what he called 'the lower classes.' 'They are easily led,' he wrote, 'and always look for guidance, being ready to follow any one who will take the trouble of thinking and deciding for them.' Patronizing drivel from the English upper crust? We've certainly had enough of that through the ages. But if we judge Jukes by his willingness to jump over the side of the sealing ship, gaff in hand, and plunge into the thick of the hunt, then we would have to conclude that he is a different case. Jukes felt compelled to end his book with a tribute to the 'sterling kindness and hospitality,' of Newfoundlanders. We are left to wonder whether there was not some merit in his other observations.

If there was this subservient attitude through much of our history, from where did it arise? Was it the result of the long-standing merchant-servant relationship, and the desperate lack of schooling? Did the working classes grow submissive in the face of those whose storehouses fed their children? As master mariner Bob Bartlett observed, ' . . . the sealer is going out to decide whether his wife and babies will have molasses cakes with their boiled codfish for the next eleven months.' In choosing food over fair treatment they would have been no different than the suppressed peoples of any nation.

We do have hints of rebellion through the nineteenth century. A strike in Conception Bay had forced ship owners to pay the men in cash rather than by the abuse-prone system of credit that ruled the codfishery. Another brought a halt to increases in the 'berth charges,' the money ship owners demanded of sealers for the privilege of signing on for the hunt. But it was the sealers' strike of 1902 that most clearly demonstrated the limits to fighting the power of the merchants.

As happened every year, by the first week of March the wharfs of St. John's were crowded with the thousands of men ready to sign on for the hunt. Rumours abounded that the sealer's wage would be $2.40 per hundredweight of fat, down eighty-five cents from the year before. As it stood, their overall share of the earnings had been slashed to one-third from the one-half paid in the days of the wooden ships.

The men joined forces and headed toward Government House, demanding a price of $5 per hundredweight. By the time the three thousand embittered and hungry men reached Military Road and the residence of Sir Cavendish Boyle, their demands had escalated—elimination of any charges for signing on, food for the time spent in St. John's before the ships left port, and an end to the insidious practice of inflating the prices of goods the men bought on credit. (For a pair of boots which normally cost $4.80 the merchant deducted $7.60 at the end of the trip.)

For three days the ship owners ignored the strikers. They stood back and smugly watched as the sealers' supply of food from sympathetic inhabitants of St. John's diminished. They watched as the men were forced to spend the frigid nights of March in the streets, and as they lost the support of the townsmen—the skinners, the shopkeepers, the coopers—who depended on the hunt for their livelihood. The sealers held firm.

The owners, perhaps fearing a riot through the city, eventually offered $3.25 per hundredweight. The men rejected it. An angry Arthur Jackman, sealing captain and warhorse of the industry, hauled up the anchor of the *Terra Nova*, claiming he would man his ship elsewhere. When word reached the men that Sam Blandford was about to leave the harbour in the *Neptune*, three hundred of them boarded the ship and made off with the free end of the hawser. They planted themselves on shore and, hauling together, tried to prevent the ship from leaving. The incensed Blandford ordered full steam ahead. With 'fearful' strain the rope snapped, fortunately without injury to anyone.

The leaders of the strike seemed more determined than ever to stick to their demands. That afternoon, under pressure from the government, the owners raised their offer to $3.50 per hundredweight and dropped the charge for signing on to the hunt. The leaders again rejected it. But this time some of the sealers broke rank and began making their way to their vessels. The police, sensing an opportunity to take control, quickly cleared the wharfs of anyone out to stop sealers from going aboard.

The most radical of the strikers rushed about, in a vain effort to clear the ships of sealers. Some went looking for gaffs to attack the police. There were none to be found; the owners had removed them from every vessel. The 'extremists,' as the newspapers labelled them the next day, were vastly outnumbered. The strike was over.

Jackman and Blandford steamed back to port and by nightfall every vessel was crammed with men, ready for their several weeks of sealing, nourished on bread and tea, the icy winds blowing through their canvas shucks of clothing, every voyage a footstep away from disaster. Heralded, they were, as the 'hardiest race of men in the universe,' their gamble 'the greatest hunt in the world.'

Huddles of Frozen Men

The strike of 1902 might have alerted the owners to the deep-seated dissatisfaction among the sealers, but, ultimately, it accounted for nothing. There was more pressure than ever to fill the holds, to return to port the 'high-liner,' as the *Florizel* and its captain, Abram Kean, had done in 1910 with the largest number of pelts ever brought to shore in one trip—close to fifty thousand. From the sealing skippers, those revered giants among seamen, the sealers heard the call for bumper trips. For profit and prestige the owners pushed their boats and crews beyond the limits of safety. In 1914 their recklessness caught up with them.

The sinking of the *Southern Cross*, with the loss of all its 173 men, was the worst of it. The ship was racing to St. John's from the Gulf of St. Lawrence, weighed down with a full load of pelts, eager to lay claim to being the first ship back and to the token reward that went with it. The ship struck foul weather and, foolishly, failed to seek shelter. On the morning of March thirty-first, it answered the whistle of the *Portia* near Cape Pine. Through the blinding snow, it could barely be seen, only enough to note how low it lay in the water. The *Southern Cross* was never heard from again. Nor were any bodies ever found. Its owners had not equipped the ship with a wireless, and exactly what happened will never be known.

On that morning of the last sighting of the *Southern Cross*, another sealing ship, the old wooden-walled *Newfoundland*, found itself stuck in ice at the Front. It, too, was without a wireless. The owners, Harvey and Company, had removed it to save money.

The *Newfoundland* was under the command of Wes Kean. His father, the venerable Abram Kean, stood in charge of the pride of the fleet, Bowring Brothers' iron-clad *Stephano,* several kilometres away. (This was the

The frozen bodies of sealers with their gaffs, on the deck of the Bellaventure.

man who, years later, at the age of seventy-eight, would bring to shore his one-millionth seal, and gather in his OBE). The day before, the elder Kean had signalled to his son that the *Stephano* had struck the main herd of seals. At 7 a.m. on the thirty-first the captain of the *Newfoundland* sent all his men onto the ice, under the leadership of George Tuff, with instructions to make their way to his father's ship. From there Abram Kean would lead them to the seals.

It took nearly four and a half hours, often over rough Arctic ice, to reach the *Stephano*. They climbed aboard exhausted, to await their orders, all the while keeping an eye on the weather. It had grown steadily worse since they left their ship.

Abram Kean gave them but thirty minutes' rest. Some of them managed a mug of tea and a few chews of hard bread before they were all ordered back over the side again. They were to kill what seals they could, pile and flag them, then return to their own ship. Tuff was baffled. Weren't they to spend the night on the *Stephano*? But he said nothing to Kean. Nobody countered the orders of the legendary sealing captain.

Only on the ice, with the *Stephano* steaming away, and a storm coming on (the same one that claimed the *Southern Cross*) did the men get the full knowledge of what was expected of them. Tuff insisted they move off and kill some seals. Others sensed the danger in losing any time before heading for their own ship. A bitter confrontation erupted, and in the end Tuff won out. An hour had passed before the rising winds and drifting snow forced him to admit the foolishness of waiting any longer. He and the master watches read their compasses and started the trek in the direction of the *Newfoundland*.

Captain Wes Kean stood on the deck of his vessel thinking his men were safely aboard the *Stephano*, but with no wireless to confirm it. Surely his father would have taken them in for the night. Abram Kean would swear later that he assumed the sealers were well within reach of their own ship, a distance he took to be no more than five kilometres. No one, he said, could have predicted the ferocity of the storm that fell on them.

The men of the *Newfoundland* were left stranded on the ice, soaked first by pounding rain, then whipped by frenzied gusts of wind and snow. It had turned into the worst storm of the winter. There was no choice but to stop and do what they could to survive the night . . . and the next day and a second night, for no one came in search of them, each captain thinking them safely aboard the other ship.

Many did not survive. Their ice shelters failed them, as did the scraps of fires made from burning their gaffs and rope. Brawny young men fell away to frozen sleep. A dead father stood frozen with his arms around his two dead sons, the drifted snow piled against them. In all, seventy-eight men perished. Rescue of the survivors came only when a few of them finally stumbled within sight of the *Newfoundland* and were caught in Wes Kean's spyglass. By the time the last of the survivors was found and taken aboard the sealing fleet, they had been on the ice for fifty-three hours. The frozen dead were hoisted aboard and piled three deep on the deck of the *Bellaventure*, like so much pulpwood.

No criminal charges were ever laid, though the government ordered a three-man inquiry into the tragedy. Two of the three found Abram Kean guilty of 'a grave error of judgement.' The third found it all to be 'An Act of God.' The gods were the sealing merchants, and the captains sent to implement their greed.

When Words Fail

The spring of 1914 saw the loss of more than 250 sealers. One of the communities struck hardest by the disasters was Brigus in Conception Bay. It was the home of Captain George Clarke and many of the crew of the *Southern Cross*. As Clarke's widow 'cried to exhaustion' and his daughter 'lay in half delirium,' neighbours told them "twas the will of God.' This was a scene of grief that Brigus knew far too often.

Farewell, *a print by Rockwell Kent, 1931.*

As an outport it was a rarity. It stood trim and proper, having prospered in the nineteenth century from the dozens of schooners that annually left its wharfs for the seal and Labrador fisheries. It reminded visitors of an English seaside village, and was a summer favourite of the wealthy of St. John's. It had tea rooms and a cosmopolitan air, though tempered by the rigour of the North Atlantic.

That may have been what attracted the

American painter Rockwell Kent. Kent had been seduced by the primal qualities of the Island's landscape on his first visit. He returned in February 1914 with the intention of making it his permanent home. In Brigus he rented an isolated cottage tucked in the cliffs, fixed it up, and sent word to his wife and children in New York to join him.

His arrival coincided with the spring seal hunt. 'Wait 'til the byes come back from the ice; with them and the girls you'll have company enough,' he was told. The hillside near his home was a favourite courting spot in springtime. That spring would be different. On March thirty-first Kent awoke to a fearsome storm of wind and snow. As the news of the disasters trickled in, a pall descended on the village, as in every home people 'huddled about the stove, no thought but of the storm and the *Southern Cross*.'

The suffering of those who came to death on the ice had passed. But for the thousands left onshore it would never reach an end. Those days had a profound influence on Kent's work, coming as it did when he was struggling to find the core of his imagery. He lived with a people he saw as 'confronting the universe, not merely themselves.' On canvas and later in his prints (icons of American printmaking of the 1930s) he often depicted a single human figure weighed down by the immensity of the heavens, sometimes a cluster of shoreline houses providing a refuge.

Captain Bob

Rockwell Kent soaked up the seafaring history of Brigus. He was living among 'map makers, discoverers,' he wrote to his dealer in New York. 'I've become more intimate with our little round earth since I've been here than in all my life before.' He was living, after all, in the place that had nurtured generations of captains, some of whom had gone to the most remote regions of the globe.

None was more honoured than Bob Bartlett. While Kent was drinking tea with Bob's mother and sisters and listening to the sealing stories of his father, the man himself was adrift on a treacherous mass of ice in the middle of the Beaufort Sea. Bartlett had been hired to captain the *Karluk*, the ship taking the Canadian Arctic Expedition, led by Vilhjalmur Stefansson, north for scientific research. The ship was crushed by the ice and sank. Though the party escaped the vessel with their supplies, they were left stranded on the drifting ice pack in the dead of the sunless, minus-forty-degree winter. Bartlett decided they should stay put in the igloos they had built, and move off only when the sun returned. Four of the party, veterans of Antarctic travel, disagreed and struck out on their own. They were never seen again.

In late February 1914 Bartlett led what was left of the crew over nearly impassable ice to Wrangel Island. It took more than two weeks. From there he walked with an Inuit companion across more sea ice to Siberia, and then trekked southward all the way to the Bering Strait. They had traversed an incredible 1,300 kilometres. By ship they reached Alaska, and there Bartlett found a vessel to take him north to rescue the others. On the way to Wrangel Island he encountered a schooner with the survivors aboard.

In what has been called 'the finest example of leadership in the maritime history of Canada,' Captain Bob's initial response to the plight of the sunken ship had saved all fourteen people. Ironically, at the very moment Bartlett was walking over ice in sight of Siberia and its promise of shelter, his countrymen, ill-clad and poorly led, were perishing in their dozens on the ice off Newfoundland.

Captain Bob Bartlett

Bartlett knew more than anyone the need to have respect for the frozen sea. He navigated it with the world's great polar explorers for years. When these adventurers came looking for ships and men to get them through the worst ice conditions anywhere, it was not to Gloucester or Portsmouth they turned, but to the ports of Newfoundland. There Scott found the *Terra Nova*, and Robert Peary found a captain for the *Roosevelt*.

Bartlett's most famous trip came in 1908–9 when he commanded Peary's ship in his final thrust to the North Pole, with a send-off by President Theodore Roosevelt himself. They sailed and steamed to Cape Sheridan, at the tip of Ellesmere Island. From there the crew of explorers and Inuit, and nearly 250 huskies, sledged supplies westward to Cape Columbia. Peary's strategy was to establish caches of food at several points along the route. Once they were all in place, he would then make a relatively quick dash to the Pole, using the supplies of one cache to get him to the next.

For safety he would need a companion. Given his experience and record of endurance, Bartlett was the obvious choice. Or so Peary led him to believe.

The final cache was put in place by Bartlett 240 kilometres from the Pole, the farthest north any human had ever gone. There, in the late days of March 1909, Peary showed up with his black naval servant, Matthew Henson, dog teams, and four Inuit drivers. Peary had changed his mind, and decided Henson would be the one to accompany him to the Pole. Arguments broke out, but the decision was final. A devastated Bartlett 'got up early the next morning while the rest were asleep, and started north alone.' He covered eight kilometres and, by his own calculations, reached eighty-eight degrees before turning back. He left Peary and the others and headed south to the base camp.

Why Peary, weak and unable to walk properly, would have forsaken the man most capable of helping him reach the Pole has been debated ever since. Was it because he did not want to share the glory with another white man, someone who was not American? Was it because he realized that if he did not make it all the way to the Pole the honest Bartlett would never tell the world otherwise?

The story Peary broke to an eager public was that he stood as the first man on the top of the world, that he had indeed spent thirty hours on the fabled ninety degrees. But he had arrived back with nothing to prove it. Many people have calculated that his return to Cape Sheridan took much less time than was possible for anyone who had reached the North Pole.

Bartlett kept his own feelings on the matter secret to the end of his life. Had he been the leader of the expedition instead of Peary, there is little doubt he could have been the first man to set foot on the Pole. A moot point, of course, because he had neither the financial backing nor the citizenship to make it possible. As great an explorer as he was, Bartlett, too, was forced to be a follower, the man behind other men's dreams.

In New York, where he spent much of his life, he turned into a curiosity, a spent Arctic man always good for a story. He took out American citizenship, hoping for something more than leading the rich of the Explorers' Club on polar-bear hunts. He spent much of the First World War in the U.S. Armed Forces, and several years after in deep depression.

Arguably his final decades were his happiest. In 1925 a wealthy American friend gave him money to buy a schooner, his beloved *Effie M. Morrissey*, which he sailed out of Brigus, undertaking a spate of expeditions north for various American scientific institutions. Bob Bartlett died in 1946 in New York, but his body was brought home to Brigus. His family house, Hawthorne Cottage, is a National Historic Site and a museum of his Arctic exploits.

Captain Bob is the best known of our polar men. But before him came Richard Pike out of Carbonear, who captained ships to the Arctic for both Adolphus Greely and Robert Peary. In 1929 Jack Bursey of St. Lunaire was along with Richard Byrd on his much-heralded land expedition to Antarctica. The *Dictionary of Newfoundland English* lists dozens of terms describing ice in all its configurations. These men had first-hand experience with them all, and used it to safeguard other, more ambitious men so that ice wouldn't get in the way of their quest for fame.

Incredible, too, is the story of Victor Campbell. Born in England, Campbell would spend the last thirty-five years of his life as a fishing-lodge owner and naval officer in western Newfoundland. He was first mate aboard the *Terra Nova*, the former Bowring Brothers' ship that carried Robert Scott to Antarctica in 1910. Scott's ill-fated final quest for the South Pole overshadowed the remarkable survival story of the Northern Party, the geological expedition led by Campbell. 'Marooned at the stormiest place in Victoria Land in this the stormiest recorded year in Antarctic history' the six men lived for eight months 'in a hole in the snow on one month's sledging provisions and what we could pick up locally, and in summer clothes.' When they finally emerged at the end of the Antarctic winter, Campbell led them to safety, a walk across 370 kilometres of treacherous sea ice and glacier.

B.B. among the Floes

Ice drew the famous of various sorts. In 1930 the American filmmaker Varick Frissell arrived to shoot *The Viking*, the first sound movie shot in what is now Canada, and one of the first sound-synchronized movies filmed on location. The story centred on the annual seal hunt. One of the lead roles, that of the ship's captain, was taken by Bob Bartlett. After the first screening of the film, Frissell took another trip to the front in search of additional footage. He lost his life when the sealing ship in which he was a passenger exploded while caught in ice off the Horse Islands.

Almost fifty years later, a very different filming of the seal fishery was underway. On an icy March day in 1977 the aging sex kitten Brigitte Bardot showed up in St. Anthony on Newfoundland's Northern Peninsula. She was looking for a whitecoat to wrap herself around. It was perhaps the zenith of the media circus that had come to surround the annual seal hunt and turn it into the most vilified of Newfoundland events.

Bardot and her entourage, together with Greenpeace and Brian Davies of the International Fund for Animal Welfare (IFAW), had made the hunt into headlines around the world. Two weeks later Bardot peered out seductively from the cover of *Paris Match* cuddling a live seal pup (albeit one that had been captured and brought back with her to Paris for the photo shoot).

In the meantime St. Anthony was deluged with hate mail. The sealers, who for generations had been augmenting their meagre incomes with a few weeks at the hunt, were suddenly 'ignorant, primitive, stupid, cold-blooded people . . . a bunch of murderers . . . sick with cruelty and savagery.' It was all a brutal lesson in the power of the media. Seal blood spilled on vast open stages of white ice became immensely crueller than that drained into the troughs of abattoirs.

The orchestrated media frenzy of the late 1970s was not the first negative press for the hunt, of course. More than a century before, the writer Jukes had described his revulsion at the scene on the ice floes, as did Philip Tocque after him. Lady Edith Blake, wife of Newfoundland's British governor, penned from Government House (as far from the life of the outport fisherman as was possible in 1889) an essay published under the title 'Seals and Savages.' Newfoundland sealers, she sniffed in print, were a people whose 'intellectual faculties are decidedly in

Brian Davies and Brigitte Bardot at a Paris news conference.

abeyance.' With the advent of television coinciding as it did with a largely unregulated hunt (much of it undertaken by Norway), it was only a matter of time before images of an open-air slaughterhouse would make it to the screen. In the meantime the Canadian government had stepped in to ensure that the killing was humane and the seal population maintained.

It was not enough for the animal rights activists. They had spied an opportunity to build profitable organizations by soliciting funds from comfortable, middle-class, often ill-informed donors. The fact that it was having a huge impact on the ability of fishermen in far-off Newfoundland to make a living was not noted in their mail-outs. Why couldn't these people be given money to build factories and make toy seals out of synthetic fur ran the thinking of Franz Weber, the European who had brought Bardot to St. Anthony.

Through intense campaigning by the IFAW, Weber, and others, the European Union banned the importation of seal products. By 1984 the Canadian government had banned the whitecoat hunt. Three years later the vessel hunt to the front was shut down completely. All that remains is a modest land-based fishery. Ottawa seems willing to wait out a time when it, too, might pass away. For protests on the streets of London and Washington have never looked good for the nation, especially when they call for boycotts of Canadian products. It has only been at the insistence of successive Newfoundland governments that the federal Department of Fisheries and Oceans has shown it any support.

What irks Newfoundlanders most of all are the annual fundraising campaigns of the anti-sealing groups. Pictures of dewy-eyed whitecoats still abound in their ads, even though they haven't been hunted for years. The literature is full of misinformation about the state of the herds. The organizers know what brings in money. And as long as they can find the means (no matter how underhanded) to videotape a few men who have broken the strict rules of humane hunting, they have all they need to relight the fires under potential donors.

IFAW's annual supporter revenue is estimated at $80 million, more than half of it coming from Britain. When founder Brian Davies retired as its head in 1997, his wage settlement was reported to be $2.5 million. Such profit on the backs of sealers is impossible for any Newfoundlander to stomach, and the anger at the unfairness of it all impossible to suppress.

28 | Communications Central

If natural science ever furnished a theme for a poet, it is to be found in this achievement . . . The whole world is fast becoming one vast city.
—On the laying of the transatlantic cable from Ireland to
Newfoundland, *The Times*, London, 30 July 1866

The Great Eastern *at Heart's Content, 1866.*

Try, Try Again

It was hardly to be expected that the lack of a ship's wireless would be a factor in the deaths of so many Newfoundland sealers in the early 1900s. After all, it had been in St. John's, on Signal Hill in 1901, that the Italian Guglielmo Marconi received the first transatlantic wireless message.

In fact, for much of the late nineteenth and early twentieth centuries the Island was at the centre of the revolution in transatlantic communication. Being poked out farther into the Atlantic than any other part of North America again proved a godsend. One of the first to show up looking for a place to do business was the American financier Cyrus Field. It was Field who had backed F.N. Gisborne in connecting Newfoundland to mainland North America by telegraph cable, via the Gulf of St. Lawrence, establishing in 1856 what proved to be a vital communications link with Europe. During the time of the American Civil War, passenger ships from Britain would drop canisters of news copy near Cape Race, where a boat owned by the Associated Press retrieved them, then telegraphed their contents to New York, beating the arrival of ships by several days.

But the young millionaire Field had a much greater vision. He proposed a full telegraph connection between London and New York. The key link would be a cable that left the shores of Valencia in Ireland and ran more than 3,333 kilometres underwater to Newfoundland. To most people it sounded as if his money far outweighed his common sense.

Several mishaps reinforced that assessment. On the first attempt in 1857 the cable snapped 320 kilometres out to sea from Ireland. The following year the cable end was lost at sea three times. A fourth attempt met only with partial success—the cable made it to shore in Bay Bulls Arm (now Sunnyside) in Trinity Bay and was connected, only to go dead after twenty-seven days of use.

Yet Field had proved that it could be done. Eight years later, with new financing and a stronger cable, and the assistance of the largest ship then afloat, the *Great Eastern*, he made yet another attempt. With great caution the ship made its way across the Atlantic, sounding equipment determining the rate of the cable released from its massive storage tanks. But again the cable snapped. Finally, on 27 July 1866, the mighty vessel sailed into Trinity Bay, anchoring in the deep water off Heart's Content. A smaller ship, with the cable end aboard, headed to shore amid robust cheers from hundreds of Newfoundlanders who had assembled from all parts of the Avalon. At the cable station a message arrived for Queen Victoria from U.S. President Andrew Johnson. Two days later the *Times* of London was calling it 'the most wonderful achievement of this victorious century.' With all links confirmed in good working order, it finally struck Cyrus Field what had been accomplished. The time needed to transfer information between North America and Europe had plunged from ten days to minutes. 'I . . . went to my cabin and locked the door,' he wrote. 'I could no longer restrain my tears . . . '

By century's end Heart's Content was the terminus for six transatlantic cables. Its large red-brick cable station quickly became a landmark, and could rightly be called one of the most vital buildings on the continent. The outport itself flourished, its population swollen by the influx of workers for the Anglo-American Telegraph Company, and later Western Union. The foreigners established schools and social clubs, and generally walked about thinking and sounding superior. It was a price the people accepted for a degree of prosperity little known in most of outport Newfoundland.

A Genius on the Hill

Atop Signal Hill in 1897 Cabot Tower had been built to commemorate the anniversary of John Cabot's landing. Nearby was an old masonry barracks converted several years before into the Diphtheria and Fever Hospital. It was here, in a vacant wing of the hospital, that the twenty-seven-year-old Marconi was given 'a small dark room furnished with a table, one chair and some packing cases.' It was early December 1901. On the table he set up his wireless receiver— 'a few coils and condensers and a coherer, no valves, no amplifier, not even a crystal.' To avoid being hounded by the press, he told only his assistants George Kemp and Percy Paget his exact intentions. A sole foreign reporter arrived from the *Herald* in New York, thinking Marconi was testing his equipment with a Cunard liner approaching North America. One of his despatches casually observed that 'St. John's merchants are considering the advisability of having the system installed on the sealing steamers.'

Via the transatlantic cable, Marconi sent a coded message to the transmitter station at Poldhu in Cornwall instructing the operator to send, at predetermined times, the three dots of the letter *S* of Morse code. Marconi and his assistants turned their attention to elevating their aerial, securing it to a four-metre balloon inflated with hydrogen. But when the hill's infamous winds took charge, the rope broke, plunging the balloon into the sea. Kites proved more successful, and on the morning of the twelfth a second attempt reached an altitude of 122 metres. Its violent surges amid the howling wind kept changing the electrical capacitance of the aerial, forcing Marconi to use an untuned circuit.

It did not look promising. But at noon that day, with wind and rain lashing the building, Marconi put aside the cup of cocoa he had taken to warm himself and held in place a single earphone. Several of the world's most prominent scientists had told him he would be wasting his time, that the curvature of the earth would doom such an experiment. He listened patiently through the random crash and crackle of atmospherics.

Suddenly, at 12:30, 'there sounded the sharp click of the tapper as it struck the coherer . . . ' Then, 'unmistakably the three sharp clicks corresponding to three dots sounded in my ear.' He handed the earphone to Kemp. The man eagerly confirmed the signal. At the end of the allotted time, Marconi jotted in his diary, 'Sigs. at 12:30, 1:10, and 2:20.' In all, they had heard it about twenty-five times, each transmission 'serenely ignoring the curvature of the earth.'

Marconi (far left) and his assistants attempt to get their kite aloft.

On December fourteenth he broke the news to the press in St. John's, who telegraphed it to the world. The front page of the *New York Times* the following morning declared it 'the most wonderful scientific development in modern times.' As for the man from the *Herald*, after he'd spent several days climbing Signal Hill to find little of excitement, other charms of the city diverted his attention. He missed the event and lost his scoop.

The citizens of St. John's were eager to share in Marconi's excitement. Young girls showed up at his receiving station with bouquets of flowers. The governor threw a reception in his honour. Everyone sensed the beginning of a new era, and wanted Newfoundland to play out its part. Everyone except the Anglo-American Telegraph Company, which still had two years remaining on its exclusive contract for telegraphy in Newfoundland. The value of its securities on the London Stock Exchange had already tumbled, despite the attempts of some telegraph officials to discredit what Marconi heard as the workings of lightning and ground current.

On the sixteenth, Marconi took a trip to Cape Spear to check out the possibility of erecting a permanent wireless station there. The estimated investment would be $50,000. The Newfoundland government could hardly contain its excitement. But when Marconi returned to the city he was handed a letter from a lawyer representing Anglo-American. It threatened legal action if he didn't remove his equipment immediately from the Island.

The government and general public were outraged. The full cabinet ascended Signal Hill to encourage Marconi to stay. Governor Boyle cabled King Edward VII. But it all came to nothing. Marconi wasn't up to the fight . . . and besides, he had already received invitations from Nova Scotia, one from the government, the other from Alexander Graham Bell, offering him property there. Marconi was soon on a train to Port aux Basques. On Christmas night he was aboard the *Bruce* on his way to North Sydney. Rushing to meet him as he disembarked was the local federal Member of Parliament. Within hours Marconi was being wined and dined along the coast of Cape Breton, where, at the pull of a cord, his train was brought to a stop. He had sighted the ideal location for his station. The next day he was on another train to Ottawa, and there found Prime Minister Wilfrid Laurier with a pot of Canadian money ready to invest in the project.

In less than a month after the letter *S* had found its way from Cornwall to

Newfoundland, the deal with Ottawa was signed and sealed, and Marconi was on his way to New York for a dinner in his honour at the Waldorf Astoria. Seven years later it would be Stockholm and the Nobel Prize for physics.

The Anglo-American Telegraph Company, feeling very much like yesterday's news, continued on at Heart's Content. In fact, the demand for its telegraphy increased dramatically with the onset of the First World War. Still it was only a matter of time before cumbersome underwater cables would give way to the magic and glamour, and cheaper rates, of transatlantic wireless.

Signalling Disaster

New inventions lure the wealthy. Their application for the common good takes time . . . too much time in the case of the *Titanic* and the Marconi wireless station at Cape Race.

Cape Race lies 740 kilometres to the north of where, on 14 April 1912 at 11:40 p.m., the *Titanic* struck the infamous iceberg. Icebergs were not uncommon in these waters, of course, and it became customary for ships to notify each other by wireless of the positions of the larger and more dangerous ones. Such was the case at 11 p.m. on the fourteenth when the *Californian*'s wireless operator sent a warning of an iceberg less than thirty-two kilometres from the position of the *Titanic*. The reaction of the wireless operator aboard the luxury liner was an abrupt 'Keep out! Shut up! You're jamming my signal. I am working Cape Race.'

The iceberg report was never taken. The *Titanic*'s Marconi Marine man was too busy sending personal messages from first-class passengers to the Newfoundland promontory, Cape Race, for relay to the rest of North America. The wealthy used the wireless to do business and to let their relatives know what a wonderful voyage it had been so far. As on that night, such messages were often given priority, for it was through them that most of the company's profits were made. Profits, the inquiry into the disaster found, which came from the work of operators overworked and underpaid.

When the *Titanic*'s captain rushed to the wireless room shortly after midnight and ordered the distress signal—CDQ—to be issued immediately, the signal was picked up at the Cape Race wireless station by its chief operator, W. J. Grey, and from there news of the impending disaster reached New York and the rest of the world. As the tragedy unfolded, transmissions from the rescue ship *Carpathia* carried none of the details the world was waiting to hear and Cape Race was eager to transmit. The inquiry later revealed that the wireless operators (including one rescued from the *Titanic*) held back information in order to sell their stories to the *New York Times*, an endeavour sanctioned and arranged by Marconi himself.

Though the public proved forgiving, Marconi had lost a little of his shine. What did endure was the perception of wireless as a lifesaver. Unfortunately for Newfoundland sealers it was a message that didn't sound as clearly as it should have back in the land where Marconi had first conducted his famous overseas experiment.

Men and Their Flying Machines

A few years later public attention was taken up with another crossing between the continents, this time in the opposite direction. Newfoundland proved the natural jumping-off spot for the intrepid young pilots anxious to be the first to fly non-stop across the Atlantic. Stirring public interest was the sum of £10,000 offered by a London newspaper, the *Daily Mail*. In the spring of 1919 crews began to show up in St. John's to take up the challenge.

First to arrive was Harry Hawker, dashing RAF ace of the First World War, and

The airfield at Harbour Grace, 1927.

his navigator, Kenneth Mackenzie-Grieve. They were to fly a newly designed Sopwith, the *Atlantic*. The equally dapper test pilot Freddie Raynham arrived two weeks later with C.W.F. Morgan, and their Martinsyde *Raymor*. An advance party for the Martinsyde team had reserved a field near Quidi Vidi Lake. The Sopwith twosome scouted the area and agreed on the Glendenning farm in Mount Pearl. First came the job of reassembling their aircraft and undertaking test flights. They settled into the Cochrane Hotel and saw a rainy and foggy April give way to a rainy and foggy May.

In the meantime American seaplanes showed up in Trepassey Harbour, 128 kilometres south of St. John's. There had long been rumours that American navy pilots were about to attempt an Atlantic crossing. Though they weren't part of the competition, since they didn't plan to fly it non-stop, just getting to the other side had the potential to dampen the acclaim due any Brit winning the *Daily Mail* prize.

To add insult to injury, on May fifteenth the American dirigible C-5 arrived in St. John's from New York and moored at Quidi Vidi in the midst of the English camp. Its crew, too, was talking as if it might attempt an Atlantic crossing. The English were left cursing the weather.

But at least they gave it the respect it deserved. Unlike the crew of the blimp. The day after its arrival the wind rose and snapped the airship's steel mooring cables. It drifted across the field as three men jumped seven metres to safety from its control car. Out over the Atlantic it sailed, never to be seen again by its airmen. It was last sighted by the crew of one of the American seaplanes in Trepassey who reported it 'moving just above the icebergs . . . apparently out of control.'

The team of Americans, aboard their three Curtiss 'flying boats,' had just lumbered into the sky over Trepassey, heading for the Azores. They had rid themselves of whatever wasn't riveted in place (including one of the weightier crewmen) in order to get airborne. The English dismissed the American venture. The U.S. Navy, after all, had stretched a line of some sixty ships between Newfoundland and Portugal, their searchlights to act as guides for the aircraft. Where was their sense of sport?

By the next day one of the three had landed in the Azores and was waiting for the fog to lift so it could continue on to Portugal. The English had enough of sitting in idleness. On May eighteenth, without a promising weather report, Hawker and Mackenzie-Grieve cleared the field (though just barely) in Mount Pearl and headed out over the open ocean. Within hours, Raynham and Morgan were roaring down the field past two thousand onlookers at Quidi Vidi, intending to give the *Atlantic* a race for the money.

At ninety metres down the airstrip the extra fuel and the wind were still proving too much to overcome. When the *Raymor* did finally clear the ground, a crosswind drove it back to earth, crushing its landing gear. The airplane struck a soft spot at the end of the field and pitched nose-first into the ground.

The *Atlantic*'s fate was not quite as ignoble. But eight hundred kilometres out the Sopwith struck thick cloud and high wind, and worse still, had an overheating engine. Hawker cut the engine and dove in a daredevil attempt to drop the temperature of its coolant. When he tried to restart the engine, it failed, and only at the last possible second sputtered back to life. The flight problems persisted, and all hopes of reaching Ireland were dashed. Their only recourse was to search the shipping lanes for a boat that would rescue them. In the end the pair came away with their lives, though they lost the plane. On May twenty-fifth the rescue ship made the coast of Scotland. Two days later the American flying boat, the C-4, landed in Lisbon Harbour.

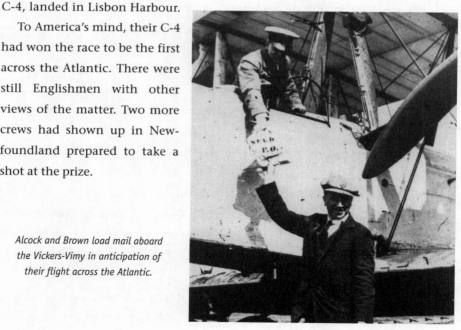

To America's mind, their C-4 had won the race to be the first across the Atlantic. There were still Englishmen with other views of the matter. Two more crews had shown up in Newfoundland prepared to take a shot at the prize.

Alcock and Brown load mail aboard the Vickers-Vimy in anticipation of their flight across the Atlantic.

One was the pair of John Alcock and Arthur Brown flying a twin-engine Vickers-Vimy biplane, the other a four-man team aboard a Handley Page bomber. The bomber was mammoth, and the search for a level field long enough to handle it took the team all the way to Harbour Grace.

Alcock and Brown finally settled on a strip of farmland in the west end of St. John's known as Lester's Field. It required a crew of thirty labourers to patch and level it into something capable of getting them off the ground. And on the afternoon of June fourteenth, fortified with sandwiches and coffee from the kitchen of the Cochrane Hotel, the duo donned their electrically heated flying suits, their fur-lined gloves and helmets, and climbed aboard.

It was a rough takeoff, desperately close to what the *Raymor* had experienced. And when the Vickers-Vimy did start to lift, its wheels skirted the ground for an agonizingly long period before the plane started to climb. 'Several times I held my breath,' Brown later wrote, 'from fear that our under-carriage would hit a roof or a tree-top.' Only Alcock's skill at the controls saved them. They would need that 'clever-piloting' of his many times during the hours ahead.

Through much of the way they were forced to run through dense cloud, with only rare glimpses of the sun or stars. So thick was it at one point that they lost sight of the wing tips and the front end of the fuselage, and all sense of the horizontal. As Alcock tried to regain equilibrium, the engine suddenly stalled, sending them into a deep spiral. They plummeted in deathly silence from twelve thousand metres, breaking through cloud with the gauge showing less than thirty metres between them and the ocean. Alcock pulled the throttles wide open and the engines suddenly roared back to life. They jolted out of the spin. So low were they, Brown recalled, that 'it appeared as if we could stretch downward and almost touch the great whitecaps that crested the surface.'

Their ordeal was not over. In the early morning they were forced to beat their way through rain, then snow, then hail. Icy snow covered one of the vital exterior gauges and clogged the air intakes. Brown had to extract himself from his seat several times, braving the frigid exterior to position himself on top of the fuselage in order to clear away snow.

But at 8:15 a.m. they sighted the coast of Ireland, and by 8:40 they were safely on the ground near Clifden, if upended in a bog. It had been fifteen hours, fifty-seven minutes since they'd left Newfoundland. They captured the attention of the world, the £10,000 prize, and knighthoods. They were shouldered through the streets of London, heroes for the Empire.

Back in Harbour Grace the crew of the Handley Page were crestfallen. They abandoned their plans, and instead decided to fly to New York on a promotional tour of their aircraft. That flight ended abruptly with a forced landing in Nova Scotia. Though better Nova Scotia than the Atlantic.

Amelia Over the Atlantic

Dozens more adventurers made the Island their starting point, including the indefatigable Amelia Earhart. She arrived in Trepassey in June 1928 aboard the *Friendship*. Although a pilot in her own right, Earhart was officially a passenger, hoping to become the first woman to cross the Atlantic. Three women who had attempted the feat had already lost their lives. Another, Mabel 'Mibs' Boll (the flashy American heiress, 'Diamond Queen of the Twenties') was at that very moment in Harbour Grace with the crew of the *Columbia*, waiting out the weather.

The *Friendship*'s crew spent close to two weeks in Trepassey also waiting the promise of reasonable weather over the Atlantic. At the invitation of the Presentation Convent, Earhart vis-ited the local girls' school. The Sisters were left somewhat aghast at her boyishly short tangle of curls, her forthright manner, and (most of all) her tight-fitting fly-ing pants. Needless to say, there was no invitation forthcoming from the boys' school.

The long wait in Trepassey was punctuated by Earhart's quarrels with her pilot, who, she discov-ered, was alcoholic. The arguing continued right up to the time they boarded the aircraft. But the flight proved a success, ending at Burry Port, Wales, nearly twenty-

Amelia Earhart at Harbour Grace, 1932.

one hours after leaving Trepassey. A heartbroken Mibs was still on the ground in Newfoundland. The flight carrying Earhart was turned into front-page news, and the beginning of the newspaper mania that surrounded her the rest of her life.

What she wanted, of course, was to conquer the Atlantic on her own. On 20 May 1932 she was back in Newfoundland, this time at Harbour Grace, with a single engine Lockheed Vega. She boarded the aircraft alone, smiling and clutching a thermos of chicken soup made for her by the proprietress at Archibald's Hotel. To the cluster of reporters she was her usual reticent self. 'You will hear from me in less than fifteen hours.' At 7:12 a.m., with the press and a throng of local people cheering her on, she took to the air.

She was true to her word. Fourteen hours and fifty-four minutes later she landed, though the flight had been far from uneventful. Flame darting out from a crack in the manifold was a constant, unnerving sight, worse in the blackness of night. Her altimeter broke. As did her tachometer for a time when, climbing to evade an electrical storm, the aircraft began to pick up ice. 'The last two hours were the hardest,' she later wrote, the peril cloaked in understatement. 'My exhaust manifold was vibrating very badly, and then I turned on the reserve tanks and found the gauge leaking.'

She was not long over Ireland when she ended the flight in 'a long, sloping meadow.' Her flying suit wet with the leaking gas, she emerged from the cockpit where for a blissful few moments she alone savoured her accomplishment. First the local cattle herder, and then a world eager for relief from the drudgery of their own lives, raced to share it with her.

Lindbergh's Legacy

It was a world not far from another great war. On 12 July 1933 a squad of twenty-four flying boats out of Fascist Italy stopped overnight in Cartwright, Labrador, on their way to the Chicago World's Fair. It was their grand propaganda tour. An Italian ship had arrived in advance of General Balbo and his aviators, with fuel, mechanics, and all the supplies for a lavish, wine-soaked banquet. The many reporters who had found their way to Labrador were suitably impressed, down to the portrait of Mussolini on the wall. Most of the local men were away at the salmon fishery, and it was left to the women to work late into the night to help refuel the planes for takeoff the next morning.

General Balbo welcomes the last of his flying boats to Cartwright, 1933.

On the way back from Chicago the Italians stopped for eleven days in Shoal Harbour in Trinity Bay. To the British and Americans it was all a startling revelation of air power. The strategic importance of Newfoundland and Labrador in the growth of aviation was never clearer.

On the same day that the Italians flew into Cartwright, Charles and Anne Morrow Lindbergh stepped ashore from a seaplane in Bay Bulls Big Pond, just outside St. John's. Lindbergh's famous flight from New York to Paris in 1927 had taken him over the city. He had flown deliberately off-course and low so there would be people to confirm he had reached that far should he encounter trouble over the Atlantic. This time Lindbergh, together with his wife, came to escape the constant harassment of the press, following the kidnapping and death of their infant son. As a technical adviser for Pan American Airways, he came also to scout possible landing sites for commercial transatlantic routes. The Lindberghs flew on to Botwood, and then to Cartwright, where they found themselves weatherbound for a week, just as the place was recovering from the Italian invasion. They touched down in North West River, Hopedale, and Hebron. The Lindberghs had flown over a supply ship steaming north and on their arrival in Hebron were able to bring the good news of its whereabouts. 'We are almost

The Lindberghs at Botwood, 1933.

starving, literally,' the Moravian missionary told them. His wife set the table, though it was the Lindberghs who supplied food for the meal they shared. The meeting was especially poignant for, as Anne wrote in her diary, the missionary's four-year-old daughter was an instant reminder of 'my little boy who had curly light hair . . . and blue eyes like her.' The following day the Lindberghs were on their way to Greenland, and over the next few months would completely circle the North Atlantic.

The Botwood that Lindbergh scouted already had a long tradition of aviation. Sidney Cotton, First World War pilot and inventor, had arrived there in 1920. His work in winter flying, including the delivery of mail to Labrador, was some of the first of its kind in the world. He was a pioneer of aerial photography, which he put to use to locate timber stands and seal herds. As a skill it came in handy when he was recruited for British and French Intelligence during the Second World War. By 1937 Botwood was the refuelling stop for Pan Am's *Clipper III* and British Imperial's *Caledonia*, the airships that provided the first regular transatlantic service.

Sidney Cotton and the mail plane he piloted to Labrador.

But it was the provision of a land-based facility that would keep Newfoundland at the centre of transatlantic aviation. During the mid-thirties, with military might building in Germany and Italy, the British air ministry came searching for a site to build an airport. They settled on a large plateau near mile 213 of the railway line. In 1936 construction began on what for a time was known simply as the Newfoundland Airport. What the site eventually held was the largest airport then in existence. 'Five runways, each 5000 ft. [1524 metres] long and 1200 ft. [365 metres] wide spreadeagle the field in ten directions. LaGuardia Field could fit snugly in one corner of it.' As a substantial community grew around the site, it was given the name Gander. And for good reason, it also came to refer to itself as 'the Crossroads of the World.'

The Second World War brought an enormous increase in the use of the airport. From here were ferried the Hudson bombers built in the United States for the use of the Allied Forces in Europe. The first seven of them made a nighttime crossing on 10 November 1940, led by the Australian-born RAF ace Donald Bennett. And when the war ended Gander became a hub for overseas air travel, with all the major airlines that spanned the two continents using it as a refuelling stop.

With so much air traffic, misfortune was inevitable. On 21 February 1941 the co-discoverer of insulin, Dr. Frederick Banting, perished when the plane in which he was a passenger lost one of its engines and failed in its attempt to return to Gander. Banting escaped the wrecked plane, but died of exposure, after bandaging the injuries of the one person to survive the crash. A total of sixty-three lives were lost in two later crashes, one of a Belgian airliner in 1946, the second of a Czech airliner in 1967. And on 12 December 1985 Gander was the site of the worst-ever Canadian air disaster. It killed all 256 people aboard an Arrow Air DC-8 carrying American peacekeepers on their way home to Kentucky for Christmas following a tour of duty in the Sinai Desert. Just seconds after liftoff the aircraft plunged into woods near Gander Lake. The cause of the disaster remains a mystery, at least to the public. The official investigation (of what stands as the worst U.S. military peacetime disaster) suggested ice buildup on the wings. But a strong dissenting opinion among commission members pointed to an on-board explosion. This has led to a widely held theory of the planting of a terrorist bomb. The U.S. government has refused to reopen the investigation.

The international lounge at Gander's air terminal remains a superb example of 1950s design. It still caters to the likes of Tom Cruise, Fidel Castro, and Yasser Arafat.

Gander was Newfoundland's first 'planned' town. Its streets continue to be named after famous aviators. Gander grew out of wilderness and into a place of international repute. The rich and famous, queens and politicians, continue to stop here. In its early days especially it was worldly and exciting, bringing an outlook that was less insular than much of Newfoundland of the day. Over time, as jet aircraft filled the skies and the need for refuelling stops lessened, Gander lost some of its speed. Yet the romance and intrigue of overseas aviation permeate the place, and its importance often resurfaces, as it did in the late 1980s when it was the scene of mass defections by Eastern Bloc travellers flying between Cuba and the Soviet Union.

Connected

Newfoundland is often depicted as being isolated and out of the mainstream of world affairs. That view is not true today, nor was it true through most of our history. In the early years of rediscovery and exploration, it was the first point of contact in North America, and it was by way of Newfoundland that much of New England, for example, was settled. (The *Mayflower* stopped at Renews in 1620 to pick up fresh water and supplies before sailing on to Plymouth Rock.) In the seventeenth century captains gathered in the larger ports of the Island to trade stories for a sense of what was happening throughout the new world. This was the start of the strong ties between Newfoundland and what people here came to call the 'Boston states.'

And in the heyday of the salt cod trade, after Newfoundland-owned schooners replaced the ships of the migratory fishery and before they themselves were replaced by large steamships, there were many whose contact with the outside world was intimate and far-ranging. Vessels regularly sailed from all the larger outports to the markets of North America, Europe, and the Caribbean. Newfoundlanders were found where good seamen were required, whether plying the Great Lakes, or serving in foreign navies.

The irony is to be found in the fact that although we were the chosen spot for the development of new means of communications in the early part of the twentieth century, we failed to seize on innovation to develop our economy. Through many of the decades that followed we allowed our geography to work against us, rather than for us, as it once had done.

It is fitting, then, that we have come into the twenty-first century with an optimism based in large measure on developments within the field of communications. Our schools are in the forefront of Internet literacy. Our IT graduates ply a trade with great success where geography has no relevance. Our entrepreneurs have seized the latest advances in wireless communication. Marconi would have nodded his approval (and grasped the opportunity to make a little money).

29 | War and the Aftermath of War

The Newfoundland Regiment is getting served pretty badly; in the last attack nearly all the officers were killed . . . cannot think how the ranks are going to be filled again; yet they are still coming . . .

—Frances Cluett, nurse in France, letter to her mother
in Belleoram, Fortune Bay, 9 December 1917

A section of a Newfoundland Regiment platoon, during training in Scotland.

Words from the Front

It is unlikely that Owen Steele of St. John's and Frances Cluett of Belleoram ever met, though it's possible, for prior to the war Steele did travel from St. John's to the outports (including some in Fortune Bay) as a salesman for his family's china business. What we do know for certain is they would never share their war experiences. Lieutenant Steele, in charge of billets for the Newfoundland Regiment, was killed by an enemy shell near the Picardy village of Englebelmer before Nurse Cluett arrived in France to take up her duties at the military hospital in Rouen. Yet in their words—his journal and her letters—they are drawn together, at least in the minds of those seeking to understand what it was to be Newfoundlanders in the thick of the First World War. Together they left us the most complete and personal accounts of that ordeal.

Steele, the consummate enlisted man, joined up soon after war was declared in August 1914, as part of the wave of young sons of St. John's fuelled with an impatience to serve the Empire. Like many, he was a member of one of the several church-affiliated, quasi-military brigades common in the city at the time. He heard the call to arms from his fellow Newfoundland Highlanders, from the pulpit of his Congregational church, from his former teachers at Bishop Field College. He could hardly resist such pressure, especially when the Catholic, Methodist, and Anglican boys were thronging to the armoury on Harvey Road to be among the first contingent of five hundred, the so-called Blue Puttees (named for the colour of

Owen Steele in Gallipoli.

The regiment's Cluny Macpherson designed an early prototype of the gas mask.

their leggings when no suitable khaki material could be found).

'These Germans, shoot them! Go to the meeting and get ready to fight,' had been the call to his fellow enlistees from the pulpit in Ferryland. 'Kick them to blue blazes!' Some lied about their age, lads years younger than the nineteen regulations stipulated. Steele was twenty-seven and a perfect specimen for the reactivated Newfoundland Regiment—intelligent and congenial, a champion athlete, a man whose moral fibre and social class quickly pushed him up the ranks to sergeant-major. On the sea voyage to the training grounds of Scotland and England, it was Steele who took charge of the ship's music concerts, and added his own choir-tuned voice to the assembly.

'We are all very particular here that we should not be classed as Canadians,' Steele wrote in his diary while training on Salisbury Plain. There was to be none of the shenanigans the drunken Canadians got up to while on leave in London. 'We have received the highest praise from several Colonels and Generals,' he added, as boastful as his upbringing would allow. Though initially a ragtag lot of merchants' sons, fishermen, and woodsmen, the regiment was soon in a physical shape and a frame of mind that would endear them to the British brass. As good a troop of colonials as they would ever use to feed the front lines.

The regiment's first assignment was Gallipoli. They arrived in September 1915, by way of the nightlife of Cairo and camel rides in thirty-seven-degree C heat to the base of the pyramids. It had been a long way from jumping ice pans off the Newfoundland coast. Gallipoli proved a rough baptism. Thirty men were lost to Turkish gunfire, another ten to disease carried by the hordes of flies. It paled compared with what the Anzacs endured, of course. And by the time the Newfoundlanders showed up, the plans to withdraw all troops from the Peninsula were already in place, though torrential rains and plummeting temperatures in late November made the evacuation a horrendous affair. The men of the regiment who survived the frostbite and the dysentery were among the last to leave Suvla Bay, and when the final evacuation of the Peninsula came at Cape Helles in January 1916, Owen Steele and his men were among the last boarding the ships.

The next stop was northern France. The Newfoundland Regiment was to be part of the 'Big Push,' the massive Allied campaign along the river Somme. 'Every road in every direction was clouded with dust,' Steele wrote in witness to the preparations, and 'everyone seems so cool about it all.' Major-General Beauvoir de Lisle, British commander of the 29th Division, addressed the regiment on June twenty-sixth. From atop his steed, he gloried in the 'honour and credit' he said the men would bring to themselves and their Island home. He assured them that in numbers and artillery, in battlefield strategies and sheer determination, the Germans were hopelessly outclassed. 'So we fear for nothing,' Steele wrote. The men marched off to the trenches, whistling and singing. Expectations ran extraordinarily high— 'to march on to Berlin and end the war.' There was talk of spending Christmas back home.

Daylight on 1 July 1916, the day of the Battle of Beaumont-Hamel (as the regiment's part in the Somme Offensive came to be called), was far from reason for celebration. Fear had come rushing in to fill the trenches. German machine-gun fire lashed the air as the eight hundred Newfoundlanders stood ready, in agonizing anticipation of what their orders would be. The Welsh regiments who had gone over the top ahead of them were devastated. The machine guns had their pick of targets. Just past 9 a.m. the British generals surveying the scene from behind the lines, in a display of unfathomable stupidity, sent word that yet another regiment would be sent into the brunt of the German fire. Many of the Newfoundland Regiment died, unable to get past their own barbed wire; many were felled in no-man's land like so much colonial excess. One or two at most reached the enemy trenches.

Left to answer the roll call the next day were 68 men. The battle buried 272 of their comrades, and wounded the rest. It is the single greatest tragedy in the history of Newfoundland and Labrador. For a country of a quarter million, still reeling from the great seal hunt disasters of two springs before, it was a monstrous cruelty to bear.

Steele had not made it to the battlefield that day. Against his wishes, he was held back with the 10 per cent of men kept in reserve (in part because of an injury to his knee in a road accident the week before). Every one of his fellow officers who rose up from the trenches was killed or wounded. But Steele's distance from the action would prove no godsend. He died on July eighth, victim of an enemy shell that fell as he organized billets for the men who had survived the slaughter. He had not written a word since the last day of June. He'd had no time, or found himself in a hopeless struggle to account for what had been done to his regiment.

It was well into July before full notice of what had happened reached Newfoundland and Labrador. At that, the story was cloaked in patriotic rhetoric. The incredible courage of the men drew attention away from the unanswered questions about the event itself. Why were there so few routes cut through their own barbed wire? Why was the artillery barrage so badly bungled? Why was the carnage allowed to continue when they had no defence whatever against the enemy machine guns? And—most painful of all for a country that throughout its history had given so much to Britain—were they sent into such a hopeless situation merely to satisfy the egos of the brass who knew there would be less to answer for than if they had been the sons of London merchants or the fishermen of Cornwall?

Tommy Ricketts with his Victoria Cross.

It would take decades before these questions were allowed to emerge. No regiment, of the hundreds up and down the Somme that day, suffered more. It left a wretched pall over the country. At the time the relatives of the dead found themselves clinging to the words of the same general who had stirred their fathers and sons to battle. 'A magnificent display of trained and disciplined valour,' de Lisle now called it, in a cable to the prime minister of Newfoundland. And, as for the battle itself, it failed, in the general's mind 'because dead men can advance no farther.'

A perverse message of comfort if ever there was one. Newfoundlanders took the British military at their word, desperate to hold to the notion their young men had died for good cause. And when the commander-in-chief himself, Douglas Haig, arrived in St. John's in 1924 to unveil the noble monument to the war that rises above the east end of Duckworth and Water Streets, he was welcomed with a display of pomp and pageantry termed 'the largest and most spectacular of its kind in the history of the country.' Royalty itself would hardly have been paid more homage.

Following the ravages of Beaumont-Hamel the Newfoundland Regiment would go on to distinguish itself on other battlefields in France. For its exceptional courage at Ypres and Cambrai it would be given the designation 'Royal' by King George V, the only regiment to be so singled out during the First World War. Seventeen-year-old Tommy Ricketts of White Bay would become the youngest

Frances Cluett

soldier in the war to be awarded the Victoria Cross, for his fearlessness in racing twice across open terrain under heavy gunfire to retrieve ammunition, enabling his platoon to capture several enemy gun positions and take eight prisoners. In addition to the men of the regiment, close to two thousand others served on the ships of the Royal Navy and another five hundred formed the Newfoundland Forestry Corps, woodsmen brought to the U.K. to alleviate the shortage of timber created by the demands of war.

In the military hospitals of England and France were the Newfoundland women who went overseas to serve in the Volunteer Aid Detachment. They were semi-trained nurses, at least thirty-eight of them, mostly from well-to-do families of St. John's. For some it proved a rough existence to which they were ill suited. Coping with bed pans and open wounds of the common soldier blurred the class distinctions that had been so much a part of their upbringing.

Frances Cluett stood out from many of them. A Fortune Bay woman in her early thirties, she took on whatever the war demanded. 'Many a bedside have I stood by and watched the last breath, with the rats rushing underneath the bed . . . ,' she wrote from Rouen to her sister in Belleoram. When she worked alone on a ward of German prisoners it was with a constant dread, something she revealed only in her letters. The suffering she witnessed was compounded by her thoughts of the men in the Newfoundland Regiment facing the horrors of the front lines. She questioned any of her patients who might have had contact with them, and grieved to her mother over what was told to her.

In all, five thousand of the regiment went overseas. A quarter of them were killed, a rate much higher than that of any other overseas country. In St. John's alone, fully one in seven of its male population aged eighteen to twenty-two died in the war. Rare was the street that did not mourn the death of a son. One Water Street merchant and his wife lost four grandsons to the battle of 1 July 1916.

Today, in the military cemeteries of Gallipoli and northern France can be found the names of men cut from the ranks of potential leaders of the Island and Labrador. And in the Beaumont-Hamel Memorial Park, an ocean away from our coast, is to be found Newfoundland's most sacred soil. Following the war, its people purchased the sixteen hectares of land on which the battle had been fought. The trenches from which the regiment rose at their colonel's whistle are still distinct, as is the remnant of the 'Danger Tree' that marks the spot in no-man's land where so many men were killed. Rising above the park, on a outcrop of granite, is a bronze statue of a caribou, the regiment's emblem, its neck stretched to the heavens in a mournful, unknowing pose. And on a commemorative plaque at the entrance to the park is cast in bronze the commissioned heroic verse of an English poet of the times, as if a foreigner could better interpret our loss, as if our own witness to the war were not enough.

The place would do well to bear the words of Frances Cluett to her mother: 'This is a very wicked world . . . you cannot realize what sufferings there are. Some of the misery will ever live in my memory. It seems to me now as though I shall always have sad thoughts in my eyes.'

Or the achingly blank page at the end of the journal kept by Owen Steele.

At What Cost?

The war effort had mixed social class and geographic region. John Shiwak, an Inuit trapper and diarist of Rigolet (in 1917 the 'premier sniper' of the regiment), fought and died alongside 'corner boys' of St. John's who had rarely set foot past Empire Avenue. His commanding officer, R.H. Tait, would go back to his law office in the capital city with stories of this 'excellent scout and observer . . . a great favourite with all ranks.' Shiwak and the other volunteers from Labrador had commanded a new respect for their homeland. Returning outport soldiers and navy men, having walked the streets of London and sailed the Aegean, took to Water Street at a stride but a few degrees short of a swagger. Their capital city couldn't lord it over them in quite the same way.

By the time peace came in 1918 Newfoundland had changed irrevocably. The war affirmed Newfoundland's view of itself as a separate nation, if but a minor one still under the considerable influence of Britain. Exports had risen sharply to keep up with the wartime demands for fish, timber, and newsprint. In Grand Falls the newsprint machines were running at top speed. On Bell Island the iron mine that had opened at the turn of the century (finally proving true predictions of mineral wealth that went back to 1610) had seen the loss of a major customer, Germany. Production fell, but then had rebounded on the strength of the Allies' massive production of military equipment and ammunition. By 1925 there was a second paper mill, this time at Corner Brook on the west coast, and in 1928 another mine, extracting lead and zinc at Buchans in the Island's western interior, started production.

Yet the Newfoundland of the 1920s was a country overwhelmed with debt. At the outbreak of the war the government, in what amounted to a colossal evasion of its constitutional responsibility, had turned the war effort over to Britain's proxy in Newfoundland, Governor Davidson, who appointed an autonomous committee of the business and professional élite of St. John's. This 'Patriotic Association,' all for the good of the Empire (to which the people of the colony were unquestioningly loyal), forged ahead with zealous efficiency. With only superficial involvement of the outports (other than the recruitment of its fittest men) Davidson and his committee led the government into war loans of over $13 million. The colony's commitment to the war far exceeded what was ever expected of a quarter million people, many of whom, unlike the decision-makers of the Patriotic Association,

Unveiling the country's War Memorial, Duckworth Street, St. John's, 1924. July first would remain a Day of Remembrance, even after it also became Canada Day.

were impoverished. In striding toward Dominion status, in answering Britain's call with such a financially unbridled show of patriotism, Newfoundland had done its own people a disservice. When all was calculated, including pensions resulting from the heavy physical toll of the conflict, the cost soared to over $34 million. Piled atop this was the cost of railway construction, including the extravagance of branch lines at a time when the debt was already out of control. Then a decade later the Depression hit. By 1934 interest on the public debt had multiplied to an astounding 63 per cent of revenues.

The electorate had lost all confidence in its politicians. It was a government, of course, that still had the upper classes of St. John's at its centre, rife with political nepotism. While the outport voice had been strengthened, it was still relatively weak, with many of the men who represented the outports born and bred in the capital city. In December 1917, the long-standing prime minister of the day, Edward P. Morris, in London to attend sessions of the Imperial War Cabinet, was offered a British peerage, in recognition of his unwavering show of support for the Empire. Such a graceful way it was to end his political career (and avoid having to enact conscription), that Morris didn't bother returning to the colony, choosing instead to cable the people of the Island with his resignation. The following day the Lime Street son of a poorhouse keeper was elevated to Baron Morris of Waterford. His priorities standing naked, he strode on to the House of Lords.

Back in Newfoundland, his place was taken by William Lloyd, who can't help being remembered for the day in 1919 when he stood in the House and himself

Richard Squires as prime minister.

seconded a notion of non-confidence that had been brought against his government. It was a moment of lunacy, 'a scene that had no parallel in the political history of any country,' topped only by a vote on the motion and its unanimous passage. Between 1923 and 1924 five different governments held office. The last of these was led by Walter Monroe and a cabinet stocked with the inert merchant class. In the name of reform they abolished the modest income tax that had been in place since the end of the war. They raised the tariffs on a list of imported goods that included tobacco products, fishing gear, and butter. High on the list of shareholder names in the city firms of Imperial Tobacco and Colonial Cordage (the country's sole maker of rope and nets) was that of the prime minister. And just weeks after the legislation was passed, John Chalker Crosbie, his minister of Finance, personally invested in a plant to manufacture margarine. It was as much a coincidence as the fact that the Monroe minister who initiated repeal of prohibition, J.R. Bennett, was also partner in the Bennett Brewing Company. In 1928, his agenda apparently complete, Monroe resigned and handed the leadership of his party and the prime ministership of the country to his cousin, the managing director of Colonial Cordage, Frederick Alderdice.

But it took a second round of dirty tricks of another prime minister, Richard Squires, to sink the country completely. In 1923 Squires had been driven from office by allegations that one of his ministers, Alex Campbell, had used public funds in his election campaign, and that Squires himself had pocketed money from the operators of the Bell Island mine as payoff for favourable legislation. A public inquiry into the matter not only upheld both allegations, but pointed to corruption even more vile—some of the funds diverted into re-election accounts had been intended for poor-relief projects. Criminal charges were laid, yet Squires, out on bail, manoeuvred behind the scenes until the government that replaced him was defeated. A grand jury dismissed the charges, the Supreme Court agreed, and after a few years of lying low (though not low enough to escape charges of tax evasion), Richard Squires was politically reborn in 1928. Of all things, he cast himself as the one to save Newfoundland from the corruption of merchant-led governments!

The choice was between Alderdice and Squires. Squires campaigned on his past record, at least the more savoury aspects of it, especially the building of the pulp-and-paper mill in Corner Brook. 'Who put the Hum on the Humber' ran the simple-minded campaign slogan. There was little surprise when Squires was returned to office, and probably even less surprise when four years later charges of corruption again erupted in the Colonial Building. This time the allegations came from his former minister of Finance, Peter Cashin. Squires was accused of falsifying the minutes of the Executive Council in an attempt to cover up the diversion of money into a personal bank account, and into the accounts of several of his cabinet, including Alex Campbell, the disgraced minister of Squires's last debacle. Campbell was also accused of evading income tax and of receiving payment for work as Immigration officer, at a time when the country had no immigration. Two weeks later came an even more damning claim.

Peter Cashin, himself wounded while serving in the war, rose in the House and charged Squires with pocketing $5,000 a year from the accounts of the War Reparations Commission. The public was incensed. Income for most of them was so low that even those who had jobs were being forced to seek dole to feed their families. (With the Education Grant slashed, married teachers with families, for example, were expected to live on $33.75 per month, and at that they were doing better than most.) Squires sidestepped the setting up of a commission of inquiry into the allegations, and weeks later, in what was ostensibly a further measure to deal with the country's financial crisis, he raised tariffs on imports and reduced the pensions of war veterans.

For the electorate it was the last straw. On April fourth a massive rally filled the Majestic Theatre in St. John's, overflowing into the Longshoremen's Protective Union Hall. Thousands more heard it on radio. More than sixty speakers for a 'Citizens Committee' took to the stage. 'The country is nearing the breakers,' declared one. 'If it has to be a revolution, let it be a revolution.'

There had been the sealers' strike of 1902 and a march of the unemployed through the streets in 1921. But such defiance was rare. Even this protest was not a spontaneous rising up of the masses. Behind it were merchants, out to save themselves from Squires's brand of financial ruin as much as reclaim any ideals of democracy.

They were surely not wanting violence. But the anger of the ordinary citizen had been boosted by new accusations from Cashin—that in the election campaign of 1928 Squires had illegally imported two hundred cases of Teacher's Whisky and used it to bribe voters, and that the Montreal distiller of the whisky had donated $15,000 on the commitment from Squires of future business.

The leaders who gathered with the crowd outside the Majestic Theatre at 2:15 the next day pleaded for restraint. Led by a brass band of Methodist Guards, it was to be an orderly march to the Colonial Building for the presentation of a petition calling for an official investigation into the charges against the government. But workers in the city had left their jobs and swelled the crowds along Duckworth Street to a 'mass of moiling humanity,' ten thousand strong. By the time they reached Military Road and swarmed before the doors of the House of Assembly, they were barely civil. The air was taut with the threat of violence.

Police met them at the steps of the Colonial Building. They were denied even the vacant seats in the visitors' gallery. Eventually a delegation of four was led inside and the doors barred. Squires reacted with characteristic wiliness to their petition, moving a motion to have it referred to a select committee. The House erupted into a great round of quarrelling.

While members wrangled over procedure, the crowd outside was losing patience. The boldest tried to crash through the doors. The commotion drew out their leaders, and in a move to restore order, they led the way back to the meeting halls.

But not everyone followed. The front doors of the Colonial Building were stormed again. This time protesters broke through. They came face to face with baton-wielding policemen who drove them back and charged the crowd outside, reinforced by more police on horseback. The crowd pelted the building with rocks, smashing every window. They brandished pickets from the fence surrounding Bannerman Park, attacking the police, dragging those on horseback to the ground. Others rushed inside and ransacked the government offices. They overturned furniture, scattered files, dragged out a piano and wrecked it. They tried, but failed, to set the place on fire.

Newfoundland suffragists take their campaign to Carbonear.

Meanwhile, Squires was trapped somewhere in the bowels of the building. As night fell he slipped out, surrounded by a dozen men. With a crowd in pursuit, he ran down Colonial Street, escaping into number 66 and out the back door while a multitude of clergymen surrounded the grounds, desperate to prevent violence.

Squires was rushed off into hiding. Eventually the crowds dispersed, though not before a few 'irresponsible youths' among them had broken into the two downtown liquor stores and smashed a few windows of businesses along New Gower Street.

The day's events were the beginning of the end for responsible government in Newfoundland. The fledgling dominion had been betrayed by its own politicians. And by the time those who elected them had risen up it was too late.

The March of Women

Pictures taken on the day of the riot show a sea of men, with just a few women scattered among the crowds. Though she would have scorned the vandalism, in the thick of the protest no doubt was the city's leading advocate for the poor and underprivileged—Julia Salter Earle.

In 1921 Salter Earle had been the one to lead a march of unemployed men to the Colonial Building (with a stiff warning to those carrying liquor to 'get rid of it'). As head of the Ladies' Branch of the Newfoundland Industrial Workers' Association she was constantly calling to task merchants and government officials for the deplorable conditions under which many of the city's factory workers had to toil. The stories are numerous of her giving up her own food so the poor would not go hungry.

In her ability to balance her roles as a career woman and social activist she was truly remarkable. The mother of six, she worked for thirty-five years as an engrossing clerk in the offices of the House of Assembly, the very place to which she led protests. (It was her job to prepare and handwrite the official documents signed to enact new laws!) She took as leading a part in her church as a woman could, and in 1925 was the first woman to run for a seat on St. John's municipal council, losing by only eleven votes.

She was a strong voice in the Ladies' Reading Room on Water Street, where the women at the upper levels of St. John's society met to discuss the issues of the day, though her company must not always have been appreciated, given that several of the other members were wives of factory owners. And when the issue of woman's suffrage peaked following the war, she was at the heart of the campaign.

The groundwork for their struggle had been set during the height of the temperance movement in the 1890s, and continued with the establishment in 1914 of the colony-wide network of the Women's Patriotic Association. Talk of their right to vote filled many of the hours spent in knitting and sewing 'comforts' for the soldiers overseas. The famed 'Newfoundland sock,' greatly sought after by all Allied soldiers, had in its stitches the resolve of women to get their own fair treatment.

After the war rose the Women's Franchise League, led by Armine Gosling, Fannie McNeil, and many of the prominent women of the city. A notable exception was Helena Squires, wife of the prime minister. Her husband's reaction to the issue of women's suffrage epitomized the narrow-minded, self-serving attitudes that so harmed the country.

Richard Squires had no time for the suffragists, despite the fact that his country and South Africa now stood alone as the only part of the Empire where the vote for women had not become law. At meetings with the League he continued to puff on his cigar and reject their arguments with disdain. Like many in his government, he dismissed the League as foreign élitists (several had been born or educated elsewhere) out of touch with the ordinary women of Newfoundland. It took thousands of names on petitions from across the Island to make him reconsider his government's position, and even then he broke his promise to introduce a bill in support of their cause. The letter writing, meetings, and petitions continued, despite setbacks. In Fortune Bay a clergyman burnt the pages of signatures his daughter had so labouriously collected (including, no doubt, that of Frances Cluett, the frontline nurse of the First World War).

By 1925 Squires was out of office, scandal at his heels. Newspapers had come out strongly in favour of the cause. Women were able to vote and run for office in the city's municipal elections. (The suffragist Armine Gosling had worked on her husband, the mayor.) The new government, under Walter Monroe, introduced a bill to bring women into the election process. It passed unanimously.

Victory was sweet, and celebrated in style. Before long the women who led the fight were turning their attention to the other social issues that had always accompanied the struggle for enfranchisement—the rights of working women, child labour, family health and poverty, issues that women such as Julia Salter Earle carried into the decades ahead.

In 1928 the objectionable Squires was re-elected. Some would say he bought his way into office with promises of money and liquor. In 1930, in a by-election in the district of Lewisporte, the first woman was elected to the House of Assembly. In a galling turn of events for the victorious suffragists, the person voted in was no other than Helena Squires. The prime minister, the dominant male, had ushered her into a safe government seat.

Squires's cunning tactics knew no bounds. When, two years later, the government came down around his ears, it was he who all the voters, male and female, would point to for losing the country's self-government. The women's vote had lasted but a few years, but eventually it would re-emerge, in a new context, and with a new measure of political power. It would be their vote in 1948 that would change Newfoundland and Labrador more radically than any vote before it had ever done.

30 | Surviving

On the island of Iona [Placentia Bay] . . . these fishermen were struck hard by the Depression . . . living on a small barren island with a low supply of food on hand, seven miles from the nearest merchant. Sometimes in winter when the bay was packed with ice, they would go two months without having their dole orders filled . . . Root vegetables could not be grown on the island as the soil was not suitable . . . Those people suffered unbelievable hardships and privation through the years. If it had not been for the seabirds they shot, they would have starved completely.

—Victor Butler, *Sposin' I Dies in D' Dory*

The Knee family of Badger's Quay, Bonavista Bay, late 1930s, doing better than many.

Lured to the Wilds

At the time of Wilfred Grenfell there were still but a few thousand permanent residents in the whole of Labrador, with vast sections of the interior still familiar only to native people. For Americans seeking to recapture the romance of wilderness, now that most of their own country was tamed and foot-worn, it was fascinating country, all the more so as Grenfell and his exploits became widely known. Together with the compelling accounts of the separate Labrador expeditions of Mina Hubbard and her husband, Leonidas, they rekindled the dreams of many an early-twentieth-century adventurer.

Leonidas Hubbard was a New York journalist who in the summer of 1903 (declaring his intention 'to get into really wild country') left North West River in a five-metre canoe in pursuit of an inland route to Ungava Bay. He starved to death in the process. It was left to his partner, the lawyer Dillon Wallace, to tell of their expedition in *The Lure of the Labrador Wild*. The tale of stoicism in the face of 'the vast solitudes of desolate Labrador, over which still brooded the fascinating twilight of the mysterious unknown' fed the armchair urban thirst for 'true-life' adventure. The book went into twenty-three printings.

If the truth of the tale were told (and for that the public would have no appetite, as Wallace well knew), the pair were incredibly naïve. They started far too late in the season. They each took just one pair of boots, moccasins that quickly wore through, making portaging an ordeal. On the second day out they mistook the Susan River for the Naskaupi, and turned into a water supply so shallow that anyone with a basic knowledge of geography would have known it couldn't possibly lead into the hinterland of Labrador. And, most absurd of all, though they hired George Elson, a mixed-blood Cree from Ontario, they failed to take with them any local person with first-hand knowledge of the terrain. Their bravado was no match for the wilds of Labrador.

Wallace's dramatic version of events earned him considerable fame and fortune. But in the view of the widowed Mina Hubbard, it was at the expense of her husband's reputation. She accused Wallace of portraying himself as a hero, someone pushed on by Hubbard long after the point they should have turned back. She was determined to set the record straight. Once she heard that Wallace intended to go back to Labrador and again commence a canoe trip to Ungava, she declared that

Innu, such as Chief Ashini (seated on the shores of Grand Lake, ca. 1920),
could have been a great help to Hubbard and his brand of adventurers.

she herself would undertake a second Hubbard expedition through the interior. Not only that, but she would get to Ungava first and in the process complete what her husband had set out to do.

And in 1905, starting earlier in the season, Mina Hubbard departed North West River in two canoes. With her were George Elson and two Cree trappers, also from Ontario, and wisely, Gilbert Blake, a native-born young man of nineteen. There would be no mistaking the Naskaupi River this time. Blake knew it well, having travelled it with his brother to get to their winter traplines.

Wallace and his crew (still with no one native to Labrador) left North West River the very same day. In exactly two months Mina Hubbard, hardly ruffled, reached the Hudson's Bay Company post on the shores of Ungava Bay. A month later, a weary Wallace emerged at the same spot, lucky to be alive. The lady who had traversed the forbidding interior in 'a short skirt over knickerbockers' and 'a rather narrow brimmed soft felt' holding up fly netting, had proved her point, and managed it with her Victorian femininity intact.

In recent years it has been Mina Hubbard's turn to gather public attention. Her feat was indeed remarkable for an urban woman of the times. The maps she drew and her accounts of the Innu on their traditional hunting grounds are invaluable. But, basically, like her husband before her, she was an incongruous sight on the

Labrador landscape. She agreed to be led (and sheltered) by native people who knew the wilderness intimately. If her husband had been unpretentious enough to do the same, he would have survived.

On the Island, excursions by foreigners into the wilds became even more commonplace. They were prompted by a multitude of accounts in angling and hunting magazines, and in such books as *Newfoundland and Its Untrodden Ways* by the Englishman J.G. Millais. No one had ever made the pursuit of caribou for their antlers such a devout enterprise. (Caribou, wrote Millais at his most alien, are 'like some beautiful women, whose charms are undeniable . . . palpitating life . . . a sum-total that is magnificent.') Taking him at his word were a stream of monied Americans, all lusting after the trophy caribou head to display in their mahogany-panelled dens back home. Among them were du Ponts and Vanderbilts, one of the latter declaring Newfoundland 'a veritable Sportsman's Paradise.'

The Reid Newfoundland Railway quickly joined in the free flow of superlatives, boasting to the potential visitor that Newfoundland had the 'best salmon and trout streams that have yet been discovered.' And that much of our 'trackless waste' was within walking distance of the railway line. It was all the start of our tourist industry, of which hunting and salmon fishing are still integral parts. They continue to lure the rich. These days it's men such as the former American president George Bush who have been seen stepping gingerly over the bogs of Newfoundland (and occasionally falling through).

Local Blessings

Of course, it is not foreign visitors like the Hubbards who have made an impact on this country of ours. It is rather the people who came and stayed. Medical people following in the footsteps of Wilfred Grenfell—Dr. Charles Curtis, Dr. Harry and Nurse Mina Paddon, and their son Anthony, also a doctor, all of whom devoted their working lives to the people of northern Newfoundland and Labrador, often travelling great distances by dog team in winter and hospital boat in summer. Or Nurse Myra Bennett, who arrived in Daniel's Harbour from England in 1921 and for decades was the only medical practitioner along 320 kilometres of the Island's west coast. Or Dr. J.M. Olds, of Yale and Johns Hopkins, who served the people of Twillingate and the hundred communities in Notre Dame Bay for half a century. When, in 1934, the grant to the hospital in Twillingate was cut, Olds introduced a

The salmon rivers of Newfoundland and Labrador were a sportsman's gold.

subscriber scheme for basic medical care, at forty-four cents per year, in cash or its equivalent, one of the earliest forms of medicare on the continent.

Had not the St. John's–based Newfoundland Medical Board been so self-serving, there might well have been many more medical personnel in the outports. In 1934 a proposal was put forward to the Commission of Government to relocate forty Jewish families fleeing Nazi Germany. Among them were two dozen doctors, nurses, and dentists requesting to take up residence in rural Newfoundland. The chief commissioner of Immigration turned down the offer, largely because of pressure from a medical board that feared the doctors would eventually give up their rural practices and head to St. John's. An overburdened nurse in Burgeo lamented, 'The Royal Commission report says that the number of doctors has decreased from 119 in 1911 to 83 in 1933 so there should not be much reason to fear competition. Is it right for 83 Newfoundland citizens to prevent thousands of other Newfoundland citizens from receiving medical care?'

Through much of our history it was individuals pushing themselves past the indifference of the establishment in St. John's that led to significant improvements in the standard of living in rural Newfoundland and Labrador. In 1919, when a request reached St. John's for medical aid and food from Labrador for survivors of the Spanish flu epidemic, government officials responded by sending several thousand metres of dressed lumber to Cartwright to build coffins for the victims, as if they had not been buried months before! The incensed Anglican minister, Henry Gordon, diverted the lumber to school construction. With the help of Dr. Paddon, he raised money outside Newfoundland to erect a building to serve both as a school and an orphanage for the children who had lost their parents in the epidemic.

In 1935 Newfoundland's per capita spending on education was roughly one-third of what it was in Canada. A survey showed that there were still fourteen thousand children of school age who were not receiving any education. If rural communities did secure a teacher (often it was only for part of the year), more likely than not it was clergy and doctors who did the recruiting. Where the Grenfell Mission operated, often young men and women (green, but eager) from England or the U.S. would be dropped into coastal communities in September without the opportunity to emerge until spring. In other parts of Newfoundland and Labrador they were young people whom the clergy deemed to be of good character and who had completed some high school. The most qualified of them were graduates of Grade 11 from more populous outports, perhaps with a summer school of teacher training in St. John's. New teachers assigned the higher grades commonly found themselves in charge of students older than themselves. On weekdays they gathered their several grades in a single classroom heated by a pot-bellied wood stove. Leslie Harris, future president of Memorial University, remembers his first year of teaching, in Harbour Buffett, in 1945. 'I could essentially take charge, not only of a school, but of a community. Adults . . . would follow my orders in organizing concerts and times and sales and dances and whatever things you had to do.' Things that included conducting the Sunday church services. He was fifteen.

The church remained at the centre of most communities. And as educational opportunity increased (those who made it to college from the outports 'were destined to be either teachers or preachers'), the outports

A fresh group of officers for the Salvation Army.

began to see more regular visits from clergy. And clergy, in turn, discovered new methods to better serve their congregations. In Labrador Methodist minister Lester Burry kept contact with trappers, in the bush for months, by setting up a radio station. In later years, clergy there replaced their dog teams with snowmobiles, and, in one instance, the case of my oldest brother, with an airplane.

In Newfoundland, it was the railway and regular coastal boat services that reduced the isolation, though for the established Churches the better access proved a mixed blessing. Some areas, especially non-Catholic ones, became easier targets for religious conversion. An eager Salvation Army had made its first appearance in Newfoundland in 1885 (just two decades after its founding) and by 1910 it was training its own officers at its headquarters in St. John's. Deterred neither by insults nor stone-throwing, Booth's Army spread across the Island and was setting down deep roots, especially in several bays on the north coast. Soon Salvationists were taking briskly to the streets of the new mill and mining towns. Today fully one-third of the Canadian faithful are based in Newfoundland and Labrador, where the Salvation Army is an established religion, not solely a service organization. Several Newfoundland-born officers have risen to the highest ranks of the Army, most notably Clarence Wiseman of Notre Dame Bay, who in 1974, became the first Canadian to head the organization worldwide.

'The flock is there in the fold, but the gate is open,' the venerable Anglican priest, Canon J. T. Richards, had warned in 1919. In places where Methodism had lost its evangelical edge (it was absorbed into the United Church of Canada in 1925) the gate opened wider. Many women welcomed the greater leadership role offered them by the Salvation Army, and by Pentecostalism, as it, too, spread across the Island.

The arrival of New England schoolteacher and preacher Alice B. Garrigus in St. John's in 1910 marked the start of the Pentecostal movement in Newfoundland. But it was through union with a separate mission headed by Eugene Vaters in Victoria, Conception Bay, that Pentecostalism gained a foothold in Newfoundland.

From age seventeen Vaters had been a teacher and Methodist preacher, but, disillusioned with its modernist leanings, broke from the Church. He headed to the Moody Institute in Chicago. (The revivalist Moody had been a strong influence on the young Wilfred Grenfell.) It was Vaters's brief time at a Pentecostal Bible school in Rochester, New York, that set his new direction. He and his wife

Pentecostal baptism in the waters of Carmanville, ca. 1940.

were soon back in Conception Bay and building a Pentecostal mission, largely made up of others who had also turned away from 'the Church of their fathers,' as Richards called it.

For thirty-five years Vaters headed the Pentecostal Assemblies of Newfoundland. By the mid-1930s it had established itself in Labrador, though its biggest gains were in central and western Newfoundland. Its fundamentalist style, like that of the Salvation Army, attracted a strong following, especially in the new towns that had sprung up, where a faster-paced society was challenging traditional outport values. It wasn't long before both groups were seeking a share of the meagre educational dollars. Building their own schools allowed both new movements to solidify their hold on an education-hungry society. As they learned from the experience of the long-established Churches, only in places where a church provided both religion and education could it ever hope to thrive.

The Rumble and the Fury

In every generation Newfoundlanders have been tested by an unpredictable ocean. In 1925, a hurricane struck the southwest coast, sinking dozens of boats fishing offshore. Nearly thirty men were lost. Then, in the midst of the malaise of low fish prices and the onset of a worldwide Depression, the south coast was dealt an even

The aftermath of the 1929 tidal wave.

greater blow. Late in the afternoon of 18 November 1929, an earthquake—at 7.2 on the Richter scale—split the ocean floor 250 kilometres off the Burin Peninsula.

It was felt as far away as New York. The tremors rocked dishes off shelves throughout Newfoundland, though it was the forty or so communities along the southern tip of the peninsula that took the worst of it. In Port au Bras 'all the houses and the ground shook for about five minutes,' leaving people 'screaming and praying,' in a desperate panic to know what might have caused it. Most concluded it had to be the explosion of a cargo ship heading toward the Gulf of St. Lawrence.

Darkness fell, two hours passed, and with it the initial dread. No one realized that an earthquake had set off a giant underwater landslide, ripping apart a dozen seabed cables, and causing the surface to swell into a tsunami, a tidal wave that was now surging toward the peninsula at 140 kilometres per hour.

Prior to it striking land, water was sucked back from the shoreline. Those who saw this rushed to higher ground. But most were caught unprepared for the wall of water—in places fifteen metres high—that came crashing in, channelled with particular fury into the narrower bays and inlets. 'The noise of smashing timber, the roar of the sea, the movement of thousands of tons of rocks and beach gravel, the screams of horrified people, all blended into one indescribable crescendo.' It flung boats from their moorings, crumpled wharfs and fishing sheds, and swept homes out to sea. 'It seemed as if all the demons in hell were let loose.'

In Lord's Cove the wave cast the Rennie home, with a mother and four children, into the harbour. The surge of water that followed threw it back on shore and left it partly submerged in a pond. Rescuers found the mother and three of the children drowned in the kitchen, and the fourth child, a three-year-old girl, miraculously still alive in an upstairs bedroom. In all, twenty-eight people on the Burin Peninsula were killed. It was the most devastating earthquake ever to strike what is now Canada, and the only one ever to result in the death of more than one person.

Fishing the Banks

Destruction of the sea bottom caused by the tidal wave ruined the inshore fishery for a full decade, making the 1930s along this coast even more arduous. Fortunately, by this time the offshore fishery to the Grand Banks had become completely centred here. In 1911 there were forty-eight banking schooners sailing from the port of Grand Bank alone. These schooners, with sails catching the wind or docked five and six deep, grew to be the defining image of this coast.

As beautiful a sight as they were, banking schooners produced a workday that was far from romantic. An average-size schooner would sail to the fishing grounds with a crew of two dozen, and ten dories stacked on deck. At one in the morning the men would rise from their bunks to bait the tubs of trawl lines, a hand-numbing task lasting until daybreak. Then over the side with their gear they went, two men to a dory. Taking measure from the compass, they dispersed from the schooner, like spokes of a wheel. More often than not they spent the day in thick fog. If the weather was particularly bad, the captain might decide to drop the dories one at a time (in what was known as a 'flying set'), allowing space between them to set the gear, after a time circling back to pick them up.

On some days there was barely time for a meal break, for the same men who caught the cod, once back aboard the schooner, cleaned and salted it in the hold. A good run of fish might give a man three or four hours of rest before the call came to bait the lines for the next day. Arch Thornhill, who first went as a doryman to the Banks at seventeen, remembered twice working at the fish seventy-two hours straight without sleep. Still, for men with little education on a coast with few other opportunities for work, there was no choice but to do what was expected of them. 'You had to work, by God! If you didn't work, you didn't get any fish. That's all.'

A fortunate few found work as crewmen on vessels out of Nova Scotia, where the hours were more civilized, the food aboard ship more substantial, the pay higher. Much of the wages of the Newfoundland crews had to be taken in credit from the fish merchant, the same man who set the price of the fish, and the same man who then charged higher prices for goods taken on credit than those paid for in cash. 'Clear roguery,' Thornhill called it, echoing the opinion of the many who in the twentieth century were still forced to live a near-feudal life.

The women had it no better. It was their job to spread and dry the fish that the schooners brought to shore. In Grand Bank they were known as 'beach women,' and were distinguished by their white aprons and sun bonnets (black if the woman had been widowed). One of them was given charge of a crew of nine. They worked on the stony beaches from daylight until dark, often with only one chance to get home to provide meals for their families, and with only the hours before sunrise to do their housework. Older children and relatives cared for the younger ones, while mothers laboured with the fish, much of the day bent over, even when they were pregnant. At the end of the season earnings might come to one hundred dollars each if they were lucky. Only ten dollars of that would be in cash, the rest given in credit, and with the same two-price system that was forced on the dorymen.

There was some relief on the Burin Peninsula when a fluorspar mine opened in St. Lawrence in 1933. But that proved a mixed blessing. Though it did much to raise the standard of living, its long-term effects on health—silicosis and lung cancer from the lack of ventilation in the mine—would eventually devastate the male population.

As throughout Newfoundland, the disparity in the opportunities available to the few well-to-do and the rest of the population was hardly questioned. While the merchants of Grand Bank could afford to send their children to university in New Brunswick, even the families of the men who captained their banking schooners led simple, almost cashless lives. People grew root crops where they could, kept hens and a few animals. They smuggled cheap liquor from the nearby French island of St. Pierre (whose best-known employer during Prohibition was rum-runner Al Capone). Their few luxuries came from the merchants' stores in years when the fish were particularly plentiful.

Medical service was the other great lack along the south coast, as it was in most of Newfoundland and Labrador. For much of the year it remained out of reach of the more remote outports. Grand Bank could boast a doctor, and of their own initiative the residents had built an eight-bed hospital, the Seaman's Institute. Yet there was only one doctor to serve all the rest of Fortune Bay. When the Spanish flu struck in 1918 it proved overwhelming.

As amazing as it is, like most outport people, they didn't grow embittered or lose their generous nature. The source of their strength was often their religious faith, though they didn't allow it to cast a pall of puritanism over their lives as people in northern climates have been known to do. (Maybe the cheap French rum had a role in this.) It was a practical faith, and one that they were not beyond leveraging for earthly purposes. The people of the Anglican community of Anderson's Cove, deep in Fortune Bay, were so determined that their children get some education (and not end up as their parents did— 'born and died of old age and couldn't write their own name') that at the turn of the century they struck a deal with the Congregational church eighteen kilometres along the shore in Little Bay East. They agreed to convert on condition their community be provided with a teacher. True to the minister's word, a teacher came. And true to the community's word, construction of a Congregational church was started soon after he arrived. In time families from other, smaller communities moved to Anderson's Cove so their children, too, could be educated. It produced a generation who not only could 'write our own names before we went to the Grand Banks,' but who found the confidence to question the way they were treated by the merchants who hired them.

The Rich, the Poor

If hard work, not material gain, be the measure of a people, in Newfoundland and Labrador stood some of the most praiseworthy anywhere.

Yet poverty was destined to remain the lot of fishing families in the 1930s, in a country where two-thirds of the people still depended on cod for their living. For that matter it was the lot of the logger or miner on whose labour the few new industries were being built. And the factory worker in the capital city.

Their circumstances were staggeringly needy in comparison to those of the upper classes. The proof is still all around us. As close as 'Winterholme' and the other former merchant manors set back from the roads bordering Bannerman Park

British Prime Minister Ramsay MacDonald enjoys the ambience at Government House, St. John's, 1934.

in St. John's. Or the Harmsworth estate in Grand Falls, where the mill's owners could bring their English sporting friends for a go at the renowned salmon rivers nearby. Or the mansion houses of the sealing captains of the northeast coast. The merchants and lawyers and aspiring middle class had their golf courses and their summer garden parties where the offspring could meet others of comparable position and acceptable wealth.

What many of them also had was isolation from the great numbers of poor, especially the rural poor. 'They are used to nothing else,' ran the after-dinner conversation of some merchants of St. John's. 'They are perfectly happy. They have blueberries and pay nothing for their firewood. In winter, they can snare rabbits.' By trying to raise the standard of living, warned Frederick Alderdice, 'we only make the people discontented.' Such attitude in the third decade of the twentieth century, such impatience to embrace a colonial mentality, could only perpetuate the economic blight that gripped hundreds of outports. To confirm the merit of their ways the merchant élite stroked their knighthoods, honours handed to them by the country that had misused the forebears of these very same communities.

It is troublesome to accept the fact that conditions in some areas deteriorated to the level of starvation. Many would prefer to speak in celebration of the hard work and indomitable spirit that freed communities from such dire straits. It was in the midst of the Depression, for example, that the Bonavista Bay community of Burnside built its imposing church. And there were indeed many such fortunate places, communities where fate was less cruel than other parts of North America. (Newfoundland of the 1930s, in fact, donated boxcar loads of salt cod to the hungry on the parched agricultural lands of the Prairies.)

But the people who did suffer deserve better than to be forgotten. With the onset of the Depression, more than one-quarter of the population was on poor relief. The 'dole' was a miserly ration of food that was by no means freely given, a result of the outcry of the merchant class who saw it as leading a great decline in self-sufficiency. The much-hated relief officer appointed to deal with the 'several family men facing starvation' in Battle Harbour, Labrador, was said to 'screw them down to the very smallest allowance per family.' The starving fishermen threatened to break into the storehouses of the merchant (Baine, Johnston) and 'shoot anyone who prevents them.' The government's telegrammed response? Starvation was no reason to be breaking the law.

Many who did have jobs found it impossible to meet the needs of their families. The Bradley Report of 1934 estimated that the minimum income needed to support an outport family was $600 per year. In 1935 the average annual income of the Newfoundland fisherman stood at $135.82. The great influx of young rural women working as domestics in St. John's could expect to earn no more than $100 per year. (Some were paid nothing, hired for room and board and some clothing.) A logger supplying the mills in Corner Brook and Grand Falls took home $30 a month. My father was one of them.

Dismal prospects in years before had sent men off the Island to earn money to feed their families, mostly to Boston and New York (where many made a name for themselves in the high-steel construction boom of the 1920s). Domestics and female factory workers were enticed to leave the Island by wages of more than twice those offered in Newfoundland. But the Depression brought an end to this migration, and many who had ventured to the mainland returned home.

With low fish prices, merchants cut the credit that in other years they had advanced to fishermen. Plots of cabbage and potatoes lay devastated by insects and crop disease. Beri-beri and tuberculosis were rampant. In Bonavista it was said that people were so desperate that many 'who possess gardens behind the settlement lose their fences each winter by the depredations of people in search of fuel.' Welfare officers handed out starvation relief that started at six cents per person per day.

'The saddest sight of all was the starving children . . . ,' recalled Milley Johnson. 'Mothers starved themselves for those children already here, not caring too much about the child on the way, which only meant another mouth to feed. It was not unusual to see babies with bloated stomachs, their arms and legs just bones, their heads out of shape . . . Outport cemeteries are full of young people who died from consumption and babies who never had a chance.'

For every such story there is another to counter it, of stretching what little was to be had and getting by. Some coasts fared better than others; some families were less impaired by disease or disability to begin, and so could mount a stronger fight. But for the urban poor of St. John's and the rural poor of the outports, the 1930s was nothing less than a devastating decade.

31 | To Each His Own

The woodsmen and the fishermen . . . are in fact serfs. For 300 years . . . the major part of their earnings has gone to create about 300 wealthy families. And that system of sweating still exists.

—John Hope Simpson, 1934

Woods camp at Botwood, 1906.

Fishermen United

Was there not a public fight to be waged against the poverty, against the thinking that led to so much of the wealth falling into the hands of a few? There was one person who had given himself to the cause of the ordinary worker, whose driving ambition had been to unite the fishermen and change the fundamental structure of Newfoundland society.

His name was William Coaker. In 1910 he had railed against a government that supported 'five splendid colleges at St. John's . . . while thousands of fishermen's children are growing up illiterate,' that maintained 'a hospital at St. John's while fishermen, their wives and daughters are dying in the outports for want of hospitals.' He called for broader opportunity for education and health care, and power redirected to the rural population through the establishment of local government. The foundation of this restructuring was fair payment for the work of fishermen.

As a boy Coaker had attended one of the city colleges, only to be forced to quit at thirteen to help support his family. He took a job on the city's waterfront as a fish handler. From his father, a master watch on sealing vessels, the young Coaker had learned of the wretched conditions under which sealers worked. In his own job he was to quickly discover that fish merchants paid as little as they could get away with. Coaker, the young man with big ideas and the nerve to back them up, led a strike of fish handlers his own age against Job Brothers for higher wages, and won.

At sixteen he left the city for Herring Neck in Notre Dame Bay. There, as branch manager of a St. John's merchant firm, he saw first-hand the conditions under which fishermen were working. When the bank crash of 1894

William Coaker

took his livelihood, he turned to farming, and to deep preoccupation with the inequity between the fishermen and the mercantile firms that employed them. His frustration came to a head in 1908 when, at a public meeting in Herring Neck, the Fishermen's Protective Union (FPU) was born. Coaker would rise to become one of the most powerful men in Newfoundland.

Yet by 1932 the FPU was spent and Coaker a man no longer with any hope of bringing his vision of change to the country. The country, in fact, had ultimately changed for the worse. What had happened to the dream of fishermen united and a class structure shaken to its core?

The task Coaker had set for himself was enormous. The fishing industry had been badly mismanaged for years, plagued by a poor-quality product and cutthroat competition between exporters. The merchants saw Coaker only as a cause of more headaches. Joining in the fight to put a stop to him were the Churches, who viewed his call for non-denominational schools, and elected school and road boards, as a threat to their power. The Catholic Church was particularly hostile. Its head, Bishop Howley, saw Coaker and the FPU as out to 'cause . . . an upheaval of our social fabric; to set class against class; . . . the outport man against the St. John's man, all of which things are fraught with mischief for our peace and prosperity.'

The Churches weren't asking the fundamental question—the prosperity of whom? Their own place of privilege and position stood in deep contrast to that of many who filled their churches. They made the morally questionable choice of aligning themselves with the self-serving mercantile and governing classes. When Catholic fishermen along the Southern Shore set up branches of the FPU they were confronted with Howley's indictment of the union. Rather than face the wrath of their clerics, the branches disbanded. Coaker's efforts to expand from his base of power on the mainly Protestant northeast coast would prove futile. His union never grew to include all the fishermen of Newfoundland, a critical element in its ultimate demise.

Coaker realized from the beginning that a political arm of the FPU was essential to his cause. His initial plan was to gain enough seats to hold the balance of power, but eventually Coaker agreed to form an alliance with another political party. This strategy, while potentially effective, was a dangerous game in Newfoundland politics, especially when the leader of that other party was the chameleon-like Richard Squires.

After the election of 1919 Coaker, under Squires, was appointed minister of Marine and Fisheries. It had been less than a dozen years between his first union meeting and the passage of legislation to reform the fishing industry. Minimum prices for cod were set, a government-regulated system for culling the fish put in place. It was a noble effort at giving the fisherman a fair return for a quality product.

But the attempt at reform came just as the world markets were recovering from the First World War. Renewed competition from other countries weakened Newfoundland's export position. Sudden fluctuations in foreign currencies strained the credibility of the new controls. Some fishermen feared a loss in markets and supported exporters who openly defied the reforms by selling their fish below the set price.

Backing for the Coaker reforms by the Squires cabinet (of which only two members belonged to the FPU) had never been more than half-hearted. The economic turmoil played directly into the hands of the merchants and the Catholic hierarchy. In the end, the FPU members of the House, outmanoeuvred by Squires and his allies, were not strong enough to fend off the attacks. (It reflects back, of course, to the state of schooling in the outports from where the FPU candidates had come. The loathsome lack of educational opportunity meant that most of the elected members possessed neither the confidence nor the skills to challenge the very governments who had denied them an education.)

By 1921, in a moment of great personal defeat for Coaker, the fishery reform legislation was repealed. The man was left disillusioned and bitter. Not long after, he found himself allied to a government encircled by scandal. His only choice was to leave politics behind.

Coaker's direct involvement in politics, with its inevitable compromises and sullied allegiances, had been his undoing. His knighthood, while he was still under the colours of Squires, was seen by some as an effort to dampen whatever passion for the cause remained in him. The heart was out of the union, and in the end many of the members turned their backs on its leader.

Port Union, the town in Trinity Bay that Coaker and the FPU had built, remained as the symbol of what the union had been capable. At its height it stood proudly self-sufficient, boasting its own fish processing plant, shipyard, convention hall, newspaper office, and rural Newfoundland's first electric generating station. It

The pseudo-grandeur of Coaker's gravesite at Port Union,
adjacent to the once mighty Congress Hall of the FPU.

was evidence that change in the treatment of fishermen was possible, indeed it was essential if Newfoundland was ever to rightly make a claim for prosperity.

Coaker's legacy was in the passion of his ideas that led him to organize the FPU. His was the loudest and most resonant voice. There were others, of course, most notably those behind the irascible Longshoremen's Protective Union (LSPU) in St. John's. By the late 1940s Newfoundland's per capita affiliation with trade unions was double that of Canada. Yet their effectiveness in an unstable economy and with a business-dominated legislature was minimal. The wages of the female shop clerks along Water Street were so low 'they would have to go on the streets if the Y.W.C.A. did not give them a home.' Some days they worked from eight in the morning to eleven at night. The men making deliveries might be on the streets of St. John's with their horse and cart until 1:30 the next morning.

But a tradition of trade unionism had been established. In the decades that followed it would be the voice of unions that would do much to rid Newfoundland and Labrador of the destructive attitudes of the affluent, which for far too long had impeded our maturation as a society. At times the confrontations were raw and impassioned, with unions at the centre of political turmoil, a loggers' strike of 1959 being the prime example. Some of its leaders, such as Nancy Riche, now secretary-treasurer of the Canadian Labour Congress, would take their Newfoundland experience and rework it in a national context.

Ironically, given Coaker's experience, it would be a Catholic priest, Father Desmond McGrath, who would initiate a movement to again bring fisheries workers under a union banner. His response to their treatment was first heard in 1970 in Port au Choix, on what had once been the French Shore. With Richard Cashin as its president for more than twenty years, the new fisheries union would rise to become the largest in North America. The descendants of the people whose work was the basis for our settlement and character were at last being heard. By necessity it was a strong voice. But at its strongest it was no longer celebrating gains made for its workers. It was forecasting overwhelming crisis.

The Suspension of Democracy

In 1926 William Coaker had predicted the demise of Newfoundland as a self-governing Dominion. Corruption and overspending would lead to it being ruled by 'a Commission . . . of the British Government.' Or, worse yet, as 'a poverty stricken Godforsaken Island administered as a province of Canada.'

Hardly a position to which a self-respecting people would want to descend. And one you would think a country that had fought for responsible government would bemoan and defy. Yet, 'a rest from politics,' as the last prime minister of the Dominion called it, fell in place with little more than a controlled whimper.

The prime minister was Frederick Alderdice. He had been returned to office in June 1932 in the wake of the riot on the Colonial Building and the obliteration of Richard Squires at the polls a few months later. Alderdice inherited a country on the extreme edge of financial ruin.

A loan from Imperial Oil (in exchange for a monopoly on all oil products in Newfoundland) had added enough funds to the treasury for a six-month reprieve. Now began a desperate search for further revenue. The doors of the banks were shut. Floating more bond issues was out of the question. Alderdice, as Squires before him, held up the Dominion's most saleable asset—Labrador. He touted it as a treasure trove of natural resources. Canada was not interested. And although a group of British financiers came close to leasing the territory for a period of ninety-nine years, in the end the deal fell through.

Alderdice saw no way of meeting the next interest payment. Britain recoiled at the thought of the 'damage to the prestige of the Empire which default might cause.' There was a scramble to avoid it. A meeting was called between Neville

Chamberlain, Britain's chancellor of the exchequer, and R.B. Bennett, the Canadian prime minister. Each agreed to a loan sufficient to meet the impending interest payment on Newfoundland's debt. There was a condition, however, one Alderdice saw no choice but to accept.

A commission of three, two representing Britain and one representing Britain's oldest colony, would be set up 'to examine the future of Newfoundland' and make recommendations on its finances and how it should be governed. On 17 February 1933 the commission was born, headed by a Scottish barrister, the first Baron Amulree, W.W. Mackenzie. Inexplicably, Newfoundland's choice to represent it was not one of its own, but its Canadian financial adviser, William Stavert, a strong advocate of confederation with Canada and agent of the Bank of Montreal.

Over the next four months the Amulree Commission held hearings in Newfoundland (but not the saleable Labrador), Ottawa, and Montreal. In all 260 witnesses offered their assessments of what was wrong with the country. They ranged from merchants swelled by their self-serving wisdom, to common fishermen hard-pressed to find words that could express how their country had betrayed its rural communities. Two of the Island's largely Protestant mercantile élite suggested that the right to vote be taken from the poor and illiterate. One chaired the St. John's committee for poor relief, the other was the great grandson of William Carson! Like most of their Board of Trade compatriots, they welcomed a return to government by Britain. Their predecessors in business had fought against responsible government when it was proposed eighty years before. It had never served either of them well enough.

In the outports there was widespread cynicism that merchant stores were the true beneficiaries of 'the dole,' that even William Coaker had forsaken his own people, trading Port Union for the luxury of retirement in Jamaica. 'We will never be in a better state of affairs till politics, as they have been served out to us in the past twenty years or more, are driven out of our land,' one man from Notre Dame Bay told the Commission. And privately, other influential views in favour of a new system of governing the Island were making themselves heard. The Catholic Archbishop Roche let it be known that he was cheered by the prospect that 'self-government had gone for good.'

So when the Amulree Report was delivered to Newfoundland, with its recommendation of a Commission of Government from Britain, few people balked. At its condemnation of Richard Squires and his kind and its stark depiction of the economic abuse of much of its population, there was but silent nodding. What the report failed to point out was that one of the paramount causes of Newfoundland's financial crisis was not of its own doing. It was rather the worldwide Depression, especially the drastic slump in fish prices.

Yet there was no outcry at the loss of the system of government for which the people's forebears had fought so hard. How, in the name of heaven, could a people ever allow its democratic rights to be swept away? This is the question many modern-day Newfoundlanders have been struggling with. More appropriate questions might be, Why had a people been driven beyond caring? And by whom?

Government by Commission

In November 1933, the Newfoundland House of Assembly passed a motion that would see it cease to exist. Most voices of dissent had been silenced by the vague addition 'until such time as Newfoundland may become self-supporting again.' An all-night session of the British Parliament ended with a similar motion of approval. And on 16 February 1934 Frederick Alderdice's signature put the country once again under foreign rule. Newfoundland and Labrador would be administered by a Commission of Government.

I first heard the words 'Commission of Government' from my father. They

The last session of the Newfoundland House of Assembly, 1933.

weren't spoken in anger or shame. Any anger was directed toward the governments preceding it who expected widows to keep from starving on relief of six cents a day. From my mother I had gathered a more subtle condemnation of the self-centredness of governments. Her reaction to anyone who put on airs was invariably, Who does she think she is—Lady Alderdice? (Though the especially pretentious might warrant allusion to a governor's wife: Who does she think she is—Lady Walwyn?)

Newfoundlanders entered the period of Commission of Government with some optimism. Anything would be better than what they had already faced. Many, like the parents of Leslie Harris in Placentia Bay, 'distrusted—utterly, totally—self-government.' And there was a measure of security in knowing the British and their treasury, while not about to turn generous, were at least committed to making the experiment work. The wife of one of the newly appointed commissioners was to observe shortly after her arrival, 'The story of Newfoundland is not one of which we as English people can be proud. We owe her a debt long overdue.' Not many people would have seen Commission of Government as an opportunity for Britain to right the wrongs of the past, but it was clear that this new government arrangement was far from a handout.

It consisted of six commissioners, three appointed by Britain and three by Newfoundland. There would be a British governor, but he would perform his duties only 'by and with the advice of the new Commission.' Alderdice (inevitably one of the Newfoundland appointees) termed the country 'betwixt and between a Crown Colony and a Dominion.' Whatever its label, beyond Water Street the country was in the mood for fundamental change.

The commissioners were each assigned several portfolios, with the policy-making departments directed into the hands of the British. The tenure of the foreigners was marked by an eagerness for reform, though its speed and direction were often at odds with what their Newfoundland counterparts had in mind. The native-born arguments had few teeth, however, and generally the British got their way, though not always with the results they had hoped for.

Most significantly, the reforms reached across the whole of the country. The new administrators, John Hope Simpson in particular, took first-hand knowledge of life beyond their living quarters at the Newfoundland Hotel as a necessary part of the job. (The commissioner's trip with his wife, Quita, to Labrador—that in itself a

welcome change—is commemorated in the name given a new logging community—Port Hope Simpson.) To judge by the letters they wrote to their relatives in
England, the Simpsons had a better appreciation of the immense gulf between the
rich and poor than did generations of civil servants who had preceded them. 'The
poverty of the outports—and indeed a lot of the city—is appalling, and I wonder
that they have not had a revolution long ago . . . Yet I am convinced that ultimately
even N.F.L. will come through—if we begin at the bottom. That means education.'

In social policy change was swift and eagerly embraced. In some cases the
reforms—such as a substantial network of cottage hospitals for the bigger out-

The medical ship
Lady Anderson
leaving Rencontre East.

ports—had been proposed by earlier governments but never brought about. The
administration commissioned a hospital ship, the *Lady Anderson*, to bring medical
services to the southwest coast. The fight against tuberculosis, together with a program of childhood immunization, became priorities. For schoolchildren, a glass of
'cocomalt,' a nutritional supplement, became a daily routine.

The Newfoundland Ranger Force, with detachments throughout the Island and
Labrador, was established to carry out government policies in rural areas. It proved
to be one of the finest initiatives of the Commission, drawing to its ranks individuals of outstanding pioneer spirit and character. Rangers were much more than
policemen. They were game wardens, truant officers, and health inspectors. They
supervised road construction, collected customs, and dispensed government relief.
Many became legendary in their own time. In the winter of 1936 Frank Mercer
carried a corpse by dogsled down half the coast of Labrador so that an autopsy
could be performed. Another Ranger made a trek through 225 kilometres of

wilderness to verify the report of a plane crash. The Rangers were examples of the outstanding individuals who would emerge to build a country when its people were given a decent chance to prove themselves.

Lack of well-equipped schools and properly trained teachers, as Amulree had suggested, was the source of much of the country's problems. Within the tenure of the Commission of Government the number of schools doubled. School attendance was made compulsory and free, the curriculum expanded and updated. The Commission instructed Memorial College, which had opened on Parade Street in St. John's in 1925, to initiate a Teacher Training Department. A summer-school program was begun for teachers who could not afford a full year at the college. There was now broader hope for higher education among those children who had come into the world outside the mill and mining towns, or beyond the roads of the Avalon.

Yet the poorer children in the capital city continued to be at a disadvantage, since the existing denominational facilities were already crowded. The Commission recommended the building of state schools to alleviate the problem. Foolishly, the Commission thought 'efficient schools managed by efficient teachers' was a virtuous solution. What it hadn't anticipated was the stone wall put up by the Anglican Bishop White and the Catholic Archbishop Roche. In their view only Church-run schools were acceptable.

The struggling population of 120 families in Moreton's Harbour, Simpson pointed out, were serviced by four schools—Catholic, Anglican, United Church, and Salvation Army. No matter the cost to the students, the Churches were not about to relinquish their control. They adamantly opposed what the Commission took to be a progressive step—that an Education Department administer the grant to education, rather than have it split and handed over directly to the Churches. Archbishop Roche is said to have warned the Commission that if a move were made to pass the bill, then it 'would be formally condemned from the altar of every R.C. Church in the island.' The Church would expect the resignation of R.C. Commissioner Howley (nephew of Roche's predecessor), not to be replaced, and Catholics would be told to boycott the forthcoming Silver Jubilee celebrations for George V.

Bishop White was just as antagonistic. The Commission saw little choice but to back away. The inevitable compromise was reached. Though a new committee structure was put in place for the administration of education, its members would be nominated by the Churches. They, in turn, would nominate the members of the local school boards. It would take more than three earnest British commissioners to wrest control of education from Church hierarchies.

The Commission's economic initiatives also ran headlong into problems. Its British members saw less dependence on the fishery as the solution to the country's financial woes and set about developing several 'land settlements'—fertile areas where unemployed men and their families would be encouraged to relocate and take up agriculture. Markland, near Whitbourne, was the first of these. The second was at Lourdes, on the west coast; Sandringham and Winterland were two others. Although the scheme met with some initial success, it did not spawn the pattern of resettlement that the Commission had envisioned. Its impact on unemployment was slight.

The energy put into the plan would have been better directed toward overhauling the fishery, where the mass of the population was focused. Though some improvements were made (a fisheries board to oversee the industry

Unloading codfish, Flower's Island, ca. 1940. The methods of the codfishery had changed little since the time of Cabot.

being one), the Commission found itself at odds with the Water Street merchants who fiercely guarded their monopoly on the industry. 'They see no further than the end of their noses and have no interest outside their own profit,' Simpson concluded in frustration.

The situation was, of course, exacerbated by the continuing worldwide

Depression. At times the fishing industry neared collapse on some coasts. The number of people on relief actually increased from what it had been when the Commission took office. Economically, the new system of government had done no better than the old, as Pierce Power, Marxist-inspired leader of the unemployed in St. John's was quick to point out. 'It is now a contest between the dictators and the masses of toiling Newfoundlanders,' he proclaimed, '. . . between the proletariat and the oligarchy sent across the Atlantic to rule us against our will!' Yet, given the social improvements, and bearing in mind what might have been had Newfoundland and Labrador struggled along on its own, the Commission could better be viewed as a limited success.

In the end, it was not anything that happened in Newfoundland and Labrador that turned the economic tide. It was instead the rise of aggression in Europe. In a very real sense the Second World War saved the country.

32 | The Wealth of War

There's an American way to make new-found friends in Newfoundland. It's the cheery invitation Have a "Coke"—*an old U.S. custom that is reaching 'round the world. It says* Let's be friends—*reminds Yanks of home. In many lands around the globe, Coca-Cola stands for* the pause that refreshes,—*has become a symbol of our friendly home-ways.*

—Full-page ad campaign in *Life* and *National Geographic*, 1944.

Uncle Sam marches past Governor Walwyn, St. John's, 1942.

Military Matters

What a difference a few years made.

In 1939 Newfoundland's economy was spiralling downward once more. Import duties in Brazil cut into one of its prime markets for cod. Civil war in Spain put an end to another. A disillusioned Commission of Government forecast a deficit of $4 million. Instead of steady progress toward a rejuvenated country, as it had promised, the Commission was facing its worse economic crisis since being sworn into office.

Then, almost overnight, revenues began to swell. Within a half-dozen years Newfoundland was in the unheard-of position of holding an accumulated budget surplus of $30 million. Twelve of those millions were diverted to Britain as interest-free loans! A measure of prosperity, elusive for as long as anyone cared to remember, had suddenly appeared.

The bearer of this good fortune didn't wander up from any merchant premises on Water Street, but marched from dockside in army boots, and landed on the west coast and in Labrador in C-17 bombers. Rarely has the risk of war transformed a country so dramatically for the better. With the aggression of Hitler in Europe had come unprecedented attention to Newfoundland and Labrador. This landmass jutting into the Atlantic was deemed to be the first line of defence should the führer defeat Britain and set his sights on North America.

As soon as war was declared, Anglo-Canadian strategies unfolded for the defence of possible Axis targets in Newfoundland—the airport at Gander and the seaplane base at Botwood, the iron mine on Bell Island, the transatlantic cable stations at Heart's Content and Bay Roberts. The port of St. John's itself was determined to be a primary point of entry should invasion of North America ever be attempted. To prevent the enemy from gaining any advantage in Newfoundland that it could then use against the mainland of the continent, a 'Scorched Earth Policy' was set in place by the War Cabinet of the Canadian government. Not only were all gun emplacements and all communications facilities (including Cabot Tower) to be destroyed, but ships were to be sunk at the Narrows to block entrance to the port, and the ten thousand tonnes of fuel in storage tanks on the Southside Hills drained into the harbour and ignited. As the officers who devised the plans duly noted, 'owing to the large amount of wood used in the buildings in St. John's . . . fire provides the simplest and quickest method of destruction.' They did have plans for the population to flee the burning city, with all the food such refugees could transport!

Fortunately their transformation of the city took a more orderly course. With the Battle of the Atlantic escalating in 1941, the British entered into an agreement with Canada to make St. John's a base of naval operations. The port evolved into the primary western turnaround point for the ships escorting convoys across the Atlantic. St. John's Harbour was home to dozens of destroyers, frigates, and corvettes. The navy's own club, the famous *Crow's Nest* (up fifty-nine steps in an alley off Water Street), is still there, its memorabilia-encrusted walls a reminder of the extraordinary activity centred in St. John's during the war.

The escort duty of the Canadian navy was enhanced by patrols of the RCAF, not only out of expanded facilities in Gander, but also Botwood, where close to a thousand men of the Black Watch showed up to guard it. New Canadian air bases were built at Torbay, on the outskirts of St. John's, and at Goose Bay in Labrador, where in an amazing three months in the fall of 1941 three huge runways were carved out of wilderness. Like Gander, Goose Bay became a refuelling point for the thousands of aircraft en route to Europe from factories in the United States. By 1943 it had surpassed Gander and became the largest airport in the world, at times its maze of barracks and tents teeming with upwards of ten thousand soldiers and civilian construction workers. (By the end of the war it had handled more than twenty-five thousand military aircraft and their passengers, including many of the quarter million American troops then airlifted back to North America.)

GIs Galore

Americans had also been quick to recognize our strategic importance. It was through Western Union's cable station in Bay Roberts that U.S. President Franklin D. Roosevelt maintained direct communication with British Prime Minister Winston Churchill. It would be at anchorage just off Ship Harbour, Placentia Bay, where the two met in July 1941 to sign the Atlantic Charter, the ideological accord that set the Allied parameters for the war.

By then Goose Bay had become part of the so-called destroyers for bases agreement, in which the United States turned over to Britain fifty destroyers, in return for ninety-nine-year land leases to construct military bases in (among other Commonwealth possessions) Labrador and Newfoundland. Blueprints were rolled out for Fort

Roosevelt and Churchill meet in Placentia Bay, 1941.

Pepperrell in St. John's, naval and army bases at Argentia in Placentia Bay, and an air base next to Stephenville, a community of 250 on the Island's west coast.

Uncle Sam had come to town, and with lots of greenbacks in his pocket. Men from the outports arrived in droves hoping to find work. My father, who had spent the 1930s lobster fishing and cutting pulp in the lumberwoods of the west coast, was among them. He had left Bonne Bay for Argentia, but along the way heard word that the Americans were hiring in Stephenville. It was there that hundreds of families from throughout Newfoundland eventually settled, under the generous shadow of Harmon Field and what grew to be the largest American air force base outside the United States.

In 1942 one-fifth of the total labour force in Newfoundland and Labrador was employed in base construction. The 'friendly invasion' abruptly thrust a significant portion of Newfoundland into America's version of the twentieth century. According to Governor Humphrey Walwyn, the ex-British admiral, the new arrivals quickly 'dazzled' the locals with their 'dollars, hygiene and efficiency.' Newfoundland was due a share of dazzle. With Frank Sinatra, Phil Silvers, Marlene Dietrich, and dozens of other stars of the USO shows stopping by to entertain the troops and their Newfoundland girlfriends, at times the dazzle became positively blinding.

Because there were now three nations holding territory in Newfoundland and Labrador, the Commission of Government was left balancing their rights with fair

Fay McKenzie, Phil Silvers, and Frank Sinatra,
Harmon Air Force Base, Stephenville, 1945.
'I was amazed at the size and hustling
spirit of the base,' admitted the crooner.

treatment for its own citizens. At times its handling of the situation was less than exemplary. When American surveyors and engineers showed up in Argentia and nearby Marquise with orders to expropriate homes, the government had not yet set a mechanism in place to compensate the residents. It took weeks of wrangling to settle on a move to Freshwater, time made worse for the people when the first homes to be vacated were promptly burnt to the ground, at the same time that 625 graves in the three local cemeteries were being dug up and relocated.

What would have sparked more widespread resentment, had the workers been organized, was the issue of the wages paid the civilians by the mainland firms contracted to build the bases. American civilians received twice the rate of pay of Newfoundlanders doing the same job. The Commission of Government insisted the contractors keep wages at a lower level, something comparable to the menial income Newfoundlanders had been used to getting. Higher pay, it insisted, would undermine the fishing industry, and put the government's own wage scale (twenty-five cents an hour for labourers) in a bad light. Not only that, it just might provide 'a golden opportunity' for the growth of trade unions. And for the good of the country, in the Commission's view, all such wage discussions with the contractors were to be kept strictly private.

As it was, the average household income in Newfoundland doubled during the war years. Significant funds were injected into road construction, and into health care and other social services. Twenty-five new regional libraries were built. An Act was finally introduced that made schooling compulsory for seven- to fourteen-year-olds. And, perhaps most indicative of the impact of the war, in 1944 legislation was passed making it mandatory that wages throughout the country be paid in cash.

The impact was reaching far beyond the outskirts of the new military installations. Money was finding its way back to the outports. But old habits died hard. Some of the men who came to work in Argentia, for example, were sending home their paycheques, not directly to their wives and families, but to the outport merchant. In some communities the merchant stood as patriarch well into the 1950s. He still decided what he would supply a family or what he would scratch off their list. He was the one who called the doctor if a child was sick, the one who decided what child in a family might do well to go away for more education. The subservience dissipated only as the isolation broke down, when someone took the brave step of using the money he earned elsewhere to open up a store in competition with the established merchant. With people squirming out from under his thumb, one Fortune Bay merchant was heard to mutter, 'We let them have too much.'

Of course, the greatest changes occurred in the communities bordering the new military installations. At its peak roughly twenty-five thousand armed forces personnel were stationed here. In addition to the major bases, scattered throughout the Island and as far north as Saglek along the Labrador coast were repeater and radar stations, some eventually forming part of the Distant Early Warning (DEW) Line during the Cold War. The first of these took shape on Fogo Island, with the perimeter of the top-secret site (the local residents had no idea what its fifty-two men were up to) patrolled by K-9 dogs and defended by seven 50-calibre machine guns.

It was a far cry from the three-thousand-kilometre

American GIs and their Newfoundland girlfriends, 1944.

NORAD early detection system, stretching from Greenland to the White Hills of St. John's, that was in place by the 1950s. In Stephenville we grew up with the sounds of F-102 intercepter jets and their partners, the huge KC-97 refuellers, the 'Stratotankers.' At the height of the Cuban Missile Crisis in 1962, with the base on 'red alert,' the anxiety that permeated the community was equal to that of any place in the U.S. itself.

Indeed it was the 'Yanks' who left the most lasting impression during the war, rather than the Canadians (with their 'baggy khaki pants') or the Brits (so polite they 'talked about "Mr. Hitler"'). From the moment the first of them arrived, aboard the immense troop ship the *Edmund B. Alexander*, American soldiers gathered the biggest slice of attention. The locals found them outgoing, eager to join in community events and service clubs. They opened their ships and planes for public viewing. They gathered kids around them, handed out treats, and taught them baseball.

Especially attracted to the uniformed young bucks were, of course, single women. Some put it down to their 'strong white . . . teeth' or their verbal charms, or just the contrast in manners with the local men. They all agreed GIs 'knew how to treat a woman.' Coca-Cola and Camel cigarettes were in endless supply. The GIs' base radio stations played all the latest hits and their social clubs organized the best dances, with their own musicians. Among them were four servicemen from Philadelphia who eventually returned to the States as the Four Aces. (Their harmonies—'Mr. Sandman,' 'Three Coins in the Fountain'—turned them into one of the great quartets of the fifties.) There was a former sax player with the Tommy Dorsey Orchestra and an Airman 2nd Class, John Williams, who for his four years at St. John's was a pianist in the Starlighters, a lesser group than the one he would go on to conduct—the Boston Pops. The Oscar-winning composer of mega-movie scores would make his film score debut in St. John's—with *Happy Union*, a tourist promotion for the Newfoundland government. Doing their military stint in Argentia were Johnny Weismuller, Steve Lawrence, and Bill Cosby. John Kennedy stopped by for repairs to his PT 109. (Gene Autry and Elvis sang only a few songs as he passed through.)

Parents of eligible young women were the wary ones, put off by the swagger and the bravado about the States. Newfoundland became 'Newfy' and 'back home' became a land of riches for potential brides. To it the single Newfoundland men countered, 'If you can't get a man, get a Yank!' (which in Stephenville was backed up with many a fistfight down Main Street). That was no deterrent. In all, over the twenty-five-year history of the bases, an estimated thirty thousand women from Newfoundland and Labrador married American servicemen. Many of the brides who went 'back home' found neither the country nor the husband lived up to their expectations, and eventually returned, often with children in tow. But most stayed, contented with their new lives, reinforcing an already strong bond between Newfoundland and the U.S.

Real War

That bond had been further reinforced by the events of February 1942. When the American destroyer *Truxtun* and the supply ship *Pollux* were wrecked on the rocks at Chambers Cove and Lawn Point on the Burin Peninsula, it was the people of St. Lawrence and Lawn who risked their lives in an attempt to save the men left clinging to life on the icy shoreline. Of the nearly 400 sailors cast into the freezing and oily waters, 183 were saved, many by men who had lowered themselves with ropes over the treacherous cliffs.

(One of the *Truxtun*'s crew, Lanier Philips, had been raised a poor black in Klan-dominated Georgia. On that horrific winter's day, he found himself being gently nursed back to health by the women of St. Lawrence, something for which, he would many times recall, 'back in the States they would have been thrown in jail . . . and I would, too, for letting them do it.' These people in remote Newfoundland not only saved his life, but also inspired him to challenge the racism of the U.S. Navy. He pressed the bureaucrats until he was allowed to train as a SONAR specialist, eventually becoming the first black instructor in his field. He marched with Martin Luther King in Selma and in 1963 played a significant role in the retrieval of two atomic bombs lost off the coast of Spain. Philips credits 'the good people of St. Lawrence' with turning his life around.)

Newfoundlanders were again jolted into acknowledging the reality of the war when, in broad daylight on 5 September 1942, the German submarine U-513 torpedoed and sank two ore carriers at anchor off Bell Island. Two months later another sub, U-518, also slid undetected into Conception Bay, evading the searchlights that scanned the waters around the island. The first torpedo missed its target and struck a loading pier, giving Bell Island the distinction of being the only place in North America to experience a direct hit by a German U-boat. The torpedoes that followed sent two more ore-laden ships to the bottom. In all, sixty-nine people were killed.

In the Gulf of St. Lawrence unfolded an even more tragic reminder of the threat to North America posed by German sea power. On 14 October 1942 the finely appointed rail and passenger ferry *Caribou*, crossing the Cabot Strait from Nova Scotia to Newfoundland, came in the sightlines of U-69. The sub had been brazenly lurking about the gulf for two weeks, always managing to evade the patrols of the Canadian navy. Near Île d'Anticosti it scored a direct hit on a freighter loaded with building supplies for the new air base at Goose Bay, then took to waters off Cape Breton Island, on the lookout for grain boats it had been told were making their way toward Montreal.

At seven o'clock on the night of the thirteenth the *Caribou* left North Sydney. In charge of the crew of 46 was Ben Taverner. First and third mates were his sons, one of seven pairs of brothers among the crew. All made their home in the ferry's destination, Port aux Basques, or nearby Channel. More than half of the 192 passengers were military personnel on their way back to assignments in Newfoundland, among them two Nursing Sisters from the Prairies, Margaret Brooke and Agnes Wilkie, due to resume their duties at the Canadian naval hospital in St. John's.

The *Caribou*'s engines were coal-fired, a troublesome circumstance in wartime. On this calm, grey night what caught the attention of the U-boat's Captain Ulrich Graf was the dim hulk of a ship 'belching thick black smoke.' He must have been surprised to see a passenger ferry at all, tempting fate by plying the gulf at night when subs like his could break the surface without fear of air patrols. The *Caribou*'s captain had argued vehemently against night crossings, but the navy overruled

him, choosing to put all its faith in the minesweeper *Grandmère* assigned to escort the ferry across the gulf. Rather than zigzagging ahead of the ship, or circling it, the *Grandmère*

Young Leonard Shiers, safe following the sinking of the Caribou.

trailed the ship astern. Its hydrophones had no hope of separating the sound of a sub's propeller from that of the *Caribou*. And of the three ships, only U-69 was equipped with radar.

The *Caribou* was a hopelessly easy target. At 3:30 a.m. a lone torpedo rammed the ferry midships. The explosion instantly killed everyone in the engine room and set the rest of the ship into 'indescribable chaos.' Passengers groped for lifebelts through pitch black, struggling to get from their cabins to a badly listing deck, only to find that the two starboard lifeboats had been destroyed in the blast. Somehow they managed to get two of the remaining lifeboats into the water. Eighty people crowded into one before they discovered the seacock had been left open. The boat filled with water and capsized, throwing some into the open water, trapping many beneath, 'thumping, thumping . . . ' in a futile call for help.

Into the second lifeboat climbed Gertie Strickland and her infant child. Her husband tossed down an older girl to one of the men in the boat, and was about to climb aboard himself when the overcrowded vessel lurched to one side. The older child was swept away into the blackness. And, minutes later, just as the remaining three were free of the capsizing lifeboat and back on the deck of the ship, a wave broke over them and flung them all into the sea. Only the father survived.

The *Caribou* had lasted but five minutes before it sank. The *Grandmère*, following navy regulations, turned in pursuit of the enemy sub rather than attempt to rescue survivors. The chase proved fruitless. The U-boat went into a deep dive amid the ungodly sounds escaping the sinking ship. Graf positioned his sub near the *Caribou*, knowing full well the *Grandmère* would not set off depth charges anywhere near the people clinging to life in the waters above.

Only 101 people survived the sinking and the hours to daylight when the captain of the minesweeper, wrecked by the moral dilemma forced on him, gave up the search and began taking survivors on board. The list of dead would include all three Taverner men. (Twenty years later a new gulf ferry would bear their name.) Of the other six pairs of brothers among the crew, only one was left, and of the fifteen children aboard, only fifteen-month-old Leonard Shiers remained. The child had been lost in the water and snatched to safety three different times. His mother, three months pregnant, also managed to cling to life, though all the while separated from the baby whom she had given up for dead. Also on the list of the living was William Lundrigan, who would go on to become one of the Island's most prominent entrepreneurs, but whose experience aboard the *Caribou* would lead him to devote much of his life to community service. Nurse Margaret Brooke survived. Most of the night she clung to the capsized lifeboat and the hand of her nursing friend, until near dawn a wave washed over the boat and separated them. Agnes Wilkie was one of the last to die.

Nineteen forty-two would not end before yet another tragedy. On December twelfth fire broke out in one of the most popular social spots in St. John's, the Knights of Columbus Hostel on Harvey Road. About 350 people, many of them servicemen, had crowded into 'Uncle Tim's Barn Dance,' broadcast that night live over radio station VOCM. Throughout the city people listened in horror as the music came to an abrupt stop amid chaotic shouting. The crowd that rushed to escape the burning building confronted doors that opened inward and windows with plywood blackout shutters nailed over them. Ninety-nine people perished, making it the most deadly structural fire ever in what is now Canada.

Investigation showed that the fire had been deliberately set, and although

The Knights of Columbus fire, St. John's, 1942.

never proved, it is widely believed to have been a work of Nazi sabotage. It would not be the only time the enemy penetrated the coastal defences. In October of the following year a German U-boat slithered ashore in uninhabited Martin Bay near the northernmost tip of Labrador. There a Siemens-manufactured automatic weather station was set up. Its housing had been labelled 'Canadian Weather Service,' and before leaving the site, the men scattered empty American cigarette packs. The station was left to transmit sixty seconds of coded weather statistics every three hours, to be picked up by receiving stations in northern Europe, and then used to formulate weather forecasts for German ships and U-boats prowling the North Atlantic. No one who happened upon the site ever realized the equipment carried the name of an organization that did not exist. It was not until thirty-five years after the war that its true origins came to light.

Overseas

Of course, for many the Second World War was a time of active military service. While hundreds joined the militia and defended the home front, thousands more served overseas in both the British and Canadian forces. Ironically, with its governance in the hands of Britain itself, the country did not take on the deep financial commitment it had so eagerly embraced during the First World War. In the fall of 1939 it was even suggested that its contribution might be simply to help the cause by reducing the funds it received from the British treasury. Not a popular stance, as an editorial in the *Evening Telegram* made clear: 'Don't place restraints on loyalty. . . . Newfoundlanders demand the right to serve their King and Country!'

That they did, though it was quickly decided that a self-contained Newfoundland regiment, as had met such calamity in 1916, would not be formed. More than two thousand men enlisted in the British army, many forming part of two regiments of the Royal Artillery. In addition to defending Britain's coastline, they would find themselves fighting in the blistering heat of North Africa, in Italy, and on the beaches of Normandy. The RAF, too, would have its squad of Newfoundlanders, ground forces and airmen, defending Britain against the night raids of German fighters. And, as in the First World War, thousands of loggers signed up for work in Scotland, part of an overseas Forestry Unit.

It would be the Royal Navy that would see the single greatest number of Newfoundland volunteers, holding true to their designation by Churchill in 1939 as 'the hardiest and most skilful boatmen in rough seas who exist.' There was hardly a Royal Navy ship in the war that didn't have a Newfoundlander among its crew. Joining them in the dangerous Atlantic waters were thousands serving as part of the merchant marine.

Scattered through the regiments of Canada's Armed Forces were another 1,700 Newfoundlanders. For many their training was a first taste of Canada. More important, their service gave many Canadians a taste of Newfoundland and its commitment to the military, where today the proportion of our population who serve is well in excess of the Canadian average.

Second World War volunteers included more than five hundred women. Barred from front-line duty, many found themselves doing clerical and other duties on Canadian bases, freeing men to fight overseas. Thousands more at home undertook volunteer work with the Women's Patriotic Association, which, by the war's end, had more than four hundred active branches. They knitted thousands of 'woollen comforts' and sewed thousands more supplies for the Red Cross and the St. John Ambulance. Perhaps the most remembered female contribution to the war effort was that of Margot Davies, whose chatty broadcast on the BBC—*Calling from Britain to Newfoundland*—connected Newfoundland servicemen passing through London with their anxious relatives back home. The hospitality she extended to Newfoundlanders in Britain was legendary. Her English accent (though she grew up a St. John's girl) continued to magnetize radio listeners long after the war came to an end.

The impact of the Second World War, as with any war, was personal and often-times tragic. Newfoundland and Labrador lost close to nine hundred of its men. Among those to survive the worst of it was John Ford from Port aux Basques, a mechanic with the RAF taken prisoner in Java after the island was overrun by the Japanese. Ford spent three years in a vermin-infested POW camp in Nagasaki, his weight sinking to ninety pounds (forty kilograms) on a diet of rice. When guards discovered he was from Newfoundland they taunted him with the news that the Germans had sunk the *Caribou*. On 9 August 1945 Ford was cutting sheet metal at a shipyard in Nagasaki Harbour when the atomic bomb was dropped. It exploded just over a kilometre from where he stood. He survived. 'Just lucky,' he put it decades later. Ultimately, and in this he could be speaking for all veterans of Newfoundland and Labrador, 'There is no glamour to war.'

33 | Nudged into Wedlock

The great go-getting, twanging continent next door has not got the
Newfoundlander yet.

—A.P. Herbert, British parliamentary mission to Newfoundland, 1943

Joey Smallwood campaigning for what he liked to call 'British Union.'

Matchmaker

The Second World War had brought unprecedented prosperity. V-E Day, for all its dancing in the streets, was also tinged with uncertainty. What now for this North Atlantic buttress? The business of war was over. Could a slump in our fortunes be far behind?

The British saw a certain urgency in dealing with the 'problem of Newfoundland,' embarrassed as they were to be fighting a war over democracy in a place where democracy had been suspended. Churchill had, after all, signed his name to the third article of the Atlantic Charter—'the right of all peoples to choose the form of government under which they will live'—in the lee of our pine-clad hills. 'The biggest blot' on the British democracy, the Opposition's Independent Labour party was yelling. In September 1942 Clement Attlee, deputy prime minister and secretary for the Dominions, had paid a visit to Newfoundland to see for himself what might be done. While praising the war effort of the gallant little ally, he was taken aback by the lack of any attempt to prepare the people for a return to self-government. He blamed it partly on the choice of Newfoundland commissioners, all of whom came from the east coast of the Island. 'The west,' he concluded at the end of his travels, 'is more awake.'

Attlee viewed local politics as a natural and essential training ground for democracy. Aside from two town councils, the city council of St. John's, and a few co-operatives, there were no other elected bodies in the whole of Newfoundland. Coupled with the fact that Newfoundlanders now had a standard of living higher than anything they had ever known when elected members were yelling at each other across the floor of the Colonial Building, it was little wonder that the Dominions secretary sensed indifference toward a return to self-government. In Attlee's view, Newfoundland was like 'a man who having had a spell of drunkenness has taken the pledge . . . is tired of it and would like to be a moderate drinker but does not quite trust himself.'

Britain would wait out the war before acting, but it was clear the abstinence of the Commission of Government could not continue indefinitely. In the meantime, a delegation of three British parliamentarians, making up a 'Goodwill Mission,' were dispatched to take a closer look at the situation.

They rummaged the minds of Newfoundlanders and Labradorians for two months during the summer of 1943. The gregarious drinker among the trio discovered a people 'fond of holidays but fine workers: politically maddening but personally the salt of the earth.' The fact that he also concluded 'I do not believe I ever heard a Newfoundlander swear . . . ' would tend to indicate he kept only select company. The second of the delegates, a compulsive fisherman, may well have been swayed by the great number of prime salmon rivers set in his path.

The third showed himself to be a harder nut to crack. He was given over to dourness (never a good trait to carry to a Newfoundland outport) and was 'reputedly an ardent seeker-out of the clergy class.' One of his conclusions, that the major deficiency in our collective nature was 'a tendency to put the blame for all that goes wrong on somebody else,' proved the sorest point. But Newfoundlanders shook his hand nonetheless, and wished him well. They were sure they themselves were doing something right, considering what he termed their 'remarkable freedom from crime.' The fact that they got along with each other, and weren't out and about in the world trying to assess the damage of Empire-hoarding ancestors, had to count for a lot.

By the end of their jaunt the three scouts did find common ground. They proposed the setting up of a forum for discussion, a 'national convention' that would bring together a cross-section of loyal subjects willing to debate the possibilities and make recommendations to the British Parliament. They also advanced the notion of a ten-year reconstruction plan, one meant to avert at any cost an 'imperial slum on the back doorstep of the United States.'

An enthusiastic Commission of Government came up with the imperial estimate for the plan of $100 million. The

Most pre-confederation outports knew few luxuries.

British quickly had second thoughts. Was there not another route to solving the 'problem of Newfoundland'? One less costly and that would avoid a return to responsible government and the resurrection of free-spending politicians.

A permanent solution, as Whitehall had concluded long ago, was confederation with Canada. But throughout Newfoundland, in the words of one of the Goodwill missionaries, 'The issue of confederation is a live one with only a very small minority.' That, and the lukewarm attitude of Ottawa to taking the Island into the fold, stood as formidable obstacles. Nevertheless, the time had come to aggressively (if out of earshot of Newfoundland itself) pursue the matter. In September 1945 an emissary, in the person of Alexander Clutterbuck, was dispatched to Ottawa.

Clutterbuck was the official in the Dominions Office who knew most about Newfoundland. Through his civil service stiffness had emerged an astute observer of events in Newfoundland, from the time of his first visit as secretary to the Amulree Commission of 1933. He entered his meetings with officials of the Department of External Affairs full of confidence. There had been indications that the traditional Canadian attitude toward Newfoundland (in Clutterbuck's view, one of 'condescension and even contempt') had changed since the two had been forced into each other's company by the events of the war.

The opening exchanges fell flat, even as Clutterbuck reiterated his country's difficult financial position. To Canada's reaction, 'I did not conceal my disappointment,' he would later confess. He was forced into playing his trump card early. If neither Britain nor Canada could offer assistance, would it not be but a matter of time before Newfoundland turned to the United States? Surely the Canadians did not need reminding of how fond Newfoundland had grown of Americans and their dollar, of how many years the Stars and Stripes had left to flutter over the bases dotted around the Island and Labrador.

Before long the notion of confederation with Canada, which Clutterbuck saw as Newfoundland's 'natural destiny,' had become for Mackenzie King, the Canadian prime minister, 'natural, desirable and inevitable.' Besides, Canada had acquired a new confidence internationally, and rounding out its country with additional territory, taking it from the Pacific to the land's end of the Atlantic, would add considerably to its stature.

Ruben Lewis, chief of the Newfoundland Mi'kmaq and his family, ca. 1905.

The Attraction

Britain and Canada were soon discussing the economic details. It became clear that Newfoundland's finances were in better shape than Canada had realized. With the iron ore reserves and hydro-electric potential of Labrador and the international centre of aviation at Gander added to the discussions, there was much to smile about.

And when Ottawa saw the homogeny in our population, the picture of a tenth province brightened even more. Nowhere else in North America could such a vast majority of a population be traced to such a small geographic area. The innate discord between the English and the Irish seemed to have been worked out, except for the occasional fight in hockey and baseball stands, and that was largely in the name of denominational education. There had been a modest influx of Scots into the Island's west coast which, to any Upper Canadian, could only be reassuring. The same coast also bore a few small settlements of Acadians and of Frenchmen who had jumped ship in the days of the French Shore. But with Leblancs changing their names to White, Aucoin to O'Quinn, and Jesseau to Jesso, assimilation was well underway.

The census of 1945 showed that more than 98 per cent of the population had been born in Newfoundland and Labrador. Of foreign cultures there was but a scattering, immigrants mainly of Lebanese and Chinese background. As Canada itself had done, Newfoundland enacted severe restrictions on immigration in the decade prior to the First World War. A head tax of $300 had been imposed on Chinese males, while Chinese women were excluded altogether. By 1932 Newfoundland's immigration had become so narrow that it denied entry to Asians, Africans, central and eastern Europeans, exempting only those whose countries imported its fish. As the Nazi influence in Europe accelerated, Jews and political refugees turned to Canada and

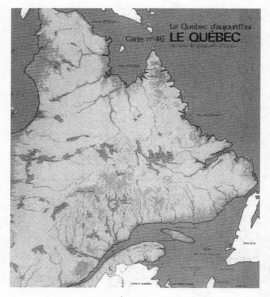

This Quebec map of 1985 chose to ignore the decisions of 1927.

Newfoundland, and were rejected by both. In Newfoundland the xenophobia was reinforced by a merchant and professional class determined to thwart the entry of anyone who might be competition for their business. In their racist immigration policies Mackenzie King discovered two governments speaking the same language.

Ottawa, unsettled by the rising discontent of its own aboriginal peoples, found little to be concerned about in the native populations. The Mi'kmaq, small in number, were mainly concentrated in one area of the south coast, and had taken English as their common language. As for the Innu and Inuit of Labrador, it was assumed they would want to join Canada, where they would find people of a common ancestry.

For the Innu it would be a reunion of sorts after the division of their territory created by the Labrador boundary settlement of 1927. Following a quarter century of wrangling between Quebec and Newfoundland, the issue had been brought before a judicial committee of the Privy Council in London. Given the Island's traditional use of Labrador as a fishing station, Canada (on behalf of Quebec) had argued that Newfoundland should hold rights to only a thin coastal strip one mile (1.6 kilometres) in width. Newfoundland's case (backed by intense archival research by dogged native son P.T. McGrath) countered that its rights followed the rivers inland, beyond the Grand Falls to the 'height of land' frequented by Innu and white trappers. The judgement fell to Newfoundland. (Seventy-five years later some in Quebec still refuse to accept it. On provincial maps Quebec regularly includes all of Labrador.) In 1945 Ottawa may well have been thinking that with Labrador in the fold of confederation, some of the sting of the Privy Council judgement would dissipate. And would there not be more of an opportunity for a disgruntled Quebec to benefit from the Labrador resources that had fallen out of its hands? A momentous consideration indeed.

Popping the Question

The matter of confederation now became not 'if' but 'how.' Britain would do what it could to set the stage. Canada would linger in the wings, there as unseen support for the Newfoundland proponents of confederation, whoever they might turn out to be. Would there spring to life some energetic Newfoundlander to capture the imagination of the populace with the notion of union with Canada? It was doubtful. He surely wouldn't rise from the ranks of the upper classes, who feared what confederation might do to their tidy business arrangements. And a broadly educated, politically obsessive upstart from off the Avalon was a rare bird indeed.

Britain set the guidelines for the National Convention. A key factor was the geographic origin of the delegates. To avoid a rush of St. John's lawyers and merchants to fill the outport seats (and thus guarantee a return to responsible government), the Dominions office required that a candidate be resident in a district for a minimum of two years. Among those signing up to run was indeed a man of rare plumage: ex-reporter, ex-union organizer, ex-broadcaster, and now resident pig farmer of Gander—Joseph R. Smallwood.

Smallwood was a man eager for his time in the sun. On 12 December 1945 he was passing through Montreal (on his way back from Ontario, where he had gone to research feed mills) when he picked up a copy of the Montreal *Gazette*. A headline on page twenty-one stopped him dead. 'SELF-RULE IS PLAN IN NEWFOUND-LAND: Colony Soon to Have Own Government After 12 Years of Commission.' Instantly Smallwood knew he would be a candidate. Before the day was out he knew exactly what platform he would embrace—the only one for which he had any chance of emerging as leader. He had talked and argued his way into believing that Newfoundlanders would, once they realized the benefits, give up their political independence forever. At that moment Smallwood 'chose Canada.' His absolute conviction that it was the right move for Newfoundland and Labrador (and for himself) would come later, on election day.

He had much to draw on for his campaign. Born in Gambo, a hamlet in Bonavista Bay, Smallwood spent his youth in St. John's. He was eccentric even by 'townie' standards and had felt the sting of the rich and arrogant during his school days at Bishop Feild College. He also came to know the gross deficiencies of many outports. In 1925 the diminutive, bespectacled young man had trudged a nine-hundred-kilometre length of the Island's railway line to organize section men facing a cut in pay. He'd worked to set up a fishermen's co-operative on the Bonavista Peninsula, at a time when he was as dirt poor as any of those he was trying to organize. He published a newspaper in Corner Brook. He'd spent four years in New York soaking up socialist ideals, and another six months in London following the grassroots of the Labour Party. He published the weighty two-volume compendium *The Book of Newfoundland*. But most important for his future as a politician, from 1937 to 1943 Smallwood worked as a radio broadcaster, host of *The Barrelman*. His nightly mixture of Newfoundland history and humour was heard across the Island, his concern for the outports an inherent part of every broadcast. His was the most recognized voice in Newfoundland. It was not a bad headstart for a politician.

To this experience and his encyclopedic knowledge of Newfoundland Smallwood brought an inexhaustible energy. He had never taken on a task in his life without giving to it his heart and soul, and almost his every waking hour. Once back in Newfoundland, he wrote to the prime minister of Canada and all nine provincial premiers, telling them his intentions and requesting material to help him understand the workings of their governments. He buried himself in the deluge of books, pamphlets, and reports for several weeks, and by March 1946 had wrung out a series of eleven articles for the *Daily News* extolling the virtues of confederation. In June he marched victorious in Bonavista Centre, having trounced his opponent with nearly 90 per cent

Confederation supporter William Keough fires up the National Convention.

of the vote. It marked the start of one of the most extraordinary political careers of modern times.

The National Convention took place over several months in the Lower Chamber of the Colonial Building. Smallwood manoeuvred himself into the centre of whatever attention was being paid to the meetings. In the beginning it was very little. From most of the other delegates spewed a tiresome, old-style harangue. They spent their time berating the Commission of Government, their rhetoric confirming that Newfoundland was destined to return to the self-serving bedlam of the Richard Squires era. The masses ignored them. As one report from Englee on the Northern Peninsula put it, 'The majority of the residents took a great deal more interest in the Louis-Walcott boxing bout than they did in the whole Convention . . . '

Only Smallwood drew them out of their lethargy. And on 28 October 1946—the first day of live radio broadcast—he stood in the chamber and brazenly called for a delegation be sent to Ottawa to determine the 'terms and conditions' for union with Canada. It set off an avalanche of criticism. The motion was 'premature' and 'unconstitutional' and (out of earshot) the fellow who made it was no better than his previous constituents—'swine.' The overreaction was exactly what Smallwood had anticipated. The passion in his old familiar Barrelman voice stretched far beyond the chamber, and far beyond the Avalon. He had planted the seed of confederation, and sat back to watch the townies who berated him heap fertilizer on it.

In the meantime the convention passed a motion to send a delegation to London to determine just what Newfoundland could expect from Whitehall if there were a return to responsible government, or if the Commission were asked to continue. In bringing some order to the turmoil purposely brought on by Smallwood, the mood of the convention changed to one of clarifying the country's options. By the time the issue of sending a delegation to Ottawa resurfaced Smallwood had allied himself with a group proposing to dispatch a third delegation, this one to Washington to investigate the possibility of a new economic alliance with the United States. Each group agreed to support the other. Both motions passed.

And just as Smallwood suspected, the Commission of Government quickly rejected the Washington venture. With the Dominions Office nodding its approval,

the convention was told it had no mandate to hold talks outside the Commonwealth. That required a return to responsible government.

Britain had matters well in hand to thwart that particular scenario. The eager
group that arrived in London received a polite but decidedly cool reception. From
the outset it was made clear that Newfoundland could not count on any financial
support should it restore self-government. The war had tied Britain's hands, it was
told, and even if the choice were a continuation of the Commission,
Newfoundland would have to face the fact that Britain was 'burdened with terrific
debts.' It couldn't even afford to pay interest on the loans Newfoundland had
advanced it during the war. 'However kindly our disposition,' ran the line, Newfoundland, regrettably, would have to go it alone. As if it all wasn't plain enough,
the Dominions Office had its position neatly laid out in a document for the delegates to take back home with them.

Two weeks later it was a stunned and indignant group of men that returned to
St. John's. The most vocal of them, the old political foe of Richard Squires, Peter
Cashin, charged Britain and Ottawa with conspiring to foil the legitimate pursuit

*Boat builders in Bonavista
Bay, ca. 1940, like other
outport people beyond the
Avalon, would reject
responsible government in
favour of change.*

of the convention. 'I say to you that there is in operation at the present time a conspiracy to sell . . . this country to the Dominion of Canada!' His outrage only intensified when news reached him of the reception given the Ottawa delegation.

On the first day the delegation arrived Prime Minister King toasted Smallwood and his colleagues over dinner at the Ottawa Country Club. King chaired the first of their meetings, before Louis St. Laurent, head of External Affairs and the cabinet's most ardent supporter of confederation, took over. Only slightly in the background was the familiar face of Alexander Clutterbuck, Britain's new high commissioner in Ottawa, appointed undoubtedly to help Canada jostle Newfoundland along the right course. Cordial discussions stretched out over three months during the summer of 1947.

By the time the delegation had finally made it back to Newfoundland (irate telegrams about their long absence having failed to speed their return), the mood of the National Convention was even more anti-confederate. That didn't stop Smallwood from keeping the issue at centre stage. The debate rose to a boiling point with the tabling in October of the terms of union put forth by Canada. By January fisticuffs threatened. Finally, in the heat of its final days, the convention passed a motion to define the referendum on which Newfoundland would decide its political future. There would be two choices. A return to responsible government. Or maintaining the Commission as it now stood. The very next day Smallwood rose and made a motion that a third choice—confederation with Canada—be placed on the ballot. After debate that lasted all night, a vote was taken. The motion was sunk, by a vote of twenty-nine to sixteen.

Romancing the Voters

In Britain's view the convention's ruling was irrelevant. Confederation with Canada had support across Newfoundland. It would be added to the ballot.

It was arguably the pivotal point in the history of Newfoundland and Labrador. It was the culmination of Britain's dealings with the country it had rediscovered 450 years before, its 'oldest Colony,' the 'great English ship moored near the Grand Banks . . . for the convenience of the English fishermen,' the wellspring of its West Country fortunes, of men to fill its navies, to bloody its battlefields. In Britain's view the cost had become too great. All that was to follow hinged on this silent decree. It was the unclean break from the past. Disassociation by deception.

Yet we could hardly expect otherwise. Modern-day Newfoundland nationalists argue that we should have first taken back self-government, then decided for ourselves whether we wanted union with Canada. But Britain believed that if there had been a return to self-government, it would have been dominated by merchant interests who would never have allowed such a vote to take place. Many in the outports would have agreed. And to Britain's mind those who wanted independence expected it with a subsidy. We might have argued that it was only fair compensation for all that Britain had gouged out of us over the centuries, but if it was self-government we wanted, we had to be prepared to go it alone. To have been beholden still to Britain, with a fake hold on our own destiny, would have been a far uglier sight than going into partnership with Ottawa.

What the advocates of responsible government presented was an irksome face from the past, and nothing to make its outport majority think they could rise up out of the poverty that the merchant class had inflicted on them. In Conche, in the final weeks of the National Convention, one woman summed it up. 'It makes no difference what kind of government we get; we live hard, we die hard, and when we go to hell, it's damn hard.'

In the new paper-mill towns and the American bases some of these people had had their first taste of comfort. They saw what cash could do for them. They weren't about to chance giving it up for the sake of something that had failed them in the past. There was no leader claiming the wealth concentrated in St. John's would be matched with the hard workers of the outports to produce a new, more equitable society. If anything, based on the arguing they heard from the floor of the Colonial Building, there was a chance life would be worse. Our geography, our history, had hopelessly skewed the wealth of the country so that

No Canadian wolves dared sniff at this door.

it rested, for the most part, in a few pockets in one end of the country. Perhaps it would have to take an outside force, one impervious to family ties and favours, to rectify the imbalance.

The referendum ballot offered three choices: 1. COMMISSION OF GOVERN-MENT for a period of five years 2. CONFEDERATION WITH CANADA 3. RESPONSIBLE GOVERNMENT as it existed in 1933. The words were brilliantly cast in favour of confederation. The choice of continuing with the Commission was no choice at all; it merely postponed the inevitable—a decision between the other two. The words 'Responsible Government' alone might have been something for the outports to debate. But the thought of it as it existed in 1933 at the end of the Squires era, in the trough of the Depression, was altogether repulsive for most of them.

Britain and Canada might have set the stage, but in the end the decision was for the people of Newfoundland and Labrador to make. The show was between Peter Cashin of the merchant-dominated Responsible Government League and Smallwood, campaign manager of the Newfoundland Confederate Association. In profile Smallwood had long since passed Gordon Bradley, the appointed head of the confederates. Smallwood was not what Canada was hoping for in a leader, but it is doubtful if anyone else could have pulled it off. The man had twice the distance to go to win, but he also had twice the energy of his opponents, and a store of campaign tricks that left them looking like inept amateurs.

Smallwood went where politicians rarely pitched before. If there were roads he eagerly suffered the mud and potholes for a few minutes with a loudspeaker. Where there were none (by far, most of the country) he descended in a decrepit seaplane, shook every hand while proclaiming deliverance into the guarantee of Canada's social programs. He was five-foot-six-inch Joey, in bowtie and scruffy fedora, a self-proclaimed saviour, using every technique he had learned from New York evangelists a quarter century before. And the reaction to him in St. John's, where he was forced to deflect insults and the occasional stone, only strengthened his hold on the outports. The fiery, temperamental, and equally passionate Cashin rose to his bait and denounced him as 'Iscariot,' pounding a fist on the podium as if it were Smallwood himself. The 'little fellow from Gambo' smiled and shot back with a fervent vow to topple Cashin's outdated vision and the men of Water Street who stood behind it.

Confederate campaign funds came largely from outside Newfoundland. They were Canadian dollars slipped Smallwood's way by supporters of the Liberal Party, those claiming an early stake in the seven new federal seats to be contested should confederation prove a winner. When substantial dollars showed up from within Newfoundland they often came from those who had judiciously noted the way Ottawa rewarded its faithful. Senatorships proved popular trading items.

The anti-confederates, on the other hand, had nothing to offer their Water Street backers, other than influence in a new government, something the upper classes clearly assumed was their inherent right. Their contributions amounted to a fraction of what the Smallwood camp was able to secure. If, in the end, the merchant princes of Newfoundland were not even willing to spend their money to save themselves, was it ever likely they would use it to save the country?

A substantial slice of the funds on both sides went to publish propaganda sheets— the *Confederate* and the *Independent*. Teamed with Smallwood's journalistic jabs were the wit and literary acumen of Greg Power and Harold Horwood, and the wickedly funny political cartoons of Jack Boothe (hired by Smallwood after seeing his work for the *Globe and Mail*). The *Confederate* ran miles ahead of its opponent. With a headline blaring 'WATCH FOR A LANDSLIDE,' it was hardly to be taken at its word, but Newfoundlanders always admired politicians cheeky enough to turn their message into entertainment.

Smallwood's great moment of political savvy was his response to the threat from those still out to forge an alliance, an 'Economic Union,' with the United States. With their option not on the ballot, they campaigned for a return to responsible government as a first step to a future referendum. Their leader was Ches Crosbie, Joey's backer during his publishing and pig-farming ventures. Useless in front of a microphone, Crosbie had the good sense to flank himself with two young media mavericks—Don Jamieson and Geoff Stirling. They telegrammed every member of the Senate in Washington, and came up with enough half-hearted positive responses to launch a campaign.

They proved no match for Smallwood. He immediately attacked what he called the 'Comic Union' for turning its back on Britain, affixing a Union Jack to both sides of the *Confederate*'s masthead. Union with Canada suddenly became a show of loyalty to the Commonwealth and to Newfoundland's ancestral home.

'BRITISH UNION ON TOP!' the paper declared, as if voters could have their cake and eat it too.

But when the results poured in, it became clear that 'Confederation with Canada,' with 41 per cent of the vote, hadn't risen to the top. At a little more than 44 per cent, 'Responsible Government' had, but without a majority. The 15 per cent captured by the 'Commission of Government' option would now be up for the taking in a run-off election. Those leading the fight for union with the United States were quickly losing heart and falling by the wayside.

It was down to a fight between boldly going it alone, or Newfoundland's allying itself with Canada. The country had seven weeks to make up its mind. Voting day was set for July twenty-second.

Calling in the Clergy

Surprising to many, religion had not surfaced as a strong public issue during the campaign leading to the first referendum. Cashin's Catholic background had not been pitted against Joey's loose Methodist roots as would have happened decades before.

A homecoming for Archbishop Roche in Placentia. The Church still defined life in much of Newfoundland and Labrador.

But any thought that the day had passed when religion was a factor in New-foundland politics was abruptly dispelled during the second campaign. A break-down of the results of the June referendum showed what appeared to be a clear split—the predominantly Catholic Avalon Peninsula had voted strongly in favour of self-government, the Protestant majority in the remainder of the Island had thrown its support to the confederates. With a mere 15 per cent of the vote to be divided, Smallwood and his troop now decided that if the religion card had to be played to win, so be it. They would deal with the consequences later.

From the start the Catholic hierarchy had urged a return to responsible govern-ment. Editorials in the Catholic *Monitor* had made that perfectly clear, though only a few priests took the fight to the pulpit. The anti-confederate stance stemmed from a fear that Canada would insist that Newfoundland rid itself of denomina-tional schooling. Beyond that, Archbishop Roche's vision of Newfoundland was of an innocent yet fiercely proud and independent nation, a legacy of the Irish patri-otism that had propelled the first fight for self-government. Unlike the Protestant Churches, which all welcomed joining broader Canadian assemblies, Catholics in Newfoundland had grown to cherish their direct, autonomous connection with Rome. In some minds Canadian Catholicism was a tad less pure, Canadian society a great deal more so.

Now, with a do-or-die vote at hand, the Catholic stance was suddenly dragged out into the open. The catalyst was an innocuous news item that appeared in the *Sunday Herald*, Geoff Stirling's American-style tabloid. It pointed out that in the June referendum Catholic nuns and brothers for the first time had been released from their vows and allowed to vote. Confederates seized on this as evidence of an all-out attempt by the Catholic hierarchy to quash their cause. A zealous Harold Horwood bought up dozens of copies of the paper, tore out the appropriate page, circled the offending article in blue pencil, and (from a list supplied by Smallwood) mailed the page to the head of every Orange Lodge on the Island.

Meanwhile, Newfoundland's British governor, Gordon Macdonald, stood before a convention of Methodists in St. John's and declared it was 'time that the Protestants pulled together.' A supporter of responsible government took to nail-ing posters on the city's Protestant churches with the incendiary slogan 'Confederation means British Union with French Canada.' The stench of sectari-anism had returned, dredging up ethnic hatred with it. With the vote only days away came the most provocative act of all. Out of an executive meeting of Orangemen in Grand Falls emerged a letter directed to all Lodges. It asserted the Catholic Church was attempting to 'influence the result' of the referendum, and called on members 'to use every effort to bring such attempts to naught.' When the infamous Orange Letter made its way to the public, an incensed Cashin had copies of it dispersed to Catholic congregations across the Island.

In the end it was hard to evaluate what difference it all made. Though voters marched in record numbers to the polls, many with their emotions boiling over, it is likely most had their minds made up well before they marked their *X*. Much was also made of a few prominent Water Street businessmen and lawyers ambling over to the confederate side in the final weeks. Some said it gave union with Canada more credibility. Others contended the newly converted had read the writing on the wall and took the detour only to ensure themselves future patronage jobs.

The Pink, White, and Green at half-mast, marking the passage into confederation with Canada.

Perhaps the most tenable explanation of why the vote went the way it did was to be found in the Catholic congregations beyond the Avalon. The Irish-born bishop of St. George's, Michael O'Reilly, supported union with Canada despite what he was hearing from Roche or the bishop in Harbour Grace. He openly endorsed the confederate candidate, the great orator Bill Keough, the man behind the west coast co-operative movement who had implored the complacent rich to remember 'the last forgotten fisherman on the Bill of Cape St. George.' Both men knew well that neglect by the powerful in St. John's had never discriminated between Catholic and Protestant. Poor was poor. And when a degree of prosperity came it came from outside the country and was there for the whole populace to share in. When the great influx of workers arrived to build the American base in nearby Stephenville the bishop didn't hesitate to accept Protestant children in the Catholic School run by the Presentation Sisters since 1925. (Three of my siblings were among them.)

The people of the west and south coasts saw confederation as a chance at equality. Besides, they knew Canadians not to be such a bad lot. Their ancestors had traded with them for centuries, and many worked alongside Nova Scotians on the Grand Banks. The radio stations they tuned to broadcast from Charlottetown and Antigonish. The town of Corner Brook could trace its roots to woodsmen from Nova Scotia and New Brunswick, who had started a sawmill there in 1864.

On the whole, cradled together along the Atlantic coast, they all had a lot in common. The revival of 'Come near at your peril, Canadian wolf' wasn't finding many singers in this part of the Island. In fact, it wasn't heard much beyond the kitchens of the Avalon. Neither were many west of the isthmus crying in their rum the night the votes were counted. Black flags might have been flapping from the verandas of mansions on Rennies Mill Road, but they were not to be seen from the paintless saltboxes of Burgeo, Port Saunders, or Burin.

Knotted Together

Labrador voted 78 per cent in favour of confederation, the district of Burgeo-Lapoile tallied up 89 per cent. St. George's–Port au Port, with a population less than a quarter Protestant, voted 57 per cent for confederation.

When the totals for all of Newfoundland and Labrador were complete, they showed a wafer-thin 52.3 per cent victory for Smallwood and his confederates. A mere seven thousand votes separated them from Responsible Government.

P.E. Outerbridge, businessman and staunch member of the Responsible Government League, blamed defeat on the 'ignorant and avaricious outporters.' Another member asserted that 'a simple people . . . should never have been asked to vote on a matter which was so complicated and so abstruse as confederation.' It should have been, he snorted, 'a matter for experts.' In the condescension of the League was every reason for its defeat.

The self-proclaimed experts were proven wrong. Except, of course, for people like Leonard Outerbridge, P.E.'s brother and one of the last-second converts to confederation. He would come to rather enjoy his appointment as lieutenant-governor of the newest part of the Canadian Dominion.

Still, when all was said and done, the rejection of nationhood was not without remorse in every part of Newfoundland and Labrador. It was bound up with the indignity of having relinquished it in 1934.

There was a bit of Archbishop Roche in everyone who voted. The flame of a self-governing Newfoundland and Labrador burned in every one of their souls. No person who walked into a polling booth wanted anything more than a chance at building a workable nation, where independence was coupled with equality of opportunity. But a majority of voters didn't see that as one of the options before them. There had been nothing to convince them that those backing the fight for responsible government had enough willpower to remake the country.

So they opted for the next best thing. Canada. Newfoundland and Labrador would become one of ten. It was a position many in the new 'province' would have trouble getting used to. But it came with the promise of a better future. And if there is one thing as a people they were used to following, it was the promise of a better future.

34 | From Election Wave to Tidal Bore

Joey started gambling millions on new businesses, then tens of millions. Finally,
like an uncontrollable gambler doubling his bets he wagered hundreds of millions
of dollars.

—Harold Horwood

Smallwood, Roy Thomson (chancellor of Memorial University),
John C. Doyle, and two unidentified women, 1961.

The Joey Factor

Joseph R. Smallwood liked to count blessings. After a half century of beating about from scheme to underfunded scheme, he was now a Canadian premier, 'the only living Father of Confederation,' with millions to spend. As for union itself, it was no less than 'the greatest blessing, under God, next to life itself.'

In the first years as Canadians, few bothered to argue. Most were busy spending the dollars that descended from Ottawa, just as Joey had promised. Eighty thousand cheques were mailed out each month—family allowance, old-age pension, unemployment insurance, veterans benefits. One woman in Trinity Bay was buried with her cherished picture of Joey beside her in the coffin. But the issue of whether Newfoundland and Labrador should ever have joined Canada never really went away, just grew less audible with the more dollars that came our way.

It has taken a new generation of feisty artists and academics, few of them born when Joey took office, to drag it back to public consciousness. The country sold its soul for the baby bonus, they claim. That, or the vote was rigged. The pre-confederation flag—the pink, white, and green tricolour—can suddenly be spotted fluttering from yuppified row houses throughout St. John's. As celebrations began for the 'golden' anniversary of confederation in 1999, a poll asked As a first choice, what do you consider yourself—a Newfoundlander or a Canadian? Fewer than 30 per cent gave the nod to Canada. Even John Crosbie (who as a federal cabinet minister had made a strong thrust to be prime minister) never thought of himself as anything but a 'Newfoundlander first.'

At the same time no less than 85 per cent call confederation with Canada a success. So, as much as we like being Canadian, there are still those nagging suspicions that we might have made it on our own. Developed our multitude of natural resources for our own benefit. Become a thriving little bulwark of the North Atlantic. Another Iceland. If Ireland, from which nearly half of us had descended, could turn itself around, then surely to God we could as well.

A lot of our ambivalence is, of course, tied up with our feelings about Joey. Even his strongest supporters had turned sour on him by the time he finished his reign in 1972. At his death twenty years later, we still couldn't decide whether he had been an asset or a liability. What we did know was that he had been a champion of

Newfoundland and Labrador, blind to his own inept business sense and love of power. And that had proved to be far from a blessed combination.

On Speaking Terms

Nobody expected the transition to confederation in 1949 to be smooth. To begin, the Terms of Union were negotiated not by a democratically elected assembly but by a team of individuals appointed by a soon-to-be-defunct Commission of Government.

The terms had their basis in the 'Proposed Arrangements' bartered by the delegation sent to Ottawa by the National Convention in 1947. The new round of negotiations was to be an exercise in fine tuning, an ironing-out of the details that would make the idiosyncrasies of Newfoundland history fit the mould of confederation. Some have argued Newfoundland was in a hopelessly vulnerable position, having already endorsed confederation in a referendum. But by then Canada wanted Newfoundland and Labrador just as much, if not more, than we wanted Canada. The referendum vote, as the Ottawa team led by Louis St. Laurent knew full well, hadn't come about out of any great love of Canada. Most Newfoundlanders hardly knew the place. Albert Walsh, chief negotiator for Newfoundland, made it clear from the start that his delegation was willing to let confederation be 'doomed' rather than sign Terms of Union it could not live with. In the end it was a matter of compromise, by two groups committed to ending the day with a deal.

Several points proved particularly troublesome. Term 17, allowing the province to retain its denominational system of education, was something Canada adamantly opposed, fearful of Quebec's reaction. But Smallwood insisted on it, in the belief that it might reconcile him with Archbishop Roche and the Catholic Church. With Term 23 Ottawa assumed Newfoundland's debt, but only after an argument with Britain over who should be the one to take it on. Agreement on the dollars necessary to jumpstart improvements in public service, Term 28, and its infamous partner, Term 29 (setting in place a review of Newfoundland's financial position after eight years), were literally sweated over for weeks in the summer heat of an airless room of Parliament's East Block. ('I usually stripped to the waist,' Joey recalled, 'and still sweated in that oven.') Even Term 46, giving Newfoundland the right to sell lowly margarine, had to be agreed to over the heads of the other provinces and their tough dairy lobbies.

On the big issues of federal jurisdiction, there was little movement. The Newfoundland delegation knew from the outset that Canada had no intention of revising the BNA Act. The new province would be one of ten, and there was no point in looking for concessions that would then be demanded by the others. This was most evident when it came time to deal with jurisdiction over Newfoundland's primary resource—its fishery. Nova Scotia was in the wings, ready to pounce if concessions were made. In the end, the only additional right granted was retention, for a period of five years only, of Newfoundland's system of marketing its salt codfish.

Control of fisheries would become a flashpoint in relations between Ottawa and Newfoundland. The same could be said of natural resources generally. There was nothing in the Terms of Union of 1948 to cover the discovery of oil on the Grand Banks. Neither was there specific reference to hydro-electric development. Both omissions became huge blockages in the path to the province's economic development.

The Terms of Union will forever be the stuff of argument. That we ended up the only province not to have control over its primary resource is impossible to swallow. That fishing men and women had to watch as decisions made in Ottawa plunged that resource into chaos—whether seals or northern cod—irritates us no end. It seems there's no cutting free from what political pundit Ray Guy calls 'this invisible umbilical cord to some rabbit warren of bureaucrats in Ottawa.' Standing like nagging sages on the other side of the argument are those who claim that as masters of our own fishery we would have done no better. For greed, we all will admit, knows no jurisdiction.

One group that is certain it was short-changed is our aboriginal population. They are not mentioned in the Terms of Union. They came up for discussion during negotiations long enough for Mackenzie King, the prime minister, to inquire, 'What about the aboriginal peoples? What about the Beothuk you have in Newfoundland?' To which one of the Newfoundland delegates piped up, 'We don't have any, sir—we shot them all.' When the gang of old boys stopped their chuckling, it remained for King to terminate the matter with a quip: 'I suppose that's one way of dealing with a problem of that kind.'

Confederation came just at the time aboriginal issues were turning into a major headache for Ottawa. Canada arrived at the negotiation table determined not to add Newfoundland to the quagmire it had created. It convinced Newfoundland

*Innu residents of Davis
Inlet, ca. 1930.*

that the new province
itself should be the one
to administer its aborig-
inal peoples. (And it is
here the argument that Newfoundland would be treated no better or no worse
than the other nine provinces breaks down.)

Newfoundland negotiated nothing in return for this concession, at least nothing that benefited the Innu, Inuit, or Mi'kmaq. They were mostly in Labrador, after
all. In fact, so out of touch was the Newfoundland delegation with the native
people in Labrador that it 'as a whole took the very firm position that it didn't
want to divide any Newfoundlanders,' that they were 'all coming into confederation under the same terms and conditions.'

While Ottawa saved millions, the aboriginal peoples were set on a course that
denied them whatever their counterparts in other provinces were receiving. For
years after confederation Newfoundland set out nothing to replace the lost federal
programs. They did what governments in St. John's had always done—they
ignored their native populations.

Gold Pen to Paper

At a ceremony on 11 December 1948, all but one of the Newfoundland delegation
walked into the Senate Chamber in Ottawa for the signing of the Terms of Union.
Ches Crosbie had quit the committee and returned to St. John's hours before. To
Crosbie the terms amounted to 'financial suicide.' Some figured his decision had
more to do with the fact that once back home he would have to face his anti-
confederate friends.

Could Newfoundland have argued its way into a more favourable agreement?
Did we 'sell the shop,' as a premier some thirty years later liked to put it? It had been

give and take on both sides. Who's to say what might have transpired with a different set of negotiators, and without the background rumblings from Quebec—Duplessis muttering that the question of the boundary with Labrador should be revisited. Neither side wanted that. It doubled the determination to come up with a deal.

The ceremony confirming the Terms of Union went forward with much enthusiasm all around. Louis St. Laurent, now prime minister, signed for Canada, as did his deputy chairman at the negotiating table, Brooke Claxton (minister of National Defence and acting secretary of state for External Affairs). For Newfoundland six men affixed their names with the new gold pens provided especially for the occasion—Albert Walsh, Gordon Bradley, J.B. McEvoy, Gordon Winter, Philip Gruchy, and the man least able to hold back his emotion, Joseph R. Smallwood.

It had been three years to the day since Britain had announced the setting-up of the National Convention to decide the future government of Newfoundland and Labrador. For confederates what had once been a notion was now an overwhelming reality. The RCAF band played 'O Canada.' Joey wept.

The government of Canada had intended that it be followed by the 'Ode to Newfoundland,' since 1904 the much-loved anthem of Newfoundland (though not of Labrador). But the music for the Ode was not to be found in Ottawa. St. Laurent ended the ceremony with a robust three cheers for the new province.

From Newfoundland a few weeks before, the last governor, Gordon Macdonald, headed home to England, bringing an end to what Sir Humphrey Gilbert had started when he sailed ashore in 1583. Two days after Macdonald's departure there appeared in the *Evening Telegram* in St. John's what the editors saw as an innocent

Canadian Prime Minister Louis St. Laurent and Joseph R. Smallwood shake hands as confederation becomes official. Albert Walsh looks on.

public tribute to the man. More observant readers discovered an acrostic. The first letter of each line of the poem formed two words. THE BASTARD.

Onwards and Upwards and Under

A few minutes before midnight on 31 March 1949 Newfoundlanders and Labradorians officially became Canadians. In Ottawa 'The Squid Jiggin' Ground' rang out from the carillon in the Peace Tower. On the cover of *Maclean's* was a commissioned oil painting of Port de Grave on a Sunday afternoon. Many in Newfoundland and Labrador were saying confederation was a state of affairs long overdue. Others were still in mourning. Whatever the consequences, there was no turning back.

Within two months Smallwood led his Liberal Party to a sweeping victory in the first provincial election, taking twenty-two of twenty-eight seats. A short time later he delivered for his counterparts in Ottawa five of the seven federal seats. He could hardly wait for his vision of the new Newfoundland to take hold.

Improvements in the standard of living were startling. Families who 'hardly saw any cash at all before confederation' all of a sudden 'had more money than they had ever dreamed.' In the first year alone over $7 million in family allowance cheques went off to mothers across the province. The amount paid in old-age pension cheques increased more than six-fold, at the same time that pension discrimination against widows and unmarried older women was eliminated. A substantial drop in infant mortality and death from tuberculosis bore witness to the fact that although Newfoundland had gone into union with Canada carrying a budget surplus, that surplus, as the outport chronicler Ted Russell put it, 'had been distilled from the life-blood of hungry Newfoundlanders living on six cents a day.' The black armbands against confederation quietly vanished at the sight of healthier children showing up for mass and fewer hard-luck stories at the merchant's door.

Hospital, school, and road construction took a dramatic leap. Money was injected into co-operatives. More libraries and schools were built. Communities, encouraged to incorporate, saw their town councils became training grounds for the next generation of politicians. In one of his first acts in office, Smallwood initiated a move to turn Memorial College into a degree-granting university. Higher education became an option that a few years before was known only to the wealthy. For the next twenty years the outcome of every provincial election was a foregone conclusion. In the polling booths nobody had any trouble recalling the differences confederation had brought, even if the Liberal named on the ballot was a certified rogue.

Most of the clever, independent 'angry young men' who had driven Small-wood's bandwagon into confederation didn't trail behind their premier for long. They quit, too independent to follow where Smallwood would have them go. He surrounded himself with neophytes, all of them easily led. Government became a one-man show, if rife with good intentions. Voters still were charmed by the sight of one of their own (he remained Joey, with an office door open to everyone) walk-ing shoulder to shoulder with financiers and prime ministers. When, in 1959, he took on Prime Minister John Diefenbaker over his decision to bring an end to the Ottawa's financial obligations under Term 29, he had the whole of the country fol-lowing his every move. His offhand wit, his pugnacious theatrics were embraced by a Canadian public tired of rhetoric from overstuffed politicians.

Only when a succession of costly development schemes went under did his halo begin to dim. It started with man named Alfred Valdmanis. Before the end of Smallwood's political career there would be others—John C. Doyle, John Shaheen—all with their own plans for economic salvation, all, in one way or another, shady men for whom Smallwood loosened the purse strings of the province. From the start Smallwood was convinced that Newfoundland would never survive—would have to sit and watch as the more prosper-ous Canadian mainland lured all its workers—if he could not pro-

Greg Power, Smallwood, and Valdmanis, bearing bundles of rosaries, pose for a Vatican photographer following the private audience with Pope Pius XII arranged by Valdmanis, 1952.

vide 'jobs, jobs, and more jobs.' He had no confidence that the fishery could do it. He undervalued what had sustained the place for centuries in favour of manufacturing. It was 'develop or perish.'

Valdmanis was a newly immigrated Latvian economist recommended to Smallwood by federal Liberals. Sitting across from him at the Château Laurier, the dropout from Bishop Feild was more than a little impressed. Valdmanis spoke six languages, held a doctorate in law, and at twenty-nine had been the youngest cabinet minister in all of Europe. Had the Germans not overrun his country, he surely would have been on his way to becoming president of Latvia. 'Brilliant and knowledgeable' Smallwood called him, a man 'implacably determined to realize for me my dream . . . ' What Smallwood hadn't taken into account were the techniques of leading a double life that Valdmanis had learned in order to survive under the Nazis. Now, in reinventing himself for a new career, such knowledge was not forgotten. He would take Smallwood's job offer at $10,000 a year, though it was hardly in keeping with his previous stature, and nowhere near the income of the friends and contacts he was about to introduce Smallwood to in Europe.

The 'director general of Economic Development' and Smallwood flew off to Germany. Smallwood loved every second of it, soaking up the culture and the lavish reception he received at every turn. He stood enthralled by the ease with which Valdmanis was opening financial doors. Together they found interest in building some sixteen factories, though hardly a difficult task given the generous concessions and guarantees Newfoundland was providing.

He set Smallwood on the course to realize his dream, if only for a very brief time, and to the tune of $26 million, two-thirds of the money Newfoundland brought into confederation. Of the factories opened, within a few years, only four remained. Shut down were a chocolate factory in Bay Roberts, a rubber plant in Holyrood, a knitting mill in Brigus, a tannery and glove factory in Carbonear. Smallwood's promise to 'dot Conception Bay with factories' had struck a snag.

And so had Valdmanis. Before long accusations began to surface that the deals struck in Europe had come with a 10 per cent 'commission,' payable to the director general (including $50,000 in cash that one day passed through his office at the Colonial Building). Smallwood, who by this time had rid himself of Valdmanis, dropped the information in the lap of the RCMP. Fraud to the tune of half a million dollars landed the ex-deputy saviour in Newfoundland's Penitentiary. To Valdmanis the kickback had been an accepted way of doing business. To Smallwood what had transpired was no indication of the premier's own business sense. The man had deceived him. Their efforts had not been a total failure, Smallwood reminded his detractors. The concrete plant in Corner Brook was employing hundreds of people. It was time to move on.

What he would never admit was that even the director general at times had been an unwilling instrument, that Valdmanis had advised Smallwood against moving so fast. For Joey, time was forever at a premium. Newfoundland had waited whole centuries for development; it could not wait another day.

Seductive Slug or Evil Genius?

Next to appear on the scene (even before Valdmanis was out the door) was John C. Doyle. Born in Chicago, Doyle came to Canada selling coal in the 1940s. He founded Canadian Javelin, once described by a U.S. government lawyer as 'the most mysterious company known to man.' Canadian Javelin was a holding company for a succession of business schemes that turned Doyle into a high-flying promoter who sucked the best and thickest Cuban cigars and talked deals big enough to change a country's fortunes forever. Smallwood adored him. He once said, 'I wish I had one hundred, one thousand John Doyles to help develop Newfoundland.' John Crosbie, who knew Doyle at his worst, thought one 'seductive slug' loose around Joey was more than enough.

Smallwood and Doyle first met in 1952. Doyle had come to Newfoundland to collect a business debt. On the TCA flight into St. John's he happened to sit next to the province's deputy minister of Mines. Doyle's raw lust for money was piqued. He soon acquired the mineral rights to land south of Wabush Lake in Labrador for a few million dollars, backed by a gushing Smallwood and his government's guaranteed bond issues. He sold the property six years later for a down payment and yearly royalties estimated at over $200 million. Not a bad return. It was another chapter in the saga of outsiders using Newfoundland (more specifically Labrador) to make themselves rich, very rich.

In the mid-1960s Doyle was back again, this time with an even more grandiose scheme. Using wood from the forests of Labrador, he would build in Stephenville (now that the U.S. had closed out its air force base) a linerboard mill. By the time the financial intrigue had run its course, Doyle had soaked up over $250 million of the province's money. Thus the reason for the oil portrait of Smallwood that hung in his opulent penthouse offices in Ottawa, not far from *Le Petit Alchemist* by Boucher and the gilded harp Doyle liked to play for relaxation.

Smallwood was forever defending Doyle's 'imagination and dogged courage.' Without him, he argued, there would be no Wabush iron ore mine, or for that matter, no IOC mine in nearby Labrador City ('induced' as it was by Doyle's success). Together, the twin towns grew into the largest employers in Labrador, since the mid-1960s listing on their payrolls at good company wages several thousand people. A blessing in employment-hungry Labrador? For certain, though how much is attributable to a money-mad Doyle is an altogether different question.

Beginning in the late 1950s, lawsuits against Doyle began to crowd the courts in Canada and the United States. That Smallwood would continue to defend him led to suspicions that the premier himself was receiving a chunk of the multi-millions changing hands. In April 1963 Smallwood even flew to Washington and met with Attorney General Robert Kennedy ('very keen . . . a very bright fellow' the dauntless premier would note) in a failed attempt to persuade Kennedy to stop a grand jury indictment against his friend. A decade later, courts in Newfoundland had rung up four hundred fraud charges against Doyle. The man whom John Crosbie also labelled 'an evil genius' skipped bail and spent the last twenty-five years of his life a fugitive in Panama, where for much of that time he continued to reap the royalty benefits of Wabush.

Also enjoying the restorative life down south was O.L. Vardy, Smallwood's deputy minister of Economic Development during the Doyle days. With so much money in the air, the Doyle method of doing business was bound to find a few converts among Smallwood's inner circle, though allegations that Vardy had defrauded the provincial treasury of three-quarters of a million dollars never made it to court. From a home in Clearwater, Florida, he, too, was able to fend off extradition to Canada. Eventually both men who had forsaken Newfoundland did find a permanent home. Vardy died in 1980 in Florida, Doyle in 2000 in Panama.

The Golden Eagle Has Landed

Jostling with John Doyle for position on Newfoundland's entrepreneurial landscape was John Shaheen. The New York financier made his first appearance in Newfoundland in 1960 with the construction of the modest Golden Eagle oil refinery in Holyrood. For years, until it was bought out by Ultramar, Golden Eagle gas stations were dotted around the province. Newfoundlanders filled up their cars feeling confident they were doing a little something to help local enterprise.

To put it mildly, Smallwood took to Shaheen. He had the blue-chip connections that Smallwood liked, including former vice-president Richard Nixon, who acted as his lawyer. Joey just needed to get Shaheen thinking in more sizable terms about Newfoundland. Another paper mill? A bigger oil refinery? Shaheen didn't disappoint. He just didn't have the money to back up the line he presented to Joey—a giant oil refinery and petrochemical complex at Come by Chance in Placentia Bay. A good chunk of the money, of course, came from the province, another colossal commitment from Joey. By 1968 some of his cabinet ministers had finally seen enough. Joey's pledge of $5 million of bridge financing was the final straw, prompting the resignations of government ministers John Crosbie and Clyde Wells.

Tripping around the world together, Shaheen and Smallwood did eventually succeed in finding additional backers for the refinery. A deal was signed, and Joey made great hay out of the return of the $5 million. And in 1973 the refinery opened, following what must be the most extravagant lead-up to a ribbon-cutting in Canadian history. Shaheen flew hundreds of people to New York, put them up at the Waldorf-Astoria, then had them join another weighty list of oil executives, financiers, and politicians aboard ship—the *QEII*, no less—for a week-long luxury cruise to Newfoundland. Even John Crosbie couldn't resist the high-rolling event. As local residents at rainy and windswept Come by Chance gathered under giant tents, Shaheen cast forth a feast for the gathering multitudes. CBC's Peter Gzowski called in live as the rest of country chuckled in amusement at who and what money could buy.

Within three years the refinery was dead. It owed $500 million (including $42 million to the Newfoundland government), prompting an even more spectacular event—to that time the largest bankruptcy in Canadian history. Shaheen's son emerged a few years later with a bid to buy back the refinery. A U.S. Senate report subsequently revealed that the money behind the bid actually belonged to arms trader Cyrus Hashemi. The report put John Shaheen in the centre of the Iran-Contra affair.

So Much Water Over the Falls

Shaheen's refinery and Doyle's linerboard debacles pale, though, in comparison with what has became Newfoundland and Labrador's greatest fiscal and psychological millstone. At least the mill at Stephenville was eventually bought by Abitibi-Price and converted to the production of newsprint, and the refinery, in mothballs for more than a decade, went back in operation under the ownership of Vitol SA. The provincial government could cut their losses and be done with it. Not so Churchill Falls.

If there is one thing most older Newfoundlanders and Labradorians envy their children it's their chance of living to 2041, the year the hydro-electric deal finally terminates. The deal signed in 1969 brings a profit to Hydro-Québec that is approaching $1 billion a year, representing 96 per cent of the value of the power. Newfoundland picks up the remaining 4 per cent, all of which is lost by a reduction in federal transfer payments to the province.

The deepest roots of this disaster of a deal are to be found in the Labrador boundary settlement of 1927. In Quebec's view there was never any settlement. Quebec had been done out of territory that rightfully belonged to it, including the

Joey and Edmund de Rothschild at the official start of
construction of the Churchill Falls power project, 1967.

mighty river and falls that Smallwood was so determined to develop. There was an unwritten understanding within the government of Quebec that if any agreement was to be reached, its terms would somehow make up for the loss inflicted by the Privy Council decision of 1927. Negotiations were led by an entrenched Jean Lesage and his Resources minister, René Lévesque.

Facing them across the table was Smallwood, who by the time a deal was signed had worked doggedly for fifteen years to bring it about. It was the most illustrious of his one-man shows, with an opening act that included meetings with Winston Churchill and the Rothschilds in London. He renamed Hamilton River and its falls in honour of Churchill. Finding a way to develop their immense hydro-electric potential became for Smallwood a testament to his encounter with the renowned statesman, and, of course, what Smallwood saw as his parallel stature in Newfoundland. The change of name was done without consulting the people of Labrador, and needless to say, the whole undertaking completely ignored the traditional use by the Innu of the land that would have to be flooded if the project went ahead.

A consortium of international companies formed the British Newfoundland Corporation (BRINCO) to develop the site. Agreement had first to be reached with Quebec, since the only feasible route to the markets of the northern U.S. was overland through that province. In 1967 Smallwood turned the sod with his by-now-famous silver shovel, as Churchill's grandson and Edmund de Rothschild looked on.

What Smallwood touted as a good deal in 1969, when Quebec's pen was finally put to paper, failed to forecast the skyrocketing price of oil four short years later. The power Hydro-Québec bought at a fixed price (and incredibly without any consideration of inflation) was suddenly worth a fortune. Repeated efforts to reopen the contract (taken all the way to the Supreme Court in the 1980s) have failed. Quebec smirks all the way to the bank, with more money than a favourable boundary decision could ever be worth. At least until 2041, when the power contract expires. Then . . . watch out for the celebration!

A Strike against the Labour Man

After twenty years in office, Smallwood's hold on the people was turning arthritic. It might have taken a Joey to convince Newfoundlanders to join Canada, but he clearly had his limitations as a leader of a maturing, increasingly informed society. Gordon Bradley, his partner in the confederation fight, had put it to him soon after Smallwood became premier: ' . . . that is one of your great failings. You go ahead and on your own, make decisions and proceed to implement them without consulting others who have a stake in the matter and who can perhaps give you some sound advice.' In Smallwood's chamber there were no advisers, only listeners.

The beginnings of the fall from grace can be traced back to a particularly ugly labour dispute in 1959. Loggers supplying the paper mills in Grand Falls and Corner Brook, represented by the International Woodworkers of America (IWA), took to the picket line over wages of $1.05 per hour for a sixty-hour work week, and living quarters that were no more than 'dark and squalid hovels.' It was a strike that had been brewing for decades. In another era the cause would have been one Smallwood himself might have led. Now the socialist was premier and

Women take time from the picket lines to bring food to loggers arrested during the IWA strike of 1959.

the champion of industrial development. Where would his support fall and how would it weigh on the workers, and on his own conscience?

The politician Smallwood took the strike as a threat to one of the few stable industries in Newfoundland. And the rise of the woodworkers' union as a threat to his personal base of support. Smallwood still thought of himself as spokesman for the common man, the same voiceless mass he had led against the merchants and into Canada ten years earlier. Now there appeared on the scene a charismatic union organizer, and a mainlander, at that, H. Landon Ladd, leading the premier's own in a fight for equality. It did strange things to Joey's soul.

The mill management in Grand Falls rejected an arbitrator's report and blatantly refused to negotiate. In every logging community the IWA set up strike committees, with the positions equally split between men and women. With every passing week the fight grew more bitter. Strikers and their families blocked highways, refusing to let logging trucks through. By the end of two months more than two hundred loggers had been arrested. On February ninth in Botwood forty-five women openly defied longshoremen about to cross picket lines on their way to ships loading newsprint. On the same day another militant band of women stopped a convoy of strikebreakers attempting to get to camps across the frozen Gander River.

Their defiance of the law demolished one of Smallwood's most cherished images, that of the placid Newfoundland wife and homemaker. Their fist-clenched cursing of police and strikebreakers set him into action. On television he turned his famous rhetoric on the union. 'How dare these outsiders come into this decent Christian province and by such terrible methods try to seize control . . . spreading their black poison of class hatred and bitter, bigoted prejudice.'

A few weeks later Smallwood had bent his opinions into legislation. He decertified the union, then enacted some of the most repressive labour legislation ever seen in Canada, vowing to rid 'this good Newfoundland earth' of any union 'whose superior officers have been convicted of such heinous crimes as white slavery, dope-peddling, manslaughter, embezzlement . . . ' It was a flagrant attempt to link the IWA with the gangster-infested Teamsters in the United States. By implication, in H. Landon Ladd, Newfoundland loggers had embraced another James Hoffa.

Trade unionists across the country were outraged. Smallwood stood by and watched the IWA falter as public opinion turned against it. Then, on March tenth, a force of seventy officers of the RCMP and the Newfoundland Constabulary confronted strikers on the main street of the central Newfoundland town of Badger. Policemen charged the crowd and in the melee that followed Constable William Moss of the Constabulary was struck in the head with a birch billet. Two days later, in a hospital bed in Grand Falls, he died. The whole province came to a standstill.

Smallwood ordered the flag-draped coffin to be drawn through the streets of Grand Falls. The railway car that carried it to St. John's stopped at every station along the route. The public lost its last ounce of sympathy for the strikers. In Bishop's Falls the IWA office was broken into and trashed.

Moss was the only member of the Newfoundland Constabulary to have ever lost his life in the line of duty. Smallwood called on Ottawa for more RCMP reinforcements. The force agreed, but Prime Minister John Diefenbaker, partly out of contempt for Smallwood's labour legislation, put a halt to the move. The overruled commissioner of the RCMP resigned.

The IWA withdrew from Newfoundland and loggers joined the Newfoundland Brotherhood of Woods Workers, a union set in place by Smallwood's Liberal government. Meanwhile the International Labour Organization in Geneva soundly condemned his legislation. The premier's reaction? 'What are they going to do, send in UN troops?' The socialist radical, the union organizer, was to be found sitting smugly behind his curtain of power.

Within ten years the hourly wage of the loggers had almost doubled. Their camps had hot and cold running water. There were sheets in their bunks and something other than beans on their supper plates. And Lord Rothermere, E.C. Harmsworth, chief shareholder of the mill in Grand Falls (whose managers in 1959 had predicted bankruptcy if they had given into the loggers' demands of a *five-cent* hike in pay) donated $500,000 to Memorial University when Joey came looking for money to build student residents. So did Sir Eric Bowater, owner of the mill in Corner Brook.

As a student at Memorial University in the late 1960s, I lived in Bowater House. A few steps away was Rothermere House. As living quarters, the residences were veritable mansions, of course, compared with what my father had known in the Bowater logging camps of the 1930s, and what any loggers knew anywhere in Newfoundland for thirty years after that. It would be in residences like these, on the campus of the university that Joey had worked so hard to see built, that students rallied support to bring about his downfall.

35 | Here to Where

You can launch a house easy and tow it away
But the home doesn't move, it continues to stay
And the dollars you make, sure they'll keep you alive
But they won't soothe the heart and they can't ease the mind.

　　　　　—From 'Outport People' by Bud Davidge (recorded by Simani)

Some families of resettlement schemes would manage to retain their outport traditions.

Right Here

Newfoundland's first settlers laid down roots within rowing distance of their fishing grounds. 'They wanted to be as far out in the sea as possible, where fish, seals and birds were more plentiful.' The Flat Islands of central Bonavista Bay is a prime example. Settled in the early 1800s, the cluster of four islands was home to almost a thousand people a century later, many of them engaged in the lucrative Labrador Fishery. These outports were as thriving as any in Newfoundland, with substantial homes and schools, and the imposing St. Nicholas' Church.

In time settlement in the deeper reaches of the bay took hold, places such as Glovertown and Eastport, its people attracted by large stands of timber and deeper soil. First the railway, then a network of roads were laid down, in many cases replacing coastal boat services. It was these latter-day outports that reaped the rewards. Electricity and medical clinics came their way. They attracted better qualified teachers. More clergy settled among them.

Their populations soared. In the dozen years after confederation the population of Newfoundland and Labrador rose an incredible 30 per cent, propelled by family allowance cheques and better health care. The province's birth rate stood close to the highest in North America. (Wilson Kettle of Grand Bay on the southwest coast made the *Guinness Book of World Records* in 1970 by having the most living descendants—582!)

Only in the remotest outports was the population shrinking, a situation compounded by change in the fishery. The production of dried salt cod had fallen dramatically. Gone was the Labrador Fishery. When 1950s America did eat fish (which was seldom at the best of times), it was the insipid fish stick that it demanded. Processing shifted from outdoor flakes on a fishing family's own property to processing plants in a bay's bigger, more accessible communities. The industry passed out of the hands of Water Street merchants (who had by now shrewdly turned to more lucrative trades such as insurance and retail) and into the hands of a new crop of plant operators. Supplying the fish, in competition with the inshore fishermen, were fleets of offshore trawlers.

By 1951 the population of Flat Islands had shrunk to half of what it was fifty years before. Young families were moving away, closer to fish plants and to the airport at Gander, which had continued to boom after the war. Work was more secure, the opportunities for their children more assured.

The families on Flat Islands faced a dilemma—resign themselves to the isolation and lack of services, or resettle the whole community. Dozens of outports around the Island confronted the same situation. Red Island in Placentia Bay held close to five hundred people in 1920. Forty years later the count stood at 243. The same was true of nearby Harbour Buffett and Tack's Beach and Merasheen. Many people had left on the promise of work at the American bases in Argentia.

By 1961 the population of Newfoundland stood at just under 460,000, but was scattered around the coast in 1,100 settlements, three-quarters of which held less than three hundred inhabitants. Already people in several of the most isolated places had decided on their own to uproot. Before long the government took charge. Smallwood saw it as a quick method of reducing the high cost of servicing rural Newfoundland. Isolation he termed 'a deadening thing, a paralysing thing, a cruel thing.' People would do better to move to government-designated 'growth centres.' It was the same tone Joey had used to sell confederation.

But for the reluctant it had a shallow ring. Government men showed up offering financial aid for relocation. To qualify, at least 80 per cent of families had to agree to move. Communities were torn apart. Older people, the backbone of these communities, were 'unwillingly forced to decide,' amid their wharfs and kitchens and the graveyards of their ancestors.

It would prove a further strike against Smallwood, this one consuming thirty thousand people directly, and the many more who saw it as cutting at the foundations of Newfoundland society. Perhaps for the first time, legions of those who had most benefited from confederation—the once-cashless outport people—found reason to deny their saviour.

Between 1954 and 1975 more than 250 communities were resettled. Houses buoyed with oil drums, then towed across open water, had become a common sight. So, too, had the burning of churches, structures the departing people had set to flame rather than leave to vandals or see fall to ruin over time. For the last service at St. Nicholas' Church on Flat Islands five hundred people filled the hand-hewn pews. Once neighbours, they were soon to be scattered to a half-dozen different communities.

For many people throughout Newfoundland the emotional pain of resettlement would never entirely heal. When the Come by Chance oil refinery was suddenly mothballed, nearby Arnold's Cove turned into anything but the 'growth centre' it was touted as being. Some of those who had resettled from the islands of Placentia Bay found themselves in debt and on welfare.

For many others, resettlement was something they had come to see as inevitable. The opportunities it opened for their children was reason enough to accept it. Better schooling did lead to greater chance at employment, though in many cases the jobs took the children even farther away, far from the communities into which their parents had migrated. They became part of the continuing stream of Newfoundlanders driving U-Hauls over the new highway to mainland Canada. (Others went off to universities, and came back, armed with Ph.D.'s, to jobs at Memorial. On occasion some could even be found lecturing about the consequences of resettlement.)

In recent years reunions to resettled communities have become commonplace. Descendants of people who moved have even made them the sites of their weddings. All seem to feel the need to reclaim a misplaced ancestry. One woman at the Tack's Beach reunion came with her New Jersey children in tow. 'I'm going to pitch a tent on the site of my father's house and I'm going to wake them up in the early morning and I'm going to say to them, "This is what I was talking about. Right here."'

Northern Indignities

In Labrador the effects of resettlement cut even deeper. Decisions by a remote government sent struggling native cultures into further turmoil.

It was the mid-1950s. Into the Inuit communities of Hebron and Nutak came the outsider notion the people would be better served by relocating to communities farther south. A doctor with the International Grenfell Association lamented what he called 'degrading squalor and poverty.' The RCMP had reported widespread alcohol abuse. The head of the Moravians reviewed the finances of the mission at Hebron and concluded it could no longer support itself, and decided relocation of both Hebron and Nutak was the best solution. In St. John's, the government stood eager to bring to Labrador the same cost-saving deals it advocated in Newfoundland.

The Inuit themselves had no desire to move. Even the government trader living

Julius Jararuse, uprooted from Hebron, July 1959.

among them was at odds to understand the reasons for it. In his mind 'there wasn't a better place for sealing, char fishing and hunting.' The outsiders refused to think that the life of the nomadic Inuit might be anything but inferior to the houses, schools, and medical care—the 'better life'—they promised to the south.

In October 1955 the Smallwood government voted to close its government trading depot at Nutak and relocate all families. On 10 April 1959 officials flew into Hebron and gathered the people together in the Moravian Church. It has been said that the church was chosen, instead of the community hall, because for the Inuit it was a place of silence and worship, not for dissenting voices.

The meeting opened and closed with a hymn. The Inuit left Hebron without a voice, and against their will. The brass band played one last time. Open trap boats, loaded with people and their belongings, slipped away. The Grenfell nurse who went with the last of them wrote in her diary: 'Today Hebron faded into the past, to be left alone in her glory.'

Days later the exiled beheld their half-built houses crowded together on the outskirts of Nain, Hopedale, and Makkovik. It was a far cry from what had been promised. Many were forced to spend the fall in tents, and the winter in overcrowded homes with other families. The move left them humiliated and vulnerable. They were outsiders set against the permanent residents in competition for the hunting and fishing resources. Depression often led to alcoholism and trouble with the law.

Being forced to trade independence for what white officials saw as superior civilization was not unique to the Inuit. It was a tactic played against the Innu as well. Government-built houses sprang up in Sheshatshiu and Davis Inlet, as a way of gathering the Innu together, in the latter case on an island away from their traditional home on the Labrador mainland. The government thought to change a nomadic hunting culture into a stationary fishing one. It failed miserably, stripping meaning from the Innu's lives in the process.

The generations that followed have suffered the consequences—lives defined by alcoholism and abuse. Lives ended in an epidemic of suicide. Communities torn apart by clan rivalries, while governments throw money at them as if new Ski-Doos and boats and outboard motors could solve the problems. Governments trying to balance economic ventures (such as the low-level military training flights out of Goose Bay) with respect for the traditional Innu use of the land.

Any solutions are immensely complicated. Glaring evidence of that filled television screens around the world when solvent-sniffing teenagers in Davis Inlet were caught by cameras in 1993. Seven years later it seemed little had changed. This time it was Innu leaders themselves who brought in the TV cameras, desperate for help for their children, some as young as six years old, neglected by alcoholic parents, sniffing gas in the garbage-strewn woods of Sheshatshiu. To redress the fundamental damage done to native societies, it will take strong, empowered native leaders in partnership with governments who all have human dignity as their first priority.

A Final Fling with Power

Labradorians, native and non-native, together with their resources, have been toyed with by governments in St. John's forever. The people were tired of seeing candidates (as one observed, 'too old to climb up over the stagehead') being parachuted into the districts. By the 1960s there was growing talk of secession. In 1970 independent MHA Tom Burgess formed the New Labrador Party. As the next election unfolded, some voters in Labrador would at least be able to take satisfaction in the fact they played a key role in bringing an end to the Smallwood era.

In the federal election of 1968 Trudeaumania (despite Smallwood's early enthusiasm for the man) had abruptly stopped at the Cabot Strait and the Quebec-Labrador boundary. Of the seven ridings in the province, six returned Tories. A year later an unpolished John Crosbie ran head to head with Smallwood for the leadership of the Liberal Party. American students might have had the hawkish Nixon, the French the autocratic De Gaulle, but the protest-hungry student masses of Newfoundland had their Joey. When the votes were tallied at the leadership convention Crosbie came in a distant second, yet the opposition to Smallwood had never been more vigorous or nasty. In the aftermath the rabble-rousers from Memorial filled the convention with shouts of 'Ho Ho Ho Chi Minh.' They punched the air with the Nazi salute. They set fire to their Liberal membership cards.

The Tories were feeling supremely confident. Crosbie left the Liberals and donned the Tory blue. He teamed up with Frank Moores, new provincial PC leader recruited from the Ottawa six, to slog it out with a vulnerable Smallwood. The election of 1971 gave the PCs twenty-one seats and the Liberals twenty. The remaining seat fell to Mr. Burgess and his New Labrador Party. The member for Labrador West was left holding the balance of power. Unfortunately, he was hardly the man to rise above the mire that was by then Newfoundland politics.

Because they had to appoint a Speaker from their troops, the Tories were without a majority. All eyes came to rest on potential 'king-maker' Burgess. Smallwood, in the meantime, amid a barrage of criticism and constitutional head-scratching, refused to resign. He would await recounts in several districts where the margin of victory had been particularly narrow. Tabulators in St. Barbe South, awarded to the PCs by eight votes, discovered that after election night the contents of the ballot box in Sally's Cove had inadvertently been burned! The political scene was turning more incredible by the hour. Headline writers for the mainland presses could hardly keep up.

The Sally's Cove fiasco went to the Newfoundland Supreme Court, with the expectation that a new district election would be called. Liberals began to gather in the troops to prepare for an all-out assault on voters. Meanwhile, both the PCs and the Liberals had, of course, taken an immediate shine to Burgess. The red carpet race for his support was on. That much-favoured Liberal, John C. Doyle, offered to open the money box to the tune of $1 million, to be deposited in Burgess's name

Frank Moores in victory.

in any bank anywhere in the world. Burgess and Doyle boarded a private aircraft and wended their way toward the capital city. They took rooms on the same floor of the government-owned Holiday Inn.

But Burgess apparently was not to be bought. At least not with money. There followed a luxury jaunt to the Château Champlain in Montreal, where he fell into the arms of the PCs. Moores's promise of a cabinet post and a strong injection of funds into Labrador was really what he was looking for. Or so it seemed for a while. Moores and Burgess made their New Deal official at a press conference.

But Smallwood was hardly to be counted out. He seized the day, shifting the scene to Florida, a venue rather more conducive to political massage, especially for someone who had spent most Decembers in Labrador. Amid the sun and surf Joey made his pitch. He had taken more than just a shine to Burgess . . . in fact he was looking for someone to carry on his good Liberal work after he retired. If Burgess came over to the Liberal camp, Joey would clear the way for him to run for the premiership. All Labrador would have its place in the sun.

Burgess hesitated (one hopes), but did make the climb back up the fence, promising Smallwood that with a discreet passage of time he would climb back down the Liberal side. The Burgess school of ethics compelled him to consult his supporters in the New Labrador Party before making it official. Smallwood returned to Newfoundland. With public opinion pounding down his office door, Joey awaited confirmation from Burgess of his newfound Liberalism.

But just as Joey thought he was about to pull off the greatest resurrection in Newfoundland political history, the Supreme Court handed down its decision. The original result would stand. The Tories were awarded the seat.

The next day, Burgess added the second nail. He would stick to his original decision—a PC he was destined to be, after all. As good as he looked with a Liberal tan, his party faithful had refused to approve his re-reawakening.

Joey resigned. Moores became premier. And as for Burgess, he did a third about-face, and went over to the Liberals when the promised PC cabinet seat failed to materialize. He even ran for the Liberal leadership, garnering all of 82 votes. Defeated in the next election, he left Newfoundland, only to turn up several years later in Angola, as a 'freedom fighter.'

Smallwood would rise half-heartedly again under the banner of what he christened the Liberal Reform Party, and sit in the Opposition, but he was a spent force in Newfoundland politics. The country would not see a political bantam of his calibre again.

He eventually withdrew and devoted his days to compiling a projected five-volume *Encyclopedia of Newfoundland and Labrador*. In 1982 he could be found touring the province selling the first volume from a motor home. Four years later a policeman showed up on his doorstep and served a writ for nearly $200,000 in unpaid printing costs. Newfoundlanders and Canadians rallied around him and the work continued.

Just before midnight on 17 December 1991 Joey died. It was a week short of his ninety-first birthday. His passing followed several years of coping with a stroke that left him frail and without the capacity for what had been the most famous of his attributes, his speech. The only church in Newfoundland big enough to hold the multitude of mourners was the Roman Catholic Cathedral of St. John the Baptist (since 1955 a Basilica), that sanctuary of his confederation rival Archbishop Roche. Even in death, as another of his rivals, John Crosbie, had observed of him in life, Joey was 'a very accomplished politician.'

Legacy for the Father of Confederation

Joey was not about to be forgotten. Even today, if you put a half-dozen Newfoundlanders in a room, toss in a few Labradorians, and raise the topic of Joseph R. Smallwood, you are guaranteed a table-pounder of an argument. There is still little consensus on whether he was 'a scoundrel or a saint,' as one recent TV biography termed it. That he changed this place irrevocably, there is absolutely no doubt. Because of Joey, 'this poor bald rock' was no more.

It is sometimes too easy to measure Smallwood by the blunders and abuse of power that punctuated his years as premier. In numerous other ways he directed incalculable benefits our way. He dealt with four prime ministers, playing the game of federal-provincial relations with an astuteness that was the envy of the brigades of premiers that came and went in other provinces during his twenty years in office. Most productive for Newfoundland was his relationship with Jack Pickersgill, the Ottawa civil service mandarin whom Smallwood groomed into a Newfoundland MP. Among the many pots of federal funds Pickersgill laid open to Newfoundland was one that extended unemployment insurance to fishermen, and another that saw Ottawa pay 90 per cent of the cost of the paved extension of the Trans-Canada Highway across the Island. (Giving rise to that most famous of Newfoundland highway signs: 'We'll Finish the Drive in '65—Thanks to Mr. Pearson.')

A paved highway and its branch roads allowed Newfoundlanders to connect to mainland Canada with an ease they had not known before. More important, the highway connected Newfoundlanders to each other. The Avalon Peninsula was forced to rid itself of its myopic notions of what constituted Newfoundland. Townies were discovering there was more to the province than could be had from a Sunday excursion to Brigus.

But it was another dream of Joey's that would most transform the province. (It was a decidedly unselfish dream, considering the fact that it more than anything was ultimately responsible for his political downfall.) In 1961 he unveiled a new campus for Memorial University. It was an elaborate ceremony highlighted by the presence of Eleanor Roosevelt. During Joey's term in office the university's enrolment increased twenty-five-fold. Today it's the largest university in Atlantic Canada.

Many of Memorial's faculty, drawn from universities across North America and Britain, were enticed here by the opportunity of building departments from a bare foundation. Several quickly became recognized for their world-class expertise. Newfoundland and Labrador itself came to be seen as a vast, untapped research field. The university's Extension Department emerged as a dynamic catalyst for community change.

Joey was determined that it be a university where 'every Newfoundlander who wants to go has a right to go.' For a time in the mid-1960s he even took the unheard-of step of doing away with university tuition, and bringing in a program of student salaries. Budget pressures forced an end to the program within a few years, but Joey's heart remained with the students and in giving them the opportunity that he himself had been denied. Though he had a lifelong love of scholarship (and had assembled a treasure of a personal library), he envied the university education that in his youth was attainable only by the upper classes. (It underlay much of his animosity toward John Crosbie—the merchant's son, graduate of Dalhousie Law School and the London School of Economics, and who on the day of confederation in 1949 was ensconced in a private boarding school in Ontario.)

It would be M.O. Morgan, an outport Newfoundlander, who would lead the expansion of the university and formulate its intellectual objectives, though in the six years before he became president in 1973, Morgan would have to work around Lord Taylor of Harlow, a figurehead with the right stuff (i.e., a British peerage) to become winner of Joey's one-man search for president.

The university brought sweeping changes. The rise in the education level of teachers in rural areas was particularly dramatic. (In 1949 fewer than 3 per

Parade of students at the opening of the new campus of Memorial University, 1961.

cent of them were university graduates.) Students flooded in from across the province, and flooded out again with their degrees. And they took with them notions of democracy and good government that they didn't see in action in the Confederation Building. Many, such as Brian Peckford, were ready to take a substantial nip out of the hand that fed them. The irony was not lost on Joey, nor did he ever do anything but support the expansion of the university. He would have much preferred seeing the reins of power pass into the hands of someone he'd help to educate.

Frankie and Johnny

As it was, power passed to Frank Moores, who spent the year of confederation in the very same private boarding school as Crosbie, and who dropped out of Boston University after two months. Moores was the son of a fish merchant in Conception Bay, in Joey's eyes that most scornful of privileged entities—a merchant prince. Unlike Smallwood, Moores had been used to power all his life, and seemed to be able to pick and choose the form of it that suited him.

Moores, it was agreed, had 'more charm than Jack Nicholson.' Joey took to calling him 'Frankie baby,' a less than subtle reference to a predilection for the oppo-

Frank Moores and John Crosbie at a meeting of provincial premiers.

site sex. Moores often had other things on his mind—salmon fishing and partridge hunting among them—though when he set it to politics he was more than capable of initiating the much-needed change in the way the business of government was conducted. Years later, when asked for his greatest accomplishment during his time as premier, he was quick to conclude: 'We restored democracy to Newfoundland.' It was no mean accomplishment.

Of course, he didn't do it alone. He was said to have feigned long work habits by having an aide leave his Cadillac El Dorado (an upgrade from Joey's Chrysler Imperial) in the premier's parking spot late into the evening. Unlike his predecessor, he preferred to delegate power. There to receive it was John Crosbie, the man who, more than any politician since Joey, should have been premier. Had he been willing to hang on as a Liberal and let Smallwood self-destruct, he might well have been. But Crosbie throughout his career has never played the game of politics easily. He often acted on impulse, refusing to mask his frustrations when confronted with inept leadership. He came to be neither premier nor prime minister, though he made a determined run for both. He nevertheless wielded considerable power, never more so in Newfoundland than as part of the Moores's administration—minister of Finance, minister of Economic Development, and president of Treasury Board. Moores was merely premier.

The new government's first priority was unravelling the financial mess surrounding Shaheen and Doyle. The PCs took over the linerboard mill in Stephenville and manoeuvred the government off the hook for $60 million at the oil refinery in Come by Chance. They nationalized operations at Churchill Falls, and bought out the timber rights of Reid Newfoundland. They put a stop to resettlement, established a second campus of Memorial University—Grenfell College on the west coast of the Island. For the first time important government decisions were being referred to a committee of more than one.

A new working relationship emerged with the federal government. At the helm of the Department of Regional Economic Expansion (DREE) in Ottawa was Don Jamieson. (Though Jamieson had once been campaign manager for Crosbie's father, Ches, he and Crosbie did little more than tolerate each other.) Jamieson put his gift for oratory to good use in the Liberal cabinet, however, and netted Newfoundland considerable rewards. The most visible evidence of Jamieson's financial might was a string of new schools. In design and amenities they were like

nothing Newfoundland education had ever seen, and are still known as DREE
schools, including the Donald C. Jamieson Academy in Salt Pond, Burin.

In 1976 Crosbie took the leap to federal politics. He was fed up, as he said, with
'playing second fiddle' to Moores, of running the show 'and getting no appreciation for it.' In Ottawa, he got his federal feet wet by turning a quick Opposition
tongue on, among others, Don Jamieson. Before long the PCs took power and
Crosbie was donning sealskin mukluks and making his famed 1979 budget speech
as minister of Finance. It and Joe Clark lasted all of two days. Crosbie was again
faced with inept leadership, but had run out of parties to switch to.

Back in Newfoundland Frank Moores quit politics. Moores was also off to
Ottawa, but to a less fishbowl life as founder of Government Consultants International, Inc. He was about to bring 'the art of lobbying to new heights.' Moores
was the man behind the ousting of Joe Clark as PC leader and the crowning of an
old fishing buddy, Brian Mulroney. Thanks in part to Moores, Crosbie, who had
run for national PC leader and lost, was left still playing second fiddle. He went on
to play it with such wit and gusto nobody seemed to care. Still, as Crosbie later
summed it up, 'it is inevitably frustrating to work as a member of a government
led by someone else.' It was Crosbie's fate to do just that all his political life.

Fish or No Fish

There was no aspect of the Newfoundland economy that Frank Moores had known
better than the fishery. In the 1950s his father was one of the first to move toward
the production of fresh-frozen cod. Moores focused unprecedented attention on
the fishery, an industry going through major transition in the midst of the environmental turmoil brought on by the fleets of foreign factory freezer ships showing up off our coast. In the late 1960s these massive oafs of fishing technology
came from the ports of eastern Europe, trawling all day and all night regardless of
ice conditions or depth of water, plundering the 'pristine cod population, the
Hamilton Bank stock . . . the first time it was fished during spawning.'

On the Island, union activity was on the rise. A bitter strike in Burgeo in 1971
led to unionization of fish plant workers province-wide. Trawlermen struck in
1974 and came away with considerable new clout in the industry. Then, in 1976,
Canada declared a two-hundred-mile (320 km) jurisdictional limit. It slowed the
devastation to the groundfish stocks inflicted by foreign overfishing, but soon our

own deep-sea trawler fleet was expanding into the vacated seas. Struggling to be heard were the inshore fishermen, the traditional backbone of the industry. In 1980, they, too, struck for and received fairer treatment. After centuries of struggle and subservience to merchants, rural Newfoundland finally received a fair share of the profits.

From Ottawa had come new regulations to improve the balance between the inshore and the deep-sea fishery and to better regulate the industry. But the bureaucrats and a succession of federal fisheries ministers proved to be incapable of ignoring politicians at both government levels, who were noisily lusting after more jobs. It was expand at all costs. The environment was conveniently put on hold.

Each spring in rural Newfoundland, with the capelin fishery at its height, I would see high-school students regularly giving up school time to work in the fish plants. A graduation certificate was losing its lustre. For the first time parents were not discouraging their children from going into the fishery as an occupation. And to add fuel to the problem, government UI programs paid benefits to young people if they *didn't* go back to school. To judge by the new homes they saw rising around them, these ex-students would have little to worry about.

Imbedded in the thinking of young people entering the industry was the number of weeks needed to qualify for unemployment insurance. Spending from May to November at the fishery, then 'drawing unemployment' for the rest of the year became the standard. Indeed, if outports were going to survive, there hardly seemed any other options. Except in the few places with milder winters, the fishery could only be a seasonal occupation.

But in some rural communities (and this was far from unique to Newfoundland and Labrador) government programs became an end in themselves. For workers who couldn't find employment in the fishery or other traditional rural occupations there was government employment on 'make-work' projects (with building wharfs and cutting brush the standard fare). The work lasted long enough to trigger UI claims. Some outport people became hewers of wood and drawers of unemployment insurance. Ten weeks' work could get a fellow forty-two weeks of stay-at-home security, not exactly a formula to engender self-reliance or entrepreneurial spirit.

Outports embraced the handouts; the politicians pressed on to find other ways to keep the people employed. One way or another they needed their vote. (Joey might have been gone, but one of his truisms—'the first job of a politician is to get elected'—was never more relevant.) The thrust to expand the fishery only accelerated.

Straight as an Arrow

Frank Moores was gone and John Crosbie was 'back in the trenches' in Ottawa. Had Crosbie stayed in Newfoundland he would have been a shoo-in for premier. Instead the job fell to one of the feisty young men who had romped and stomped for Crosbie in his leadership bid in 1969—Brian Peckford. In a provincial election a few months later Peckford took on new Liberal leader and homecoming kingpin Don Jamieson. He trounced him soundly.

Peckford cut a novel figure in the Confederation Building. The son of a Newfoundland Ranger, he was born and raised in rural Newfoundland and related to it better than any premier before or since. In exuberance for leading government, Newfoundland had hardly seen his like before, except, of course, in Smallwood. Peckford was much less of a dictator, but his ultimate downfall, too, would be the 'grand scheme.' At his worst he was the cigar-toking, finger-jabbing defender of the indefensible. At his best he rooted out Newfoundlanders' pride in themselves, for decades lost in the put-downs of an ignorant mainland. He met arrogance with arrogance, and along the way power got the better of him.

Smallwood had bungled the first wave of development, and, in Peckford's view, Moores hadn't enough political spine to take on the federal government over who should have the right to manage the province's fishery, and (what became the prime focus of the Peckford term in office) its offshore oil reserves. Peckford saw before him a second and last chance at economic respectability. And this time, he vowed, 'we're going to do it right.' That he only partially succeeded was through no lack of trying.

As minister of Mines and Energy in the

Brian Peckford holding up his symbol of the new Newfoundland and Labrador.

Moores cabinet, Peckford had faced down the multinational oil companies out to secure drilling permits on the Grand Banks. He insisted on more jobs and a bigger financial take for Newfoundland. When Moores came close to caving in, Peckford threatened to resign. Now, it was Peckford himself calling the play-by-play. A whirlwind of political will from Green Bay settled into the premier's chair.

He set the tone with the adoption of a new provincial flag. Gone finally was the Union Jack, replaced by a Christopher Pratt–designed standard, at once honouring the past and pointing, in the words of the official description, 'the way to what we believe will be a bright future.' Neptune's trident had evolved into a golden arrow. We would not lack for confidence.

In that same opening flourish of government, a Department of the Environment was created. Newfoundland saw its first female cabinet ministers. Lynn Verge, especially, stirred government to get on track with equality issues. A matrimonial property act was passed and a Status of Women Council set in place. The smell of patronage seemed to dissipate, replaced by tangible passion to set the province aright. There was even a feeling, incomprehensible as it was to the PCs in Ottawa, that the province's concerns rose well above party politics. Peckford was looking for all the world like the leader the forces for Responsible Government could have used thirty years before.

As it stood, it was a federalist Canada he was taking on, in the same way he had taken on the oil companies. In November 1979 offshore oil exploration leapt forward with confirmation of the vast resources of the Hibernia oil field. The premier and his Energy minister, Leo Barry, held high the vials of crude, and promised at least five hundred million barrels more. Such optimism for the future we had never witnessed.

To What End?

Suddenly, in the early hours of 15 February 1982, the human cost of that optimism tore at the heart of every last one of us. We awoke to a death knell—one of the offshore drill rigs, the *Ocean Ranger*, had been sunk by a savage winter storm, taking all of its eighty-four men. Newfoundland and Labrador had been home to fifty-six of them.

The *Ocean Ranger* was billed as the world's largest semi-submersible rig, and unsinkable. The deck and drilling area were the size of two football fields. It tow-

An overturned lifeboat, after the sinking of the Ocean Ranger, *1982.*

ered thirty storeys. The upper hull rested on eight vertical columns, set in two immense pontoons each holding a dozen ballast chambers. From the corner columns ran twelve gigantic anchors holding the rig to the ocean floor.

Partway down another of these columns was the heart of the rig—the ballast control room. Through the thick tempered glass of its portholes the operators had watched the fury of the North Atlantic many times, mere child's play for a rig this technically advanced.

Just after 7:45 p.m. on Valentine's Day a wave whipped up by the cruellest storm in years smashed through one of the portholes. Another rig fourteen kilometres to the east picked up a voice from the control room: 'We have water and glass on the floor. All valves are opening on the port side . . . ' The control panel was drenched with sea water. A succession of short circuits played havoc with the ballast tank valves, causing them to open and close on their own. The rig began to list. At twelve to fifteen degrees, lockers housing the anchor chains flooded.

By 1:00 a.m. the next day the situation was beyond hope. A series of maydays erupted from the *Ranger*—to the second rig, to its supply ships, the Mobil office in St. John's, air-sea rescue centres in Gander and New York. The crew's only chance at survival was to abandon the rig.

The weather was so severe that only the supply ships could reach them. The nearest was the *Seaforth Highlander*, thirteen kilometres away. It came upon the rig to find only one lifeboat afloat. Because of the severe list the others, launched twenty-one metres above the surface, had struck the sides of the rig and broken apart. Even the one the *Highlander* spotted had a gaping hole in its bow. Floodlights revealed a huddle of men frantically bailing it out.

The crew of the *Highlander*, on deck and holding on desperately themselves, managed to get a line to the lifeboat. The survivors emerged and, in fear of being crushed against the supply ship, crowded to the port side.

Their weight caused the lifeboat to roll, then capsize, throwing the men into the frigid waters. The line to the supply ship snapped. A wave swept the lifeboat away, together with those who still had enough life in them to cling to its sides. By the time the *Highlander* reached them a second time and had flung out an inflated life raft, all the crew could discern were bodies floating lifeless, the lights of their lifejackets still lit.

A half-hour later the rig itself capsized. It went to the ocean floor less than 160 kilometres from where the unsinkable *Titanic* had gone down seventy years before. In the days that followed the loss of the *Ocean Ranger*, only twenty-two bodies were recovered.

Mobil Oil and the operators of the rig, Ocean Drilling and Exploration Company (ODECO) of New Orleans, faced two separate investigations and a torrent of questions: Why was the ballast control room in such a vulnerable location? Why was its control panel not sealed against water damage, its operators not adequately trained? Why hadn't procedures for abandoning the rig been more carefully planned, and more rescue equipment placed aboard the supply vessel? Why weren't there survival suits for the crew?

Simply put, by the control-room operator due to take over duties on the *Ranger*'s next change of shift, 'The boys didn't have a chance.' No amount of corporate damage control or verbal contortions ever proved anything different.

According to Peckford

A drilling program continued. By 1985, with Brian Mulroney's PCs in control in Ottawa, agreement was reached on joint federal-provincial management of the offshore resources. It came on the heels of two Supreme Court decisions, one striking down Newfoundland's attempt to reopen the Churchill Falls deal, the second its claim to jurisdiction over the Grand Banks. Peckford had been so badly wounded by the verdicts that he never fully recovered. The Atlantic Accord with Mulroney, though giving Newfoundland a substantial voice at the management table, only partially made up for the setback. And the time was past when

Peckford could successfully campaign on that even more profound fight with Ottawa, provincial control of the fishery.

When Peckford went to the polls two months after signing the accord, the electorate rewarded him with a reduced majority. The wisdom of his confrontational approach to governing was now more in question than ever. The fact that he had waged his battles in the midst of a recession didn't help. Unemployment wavered always between 15 and 20 per cent. Before leaving office the provincial sales tax would mushroom to 12 per cent.

The man took to being driven by limo and smoking thick cigars at press conferences. He renovated his premier's office to the tune of half a million dollars. It all had a John C. Doyle aroma that repulsed more and more voters. The idealist scrapper, the fellow who had been equally comfortable snaring rabbits with his buddies in Green Bay and duelling with Pierre Trudeau on national television, had turned in on himself. What fight was left Peckford directed at his critics. When a new investigative newspaper, the *Sunday Express*, appeared on the scene and focused its considerable journalistic skills on his missteps, Peckford flared like a spoiled child.

His government pushed on, almost spoiling for a fight with the electorate. One fist went up with an experiment in time warp called Double Daylight Savings Time. In 1988 the government brain trust decided to push our time zone another full hour past the time-honoured thirty minutes that we were already ahead of the rest of the country. Salmon fishermen and softball players loved it. Parents trying to get their kids to bed despised it. So did stockbrokers and anyone wanting to catch the Stanley Cup games on TV. In October flashlight-wielding students in Labrador City were marching to school in the mornings in protest. The radio open-line shows buzzed with 'bad-tempered zombies' for weeks on end. The government scrapped the experiment, and decided to find other ways to control the sunshine.

It came to be called the Sprung Greenhouse Affair. The very man who so berated Joey Smallwood's hare-brained development ventures sank $22 million into an unproved hydroponic scheme of Calgary businessman Philip Sprung to grow, of all things, cucumbers. As the unanswered questions mounted, the bull-headed premier pushed ahead, disaster building on disaster. An all-night glow settled over the chosen growth centre—Mount Pearl. With the mega-kilowatt lights raising the ire of its normally docile residents, rumours of crop failures abounded. It was political cartoonist heaven.

By early January 1989, the cuke business had gone under. It was time to sell the shop. Peckford himself had been sandwiched by public opinion. It was resign or face ever greater humiliation at the next election. That he left to his minister of Fisheries and premier for forty-four days—Tom Rideout.

If there was anything positive to be found in the greenhouse debacle, it was the comic relief it provided. We entered the 1990s still chuckling over cucumber jokes. And, of course, taking a page from Ralph Klein, we could blame half our misfortune on 'those western bums.' Early in the decade Brian Peckford himself resettled out west, to Vancouver Island. Newfoundland had proved a little claustrophobic for an ex-premier. He's missed, though. If secession from Canada ever catches on, the bet is he'll be back in a flash, gloves off, ready for a crack at the leadership.

36 | Sheer Will

I sometimes wonder what God's got in store for us Newfoundlanders . . . Maybe He's gonna have one more big whack at us before the good times come.

—Cabot Martin, 1982

George Story in the Newfoundland landscape, by Gerald Squires.

Creation

Long before he was premier, Brian Peckford was a teacher of English literature. His political career unfolded in parallel with a burgeoning of the arts in the province, into which he always put great store, even as he himself was being skewered in print and on stage. His government set in motion an Arts Council and Peckford invited one of the great teachers from Memorial, George Morley Story, to be its first chairperson.

Perhaps more than anyone, Story—Island-born Rhodes scholar, lexicographer, champion of Newfoundland studies—stood as an example of what influence the university had brought to bear on the province. He is best known as the man behind the remarkable *Dictionary of Newfoundland English*, but his most profound achievement was to stir a generation of students and colleagues into re-evaluating their own culture and channelling their energies into its investigation. Story had assured Newfoundlanders (as the *Daily Telegraph* would put it at his untimely death in 1994) 'that they could never be subsumed into any amorphous Canadian identity.'

This was the antithesis of the Newfoundlanders who ended up on mainland Canada and, as a survival skill, donned the 'Newfie' persona. That had spawned a glut of odious music and the caricature of the dim-witted-but-friendly, rubber-booted Newf, a situation made worse by a local tourist industry feeding itself on idiotic 'souvenirs,' joke books, and that ceremonial embarrassment, the 'Screech-in.' None of which we have yet had the good sense to eradicate. (There is even an N-word souvenir shop on the road to the designated site of Cabot's landing, complete with an outhouse.)

The creative arts in rural Newfoundland and Labrador were often lost in the struggle to put food on the table. One exception was storytelling, the other handiwork, such as the finely hooked mats of the Grenfell Mission. In larger centres the arts found some encouragement, but in career summaries Newfoundland generally didn't rise much beyond 'birthplace.' Maurice Prendergast, the famed American colourist, and Maurice Cullen, the strongest influence on the Canadian Group of Seven, both left while still young children. John Murray Anderson, raised in St. John's, ended up a producer on Broadway, with a career in the first half of the century surpassed only by Ziegfeld's.

Western Bay's E.J. Pratt left Newfoundland in 1907 at age twenty-five. He traded

CODCO's arrival was unlike anything ever seen in Newfoundland (or Canadian) theatre.

Newfoundland for academic life at Victoria College, University of Toronto, and still managed to establish himself as Canada's best-known poet. In more modern times, it was actor Gordon Pinsent of Grand Falls who made it to the semi-bright lights of Toronto. The best we could do was send them off with a storehouse of experiences for future culling.

Those that did stay, we generally ignored. The best of the writers was Margaret Duley. With *Highway to Valour*, partly set against the backdrop of the tidal wave of 1929, came our first convincing literary voice. She wrote four novels but died in 1968 in obscurity. It would have taken more than good reviews (even when they came from outside Newfoundland) to rouse the tweeds at Memorial College, the Island's bastion of British higher education.

Confederation stirred the mix. The new Memorial University set some heat under it. Smallwood himself had the gift of the pen (if mostly of the propaganda variety) and was quick to recognize it in others. Enticed to the cabinet table of his new government were three of the Island's best writers—Greg Power, Harold Horwood, and Ted Russell. None of them had lasted long as underlings of the premier. Russell eventually turned to writing his 'Uncle Mose' stories, the best-loved depictions of rural life to emerge from Newfoundland. Horwood took up journalism, using his 'Political Notebook' to eventually sink his literary teeth into his old boss. Of more than a dozen books on Newfoundland subjects, his best are works of natural history, including *The Foxes of Beachy Cove*, presaging a public awakening to environmental issues.

Horwood's first novel, in 1966, was a turning point for a new generation of writers. Up to that time writing in the province was overshadowed by those who had 'come from away,' especially Farley Mowat, who settled for a time in Newfoundland and spent several books interpreting us to the world. We needed our own voice. We needed to confirm that what we had to say had a readership elsewhere. *House of Hate* by Percy Janes and Cassie Brown's *Death on the Ice* did just that. The founding of Breakwater Books and the ISER publishing program at Memorial gave new hope that more voices would be heard. Among them was Ray Guy. His political satire was already so widely read that he became a prime factor in Joey's downfall. His impact as a writer within Newfoundland was the strongest since D.W. Prowse published his *History of Newfoundland* in 1895.

The work of Christopher Pratt and David Blackwood brought unprecedented attention to the visual arts. Don Wright set up St. Michael's Printshop, and soon, because of enthusiasts such as Edythe Goodridge, artists from across the country were making the trek to Newfoundland to see what all the fuss was about. Gerald Squires returned to the province and in his soul-searching canvases helped focus the rethinking of our heritage.

What we discovered was just how different it was from the morass of North American mainstream culture. Though rooted in England and Ireland, it had evolved into something distinct. Tourist brochures gave up the caricature image and took on a new tone, billing us as 'another world next door.' We were that and much more.

Anyone who saw the CODCO theatrics of *Cod on a Stick* in 1973 knew something extraordinary was on the loose. When not filling seats in the LSPU Hall in St. John's with wickedly entertaining forays into collective theatre, its actors performed across the province and in mainland Canada. There, journalists such as St. John's native Sandra Gwyn helped spread the word—something is afoot in the Happy Province, a 'Newfoundland Renaissance.'

It hit with an equal wallop in music. The success of Harry Hibbs and a sea of Newfoundland musicians exiled in Ontario gave way to home-nurtured talent. Figgy Duff mixed rock with traditional harmonies. Young musicians searched the

Rufus Guinchard and Emile Benoit.

outports and discovered masters of the fiddle and accordion—Rufus Guinchard, Minnie White, Emile Benoit—and a repertoire stretching back two hundred years. The cross-generational mixing was an extraordinary moment in the evolution of Newfoundland culture. From west-coast outports had emerged mentors for a fresh pool of musical talent centred in the capital city. Newfoundland's musical lineage, once in danger of being severed, stood intact, about to renew itself.

Today, the creative face of Newfoundland and Labrador is everywhere. For a population less than that of Hamilton, Ontario, we are looking extraordinarily good. When we are not wowing them on the mainland—*This Hour Has Twenty-Two Minutes*, Great Big Sea, Wayne Johnston, Mary Pratt, Buddy Wasisname and the Other Fellers—we are drawing the mainland to us—*The Labrador Creative Arts Festival, The Stephenville Theatre Festival, Festival 500: Sharing the Voices*, festivals of new dance, of new film and video, of new sound. The true measure of the vibrancy of our culture is the brilliance of the work done by the artists who live here, whether it be Bernice Morgan's words in *Random Passage*, the lyrics Ron Hynes chose for *Atlantic Blue*, the film images of Rosemary House and Gerry Rogers, Doris Saunders's assembly of stories for *Them Days* magazine, Donna Butt's vision for Trinity's summer of theatre, or the work of the several artists from Bulgaria who defected in Newfoundland and settled here in the late 1980s. We no longer await confirmation by others before we believe in ourselves. As George Story once put it, 'It is our creative ability that ensures our survival.'

Recreation

For centuries it was work at the fishery and in the lumberwoods that kept us fit. 'Randying' (sledding) in winter and 'copying' (jumping) ice pans in the spring were the sports of rural youth. In 1919, the ex-Oxford athlete Wilfred Grenfell confessed, 'There is no better fun than a randy over the snow on a light komatik.' At the time of confederation, Ray Guy was still at it: 'You can randy on anything. Bits of old floor canvas and pieces of cardboard boxes. Stave slides which your father made out of old barrels.' In the heat of summer other juveniles were found playing 'rounders,' an old English field game that vaguely resembled baseball, or 'tiddley,' the object of which was to hook into the air a stick balanced atop two rocks, then whack it as far as possible. (None of the games called for safety equipment of any sort, as a scar over my right eye from an airborne tiddley stick attests.) Even more dangerous was 'grump.' Here daredevils would take to bases at four grumps, or mooring-posts, on a wharf. While pairs of them raced to change places, a fifth player tried to steal a vacant base. It made for good runners . . . and even better swimmers.

Since these games didn't have much international recognition, grown-up athletes were forced to turn elsewhere. Here St. John's had a definite edge. Organized sports (with religious rivalries calling up that extra aggression) have been part of the fabric of the place since the 1800s. With the exception of the communities of the

Alex Faulkner gets it past Tim Horton and Johnny Bower,
making Red Wings fans of a generation of Newfoundlanders.

Avalon, the company towns and military bases, there was a lack of what could be called 'proper' sports facilities. Team sports that required a level field and a minimum of equipment (soccer and pond hockey) were the most widespread. Athletes who competed outside the country found they did best in these, or in sports that made use of the country's natural facilities—events such as running, rowing, and cross-country racing. In 1920 marathoner Eric Robertson (who four years earlier had been wounded at Beaumont-Hamel) became the first Newfoundlander to compete in the Olympic Games. It would be seventy years later, in Lillehammer, that Dwayne Norris would claim our first medal, a bronze in hockey. Six years after that in Atlanta, our second, this time a silver, was captured by Maria Maunder in rowing.

There have been plenty of athletic highlights along the way. In 1930 Newfoundland sent off its first international team, to the inaugural Empire Games. Racewalker Ferd Hayward was U.S. National twenty-five-mile champ in 1951. Bishop's Falls lad Alex Faulkner scored five goals (three of them game winners!) as part of the Detroit Red Wings' semi-final bid for the Stanley Cup in 1963. (Our greatest sports 'hero' had a chocolate bar named in his honour.) Newfoundland

curlers won the Canadian Brier in 1976. Wheelchair star Joanne McDonald set a world record at the Pan-Am Games of 1982. The 123-pound Joy Burt of Corner Brook became our second world champion with a squat of 380 pounds and a deadlift of 443 pounds at the world powerlifting championships of 1987. Brad Gushue and his junior men's curling rink captured the world title in 2001. Not to forget Carolyn Frances Hayward, who in 1956 escaped the sedate halls of Bishop Spencer College in St. John's and landed a career as a bullfighter. One of the very few *matadoras*, she

Joanne McDonald in action.

became a celebrity across Mexico and South America, putting an end to over 120 bulls, the largest in excess of 900 pounds. Our athletic prowess is nothing if not distinctive.

Now, what with a proliferation of well-equipped schools, dozens of make-work-project rinks and baseball diamonds, new arenas and pools, and world-class ski hills we are as organized as the next guy. While it's debatable whether it's all as much fun as a good game of grump, there's a lot to be said for the way we show-cased athletic achievement as hosts of the Canada Games, first in St. John's in 1977, then in Corner Brook in 1999. While many still have to leave home to do their best, we also like to bring the world's best to us, such as Olympic gold medal-list Simon Whitfield, who, with the top athletes in his sport, comes annually to the Corner Brook Triathlon World Cup.

And for years we have been doing our bit to help other provinces to Olympic glory. Alex Oakley left Newfoundland shortly after confederation to find work in Ontario. As a racewalker, he competed over a career that spanned twenty years. In 1960 his sixth-place finish in the 20km was Canada's best individual performance of the Rome Olympic Games. At fifty, more than double the age of most of his competition, he raced with two broken ribs, entering the stadium at the Montreal Olympics to a standing ovation. Competitor in an incredible five Olympic Games, Commonwealth Gold Medallist, Canadian Amateur Athlete of the Year, Member of the Canadian Sports Hall of Fame, Oakley returned to Newfoundland when he retired. At seventy-five he was walking eight kilometres a day near his home along the Southern Shore.

No Fish

Alex Oakley is one of hundreds of thousands since confederation who have left the province not because they wanted to but because the work was elsewhere. People have been our most consistent export. Few are the Newfoundland families who don't have someone in Brampton or Fort McMurray or hundreds of other mainland towns. Our labour force has become an indispensable mechanism in the industrial machine of Canada. (And let no one rant on that we don't pay our fair share in this country.)

Every politician who has ever campaigned for premier has vowed to curb the exodus. None embraced it to greater effect than Clyde Wells, the Liberal leader out

John Crosbie makes his way to a press conference to announce the cod moratorium.

to dislodge the PCs from power following the resignation of Brian Peckford in 1989. In speech after speech the theme of bringing home sons and daughters won over voters. For nothing matters more to Newfoundlanders than family. The sons and daughters didn't come home, of course. In fact, more and more of them left. So many that now the parents are mainlanders, too, gone to be near their children and grandchildren. Except for the vacation days of summer, whole outports have turned ghostly quiet.

The first day of the funeral was 1 July 1992. On the day to celebrate confederation, the day to mourn the fallen at Beaumont-Hamel, the federal minister of Fisheries, John Crosbie, had run afoul of fishermen in Bay Bulls. Word was out that Ottawa was about to shut down the codfishery. Crosbie braved a hostile crowd. When the verbal attacks turned personal, Crosbie spat out a few words that for thousands of fishermen would sum up what it felt to be Canadian that day: 'I didn't take the fish from the goddamned water!' A fisherman face to face with Crosbie shot back, 'You and your goddamned people took it! You and your people took it!'

Crosbie, of course, wasn't personally responsible for the death of the codfishery. The accusation flew at what he symbolized—the succession of federal and provincial government departments that had mismanaged the stocks. There was something else he symbolized (if again, through no fault of his own)—the merchant wealth that suppressed the fishermen's ancestors, denied them an education, a fair deal in the affairs of the country.

Crosbie stood and took the brunt of their venom that afternoon. The next day he announced a complete shutdown of the codfishery, and had to be whisked away by police. Inshore fishermen, denied entry to the press conference called to end their very livelihood, literally rammed the doors of government. They went 'berserk,' as Crosbie put it. 'In the first place, I don't frighten,' said an arrogant minister of Fisheries.

It was a pity they hadn't gone berserk twenty-five years before, at the height of the foreign decimation of the stocks. The federal government, more concerned with offending its trading partners than standing up for the Newfoundland fishermen, could have done with a damn good fright. The reasons the domestic fishery had come to such a state—a complete shutdown of what had sustained Newfoundland and Labrador since the time of Cabot, throwing out of work twenty-seven thousand fishermen and plant workers—are yet to be fully understood. Foreign plunder just outside the two-hundred-mile limit (on the 'nose' and 'tail' of the Grand Banks), overexpansion of the domestic fishery (too many fish plants, too many trawlers, too many fishermen), bad science, worse management, cold water, seals—they all contributed. Statistics abounded, and like the warnings of the inshore fishermen, all were heeded too late. One will suffice: in 1968, in the heyday of the foreign factory freezers, a record high 810,000 tonnes of northern cod were taken, at a time when the sustainable maximum catch was estimated to be 250,000 tonnes. It serves as a marker for the beginning of the end.

As a consequence of the moratorium, out-migration from Newfoundland mush-roomed. More than forty-five thousand people have gone since 1993, from the province whose birth rate has fallen from the highest in Canada to the lowest. Newfoundland and Labrador is the only province in the country to suffer a net loss of population in the last decade. Once-thriving towns, places such as Trepassey, Burgeo, and Catalina, have been turned into shadows of their former selves. In Trepassey, workers stood and watched as their plant's equipment was dismantled and shipped to South Africa.

Hope is not entirely gone. It never is, not in this place. 'Those fish are coming back,' said one fisherman, 'and I'll be waiting on this shore, by God.' But those left to do the waiting are always older and greyer (and have less time to cling to hope) than those who leave.

What to make of it all? Newfoundland and Labrador had struck hard times before, and without an income-support system for those thrown out of work. And out-migration has been a fact of life here forever and a day, if never to the extent it was in the latter half of the 1990s. The resiliency of Newfoundlanders is renowned. (It should be, given how many times we have had to display it.)

In some parts of the province, the Great Northern Peninsula especially, the cod moratorium has been particularly devastating to what was already a fragile population base. In some places fish processors and government, working together, have been able to find relief in other, underutilized species and in aquaculture. Sea urchins, once a nuisance, are now carefully harvested and their roe packaged for Japan. In Trinity Bay fishermen are sending to market fattened farmed cod. Plant operators have turned entrepreneurs, searching world markets harder than ever for places to do business. Where once there was great waste, commercial uses have been found for every part of a catch. Largely on the basis of crab, shrimp, and other shellfish, the combined landed and production value of the fishery in 2000 reached over $1 billion, its highest level ever.

Of Church and School and State

The key to long-term viability of our economy is the confidence that comes with education. Many highly skilled college and university graduates have left to do their bit for the economies of the rest of North America, but more and more are managing to stay. They're determined to get the province on its feet and keep it there.

The most striking indication that there is a new attitude at work in Newfoundland and Labrador is the reform to the school system. What seemed impossible even a few years ago has taken place. Gone finally is the duplication and fiscal waste caused by a system of denominational schools. As good a job as some individual schools had done, society was no longer willing to tolerate the inherent disadvantages of the system, including the religious intolerance it perpetuated.

That intolerance showed its destructive face (for the last time, one hopes) during the two referenda it took to bring about the reform. The government of the mid-1990s had sensed an openness to change, accelerated by the push for deficit control. With schools running on bare-bones budgets and having to constantly pound on doors with fundraising schemes, the public was in no mood for the sight of half-filled yellow buses flashing past one school just to get to another of a different religion.

It coincided with widespread revulsion at the disclosures that some religious leaders, both Protestant and Catholic, had violated the trust placed in them for the care of children. Years marked by an unrelenting stream of stories of physical and sexual abuse inflicted on young boys, together with the complicity of the Church hierarchy and police officials in the matter, had rocked the whole province. The heart-rending newspaper accounts by victims, the intensely courageous televised testimony before the Hughes Inquiry into the abuse by Irish Christian Brothers at the Mount Cashel orphanage, and the near-daily reports of the criminal trials had caused the population to question what for centuries had been beyond question— the far-reaching powers exercised by the Church. While the spiritual role of the Church was in some sense renewed by what had been revealed, blind trust in its temporal leaders had vanished. Control was delivered into the hands of the people. Though it can be but a small measure of consolation for the victims, their stories did force change in the role of religious orders in Newfoundland society. They served, as well, to inspire victims in other institutions across the country to come forth with their equally horrific tales.

The time had come to do away with the discrimination of hiring teachers on the basis of religious affiliation, rather than merit alone. Some churches forecast a godless society, holding up the public school system in the U.S. (and in one case Nova Scotia!) as a warning of what would come to pass. (The biggest instance of shortsighted rhetoric, however, had to be an early newspaper ad that pointed to Bill Clinton as an example of what a Jesuit education could do to enhance morality.)

It will take another generation before the religious prejudices will have faded from the landscape. During the debate over education reform, some parts of the province had already been left shaking their head at all the rancour emanating from St. John's. They had accepted reform and were much more concerned about putting a stop to shrinking populations. The capital city itself is now showing signs of being able to see reform in a broader provincial context, though in part that is due to an influx of people into the city who did not grow up there, many from rural Newfoundland.

With the removal of Churches from the running of the education system, their place in Newfoundland society has been realigned. Even that historic centre of religious pugnaciousness, the Basilica, will soon share its hillscape with a new provincial cultural complex, the design of which is based on the fishing sheds that for centuries were the centre of our working lives. Visitors entering the harbour (and able to turn a blind eye to Atlantic Place) will look skyward to see the two forces that have most shaped our society—the fishery and the Church. (Architectural estimates have reassured uneasy churchgoers that the Basilica will remain higher. God will stay a good two metres above the fray.)

Sense of Place

Of those leading us in the fifty years since confederation, there are none lacking in lustre of one sort or another. All of them, at their strongest moments, have proved formidable opponents. At the national level, none more so than Clyde Wells.

It is worth noting that each of our first six premiers has grown up successively farther from St. John's. Wells came from a west coast railway town of a few hundred, Stephenville Crossing. He survived its two-room school and made it to university, no mean feat considering that at the time rural Newfoundland was only just coming out of its educational doldrums. At Memorial University he encountered a student body split between those who grew up in St. John's and those who didn't. It was the time of 'speech' classes for first-year education students to rid the 'baymen' of their accents. (This culture clash was lost on the merchant rich, of course, for they bypassed lowly Memorial on their way to something with more prestige.)

In many like Wells there was an unspoken will to excel in spite of their weak academic foundation. Condescension from the more privileged middle-class 'townies' only hastened the process. Fortunately, among the faculty were several eager to spur them on, for if there

Clyde Wells, Memorial University graduate, 1959.

was anyone about to reshape the province, it would be these dogged few of the new generation of rural Newfoundlanders.

In the Trinity Bay–born M.O. Morgan (future president of Memorial), Wells found a mentor, and someone to help him realize his goal of becoming a lawyer. Wells would arrive at Dalhousie Law School a few years later, shortly after John Crosbie had graduated. (As fate would have it, walking the same corridors in 1959 was Brian Mulroney, though a less-than-shining academic record sent him packing after one year.)

In 1966 Wells was a rising attorney in Corner Brook when Joey Smallwood came looking for new Liberal blood. Wells took the district of Humber East, and at twenty-eight became the youngest person ever to be appointed to the provincial cabinet. Around the table with him was John Crosbie. Of course, as always, the last word went to Joey, and within two years the pair had resigned over Smallwood's wheeling and dealing with John C. Doyle.

Wells went back to his law practice, while Crosbie learned the political game enough to reconfigure himself and become one of the highest-profile ministers in Brian Mulroney's Ottawa. Wells was never forgotten, though, by the Liberal Party. Through the provincial PC days of Frank Moores and Brian Peckford, there was always the feeling that the Liberals had someone waiting in the wings, ready to take power when the time was right.

In 1987, with a bad smell of cucumbers starting to permeate the province, Wells was being lobbied to return to politics. In fewer than two years he was premier. On a national level Crosbie was still far better known, though sometimes the attention was not what he might have wanted. His 'Pass the tequila, Sheila' crack proved his most remembered public statement.

Oddly enough, Crosbie—a mainland-educated son of the St. John's merchant class—had made a name for himself in Ottawa by enhancing his ready wit with a beefed-up Newfoundland brogue. Meanwhile, back in Newfoundland, Wells—the first Memorial grad from the Crossing—was suddenly filling the Canadian airwaves with eloquent, finely tuned, ultra-serious ruminations on the Canadian constitution.

The matter at hand was Prime Minister Mulroney's attempt to bring Quebec back into the Canadian family—the Meech Lake Accord. Brian Peckford had agreed to it, but now Clyde Wells was proposing he would rescind his province's approval. Mulroney and the other premiers refused to take him seriously. He was only a Newfoundlander, after all.

Wells's stance would prove no joke, and soon the whole country was sitting up and taking notice. In fact, much of the country, left voiceless by a prime minister who wanted it all to be decided by eleven men behind closed doors, cheered him on. During the first round of debate in Ottawa in November 1989 Wells electrified Canadians by taking on Mulroney and the patronizing Ontario Premier David Peterson, rejecting an agreement that Wells said would produce 'a class-A province, a class-B province, and eight class-C provinces.' Within a few days, thousands of letters of support from across the country poured into his St. John's office. He was seen as a breath of political fresh air, one willing to stand up for what he (and apparently the majority of Canadians) believed. One letter writer would contend he was 'the only politician left with enough integrity and common sense to lead Canada back from the abyss.' The Newfoundland legislature passed a motion to reverse its support of the accord.

The biggest test of Wells's conviction was set for June 1990, a few weeks before the twenty-third, the deadline for ratification of the accord by all ten provinces. Manitoba, the only other hold-out, caved in. Over several days behind closed doors Wells faced a ruthless barrage of accusations, denouncing him as someone who would deliberately set the country on a path of destruction. For his part, Wells dared to accuse Mulroney and the other premiers of following an agenda set not by the Canadian people but by separatists in Quebec. In the end Wells made a deal. He would take the accord back to Newfoundland and (with no time for a referendum) put it to a vote in the legislature.

What followed was political skulduggery at its most contemptible. Any thoughts that the country could expect otherwise had been dispelled on June twelfth with the publication of Mulroney's infamous 'roll the dice' interview, in which he told reporters that the timing of the conference in early June had been calculated to create crisis, to put the heat on the holdout provinces. That Mulroney was cocky enough to admit his manipulation only further inflamed Canadians. In Manitoba, native MLA Elijah Harper (speaking for irate aboriginals excluded from the drafting of the Accord) set in motion a filibuster to stop its passage by the deadline.

Mulroney and three premiers made the pilgrimage to Newfoundland to plead the case for approval. Crosbie worked over the MHAs in the back rooms of Confederation Building. Prominent Newfoundland businessmen cornered them with predictions of doom and gloom for Newfoundland if they voted no. When nothing seemed to be getting the job done, Lowell Murray, Mulroney's field worker and manipulator of last resort, pulled one final trick from the bag. With the Newfoundland vote scheduled for the afternoon of June twenty-second, and approval in Manitoba impossible, Murray bypassed Wells and went straight to national TV to lay out a deal. The government would approach the Supreme Court to give Manitoba an extension on the deadline . . . but only if Newfoundland voted in favour of the accord. Wells and his government members were livid. If an extension for Manitoba was possible, why not for Newfoundland, as Wells had been seeking, to allow time for a referendum? For that matter, why not an extension so the whole country could properly debate and vote on the issue? The premier's telephone and fax lines were going nonstop, the pile of messages of support from across Canada reaching thirty thousand. There was little but contempt for what Wells would later call 'the final manipulation.'

As a people we tend not to take kindly to blackmail. Murray was looked upon as a conniving weasel. Of course, he and Mulroney had to know beforehand what the reaction would be, that the legislature was now certain to vote no. Elijah Harper had already killed Meech, but the federal Tories weren't about to turn on the aboriginals in Manitoba. Newfoundlanders were a different matter.

Wells would not have his province made a scapegoat. He announced he would move adjournment of the debate. There would be no vote.

Wells himself would take the brunt of the ire about to spew out of Ottawa. Before it erupted he stood in the legislature and delivered the most brilliant speech of his political career. 'Don't try to create another precipice over which to drive the people of this nation . . . ' he warned the federal government. In the course of Crosbie's telephone call to update Mulroney on the situation there emerged one last manipulative gasp. The federal government would support adjournment without a vote, and seek an extension of the deadline for both Newfoundland and Manitoba, on condition that Wells would publicly endorse the accord. Crosbie would have done better to save his breath.

Mulroney and Murray had their scapegoat, the one they really wanted. They were able to point the finger directly at Wells. The public's response to Mulroney's

In 1991 the signing of the agreement to develop the Hibernia oilfields brought
together the five men who, since confederation, had served as premiers.

tactics came in the next federal election. The Tory seat count across the country
plummeted to two. The dice were stilled.

Some deemed Wells's stance over Meech Lake as anti-Quebec. It was never that,
the Churchill Falls deal notwithstanding. As cultures go in Canada, those of our
two provinces are the most distinctive. We are the two misfits in the Canadian
mould. But no province should have to settle for anything but a fair partnership.

Meech Lake and the subsequent Charlottetown Accord would dominate the
early years of Wells's career as premier. In public constitutional debate he shone.
He made us feel more Canadian than we ever had before. And in the process had
forced the rest of the country to revise its notion of Newfoundland and Labrador.
A quaint backwater we were not, and the quicker the other provinces accepted the
fact we were making a serious contribution to the country, the stronger would
become our ties to it. David Peterson might have been making Newfie jokes with
his aides when Wells first challenged Meech Lake, and MP Don Blenkarn spewing
his moronic musings—'I sometimes feel we would be better off if we towed
Newfoundland out to sea and sank it'—but by the end of the process the humour
had been lost even on them. John Crosbie, bitter to the last about the deflation of
his friend Mulroney, called Wells 'dogmatic, and unyielding, inflexible . . . exactly

the wrong type to be in politics.' What was more to the point, Wells hadn't been one to 'play ball' in the way that was expected of provincial premiers. Yet that was exactly the appeal of the man, emerging as he did at a time when the public was extraordinarily cynical about its politicians.

Inevitably, the constitutional matters faded and provincial ones returned. Clyde Wells's record outside the constitutional arena received few of the accolades it had received within it. When he fought with labour (inevitable in one of the most highly unionized provinces in Canada) he lost the battle of public opinion, as he did in his failed attempt to privatize Newfoundland Hydro. He was often accused of being too rigid, too hard-nosed, too prone to thinking his way was the only way. His government ran roughshod over the rights of employees and violated the Public Tendering Act, costing taxpayers millions of dollars in court settlements.

Yet, under his premiership the province weathered a recession and social turmoil brought about by the cod moratorium and the protracted scandal within the Catholic Church. At the end of his time in office he could point to fiscal responsibility and the first balanced budget in thirty-seven years. He could also point to his bold initiative on education reform. Perhaps that will be the legacy of the man who emerged from a two-room school where 'the teacher taught every subject in every grade from grade five to eleven' to become premier of the province. He would leave office having started the process that would result in a school system infinitely fairer and stronger than the one he himself had experienced.

The Hibernia platform on its way to the Grand Banks.

Unlike many who get a solid taste of political power, Wells had no desire to cling to it indefinitely. In many ways he had been a reluctant politician, a man who much preferred private life and what he called the 'more civilized atmosphere' of the courtroom, where events unfolded logically, and emotion did not take control of agendas. He resigned as premier in December 1995, just shy of the maximum ten years he had promised to devote to public office. He returned to the practice of law. In 1999 he was appointed Newfoundland's chief justice.

As for his nemesis, John Crosbie, after Meech Lake he dug in and turned his attention to convincing the federal cabinet to invest the billions necessary to get the Hibernia oil project activated, no easy task following the accord's failure. His colleagues came to realize that sinking Newfoundland as Don Blenkarn had advocated was a bit short-sighted, considering that with it would sink the potential for immense revenue for many years into the future. Much of Crosbie's time was spent countering the sceptics who lined up outside the editorial offices of what was quickly turning into Newfoundland's public relations enemy number one, the *Globe and Mail*. His role in pushing ahead the largest capital project ever undertaken in Atlantic Canada proved to be his greatest contribution to the province and the country. Today the immense Hibernia production platform, built at Bull Arm by more than five thousand Newfoundland workers, pumps oil from the vast reserves beneath the Grand Banks.

John Crosbie left politics in 1993 after twenty-seven years, to retire back home in Newfoundland. In Crosbie, Canada had a colourful, 'no holds barred' politician, one at times, as he himself admitted, 'too stubborn or too opinionated or too hasty or too unheeding.' And in Crosbie, Newfoundland had an outstanding political force, a fiercely committed fighter for the interests of the province. It is only fitting he was welcomed home with his appointment by Clyde Wells as chancellor of Memorial University. There, each spring and fall he presides over the convocation of hundreds of fresh graduates, many of them Newfoundlanders and Labradorians who view the opportunity to attend university as a birthright.

A Tobin by Any Other Name

Brian Tobin was crowned premier less than a month after Clyde Wells resigned. Shortly after that he had won thirty-seven of forty-eight seats in a provincial election. It was no political neophyte who had come home from Ottawa. He was after all Captain Canada, alias the Turbotnator, alias Rat Packer. If the Tories could hold up Clyde Wells as the one to push the country to the brink of separation, then the Liberals could hold up Brian Tobin as pulling it back again with his organization of the huge federalist rally in Montreal on the eve of the Quebec Referendum in 1995.

The man could do no wrong. And except for the rare flash of bad temper (green reporters bring out the worst in him), he remains the exceptional politician— sharp, articulate, energetic, as relaxed on the campaign trail . . . as he is in the presence of the queen. He has no qualms about delegating responsibility, is comfortable in a world where women are as prominent as men. A leader for a new age? There was a time when he was a bit too smooth, displaying that political scripted charm that leaves the impression of a person too comfortable with power. Even that has dissipated. He can be humble and he can be supremely confident. What more could a country want? Just a working knowledge of French.

Tobin was the first premier born after confederation, a Canadian from the start. He was also the first premier to escape the shadow of the 'only living father.' When Smallwood left office, Tobin was still too young to vote.

Born in 1954 in Stephenville, he spent most of his youth in Goose Bay, Labrador. In both places he knew the relative prosperity brought to the province by the American

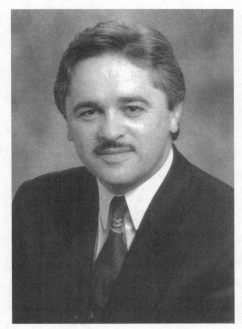

military. There was a different perspective here—neither the isolation of outport Newfoundland nor the particular preoccupations of the Avalon. There was also a wider view of career options, though when leaving high school, as his yearbook noted, Tobin didn't know what he wanted to do. He tried Memorial University, but didn't stay long. He does not even hold that much debt to Smallwood.

Barely twenty-five when he was elected federal Liberal Member of Parliament for Humber–St. Barbe–Baie Verte

Brian Tobin as federal member of Parliament (the first stint).

in 1980, he has not lost an election since. Politics has been his life, and although that marks a man, and not always for the better, from it has come the keenest political sense in the country.

His triumph was, of course, the Turbot War. It was early March 1995. Federal Fisheries Minister Tobin had convinced timid parliamentary colleagues of the need to take action on the high seas—confrontation with Spain and exposure of their scandalous fishing practices just outside the two-hundred-mile limit. For once the country would defend the stocks that straddle both sides of that limit, with something more than words and impotent diplomatic initiatives—all for the sake of a fish that few people had ever heard of, and all for the sake of the fisheries, still only 1 per cent of GNP. How un-Canadian. How like what Newfoundland had been saying should have been done years ago with the cod.

Over the bow of the Spanish trawler *Estai* rang a burst of machine-gun fire from a Canadian fisheries patrol vessel, the culmination of several hours of perilous, fog-shrouded chase through rough seas. Having cut away its nets, the crew of the Spanish trawler finally gave up and allowed Canadian authorities to board and arrest the vessel. Escorted through the Narrows of St. John's Harbour, the Spaniards came face to face with busloads of fishermen still embittered by the cod moratorium.

When the nets of the *Estai* had been retrieved, Tobin stood with them on a barge in view of the United Nations in New York, pointing to a mesh size sixteen millimetres below regulation, and an interior liner thirty-four millimetres below that. Seventy per cent of the turbot catch discovered in its hold were smaller than his hand. The Spanish could deny it no longer. The mouthpiece of the EU Fisheries Commission, Emma Bonino, had finally been silenced. Tobin, always good for the media soundbite, gave them one for the books: 'We're down now to one last, lonely, unloved, unattractive little turbot clinging on by its fingernails to the Grand Banks of Newfoundland.' For Newfoundland fishermen it proved a humourless eulogy for an industry devastated by decades of overfishing. It was a dramatic spectacle, and Canadians were probably more united over this issue than anything in recent years, but it had come far too late in the international fisheries game.

Two years later Brian Tobin, now as premier, would lead us in celebrating five hundred years since European rediscovery. For some fishermen, including those in Bonavista where the celebration was focused, it was a bittersweet moment. We were no longer an 'English ship moored near the Grand Banks,' but gone, too, was the cod that once filled its holds.

Tobin would bring that same Turbotnator brashness to the premiership. It was most apparent in the stance he took on Voisey's Bay. When INCO acquired 'the find of the century,' the vast nickel deposits in northern Labrador discovered by Albert Chislett and Chris Verbiski in 1995, they paid in excess of $4 billion. A deal with the Tobin government came with the promise of a smelter-refinery complex to be built in Newfoundland near the site of the vacated U.S. base at Argentia. Then, with falling nickel prices, INCO scratched the smelter. The government cried foul and refused the go-ahead for any mining development. The two remained deadlocked. The nickel remained in the ground.

In the meantime Bay Street, in the persons of Diane Francis of the *National Post* and Seymour Schulich, 'Toronto tycoon,' bleated in public that Tobin and his Newfoundland government should be content with the mining jobs and were 'holding out for the impossible,' that the province was 'the biggest sinkhole in the country.' Damn it all, 'there are more votes in North York.'

Get your suits in a knot, why don't you? We are talking history here—the most resource-rich province with the lowest per capita income, a devastated fishery, Churchill Falls, Shaheen and Doyle. Are we about to let it happen one more time? Tobin shot back, 'Take a pill.'

Fireworks

The years of the Tobin administration were marked by celebration—Cabot 500, fifty years of confederation, one thousand years since the Vikings. Somehow, despite disheartening news about the recovery of the cod stocks, there was good reason to celebrate. Actually, the celebrations seemed less about the past than they did about the future. We are an optimistic crowd, undoubtedly, but this time the optimism had conviction built in . . . at least in some parts of the province.

Much of it had to do with recent economic successes—shellfish production, high tech/IT companies, Hibernia. In the capital city it translated into more BMWs, $1-million condos, still more golf courses. To Jan Morris's list of adjectives describing the city could have been added 'confident.'

Tobin, as premier, prided himself on risk, the confident thrust into the uncharted. We saw it in calling a second referendum to make the decisive move to public education. And saw it again in his determination to stand his ground with INCO. He brought a wider focus to government, with female ministers taking the lead in giving social issues greater priority, in demonstrating their relationship to economic development.

Showing confidence is risky business, of course. There's no blaming others for the ruts in the roads. There is the ever-present danger of alienating those who have nothing to celebrate. And in the end, the measure of a government is not in the bluster of political discourse, or in strutting statistics about unprecedented growth in the economy. It is in its day-to-day contact with people, in how it treats its disadvantaged. A test will be the native children of Labrador. In ten years how will they have fared? And the rural communities whose populations have suffered the most devastating effects of the cod moratorium, what will be said of them?

Turbotnated

Brian Tobin is gone from provincial politics now. He resigned in the fall of 2000 and, amid shouts of 'opportunism,' struck a path back to Ottawa. He was made a federal cabinet minister even before his election to Parliament. In the industry portfolio, he argued, he is better able to serve the interests of the province than he could even as premier.

He's the guy calling the tune on federal-provincial relations, the one to work out a fairer deal for the province among the minefields of resource revenue sharing and equalization payments. He could eventually be the one to right the flaws of the deal that brought us into confederation. (For starters we assume there'll be no more blunders like the federal shrimp-quota fiasco of 2000.) One day he'll be taking a shot at replacing Jean Chrétien as prime minister. If he lands the prize, we expect a federal government more in tune than ever with the aspirations of Newfoundland and Labrador.

Interim Premier Beaton Tulk was left to hold the fort as a leadership battle took shape. Unfortunately for the Liberals, with those eager to be premier let loose, rifts in the party that were hardly noticeable under Tobin turned into gaping chasms. The Tobin brand of confidence dissipated. The Liberals suddenly had less to celebrate.

Time and Tide

In Newfoundland and Labrador we like a good 'time.' A time here is a party, a night of music and dancing, food and liquid sustenance. George Story and his university colleagues defined it as 'a communal gathering.' One of his ex-mainland friends in the Folklore Department termed it 'sanctioned deviation.'

There was a political 'time' in Mount Pearl, Newfoundland, in early 2001—the gathering of 1,300 Liberals, a deviation from their normal display of unity, sanctioned to choose a new leader, and thus a new premier. Appropriately enough, given the political landscape at the time, it was held at an arena called 'The Glacier.'

Since Tobin's departure the leadership hopefuls had been like glacial erratics, those scattered rocks left behind when the mighty icecap holding them together melts. In the end the chosen one, Roger Grimes, sat precariously on the landscape, despite the fact that his caucus comrades were there to shore him up. In second place, by just fourteen votes, stood the crestfallen populist John Efford, quick to compare his loss to that of Al Gore, the choice of the people in a vote swayed by a party establishment. The third-place finisher moved maladroitly about the convention, letting it be known that he would have no time for the new premier or his cabinet. Party solidarity at its less than perfect.

Prominent on the stage during the Grimes acceptance speech was the man whose resignation had brought about what now amounted to cracks of seismic proportions. As Grimes rallied the party faithful, Tobin did what he could to keep them from jumping into their chosen abysses. He filled Efford's ear with whatever masters of party politics say to the defeated. He slipped a one-word note to Grimes, reminding him to pay tribute to the third-place loser. It was a grim task. It didn't play well on television.

What had raised the spectacle to new heights was something taking place outside the confines of the Glacier. Tories were striding about the land, more in step than anytime since the days of the young Peckford. Leading them was Danny Williams, crowned in a neat and timely fashion just a few days before the Liberal fiasco, and by acclamation. No nasty convention. No TV cameras so all the province could spy on the games politicians play.

Leading the disparate troops in the Liberal encampment would be ex-school teacher Grimes, the man with the experience (and the scars) of numerous tough

A glacial erratic, rock perched on rock.

portfolios under Wells and Tobin. He had been long celebrated by his colleagues for maintaining a level head when arrows filled the air.

Out to fell him was Danny Williams, St. John's lawyer and multi-millionaire businessman. A fresh face, freshly monied, sporting charisma as yet untarnished by political office. (Sporting as well what has become standard issue for this province's political leaders—a sealskin jacket.)

To add to the drama, a scant four days before the convention two Northern Peninsula districts—one vacated by Tobin and never anything but Liberal since the dawn of confederation—had been lost to the PCs in by-elections. Suddenly, the townie Williams was a man of the outports. The outport-allied Liberals were looking more and more like out-of-touch townies. The old stereotypes of politics in Newfoundland—those last, lingering remnants of Smallwood era—had finally been put to rest.

The PC wins came along a stretch of the Newfoundland coast where people were anything but confident about their future. They were fuming at the neglect they felt in the wake of the cod moratorium. As more and more of their young people were sucked away by employment hopes on mainland Canada or in St. John's, as schools closed and services deteriorated, they felt abandoned, doomed to wither away, the ravaging of the cod stocks playing out some inevitable final scene.

But in this new millennium, in a province in the forefront of communications technology, even the most distant outports make themselves heard. The roar is unmistakable. Political tides are on the move.

Thro' Spindrift Swirl

When blinding storm gusts fret thy shore
And wild waves lash thy strand
Thro' spindrift swirl and tempest roar
We love thee, wind-swept land . . .

—Cavendish Boyle

Happy Adventure, Bonavista Bay.

And Tempest Roar

Try as we may, there's no escaping politics in Newfoundland and Labrador. For we don't just follow politics, we ingest it. The entertainment value alone is almost worth the high taxes.

It's one of the reasons we hold to this place. But, of course, there are a thousand more.

The unrivalled drama where the ocean strikes the land, where the rivers herald its interior. Air ripe with the scent of spruce and fir. The countless stories in the air, in the land, in the people.

Where to a stranger you're 'buddy,' or 'sweetheart.' Where a stranger's first question is, 'Where you from?', meaning where in Newfoundland and Labrador did you grow up and I'm sure to know someone who knows you.

Freshly caught lobsters cooked in seawater on a beach, tea brewed in the winter

Voices of the Newfoundland Symphony Youth Choir.

woods. Cod. The wit, the humour, the laughter that is part of every day. The optimism. Home.

Ask Harry Martin, wildlife officer and folksinger, whose songs of Labrador stir a rich, abiding love of the land and its people.

Or Susan Knight, founder of the internationally acclaimed Newfoundland Symphony Youth Choir. 'I am of this place,' she says, with the passion that stirs in people from Cape Chidley to Cape Spear.

The lyrics of the land are sung with more gusto than ever. We're getting used to 'O Canada,' but it's those tributes to Labrador and anthems such as the 'Ode to Newfoundland' that continue to stir our soul. And it's not just old anti-confederates trying to reclaim the past. Leading us are young people.

When the young people of this place sing, they sing for everyone.

> Thro' spindrift swirl and tempest roar,
> We love thee, wind-swept land
> We love thee, we love thee,
> We love thee, wind-swept land.

Acknowledgements

*We are always surrounded by the living and the dead, the present and the absent,
real, imagined and forgotten persons.*

—Stuart Pierson, historian

This book was shaped by the work of many people. When I was first approached in 1998 with the proposition of writing it I knew that the research for the most part would draw on secondary sources, that I would be relying on the expertise of those who have written on a multitude of topics related to our past. Credit goes first to them. Some aspects of the book rest heavily on the published articles of individuals, who alone have focused on a topic. To these people—the names of whom will be apparent in the bibliography—I offer particular thanks. (To Olaf Janzen of Grenfell College, for his annotated bibliography, 'A Reader's Guide to Newfoundland History to 1869,' I am especially grateful. It saved me many hours of searching in an already tight schedule.)

The library at Memorial University, in particular its Centre for Newfoundland Studies, Map Room, and CNS Archives, was invariably welcoming and helpful. Many thanks, as well, are extended to the Newfoundland Reference section of the Provincial Library, the Provincial Archives, the Newfoundland Museum, Parks Canada, the *Telegram*, the Colony of Avalon, and the National Archives in Ottawa.

To my agent, Linda McKnight, I am grateful for sound advice and unfailing encouragement. To everyone at the publishing end—in particular, Cynthia Good, Cathy MacLean, Shannon Proulx, Laura Brady, and Mary Adachi—goes my gratitude for keeping order and aiming for the best possible book. Carl and Norma Major offered much insight, especially regarding the south coast and Labrador. There are many others whom I called upon personally for quick assistance and advice, among them Linda Badcock, Allan Clarke, Joanne Costello, Ann Devlin-Fischer, Debbie Edgecombe, Richard Ellis, Michael Dove, John Fitzgerald, Mark Genge, Maxine Genge, Susan Hadley, John Hewson, Jim Hiller, Linda Kane, Paul Keough, James Overton, Shane O'Dea, Ron Pelley, Ned Pratt, Sheila Pratt, Suanne Reid, Bert Riggs, Joan Ritcey, Hans Rollmann, Jim Tuck, Gail Weir, Linda White, and Alberta Wood.

Three people—Cynthia Good, Anne Crawford, and Bert Riggs—read the book in manuscript. Their comments were invaluable and thoroughly appreciated.

The lens through which I viewed what has been written about the history of Newfoundland and Labrador is my own. Much that some people might view as significant is not to be found here, much that others might think minor brought to the fore. For any history is subjective, and works within its limits of time and space. I undertook the project not because of any great grounding in our past but because I knew there were a lot of people, like myself, seeking a general synthesis of what is known. I wrote it in the spirit of love, frustration, and good humour with which many of us view this place. From the start it was an exhausting exercise, but one there was no resisting. Now, at its end, my deepest appreciation goes to Anne and Luke and Duncan, for their endless support and patience.

Newfoundland and Labrador History . . .
on the Web, in Video and Fiction, and Live!

Newfoundland and Labrador history has a polished presence on the Internet. Head first to the *Newfoundland and Labrador Web Sites by Subject* page of the Centre for Newfoundland Studies (www.mun.ca/library/cns/links.html) for an overview. An excellent first bet would be the *Newfoundland and Labrador Heritage Web Site* (www.heritage.nf.ca) , with its labyrinth of topics. The Encyclopedia of Newfoundland and Labrador is online, as is the *Dictionary of Newfoundland English*. Hans Rollmann's *Religion, Society & Culture in Newfoundland and Labrador* is essential for anyone interested in the vigorous role of religion in our past. The site carries several early published works, including *Quodlibets*, and the discourses of Whitbourne and Mason. Among the other sites not to be missed are *Newfoundland and the Great War* and *Archival Treasures*, with Bert Riggs. For bibliographic lists, see the Web pages of Olaf Janzen and Melvin Baker.

On video, you can go back to our rock beginnings with *When Continents Collide* and *A Wonderful Fine Coast* (both available through Gros Morne National Park). *The Quest for Ancient Footsteps* (Sharon Halfyard, Curzon Village Productions, 1998) follows archaeologist Priscilla Renouf's search for Maritime Arachic habitation sites in Port au Choix. Our ancient peoples are also the starting point for *East of Canada*, the five-part television series (CBC Home Video, 1997), the most substantial attempt yet at bringing the sweep of our history to television.

Over the years the National Film Board of Canada has released several fine works dealing with aspects of our past. *The Last Days of Okak* (Anne Budgell and

Nigel Markham, 1985) presents the haunting story of the flu epidemic of 1919. *Seven Brides for Uncle Sam* (Anita McGee, 1997) grasps the joy and heartbreak of the many women who wedded U.S. servicemen stationed on the military bases here since the Second World War. The charms of St. John's, old and new, are never more apparent than in *Rain, Drizzle, and Fog* (Rosemary House, 1998.) Conspiracy as a way of bringing a reluctant Newfoundland and Labrador into confederation with Canada is the subject of the movie *A Secret Nation* (Michael Jones and Ed Riche, 1992); the tragedy of Mount Cashel the subject of *The Boys of St. Vincent* (John Smith and Des Walsh, 1994.)

The docudrama *The Untold Story* (Marian Frances White and Greg Malone, Codlessco Ltd., 1999) follows the twenty-five-year struggle of Newfoundland women for the vote. The feature film *The Viking* of 1931 (long lost, but now available on video from Newfoundland Historic Parks) is rather stilted by today's standards, but is worth seeing for its historical footage of the seal hunt and of Bob Bartlett as the ship's captain. Bartlett is the subject of a CBC video from its *Life and Times* series, as is Joey Smallwood.

Fiction remains for many their window into history. We have a several works that together make a fairly well connected trail though our past. There have been a number of novels dealing with the tragedy of the Beothuk, the most recent of which is *The Beothuk Saga* (Bernard Assiniwi, in translation from French, McClelland & Stewart, 2000). *Eiriksdottir* (Joan Clark, Penguin, 1995) brings the larger-than-life Norse woman Freydis to L'Anse aux Meadows at the turn of the first millinneum. John Cabot, in the second wave of rediscovery, is seen through the engaging mind of his wife, Mathye, in *In the Hands of the Living God* (Lillian Bouzane, Turnstone, 1999). *The Afterlife of George Cartwright* (John Steffler, M&S, 1992) gives us eighteenth-century Labrador at its most unforgettable. Permanent outport settlement in Newfoundland is the subject of what has become the most popular of our historical novels (and an eight-part miniseries for TV), *Random Passage* (Bernice Morgan, Breakwater, 1992). Labour leader William Coaker and his FPU provided the stimulus for *A Settlement of Memory* (Gordon Rodgers, Killick, 1999). *No Man's Land* (Kevin Major, Doubleday, 1995) is set in France in 1916 as the Newfoundland Regiment heads to the devastation of Beaumont-Hamel. Though creative non-fiction, the classic *Death on the Ice* (Cassie Brown, Doubleday, 1972) is novelistic in its approach as it brings to life our most dramatic sealing tragedy. Finally, with *The Colony of Unrequited Dreams* (Wayne Johnston, Knopf, 1998) we enter the modern era of Smallwood, that most absorbing of Newfoundland characters.

For those who prefer their history live, you would do well to take in the stage plays of Tom Cahill, David French, Des Walsh, and others, as well as the several community-touring pageants to be found in the province during the summer months. In the forefront of these is *The Trinity Pageant* (Donna Butt and Rising Tide Theatre), where on the landwash, wharfs, church, and fields of Trinity Bay the commotion of our past unfolds.

On the Internet you will find 'If These Walls Could Talk,' a history of the Colonial Building. Among its highlights—the greatest instance of social upheaval in our entire history, the riot of 1932.

Selected Bibliography

Alcock, J., and A. Brown. *Our Transatlantic Flight*. London: Kimber, 1969.

Alexander, David. 'Literacy and economic development in nineteenth-century Newfoundland.' *Acadiensis*, 10 (1), 1980.

Andersen, Raoul. *Voyage to the Grand Banks*. St. John's: Creative, 1998.

Antle, P.J. 'Night of terror' [tidal wave]. *Atlantic Guardian*, 14 (2), 1957.

Audubon, Maria, ed. *Audubon and His Journals*. New York: Dover, 1960.

Badgley, K. 'Rigorously applied in practice: a scorched earth policy for Canada and Newfoundland...' *The Archivist / L'Archiviste*, 116, 1998.

Baker, Melvin. *Aspects of Nineteenth Century St. John's Municipal History*. St. John's: Creative, 1982.

Baker, Melvin, Robert Cuff, and Bill Gillespie. *Workingmen's St John's*. St. John's: Creative, 1982.

Bannister, Jerry. 'Convict transportation and the colonial state . . . 1789.' *Acadiensis*, 27 (2), 1998.

———. 'The campaign for representative government in Newfoundland.' *Journal of Canadian Historical Association*, 5, 1994.

Barkham, Selma. 'The Basques: Filling a gap in our history between Jacques Cartier and Champlain.' *Canadian Geographical Journal*, 96 (1), 1978.

Bassler, Gerhard P. *Alfred Valdmanis and the Politics of Survival*. Toronto: U of T Press, 2000.

———. *Sanctuary Denied*. St. John's: ISER, 1992.

Beare, Graeme. 'Aeroplanes in Cartwright.' *Them Days*, 12 (1), 1986.

Benson, Bob. 'A bitter clash [IWA strike].' *The Telegram*, 24/01/99.

———. 'Political Primer' [Frank Moores]. *The Evening Telegram*, 19/03/95.

———. 'Saints, sinners, and John C. Doyle.' *The Telegram*, 11/06/00.

Bliss, M. 'King of the Rock'[Brian Peckford]. *Saturday Night*, 97 (12), 1982.

Bonnycastle, Richard. *Newfoundland in 1842*. London: Colburn, 1842.

Bower, Peter, et al. *What Strange New Radiance*. Ottawa: PAC, 1979.

Buckner, P., G. Campbell, and D. Frank, eds. *Atlantic Canada Before Confederation*. Fredericton: Acadiensis, 1985, 1990, 1998.

———. *Atlantic Canada After Confederation*. Fredericton: Acadiensis, 1985, 1988, 1999.

Bulgin, Iona, ed. *Cabot and His World Symposium*. St. John's: NHS, 1999.

Butler, Victor. *Sposin' I Dies in D'Dory*. St. John's: Jesperson, 1977.

Byrne, Cyril, ed. *Gentlemen-Bishops and Faction Fighters*. St. John's: Jesperson, 1984.

Byrne, Cyril, and Terrence Murphy, eds. *Religion and Identity*. St. John's: Jesperson, 1987.

Cadigan, Sean. *Hope and Deception in Conception Bay*. Toronto: U of T Press, 1995.

———. 'Battle Harbour in transition: Merchants, fishermen and the state in the struggle for relief in a Labrador community during the 1930's.' *Labour*, 26, 1990.

———. 'Whipping them into shape: State refinement of patriarchy among Conception Bay fishing families, 1787–1825,' in C. McGrath, et al. *Their Lives and Times*. St. John's: Killick, 1995.

Cameron, Bill. 'The Candidate.' *Saturday Night*, 115 (22), 07/10/00.

Campbell, Lydia. *Sketches of Labrador Life*. St. John's: Killick, 2000.

Candow, James E. 'The British Army in Newfoundland, 1697–1824.' *Newfoundland Quarterly*, 79 (4), 1984.

Candow, James E., and Carol Corbin, eds. *How Deep is the Ocean?: Historical Essays on Canada's Atlantic Fishery*. Sydney: University College of Cape Breton Press, 1997.

Cardoulis, J. N. *A Friendly Invasion*. St. John's: Breakwater, 1990.

Cartwright, George. *A Journal . . . During a Residence of Nearly Sixteen Years on the Coast of Labrador*. Newark, England: Allin and Ridge, 1792.

Cell, Gillian. *English Enterprise in Newfoundland, 1577-1600*. Toronto: U of T Press, 1969.

Charbonneau, P., and L. Barrette. *Against the Odds: History of the Francophones of Newfoundland and Labrador*. St. John's: H. Cuff, 1994.

Colman-Sadd, Stephen, and Susan A. Scott. *Newfoundland and Labrador: Traveller's Guide to the Geology*. St. John's / Ottawa: Government of Newfoundland and Labrador / Canada, 1994.

Cooke, Alan. 'A woman's way' [Mina Hubbard]. *The Beaver*, 291, 1960.

Coyne, Deborah. *Roll of the Dice*. Toronto: James Lorimer, 1992.

Crosbie, John C. *No Holds Barred: My Life in Politics*. Toronto: McClelland & Stewart, 1997.

Crowley, John E. 'Empire versus truck: the official interpretation of debt and labour in the18th-century Newfoundland fishery.' *Canadian Historical Review*, 70 (3), 1989.

Deacon, Bruce. "Mr. And Mrs. Olympics." *Athletics*, April–May 2000.

Dictionary of Canadian Biography. Toronto: U of T Press, 1966– .

Earhart, Amelia. *The Fun of It*. NY: Brewer, Warren, and Putnam, 1932.

Edwards, Ena Furrell. *Billy Spiney, The Umbrella Tree and Other Recollections of St. Lawrence*. For the author, 1991.

English, Christopher. 'Collective violence in Ferryland district, Newfoundland, in 1788.' *Dalhousie Law Journal*, 21 (2), 1998.

———. 'Development of the Newfoundland legal system to 1815.' *Acadiensis*, 20 (1), 1990.

Ennis, F., and H. Woodrow, eds. *Strong as the Ocean: Women's Work in the Newfoundland and Labrador Fisheries*. St. John's: Harrish Press, 1996.

Fingard, Judith. "The relief of the unemployed poor in Saint John, Halifax and St. John's, 1815–1860." *Acadiensis*, 5 (1), 1975.

Fitzgerald, Jack. *Up the Pond*. [St. John's Regatta] St. John's: Creative, 1992.

Fitzgerald, John E. ' "The true father of confederation"?: Archbishop E. P. Roche, term 17 and . . . confederation . . . ' *Newfoundland Studies*. 14 (2), 1998.

Fitzhugh, Lynne D. *The Labradorians*. St. John's: Breakwater, 1999.

Francis, D. 'Tobin represents the worst of politics.' *National Post*, 20/01/00.

Gilbert, William. ' "Divers places": The Beothuk Indians and John Guy's voyage into Trinity Bay in 1612.' *Newfoundland Studies*, 6 (2), 1990.

Gillespie, B. *A Class Act: An Illustrated History of the Labour Movement* . . . St. John's: Newfoundland and Labrador Federation of Labour, 1986.

Gosse, P. H., and R. Rompkey, ed. 'Philip Henry Gosse's account of his years in Newfoundland, 1827-1835.' *Newfoundland Studies*, 6 (2), 1990.

Goudie, Elizabeth. *Woman of Labrador*. Toronto: Peter Martin, 1973.

Graesser, Mark. 'Who voted for confederation?' Statistical analysis prepared for Newfoundland Historical Society Symposium, March 1999.

Greene, John P. *Between Damnation and Starvation*. Montréal/Kingston: McGill-Queen's, 1999.

Gunn, Gertrude. *The Political History of Newfoundland, 1832-1864*. Toronto: U of T Press, 1966.

Gwyn, R. *Smallwood: The Unlikely Revolutionary*. Toronto: M&S, 1972/99.

———. 'That was your fifteen minutes, Clyde Wells.' *Saturday Night*. 106 (1), 1991.

Hadley, M. *U-Boats Against Canada: German Submarines in Canadian Waters*. Montréal/Kingston: McGill-Queen's, 1985.

Hallock, Charles. 'Three months in Labrador.' *Harper's New Monthly Magazine*. 22, (131, 132), 1861.

Handcock, Gordon. *Soe Longe As There Comes Noe Women*. St. John's: Breakwater, 1989.

———. *The Story of Trinity*. Trinity: Trinity Historical Society, 1997.

Harrington, M. *Prime Ministers of Newfoundland*. St. John's: H. Cuff, 1991.

Harris, Michael. 'Citizen Peckford: A personal hail and farewell.' *Sunday Express*, 22/01/89.

———. *Lament for an Ocean*. Toronto: M&S, 1998.

———. *Rare Ambition*. Toronto: Penguin, 1993.

———. *Unholy Orders*. Toronto: Penguin, 1991.

Harris, R.C., ed., and G. J. Matthews. *Historical Atlas of Canada, Volume I: From the Beginning to 1800*. Toronto: U of T Press, 1988.

Head, C. Grant. *Eighteenth Century Newfoundland*. Toronto: M&S, 1976.

Hiller, J.K. *Confederation: Deciding Newfoundland's Future*. St. John's: NHS, 1998.

———. 'The Moravians in Labrador, 1771-1805.' *Polar Record*, 15 (99), 1971.

———. 'The Newfoundland seal fishery: An historical introduction.' *Bulletin of Canadian Studies*, 7 (2), 1983–84.

Hiller, J.K., and P. Neary, eds. *Newfoundland in the Nineteenth and Twentieth Centuries*. Toronto: U of T Press, 1980.

———. *Twentieth Century Newfoundland*. St. John's: Breakwater, 1994.

Horwood, H. *Bartlett*. Toronto: Doubleday, 1977.

———. *Joey*. Toronto: Stoddart, 1989.

———. *Pirates and Outlaws of Canada, 1610-1932*. Toronto: Doubleday, 1984.

———. 'The people who were murdered for fun.' *Maclean's*, 72 (21), 1959.

How, Douglas. *Night of the Caribou*. Hantsport, NS: Lancelot Press, 1988.

Howley, J.P. *The Beothucks, or Red Indians*. Toronto: Coles [reprint], 1974.

Hubbard, Mina. *A Woman's Way Through Labrador*. New York: McClure, 1908.

Humphreys, John. *Plaisance*. Ottawa: National Museums of Canada, 1970.

Ingstad, Anne Stine. *The Norse Discovery of America*. London: Oxford University Press, 1985.

Ingstad, Helge. *Westward to Vinland*. New York: St. Martin's Press, 1969.

Janzen, Olaf Uwe. 'Illicit trade in English cod into Spain, 1739–1748.' *International Journal of Maritime History*,' 8 (1), 1996.

———. 'The Royal Navy and the defence of Newfoundland during the American Revolution.' *Acadiensis*, 14 (1), 1984.

———. ' "Une grand liaison": French fishermen from Île Royale on the coast of southwestern Newfoundland, 1714-1744.' *Newfoundland Studies*, 3 (2), 1987.

———. ' "Une petite république" in southwestern Newfoundland . . .' in Fischer, L.R. and W. Minchinton, eds. *Research in Maritime History, Vol.3. People of the Sea*. St. John's: IMEHA, 1992.

Johnson, C. Milley. 'The Depression in the outports,' in Morgan, B., H. Porter, and G. Rubia, eds. *From This Place*. St. John's: Jesperson, 1977.

Jones, Frederick. *Edward Feild: Bishop of Newfoundland, 1844–1876*. St. John's: NHS, 1976.

———. 'Religion, Education, and Politics in Newfoundland, 1836–1875.' *Canadian Church Historical Society Journal*, 12 (4), 1970.

Jukes, J. *Excursions in and about Newfoundland*. London: J. Murray, 1842.

Kaplan, Susan A. 'European goods and socio-economic change in early Labrador Inuit society,' in Fitzhugh, William W., ed. *Cultures in Contact*. Washington: Smithsonian Institution Press, 1985.

Kearley, Linda, ed. *Pursuing Equality: Historical Perspectives on Women in Newfoundland and Labrador*. St. John's: ISER, 1993.

Kearney, Anna. *'Getting to Know Ourselves': A Human History of Gros Morne National Park, Newfoundland*. Ottawa: Parks Canada, 1979.

Kelly, G. *Rockwell Kent: The Newfoundland Work*. Halifax: Dalhousie, 1987.

Kennedy, J. *People of the Bays and Headlands*. Toronto: U of T Press, 1995.

Lahey, R. 'Catholicism and colonial policy in Newfoundland, 1779–1845,' in Murphy, T., and G. Stortz, eds. *Creed and Culture*. Montréal/Kingston: McGill-Queen's, 1993.

———. *James Louis O'Donel* . . . St. John's: NHS, 1984.

Lindbergh, Anne M. *Locked Rooms and Open Doors:* New York: HBJ, 1974.

Long, Gene. *Suspended State*. St. John's: Breakwater, 1999.

Lysaght, A.M., ed. *Joseph Banks in Newfoundland and Labrador, 1766*. Berkeley: University of California Press, 1971.

Mackenzie, David. *Inside the Atlantic Triangle*. Toronto: U of T Press, 1986.

MacLeod, Malcolm. *Crossroads Country*. St. John's: Breakwater, 1999.

Mailhot, José. *The People of Sheshatshit*. St. John's: ISER, 1997.

Mannion, John. 'Patrick Morris and Newfoundland Irish immigration.' *Canadian Journal of Irish Studies*, 12 (2), 1986.

———, ed. *The Peopling of Newfoundland*. St. John's: ISER, 1977.

Marconi, Degna. *My Father, Marconi*. Ottawa: Balmuir, 1982.

Marshall, Ingeborg. *A History and Ethnography of the Beothuk*. Montréal/Kingston: McGill-Queen's, 1996.

Martin, Ged. 'Convict transportation to Newfoundland in 1789.' *Acadiensis*. 5 (1), 1975.

Matthews, Keith. *Lectures on the History of Newfoundland 1500–1800*. St. John's: Breakwater, 1988.

———. 'The class of '32: St. John's reformers on the eve of representative government.' *Acadiensis*, 6 (2), 1977.

McCann, Phillip. 'British policy and confederation.' *Newfoundland Studies*, 14 (2), 1998.

———. 'Class, Gender and Religion in Newfoundland Education, 1836–1901.' *Historical Studies in Education*, 1 (2), 1989.

———. 'The Newfoundland School Society, 1823–55,' in Mangan, J.A., ed. *Benefits Bestowed*. Manchester: Manchester University Press, 1988.

McDonald, Donna. *Lord Strathcona*. Toronto: Dundurn Press, 1996.

McDonald, Ian. *'To Each His Own.'* St. John's: ISER, 1987.

McGhee, Robert. *Canada Rediscovered*. Ottawa: CMC, 1991.

McGrath, C., B. Neis, and M. Porter, eds. *Their Lives and Times: Women in Newfoundland and Labrador: A Collage*. St. John's: Killick Press, 1995.

Memorial University of Newfoundland. CNS Archives: 'Frances Cluett: Papers, 1916–1920.' Coll: 174.

———. 'Owen Steele: Diary, 1914-1916.' Coll: 179.

Moon, E. 'The fighting women of Foxtrap.'*Atlantic Advocate*, 49 (7), 1959.

Moreton, Julian. *Life and Work in Newfoundland*. London: Rivingtons, 1863.

Morison, S.E. *The European Discovery of America*. New York: Oxford, 1971.

Morris, Jan. *Locations*. Toronto: Macfarlane Walter & Ross, 1992.

Mowat, Farley. *The Farfarers*. Toronto: Key Porter Books, 1998.

Moyles, R. G, ed. *Complaints is Many and Various, But the Odd Divil Likes it: Nineteenth-Century Views of Newfoundland*. Toronto: Peter Martin, 1975.

Munn, W.A. *Wineland Voyages*. St. John's: The Labour Group, 1930.

Neary, Peter. *Newfoundland in the North Atlantic World, 1929-49*. Montréal/Kingston: McGill-Queen's, 1988.

———. "Newfoundland's union with Canada, 1949: Conspiracy or choice?" *Acadiensis*, 12 (2), 1983.

———. 'The Bradley Report on Logging Operations in Newfoundland, 1934: A suppressed document.' *Labour*, 16, 1985.

———, ed. *White Tie and Decorations: Sir John and Lady Hope Simpson in Newfoundland, 1934-1936*. Toronto: U of T Press, 1996.

Neary, Peter and Patrick O'Flaherty, eds. *By Great Waters*. Toronto: U of T Press, 1974.

———. *Part of the Main*. St. John's: Breakwater, 1983.

Neary, Steve. *The Enemy on Our Doorstep*. St. John's: Jesperson, 1994.

Nemec, Tom. 'The Irish Emigration to Newfoundland.' *Newfoundland Quarterly*, 69 (1), 1972.

Nicholson, G.W.L. *The Fighting Newfoundland / More Fighting Newfoundlanders*. St. John's: Government of N & L , 1964, 1969.

Noel, S.J.R. *Politics in Newfoundland*. Toronto: U of T Press, 1971.

O'Brien, P. *The Grenfell Obsession*. St. John's: Creative, 1992.

O'Flaherty, Patrick. *Old Newfoundland: A History to 1843*. St. John's: Long Beach Press, 1999.

———. 'The seeds of reform: Newfoundland, 1800-18.' *Journal of Canadian Studies*, 23 (3), 1988.

———. *The Rock Observed: Literary Responses to Newfoundland and Its People*. Toronto: U of T Press, 1979.

O'Neill, Paul, *The Story of St. John's*. Erin, ON: Press Porcépic, 1975–76.

Ommer, Rosemary, ed. *Merchant Credit and Labour Strategies in Historical Perspective*. Fredericton: Acadiensis, 1990.

Overton, James. 'Poverty, dependence and self-reliance: Politics, Newfoundland history and the Amulree Report of 1933.' Paper presented to the Newfoundland Historical Society Symposium, 24–25/03/00.

Pastore, R. 'Archaeology, history and the Beothuks.' *Newfoundland Studies*, 9 (2), 1993.

———. "The collapse of the Beothuk world." *Acadiensis*, 19 (1), 1989.

Patey, Francis. *A Battle Lost* [seal fishery]. St. Anthony: Bebb, 1990.

Penney, A. *History of the Newfoundland Railway*. St. John's: H. Cuff, 1988.

Peyton, Amy. *Nightingale of the North*. St. John's: Jesperson, 1983.

Pope, Peter. *The Many Landfalls of John Cabot*. Toronto: U of T Press,1997.

Prowse, Daniel W. *A History of Newfoundland*. London: Macmillan, 1895.

Quinn, David. *Sir Humphrey Gilbert and Newfoundland*. St. John's: NHS, 1983.

Quinn, D., ed. *New American World:* 5 vols. New York: Arno Press, 1979.

Reece, Bob. ' "Such a Banditti": Irish convicts in Newfoundland, 1789.' *Newfoundland Studies*. 13 (1–2), 1997.

Renouf, M.A.P. *Ancient Cultures, Bountiful Seas: The Story of Port au Choix*. St. John's: Historic Sites, 1999.

Richling, Barnett. 'Not by seals alone: The Moravians in the fur trade – souls and skins.' *The Beaver*, 68 (1), 1988.

Riggs, Bert. 'A Backward Glance.' The *Telegram*, various issues.

Rollmann, Hans. 'Anglicans, Puritans, and Quakers in sixteenth- and seventeenth-century Newfoundland.' *Avalon Chronicles*, 2, 1997.

———. 'Prince William Henry in Placentia.' *Ancestor*, 9 (1), 1993.

———. Various articles on Website: *Religion, Society, and Culture in Newfoundland and Labrador.*

Rompkey, Ronald. *Grenfell of Labrador*. Toronto: U of T Press, 1991.

———. *Labrador Odyssey*. Montréal/Kingston: McGill-Queen's, 1996.

Rowe, F. *A History of Newfoundland and Labrador*. Toronto: McGraw-Hill Ryerson, 1980.

———. *Extinction*. Toronto: McGraw-Hill Ryerson, 1977.

Rowe, Percy. *The Great Atlantic Air Race*. Toronto: McClelland & Stewart, 1977.

Ryan, Shannon. 'Fishery to Colony: A Newfoundland Watershed, 1793–1815.' *Acadiensis*, 12 (2), 1983.

———. *The Ice-Hunters: A History of Newfoundland Sealing to 1914*. St. John's: Breakwater, 1994.

Sager, Eric W. 'The merchants of Water Street and capital investment in Newfoundland's traditional economy,' in Fischer, L.R., and E.W. Sager, eds. *The Enterprising Canadians:* St. John's: Maritime History Group, 1979.

Schlager, Neil, ed. *When Technology Fails*. Detroit: Gale Research, 1994.

Smallwood, Joseph R. *I Chose Canada*. Toronto: Macmillan, 1973.

Smallwood, Joseph R., and Cyril F. Poole, eds. *Encyclopedia of Newfoundland and Labrador*. 5 vols. St. John's: Newfoundland Book Publishers and H. Cuff for The Smallwood Heritage Foundation, 1981-1994.

Staveley, Michael. 'Drawing the lines on the Labrador.' *Newfoundland Lifestyle*, 6 (2), 1988.

———, and Anne E. Stevens. 'The Great Newfoundland Storm of 12 September 1775.' *Bulletin of the Seismological Society of America*, 81 (4), 1991.

Steele, D.H., ed. *Early Science in Newfoundland*. St. John's: Sigma Xi, 1987.

Story, George M., W.J. Kirwin and J.D.A. Widdowson, eds. *Dictionary of Newfoundland English*. Toronto: U of T Press, 1982.

Sturtevant, W.C. 'The first Inuit depiction by Europeans.' *Études Inuit Studies*, 4 (1–2), 1980.

Tanner, Adrian. 'The aboriginal peoples of Newfoundland and Labrador and confederation.' *Newfoundland Studies*, 14 (2), 1998.

Taylor, J.G. 'The two worlds of Mikak.' *The Beaver*, 314 (3–4), 1983–84.

Thomas, John and Peter Pope (ed.). '"True and faithful account": Newfoundland in 1680.' *Newfoundland Studies*, 12 (1–2), 1996.

Thoms, James R. ed. *Fifty Golden Years*. St. John's: Stirling Press, 1999.

Thornhill, H. *It Happened in October* [SS Caribou]. 1945.

Trudel, François. 'The Inuit of southern Labrador and the development of French 0sedentary fisheries, 1700–1760,' in Preston, R.(ed.), *Canadian Ethnology Society: 4th Congress, 1977*. Ottawa: National Museums, 1978.

Tuck, J.A. 'Newfoundland and Labrador prehistory,' in *Canada's Visual History*. CD-ROM. Ottawa: NFB and CMC, 1994.

——. 'Unearthing Red Bay's whaling history.' *National Geographic*, 168 (1), 1985.

——, and R. Grenier. *Red Bay, Labrador*. St. John's: Atlantic Archaeology, 1989.

Wallace, Dillon. *Lure of the Labrador Wild*. New York: F. Revell, 1905.

Webb, Jeff A. *History of Newfoundland to 1815* [History 3110 course manual]. St. John's: Memorial University, 1998.

——. 'Leaving the state of nature: A Locke-inspired political community in St. John's, Newfoundland, 1723.' *Acadiensis*, 21 (1), 1991.

——. 'The Responsible Government League and the confederation campaign of 1948.' *Newfoundland Studies*, 5 (2), 1989.

Whalen, Maudie. 'The night the sea smashed Lord's Cove.' *Canadian Geographic*, 114 (6), 1994.

Whiteley, William H. *James Cook in Newfoundland, 1762–1767*. St. John's: NHS, 1975.

——. 'The establishment of the Moravian Mission in Labrador and British policy, 1763-83.' *Canadian Historical Review*, 45 (1), 1964.

Wicks, René. 'Newfoundland social life, 1750–1850.' *Newfoundland Quarterly*, 70 (4), 1974.

Wilkshire, Michael. *A Gentleman in the Outports: Gobineau and Newfoundland*. Ottawa: Carleton University Press, 1993.

Williams, Alan F. *Father Baudoin's War*. St. John's: Memorial University, 1987.

——. *John Cabot and Newfoundland*. St. John's: NHS, 1996.

Wix, Edward. *Six Months of a Newfoundland Missionary's Journal, from February to August 1835*. London: Smith, Elder & Co., 1836.

Yates, Anna. *Leifur Eiriksson and Vinland the Good*. Reykjavik: Iceland Review, 1993.

Yonge, James, and F.N.L. Poynter (ed). *The Journal of James Yonge, 1647–1721, Plymouth Surgeon*. London: Longmans, 1963.

Abbreviations:

CMC—Canadian Museum of Civilization

CNS—Centre for Newfoundland Studies

HBJ—Harcourt Brace Jovanovich

ISER—Institute of Social and Economic Research, Memorial University

M&S—McClelland and Stewart

NHS—Newfoundland Historical Society

PAC—Public Archives of Canada

U of T—University of Toronto

Illustration Credits

Bristol Museums and Art Gallery: 31

British Museum: 131

Cap & Gown / Memorial University: 450

Centre for Newfoundland Studies Archives: 176, 188, 226, 233, 239, 243, 246, 260, 262, 273, 282, 285, 291, 293, 294, 299, 303, 308, 314, 316, 318, 320 (bottom), 321, 326, 329, 330, 334, 337, 345, 352, 356, 362, 364, 368, 371, 373, 376, 381, 388, 395, 405, 407, 427, 440, 442

Charles P. de Volpi: 37, 66, 140, 154, 194, 201, 255, 257

Collection of the author: ii, 1, [engravings: 15, 42, 69, 123, 165, 181, 235, 265], 286, 301, 320 (top)

College of Arms, London: 98

Colony of Avalon, Ferryland / David Webber: 94, 99

Cupids Museum / William Gilbert: 80

Duncan Major: xiii

Ethnological Institute, Gottingen University: 136

Gerald Squires / QE II Library, Memorial University: 438

Harriet Irving Library, University of New Brunswick: 60

Ivor Sharp: 432

Jim Tuck: 10, 55, 102

Kevin Major: 6, 40, 417, 463

Knatchbull Portrait Collection, Courtauld Institute of Art: 142, 143

Memorial University, QE II Library (including CNS): 17, 20, 46, 50, 53, 58, 72, 88, 93, 107, 114, 120, 127, 132, 163, 174, 178, 183, 199, 205, 219, 222, 224, 249, 252, 264, 372, 386, 404, 414

Michael Burzynski: 7

NASA: 5

National Archives of Canada: 48, 104, 110, 117, 139, 149, 156, 158, 161, 167, 210, 278, 342

National Library of Canada: 63, 191

National Maritime Museum,
Greenwich: 151

Ned Pratt: 170, 464

Newfoundland Museum: 27, 28, 89,
212

Newfoundland Department of
Tourism, Culture and Recreation /
David Preston Smith: 25

Newfoundland Department of Mines
and Energy: 462

Niels W. Jannasch: 217, 223

Parks Canada: 9, 11, 21, 22

Provincial Archives of Newfoundland
and Labrador: 75, 78, 84, 146, 185,

202, 204, 208, 220, 229, 231, 240, 258,
271, 276, 289, 292, 311, 322, 325, 327,
333, 340, 344, 347, 348, 355, 359, 366,
378, 383, 385, 390, 400

Ron Pelley and Paul Keough: x, xi
(maps)

The Telegram, St. John's: 35, 306, 392,
397, 412, 424, 428, 434, 443, 446, 454,
455, 457

Tony Williamson: 421

Toronto Star: 444

Usher Gallery, Lincolnshire County
Council: 130 (detail)

INDEX